Oh My Goddess!

ああっ女神さまっ   *Love Potion No. 9*

PUBLISHER
Mike Richardson

SERIES EDITORS
Peet Janes, Greg Vest, Marilee Hord,
Robert Conte, & Dave Chipps

COLLECTION EDITOR
Suzanne Taylor

COLLECTION DESIGNERS
Julie Eggers Gassaway & Amy Arendts

COLLECTION DESIGN MANAGER
Brian Gogolin

English version produced by Studio Proteus for Dark Horse Comics, Inc.

OH MY GODDESS!: Love Potion No. 9

This book collects *Oh My Goddess!* Part I issues four and five, Part II issues six, seven, and eight, and specials "On a Wing and a Prayer" and "Love Potion #9."

Published by
Dark Horse Comics, Inc.
10956 SE Main Street
Milwaukie, OR 97222

First edition: October 1997
ISBN: 1-56971-252-2

1 3 5 7 9 10 8 6 4 2
Printed in Canada

Oh My Goddess!

あぁっ女神さまっ

Love Potion No. 9

STORY AND ART BY

Kosuke Fujishima

TRANSLATION BY

Alan Gleason & Toren Smith

LETTERING AND TOUCH-UP BY

L. Lois Buhalis, Tom Orzechowski, & Susie Lee

DARK HORSE COMICS®

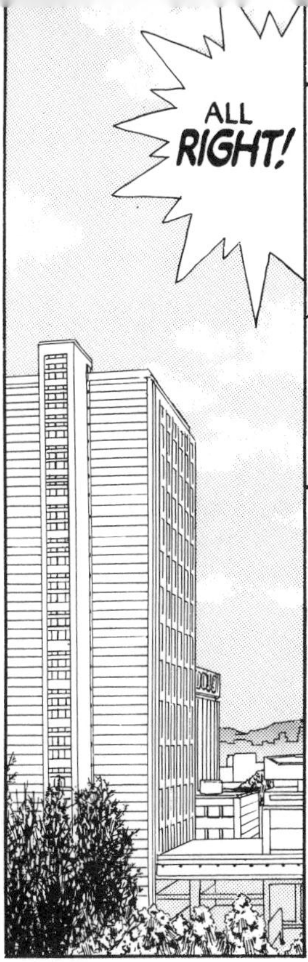
ALL RIGHT!

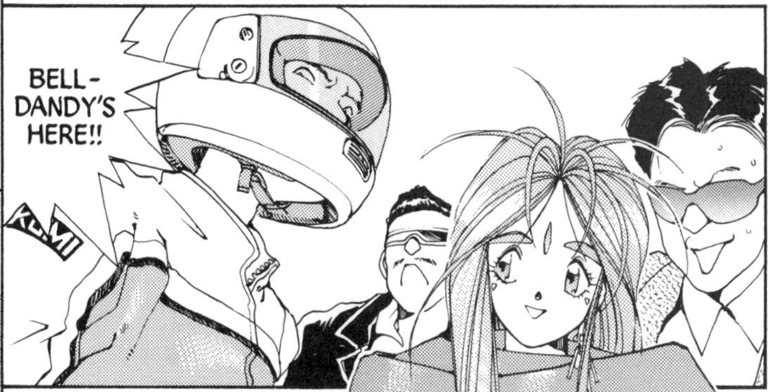
BELL-DANDY'S HERE!!

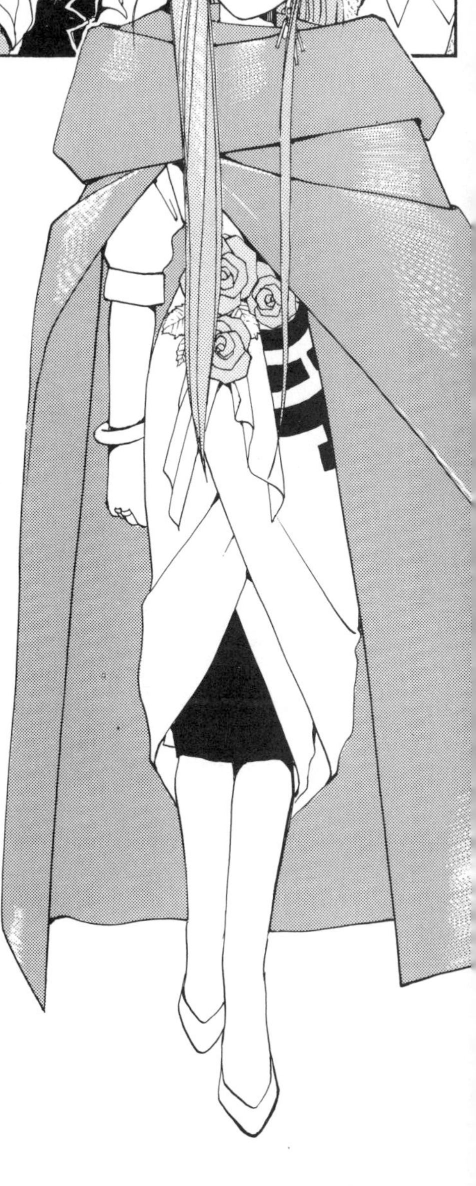

THE SECRET'S OUT!

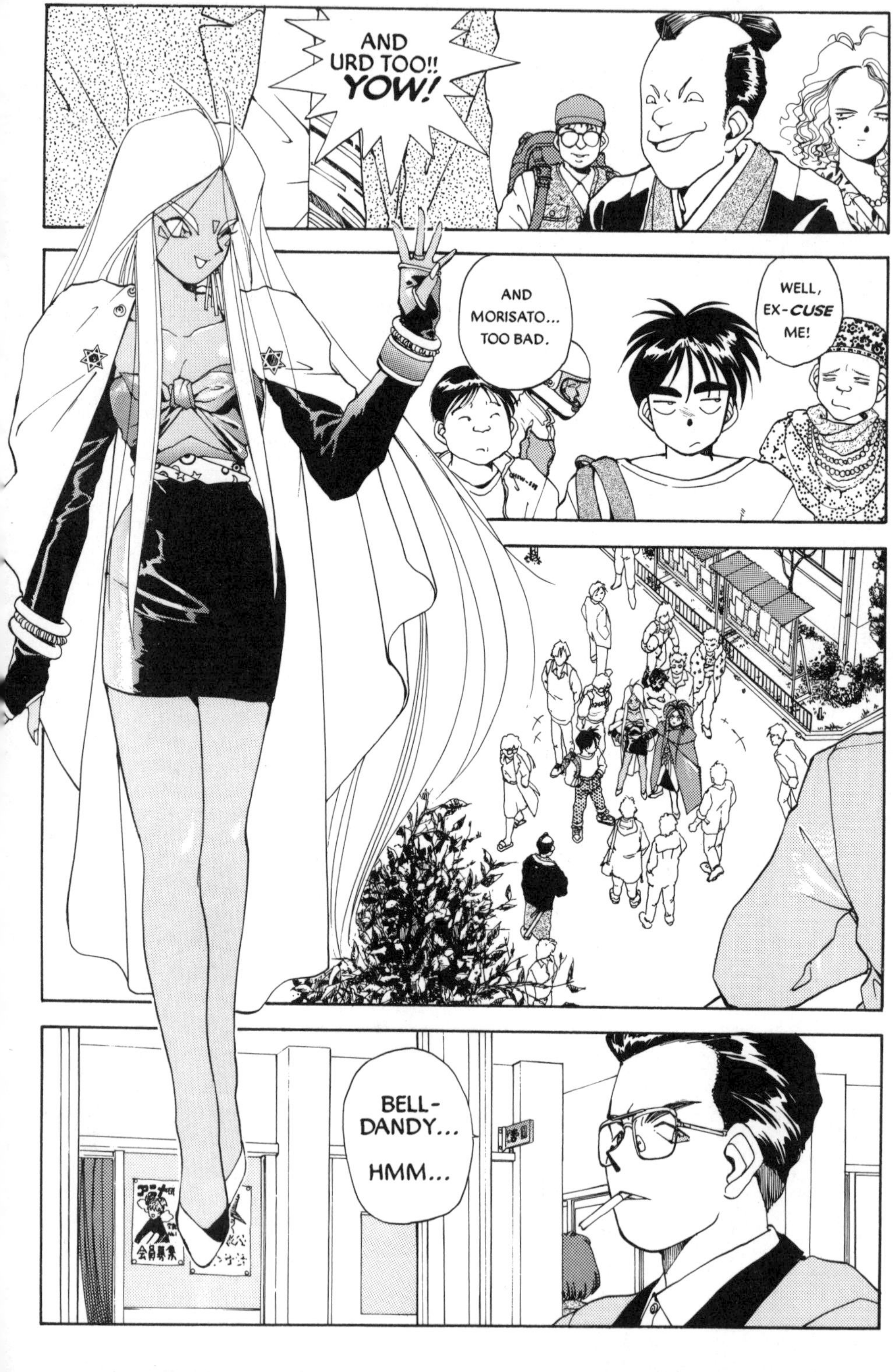
AND URD TOO!! YOW!
AND MORISATO... TOO BAD.
WELL, EX-CUSE ME!
BELL-DANDY... HMM...

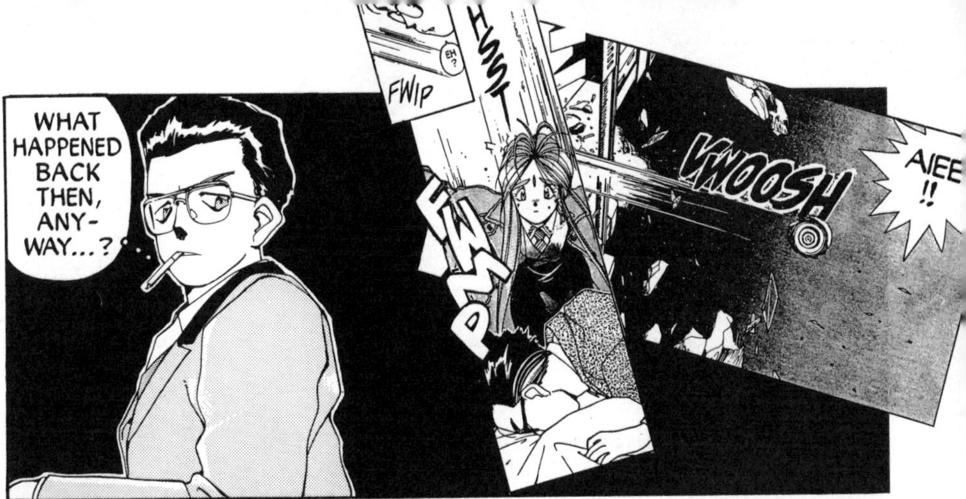
WHAT HAPPENED BACK THEN, ANY-WAY...?
FWIP
EH?
HSST
AIEE!!

Note: As seen in Oh My Goddess! Part 1, Ish #3!—Ye Ed.

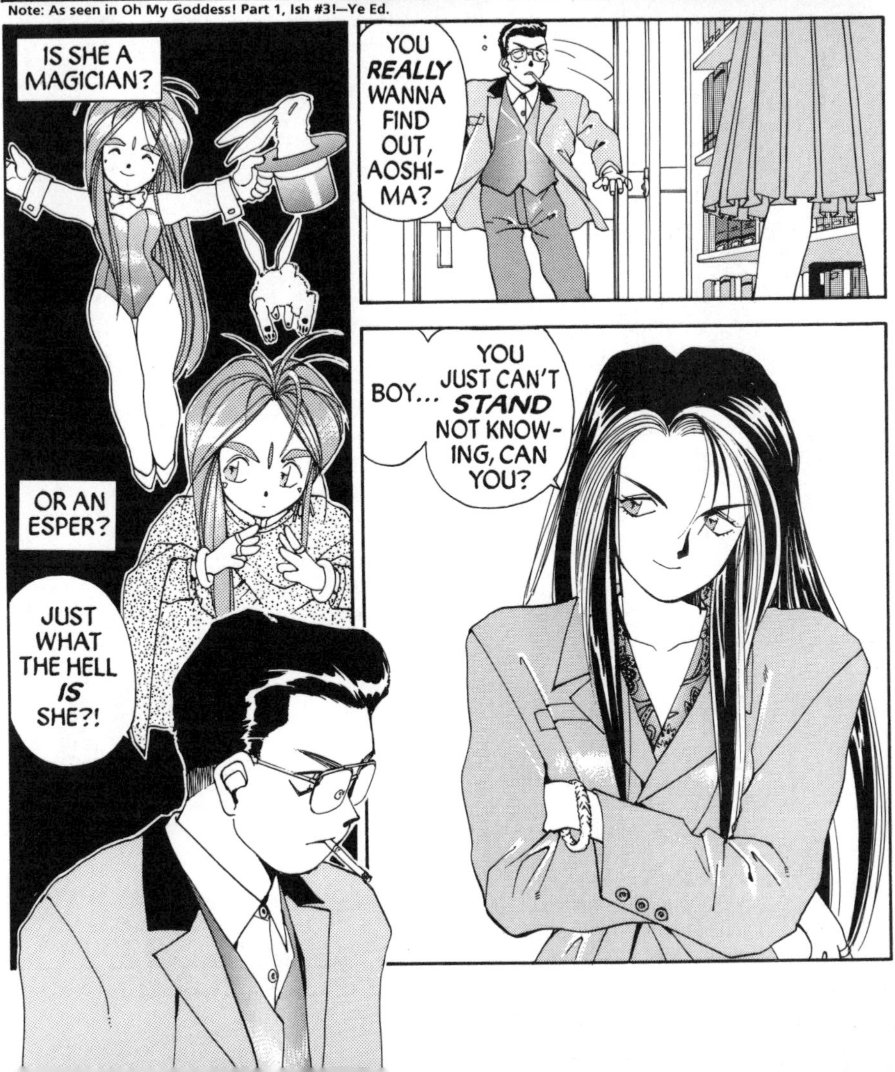
IS SHE A MAGICIAN?
OR AN ESPER?
JUST WHAT THE HELL *IS* SHE?!
YOU *REALLY* WANNA FIND OUT, AOSHI-MA?
BOY...
YOU JUST CAN'T *STAND* NOT KNOW-ING, CAN YOU?

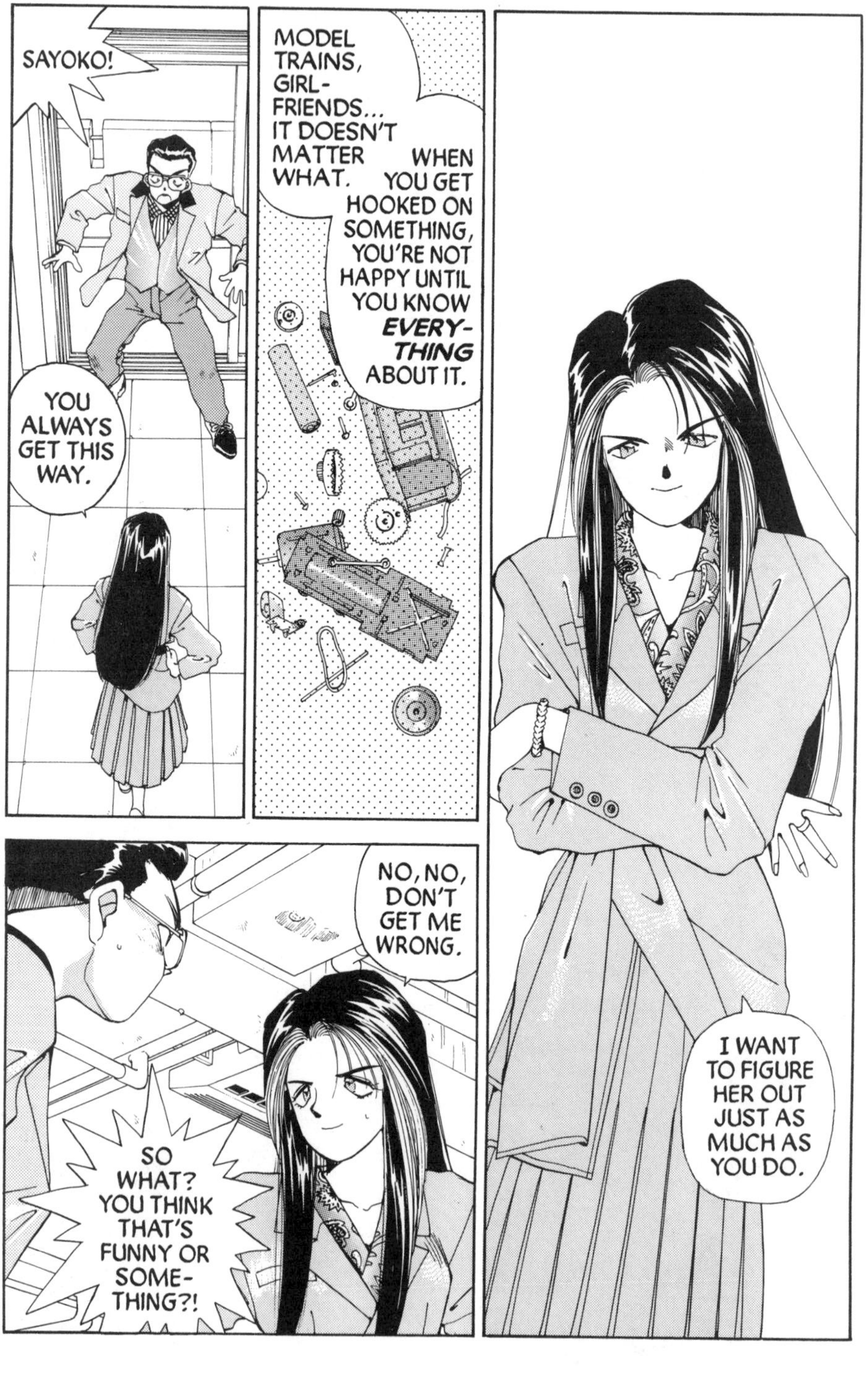
SAYOKO!
YOU ALWAYS GET THIS WAY.
MODEL TRAINS, GIRL-FRIENDS... IT DOESN'T MATTER WHAT.
WHEN YOU GET HOOKED ON SOMETHING, YOU'RE NOT HAPPY UNTIL YOU KNOW *EVERY-THING* ABOUT IT.
SO WHAT? YOU THINK THAT'S FUNNY OR SOME-THING?!
NO, NO, DON'T GET ME WRONG.
I WANT TO FIGURE HER OUT JUST AS MUCH AS YOU DO.

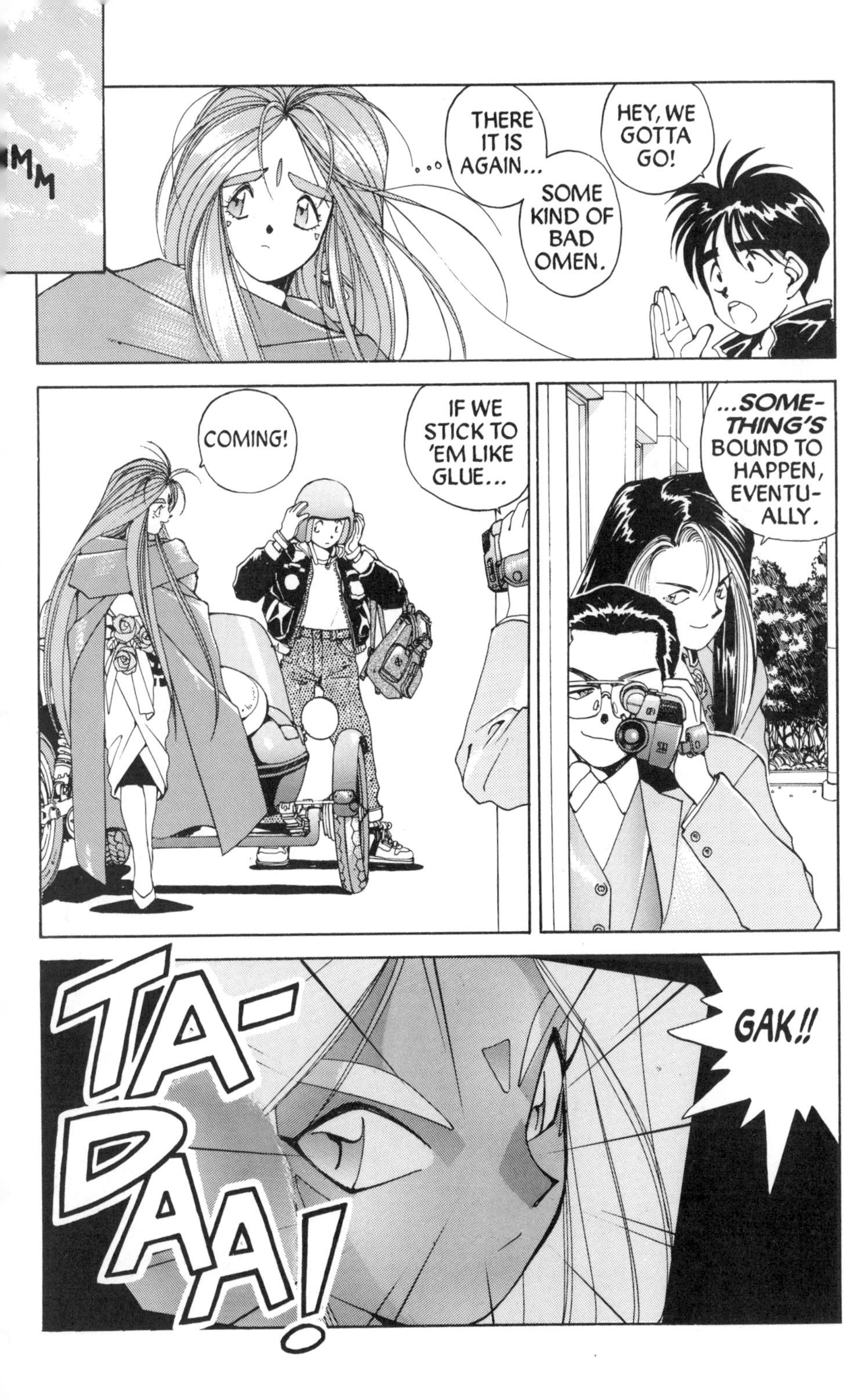
MM
...
THERE IT IS AGAIN...
SOME KIND OF BAD OMEN.
HEY, WE GOTTA GO!
COMING!
IF WE STICK TO 'EM LIKE GLUE...
...*SOMETHING'S* BOUND TO HAPPEN, EVENTUALLY.
TA-DAA!
GAK!!

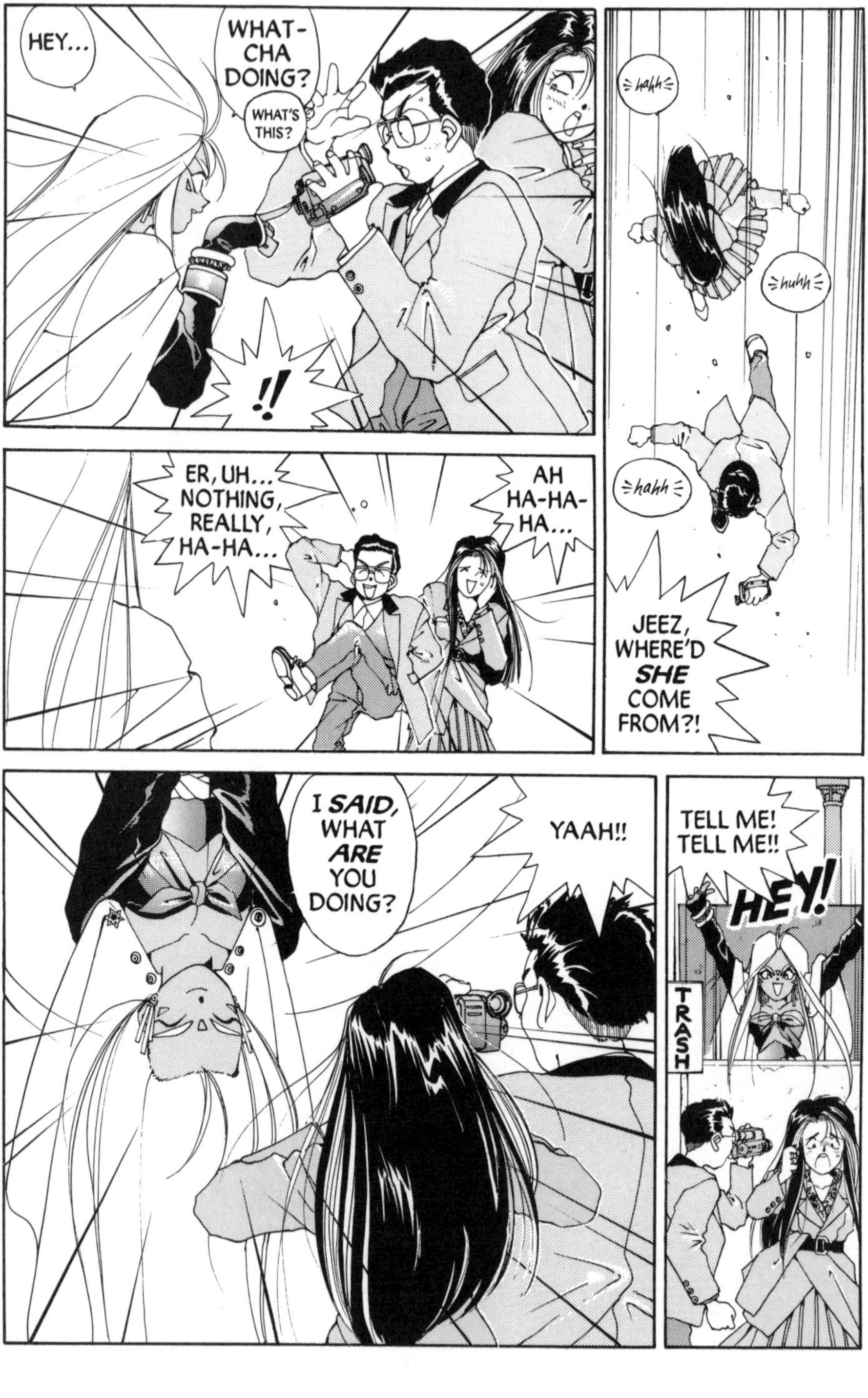
HEY...
WHAT-CHA DOING?
WHAT'S THIS?
!!
ER, UH... NOTHING, REALLY, HA-HA...
AH HA-HA-HA...
hahh
huhh
hahh
JEEZ, WHERE'D *SHE* COME FROM?!
I *SAID,* WHAT *ARE* YOU DOING?
YAAH!!
TELL ME! TELL ME!!
HEY!
TRASH

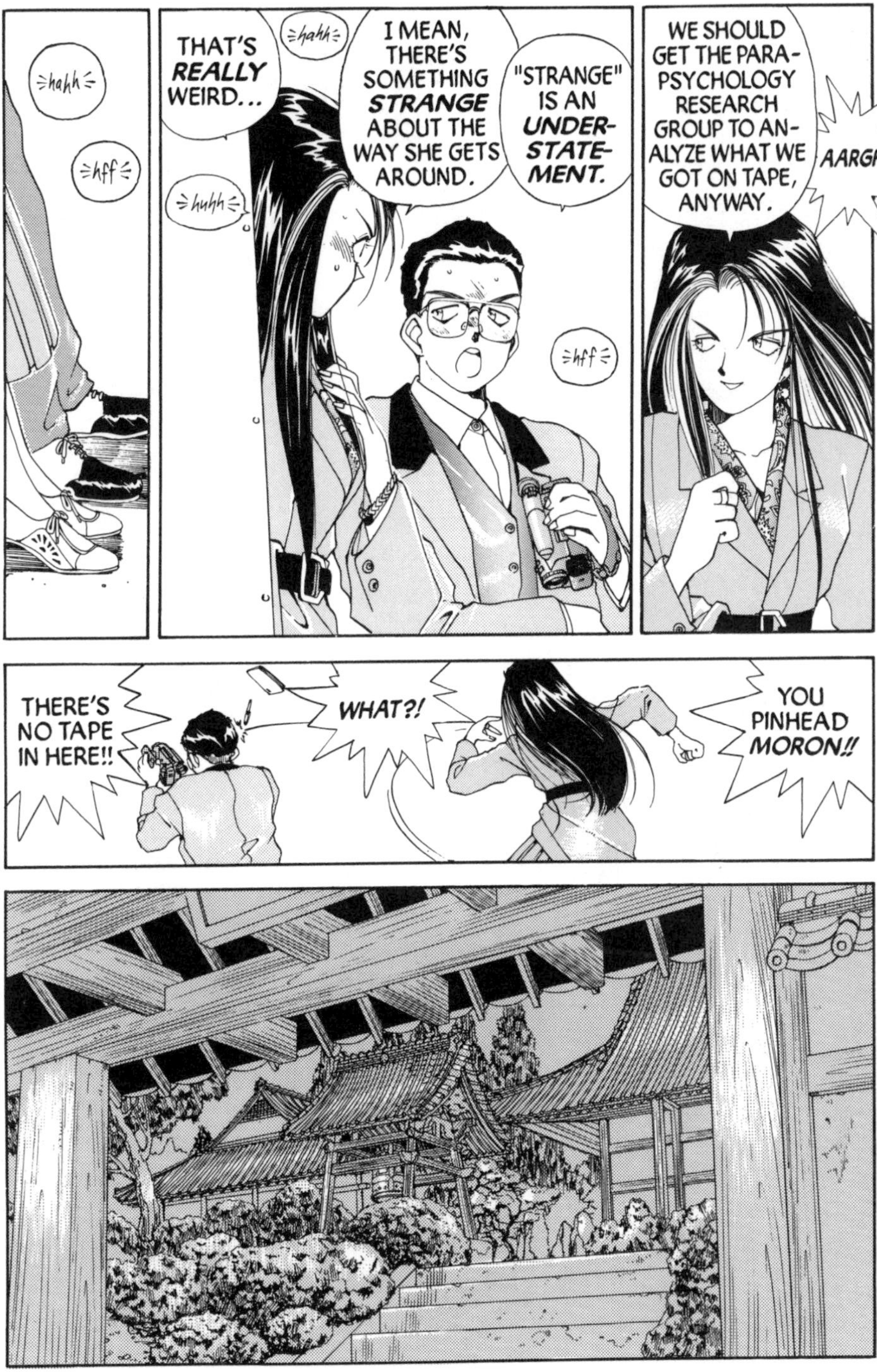
hahh
hff
THAT'S *REALLY* WEIRD...
hahh
huhh
I MEAN, THERE'S SOMETHING *STRANGE* ABOUT THE WAY SHE GETS AROUND.
"STRANGE" IS AN *UNDER-STATE-MENT.*
hff
WE SHOULD GET THE PARA-PSYCHOLOGY RESEARCH GROUP TO AN-ALYZE WHAT WE GOT ON TAPE, ANYWAY.
AARGH!
THERE'S NO TAPE IN HERE!!
WHAT?!
YOU PINHEAD *MORON!!*

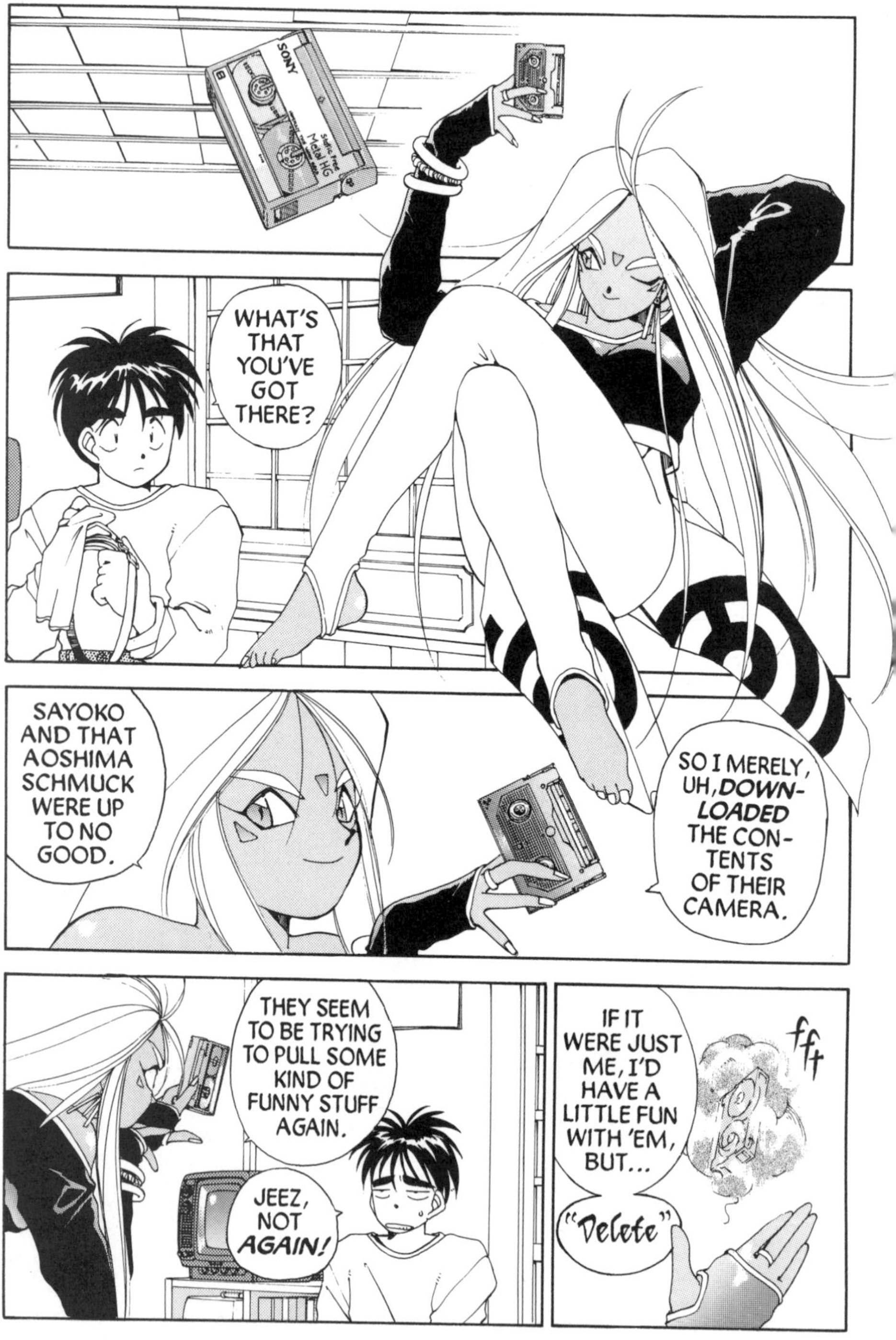
SONY
Static-free
Metal HG
WHAT'S THAT YOU'VE GOT THERE?
SAYOKO AND THAT AOSHIMA SCHMUCK WERE UP TO NO GOOD.
SO I MERELY, UH, ***DOWN-LOADED*** THE CON-TENTS OF THEIR CAMERA.
THEY SEEM TO BE TRYING TO PULL SOME KIND OF FUNNY STUFF AGAIN.
JEEZ, NOT ***AGAIN!***
IF IT WERE JUST ME, I'D HAVE A LITTLE FUN WITH 'EM, BUT...
"Delete"
fft

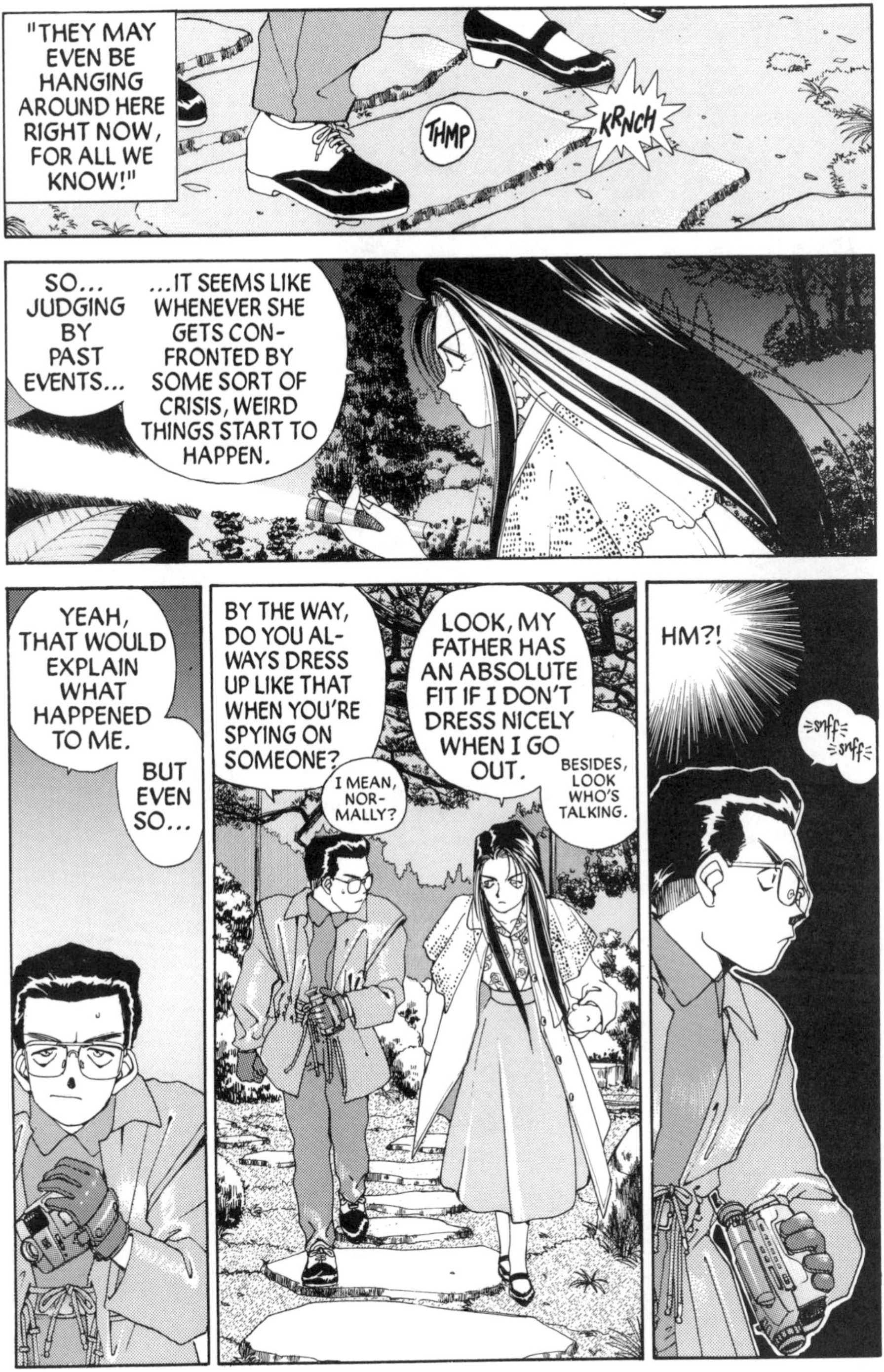
"THEY MAY EVEN BE HANGING AROUND HERE RIGHT NOW, FOR ALL WE KNOW!"
THMP
KRNCH
SO... JUDGING BY PAST EVENTS...
...IT SEEMS LIKE WHENEVER SHE GETS CON-FRONTED BY SOME SORT OF CRISIS, WEIRD THINGS START TO HAPPEN.
YEAH, THAT WOULD EXPLAIN WHAT HAPPENED TO ME.
BUT EVEN SO...
BY THE WAY, DO YOU AL-WAYS DRESS UP LIKE THAT WHEN YOU'RE SPYING ON SOMEONE?
I MEAN, NOR-MALLY?
LOOK, MY FATHER HAS AN ABSOLUTE FIT IF I DON'T DRESS NICELY WHEN I GO OUT.
BESIDES, LOOK WHO'S TALKING.
HM?!
snff snff

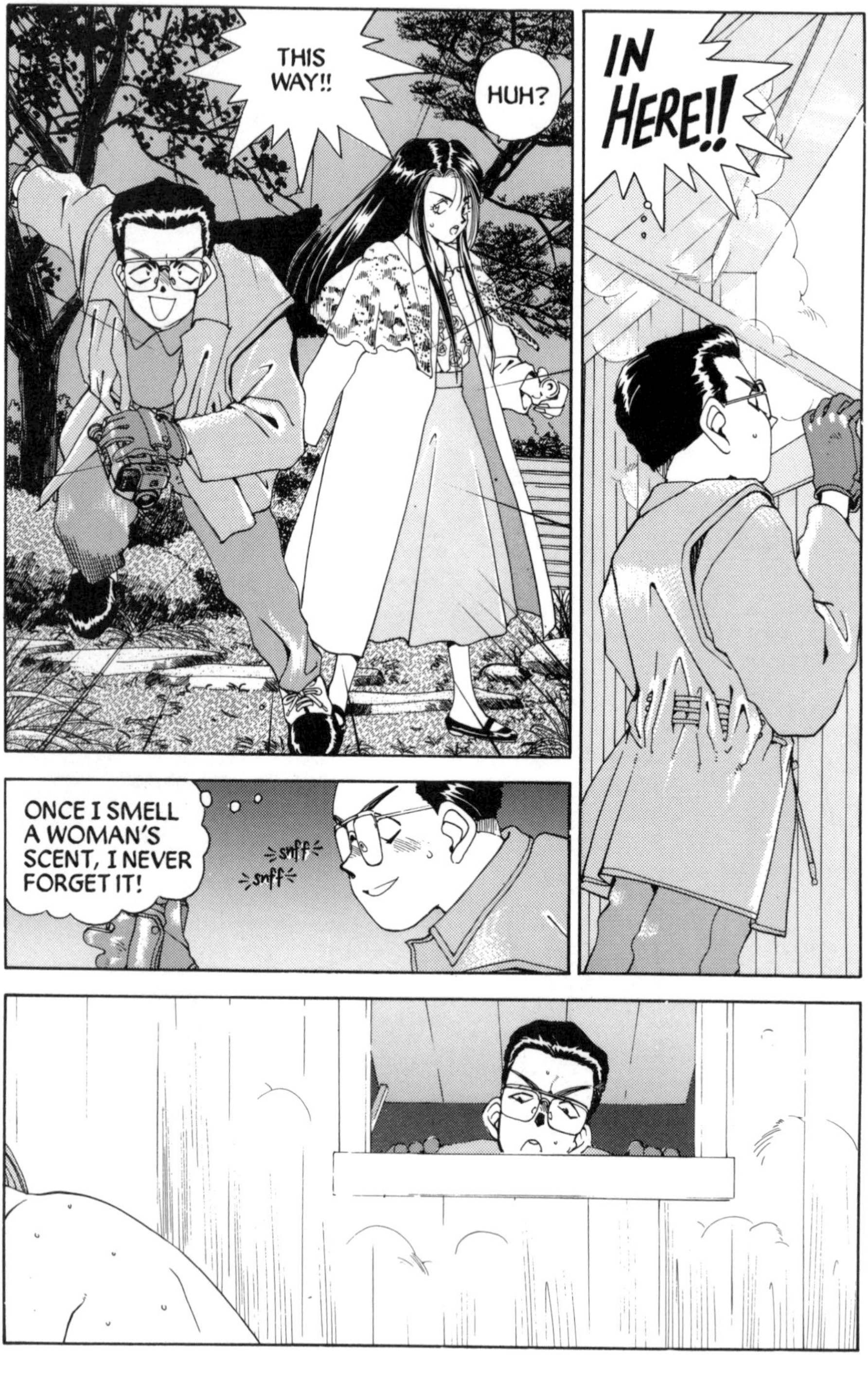
THIS WAY!!
HUH?
ONCE I SMELL A WOMAN'S SCENT, I NEVER FORGET IT!
snff
snff
IN HERE!!

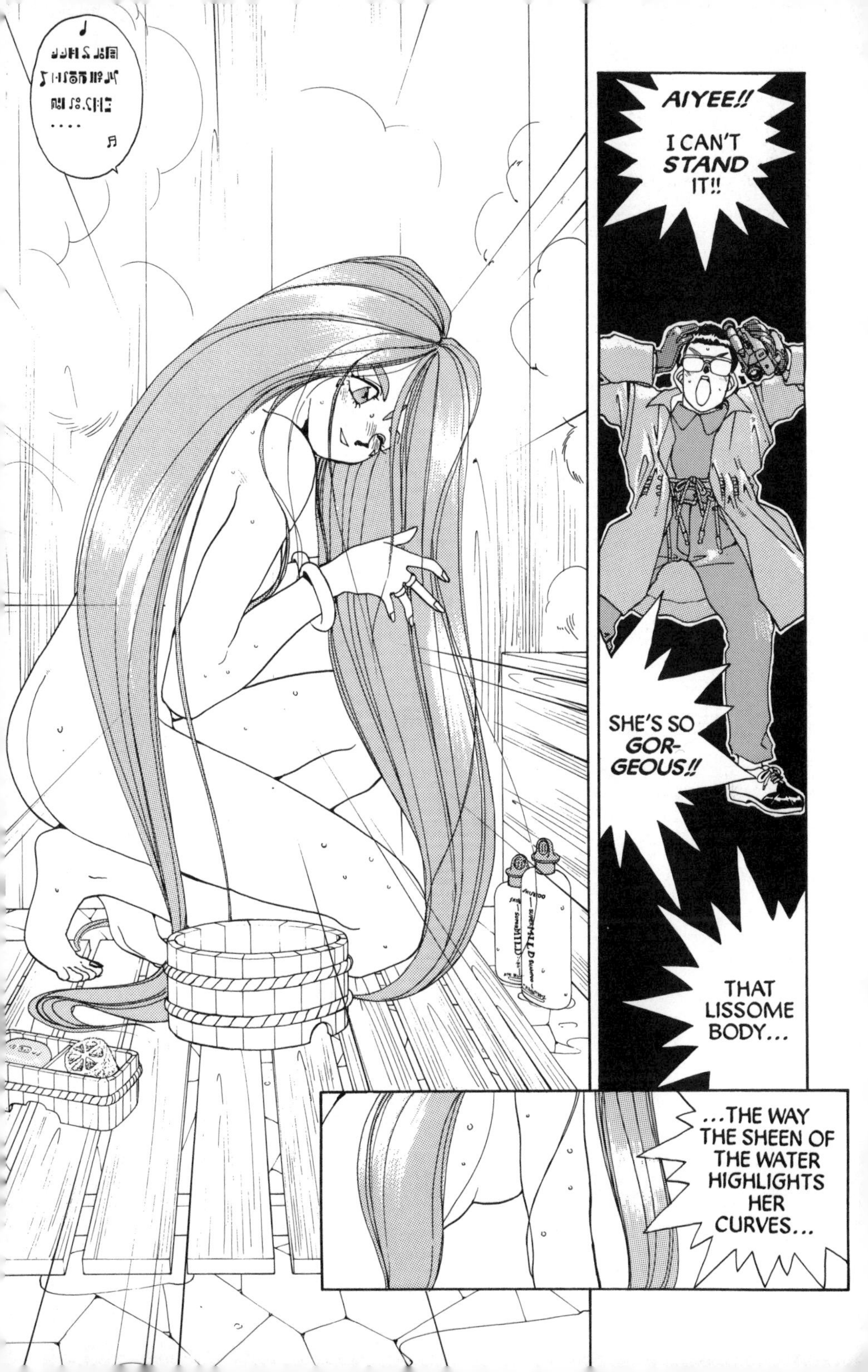

AIYEE!! I CAN'T STAND IT!!
SHE'S SO GOR-GEOUS!!
THAT LISSOME BODY...
...THE WAY THE SHEEN OF THE WATER HIGHLIGHTS HER CURVES...

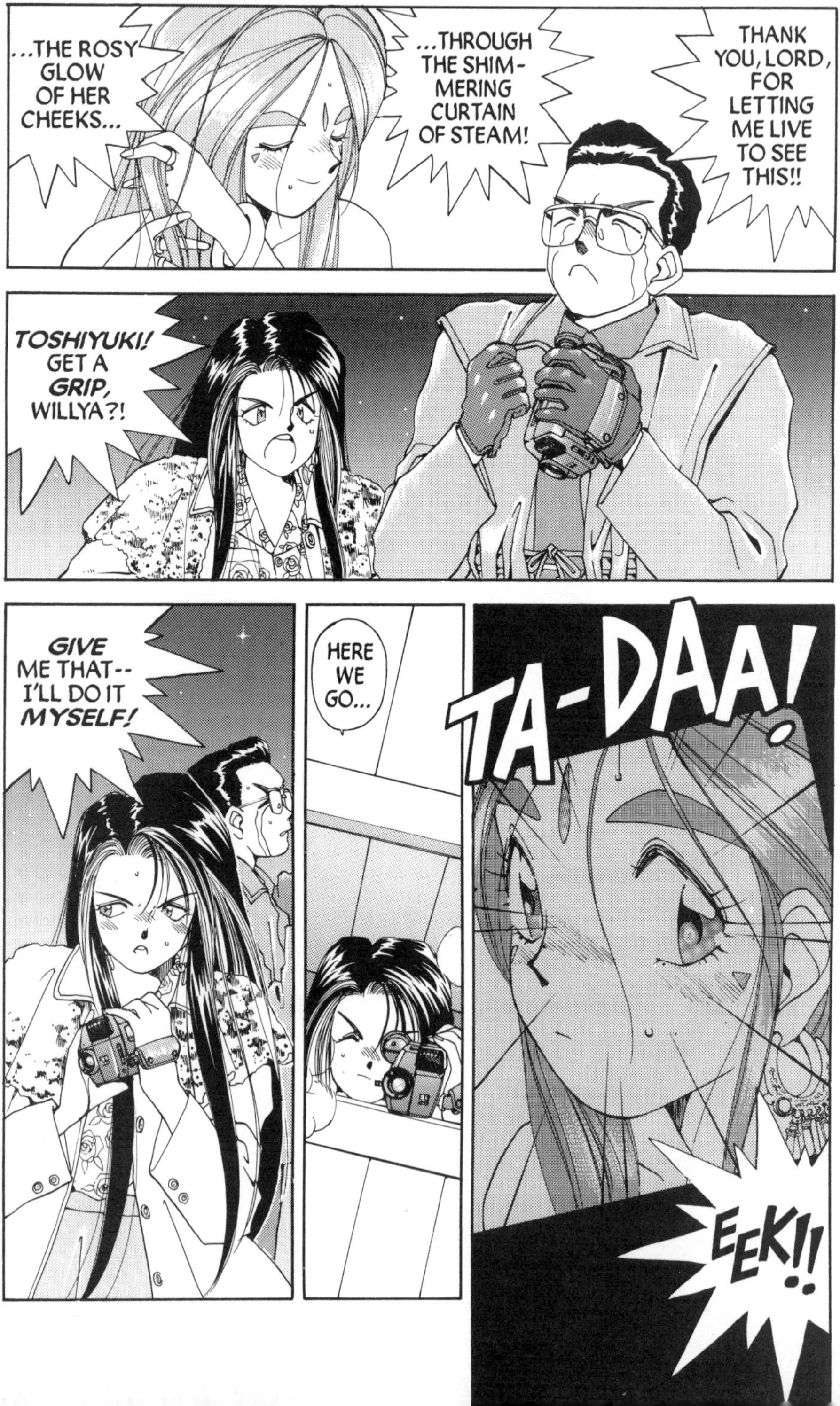
...THE ROSY GLOW OF HER CHEEKS...
...THROUGH THE SHIM-MERING CURTAIN OF STEAM!
THANK YOU, LORD, FOR LETTING ME LIVE TO SEE THIS!!
TOSHIYUKI! GET A GRIP, WILLYA?!
GIVE ME THAT-- I'LL DO IT MYSELF!
HERE WE GO...
TA-DAA!
EEK!!

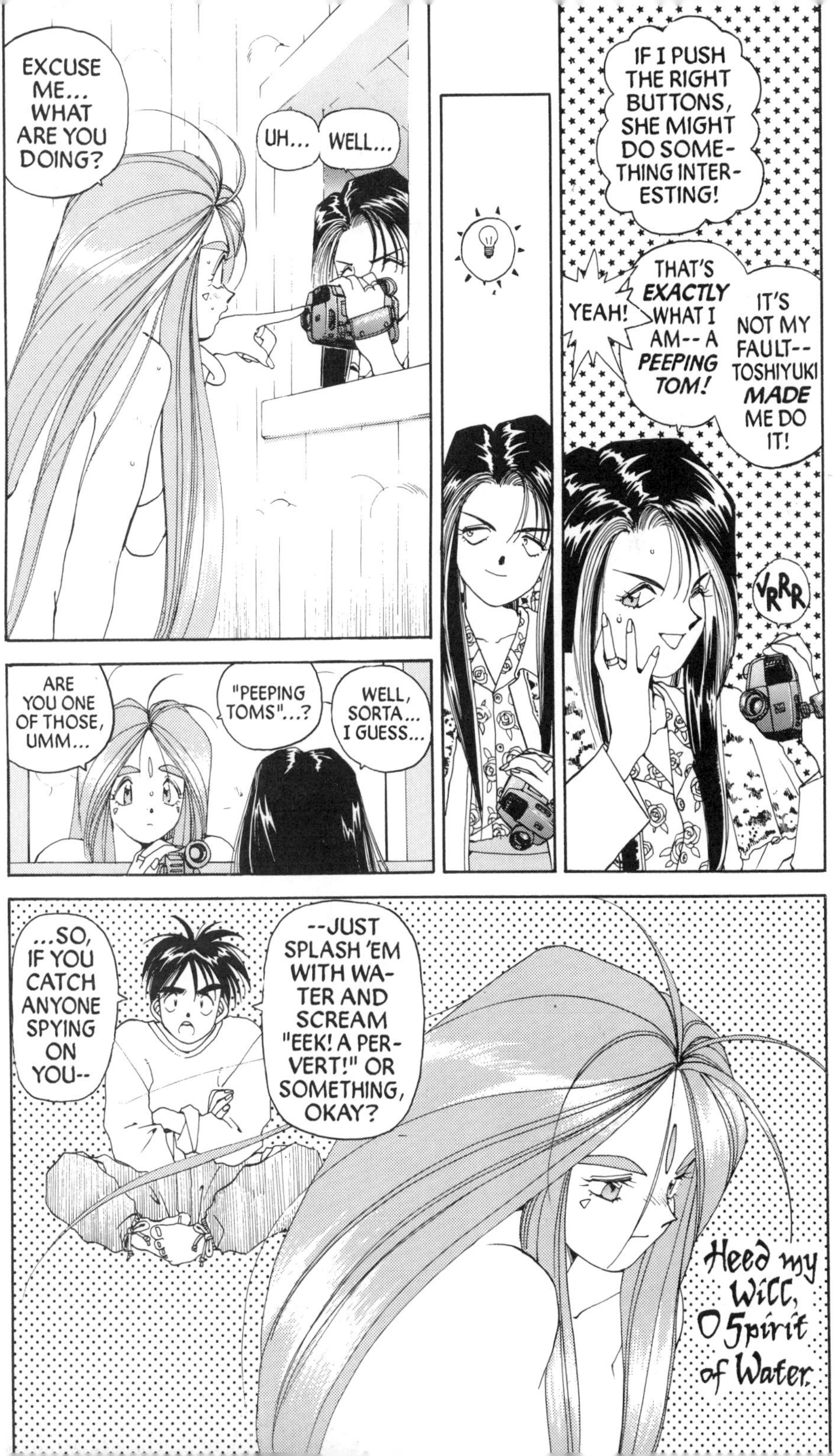
EXCUSE ME... WHAT ARE YOU DOING?
UH...
WELL...
IF I PUSH THE RIGHT BUTTONS, SHE MIGHT DO SOME-THING INTER-ESTING!
YEAH!
THAT'S EXACTLY WHAT I AM-- A PEEPING TOM!
IT'S NOT MY FAULT-- TOSHIYUKI MADE ME DO IT!
VRRR
ARE YOU ONE OF THOSE, UMM...
"PEEPING TOMS"...?
WELL, SORTA... I GUESS...
...SO, IF YOU CATCH ANYONE SPYING ON YOU--
--JUST SPLASH 'EM WITH WA-TER AND SCREAM "EEK! A PER-VERT!" OR SOMETHING, OKAY?
Heed my Will, O Spirit of Water.

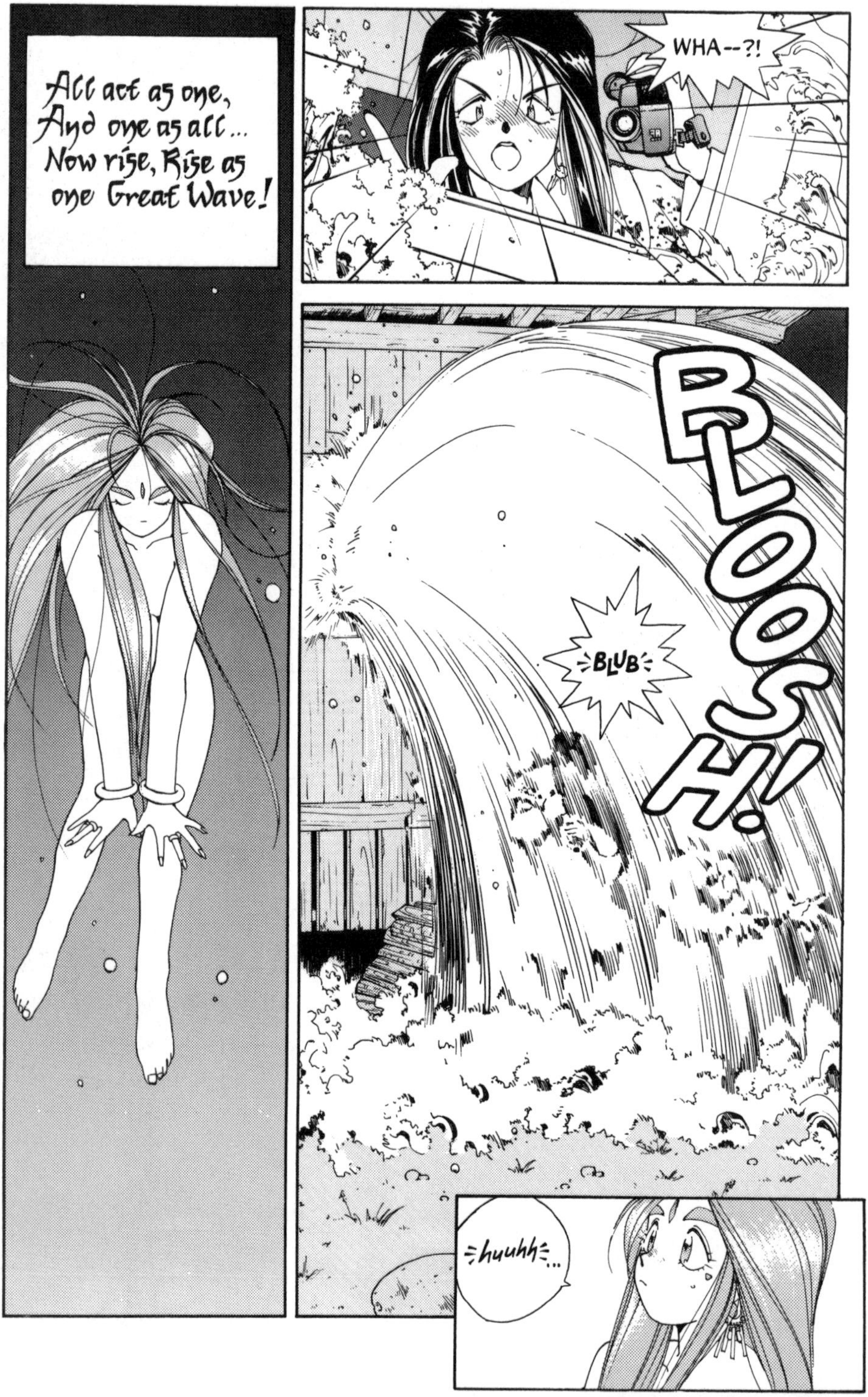
All act as one,
And one as all...
Now rise, Rise as one Great Wave!
WHA--?!
BLOOSH!
BLUB
huuhh...

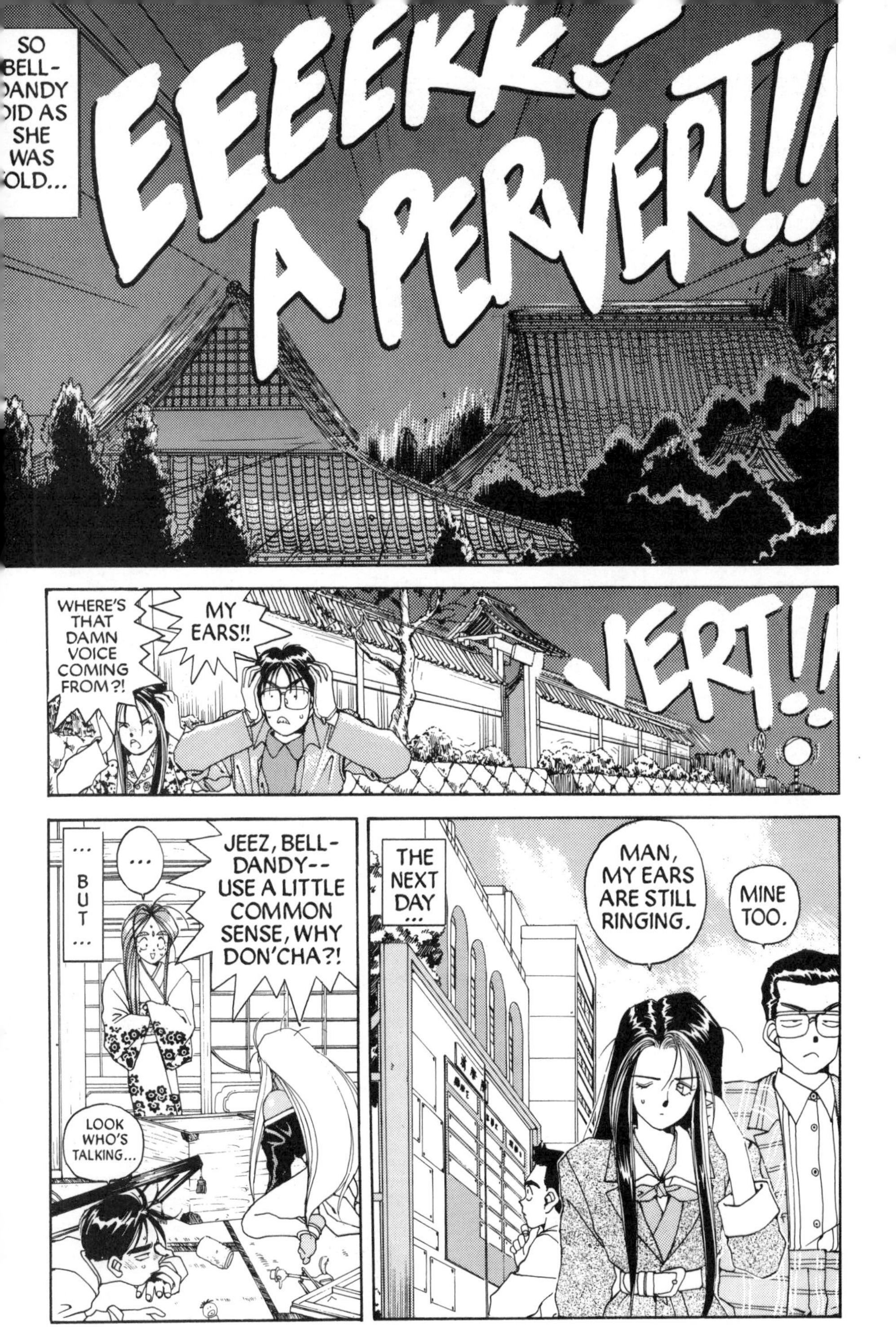
SO BELL-DANDY DID AS SHE WAS TOLD...
EEEEKK! A PERVERT!!
WHERE'S THAT DAMN VOICE COMING FROM?!
MY EARS!!
VERT!!
... BUT ...
...
JEEZ, BELL-DANDY-- USE A LITTLE COMMON SENSE, WHY DON'CHA?!
LOOK WHO'S TALKING...
THE NEXT DAY ...
MAN, MY EARS ARE STILL RINGING.
MINE TOO.

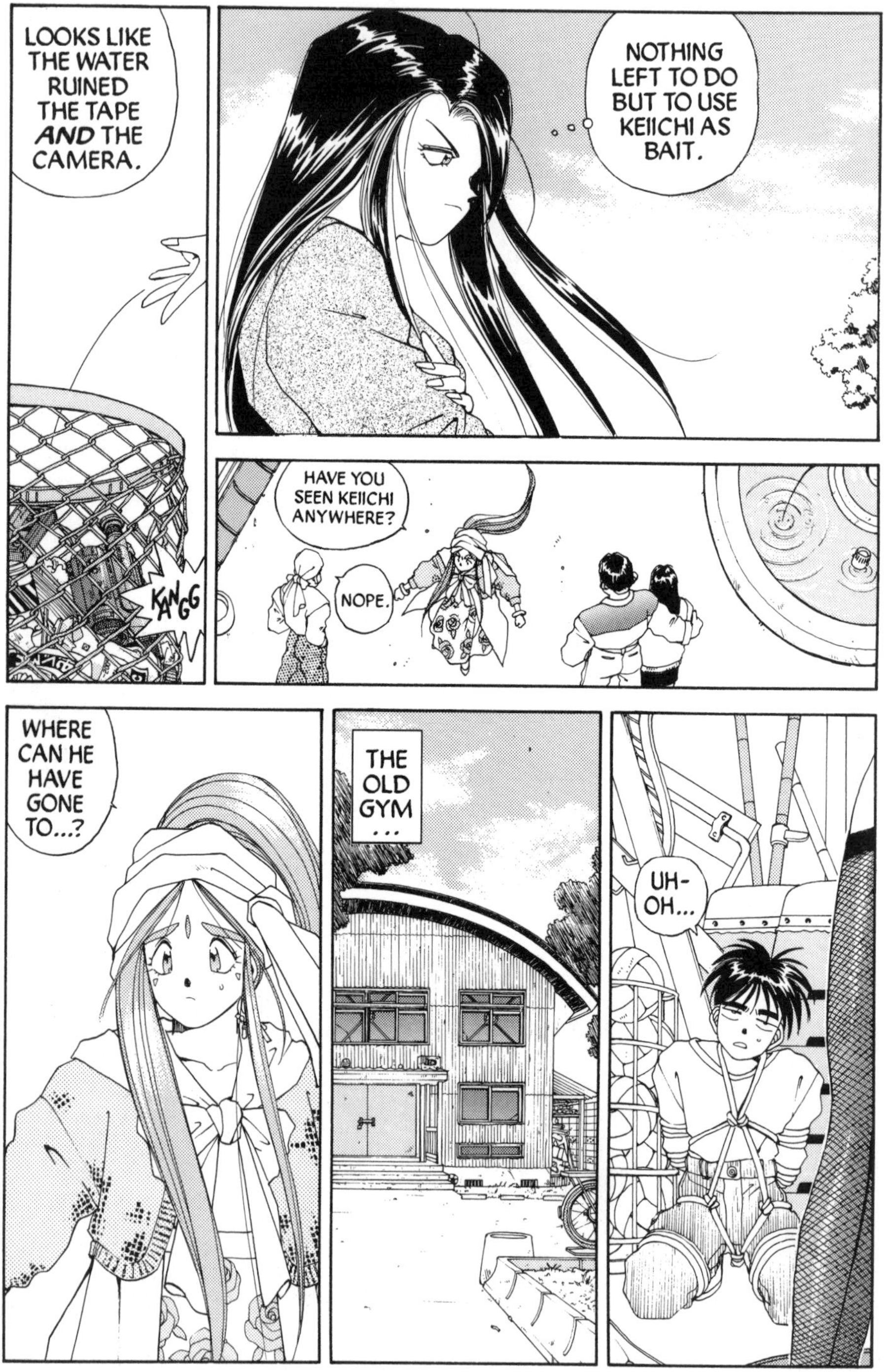
LOOKS LIKE THE WATER RUINED THE TAPE AND THE CAMERA.
KANGG
NOTHING LEFT TO DO BUT TO USE KEIICHI AS BAIT.
HAVE YOU SEEN KEIICHI ANYWHERE?
NOPE.
WHERE CAN HE HAVE GONE TO...?
THE OLD GYM ...
UH-OH...

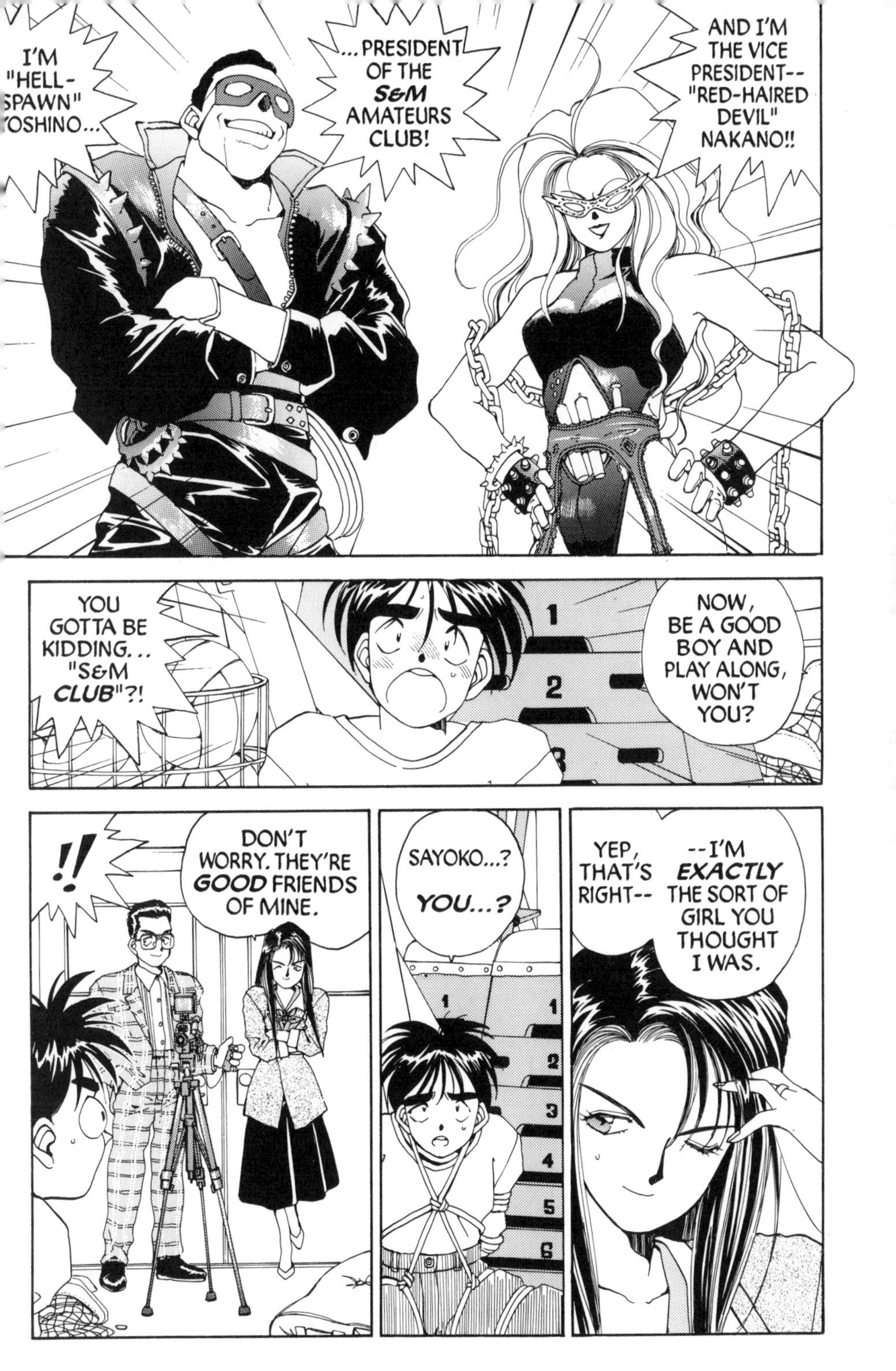
I'M "HELL-SPAWN" YOSHINO...
...PRESIDENT OF THE S&M AMATEURS CLUB!
AND I'M THE VICE PRESIDENT-- "RED-HAIRED DEVIL" NAKANO!!
YOU GOTTA BE KIDDING... "S&M CLUB"?!
NOW, BE A GOOD BOY AND PLAY ALONG, WON'T YOU?
!!
DON'T WORRY. THEY'RE GOOD FRIENDS OF MINE.
SAYOKO...? YOU...?
YEP, THAT'S RIGHT--
--I'M EXACTLY THE SORT OF GIRL YOU THOUGHT I WAS.

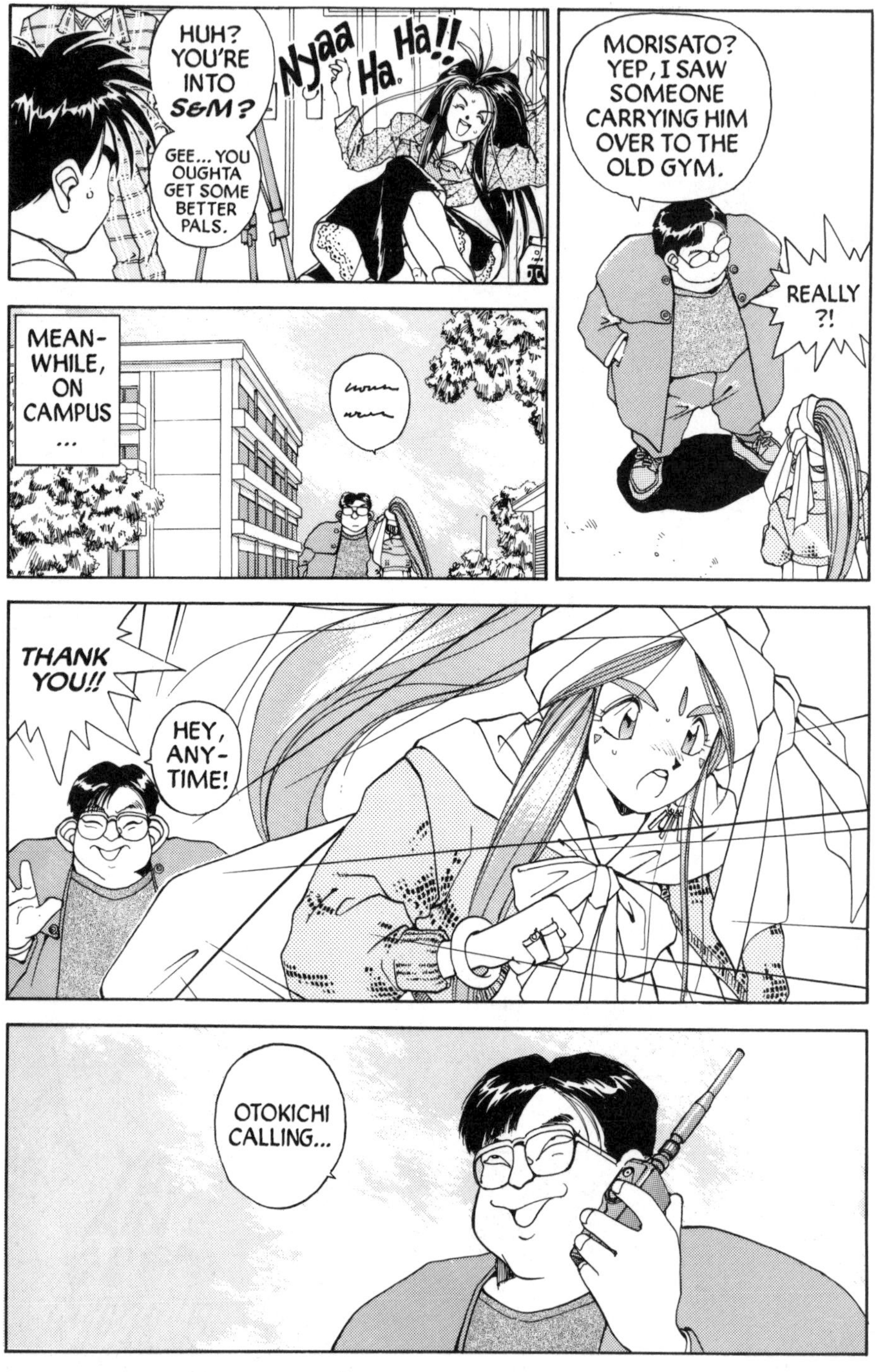
HUH? YOU'RE INTO S&M?
Nyaa Ha Ha!!
GEE... YOU OUGHTA GET SOME BETTER PALS.
MEAN-WHILE, ON CAMPUS ...
MORISATO? YEP, I SAW SOMEONE CARRYING HIM OVER TO THE OLD GYM.
REALLY ?!
THANK YOU!!
HEY, ANY-TIME!
OTOKICHI CALLING...

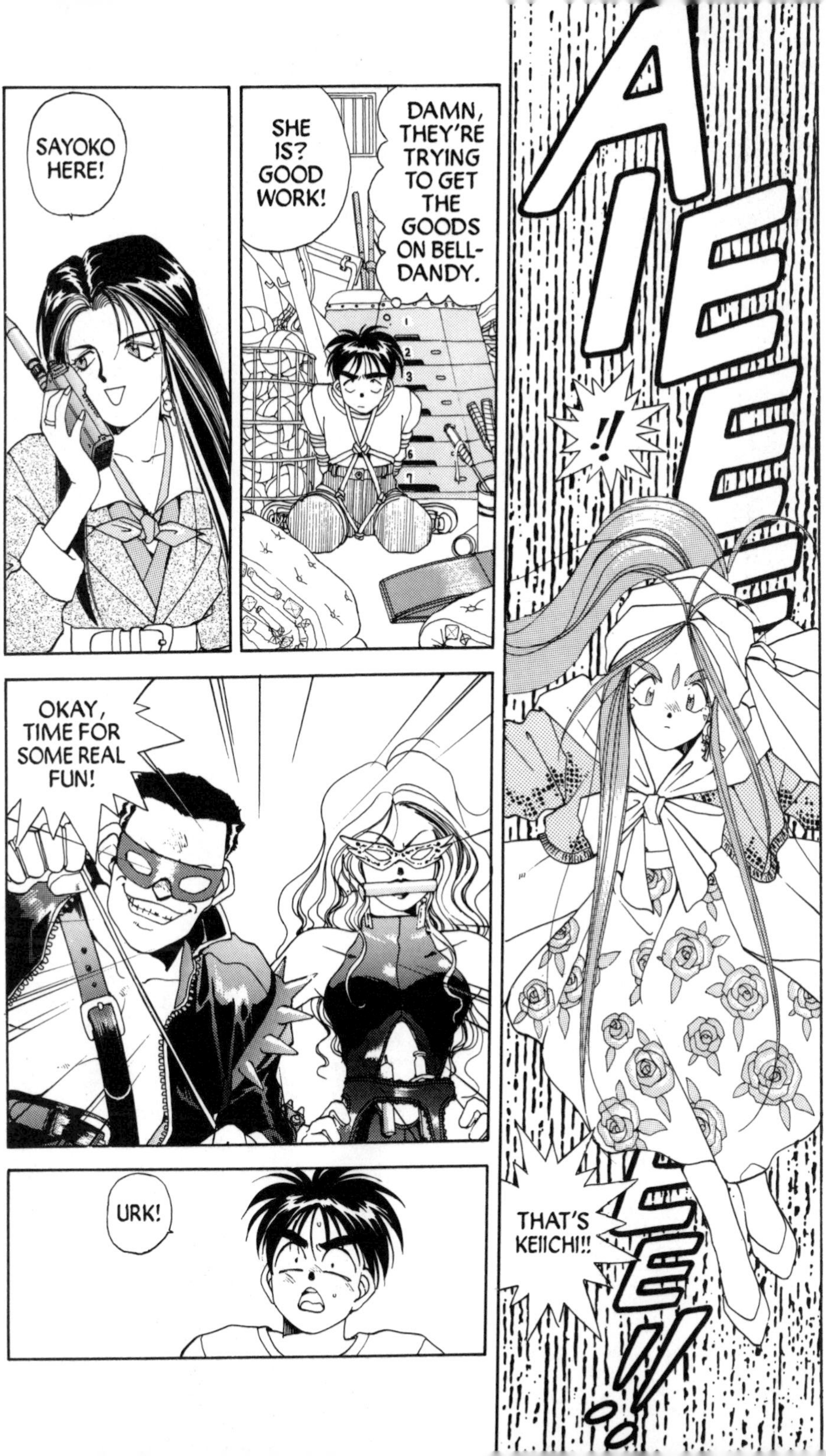
SAYOKO HERE!
SHE IS? GOOD WORK!
DAMN, THEY'RE TRYING TO GET THE GOODS ON BELL-DANDY.
OKAY, TIME FOR SOME REAL FUN!
URK!
AIEEEEEEE!!
!!
THAT'S KEIICHI!!

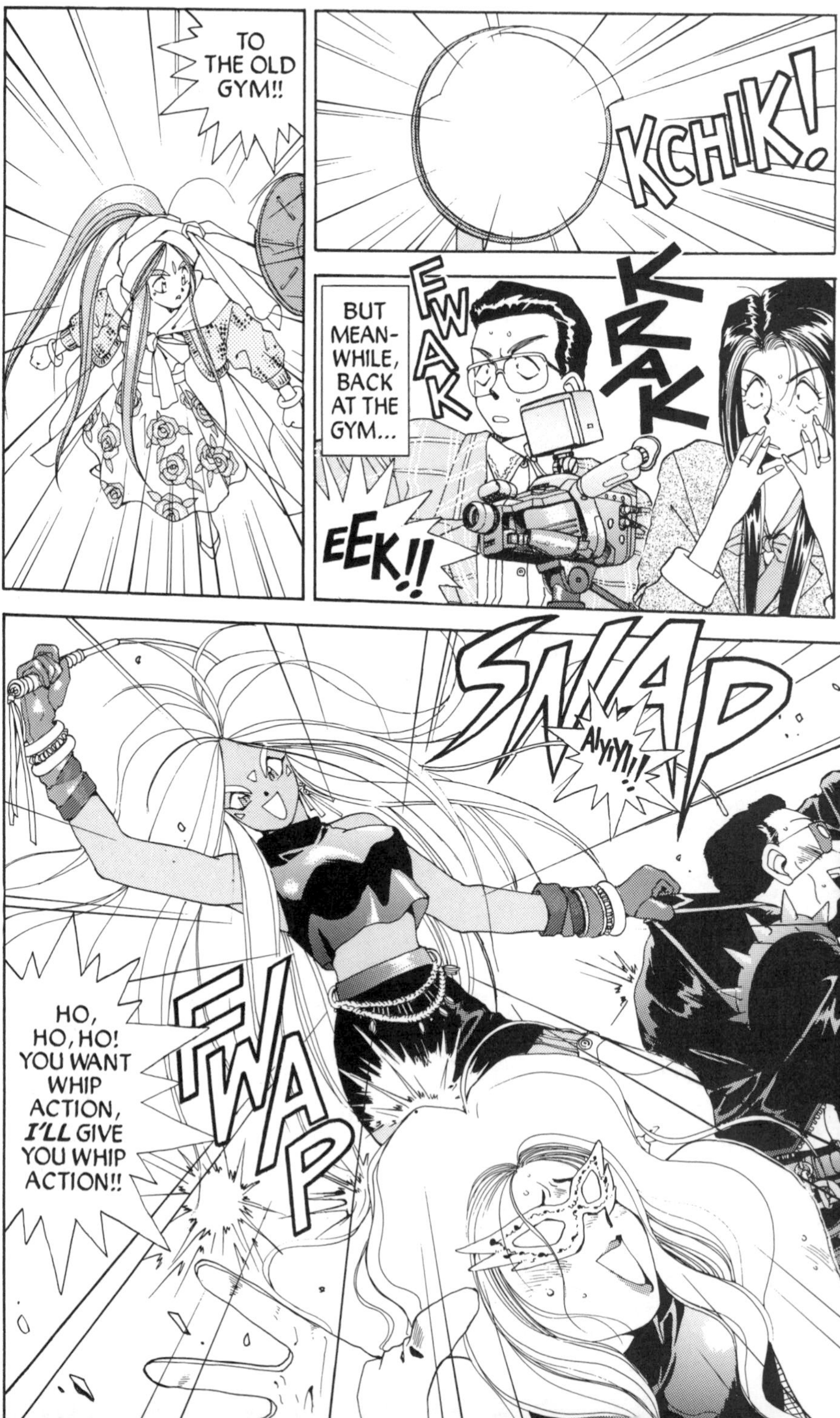
TO THE OLD GYM!!
KCHIK!
BUT MEAN-WHILE, BACK AT THE GYM...
FWAK
KRAK
EEK!!
SNAP
AIYIYI!!
HO, HO, HO! YOU WANT WHIP ACTION, *I'LL* GIVE YOU WHIP ACTION!!
FWAP

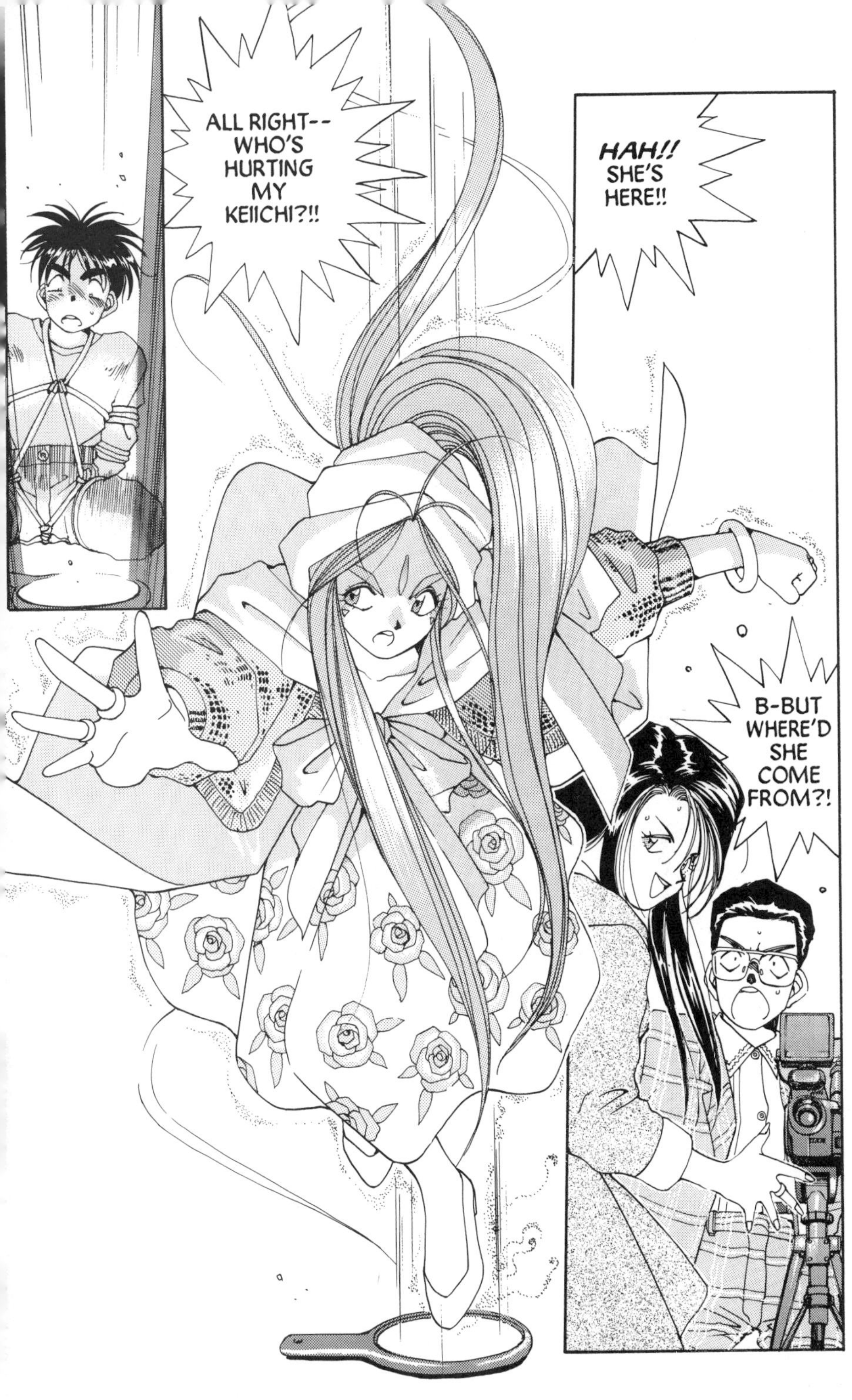
ALL RIGHT-- WHO'S HURTING MY KEIICHI?!!
HAH!! SHE'S HERE!!
B-BUT WHERE'D SHE COME FROM?!

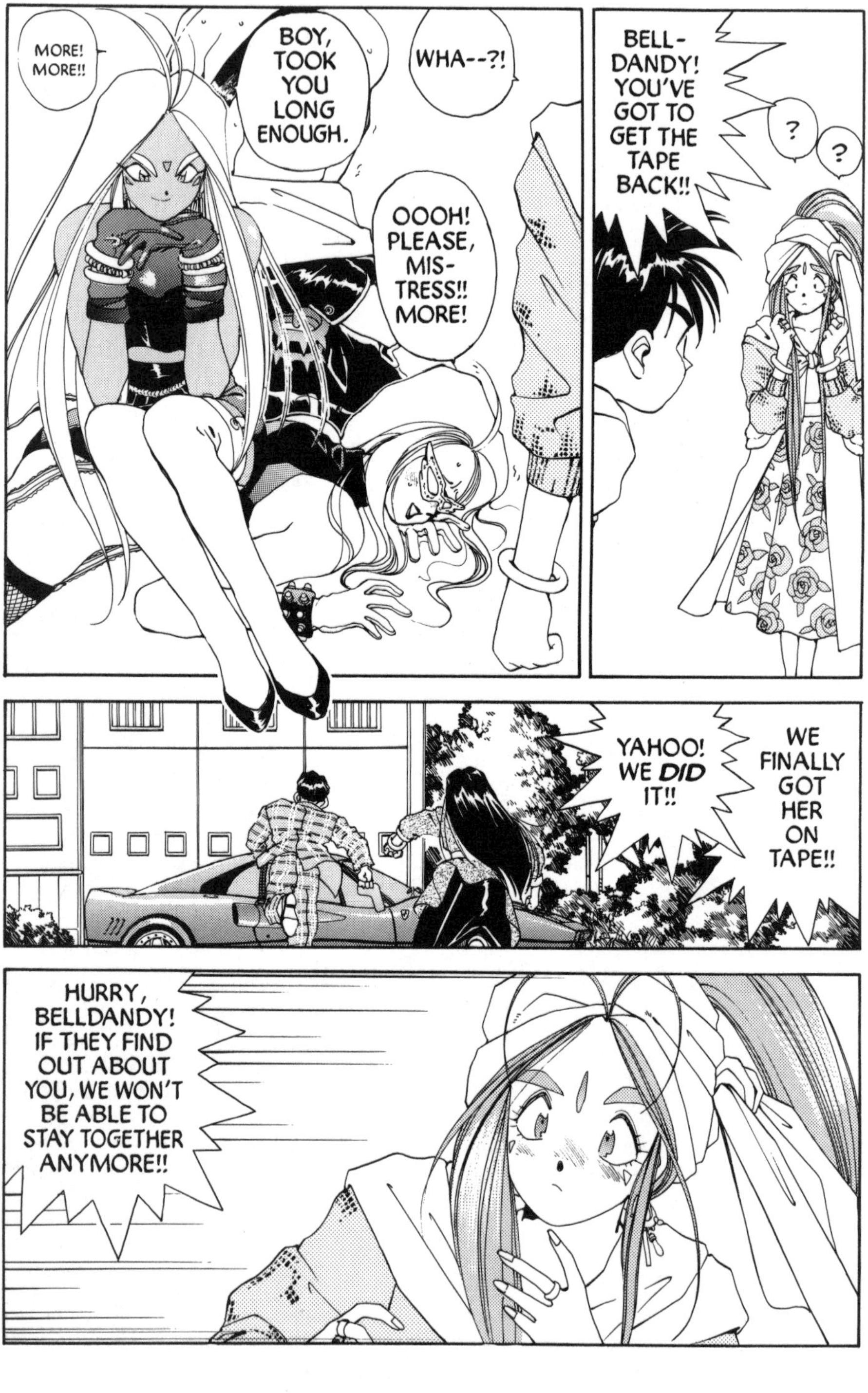

MORE! MORE!!
BOY, TOOK YOU LONG ENOUGH.
WHA--?!
OOOH! PLEASE, MIS-TRESS!! MORE!
BELL-DANDY! YOU'VE GOT TO GET THE TAPE BACK!!
?
?
YAHOO! WE DID IT!!
WE FINALLY GOT HER ON TAPE!!
HURRY, BELLDANDY! IF THEY FIND OUT ABOUT YOU, WE WON'T BE ABLE TO STAY TOGETHER ANYMORE!!

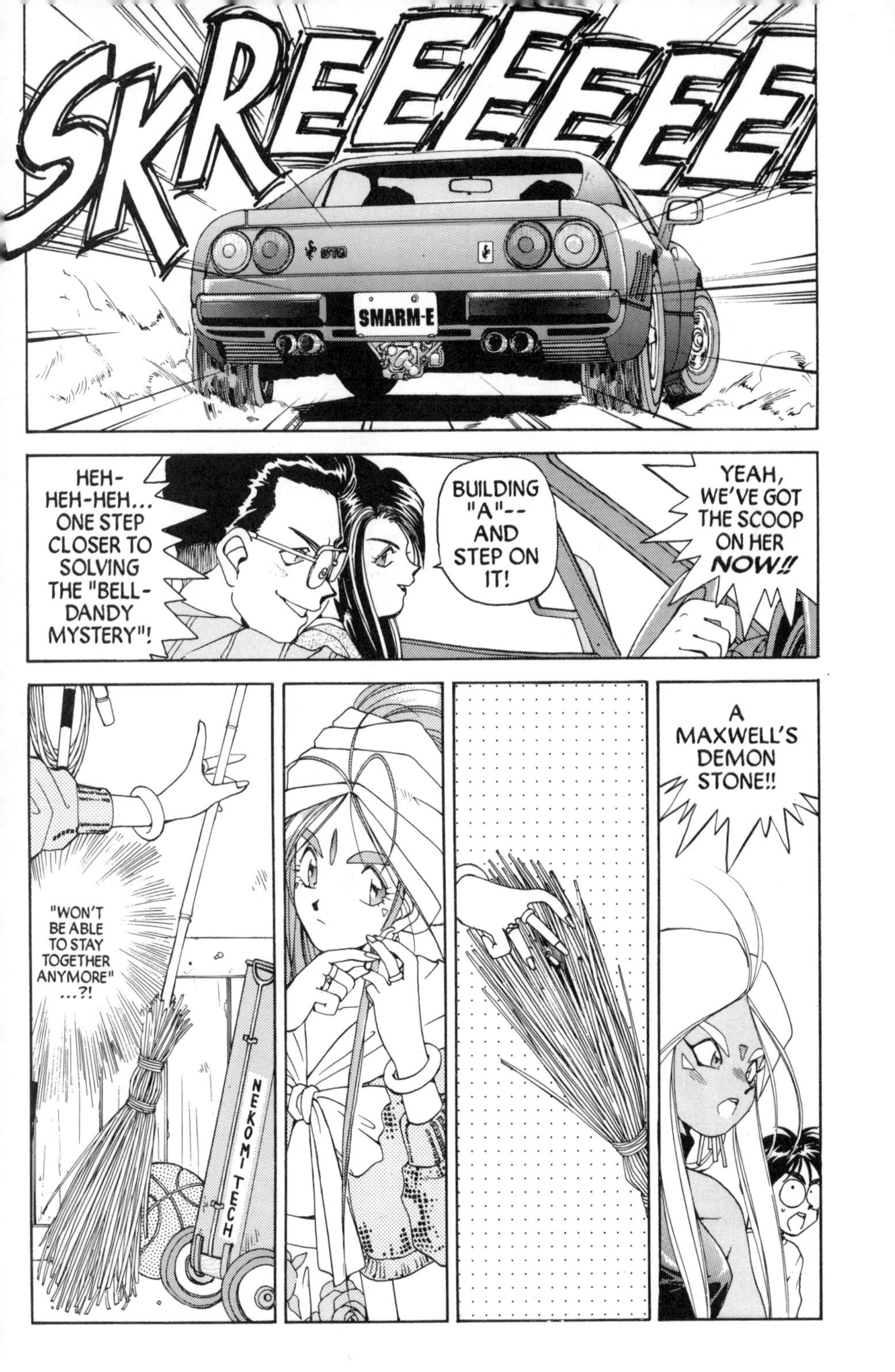
SKREEEEEEE
SMARM-E
HEH-HEH-HEH... ONE STEP CLOSER TO SOLVING THE "BELL-DANDY MYSTERY"!
BUILDING "A"-- AND STEP ON IT!
YEAH, WE'VE GOT THE SCOOP ON HER NOW!!
"WON'T BE ABLE TO STAY TOGETHER ANYMORE" ...?!
NEKOMI TECH
A MAXWELL'S DEMON STONE!!

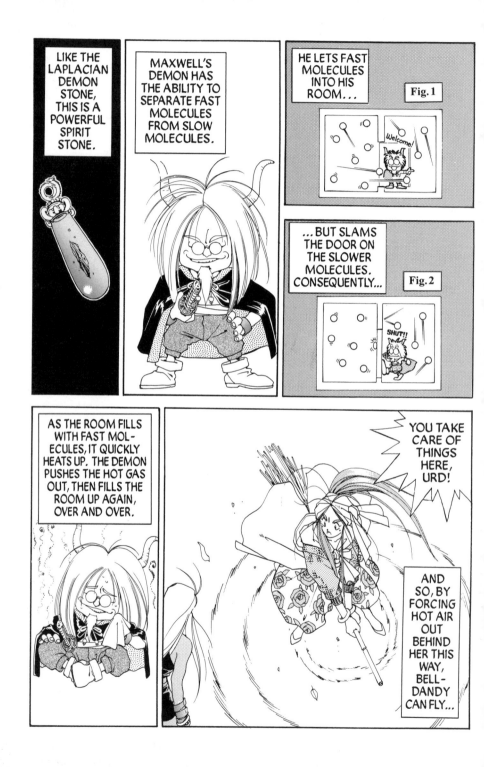

LIKE THE LAPLACIAN DEMON STONE, THIS IS A POWERFUL SPIRIT STONE.

MAXWELL'S DEMON HAS THE ABILITY TO SEPARATE FAST MOLECULES FROM SLOW MOLECULES.

HE LETS FAST MOLECULES INTO HIS ROOM...

Fig. 1

Welcome!

...BUT SLAMS THE DOOR ON THE SLOWER MOLECULES. CONSEQUENTLY...

Fig. 2

SHUT!!

AS THE ROOM FILLS WITH FAST MOLECULES, IT QUICKLY HEATS UP. THE DEMON PUSHES THE HOT GAS OUT, THEN FILLS THE ROOM UP AGAIN, OVER AND OVER.

YOU TAKE CARE OF THINGS HERE, URD!

AND SO, BY FORCING HOT AIR OUT BEHIND HER THIS WAY, BELL-DANDY CAN FLY...

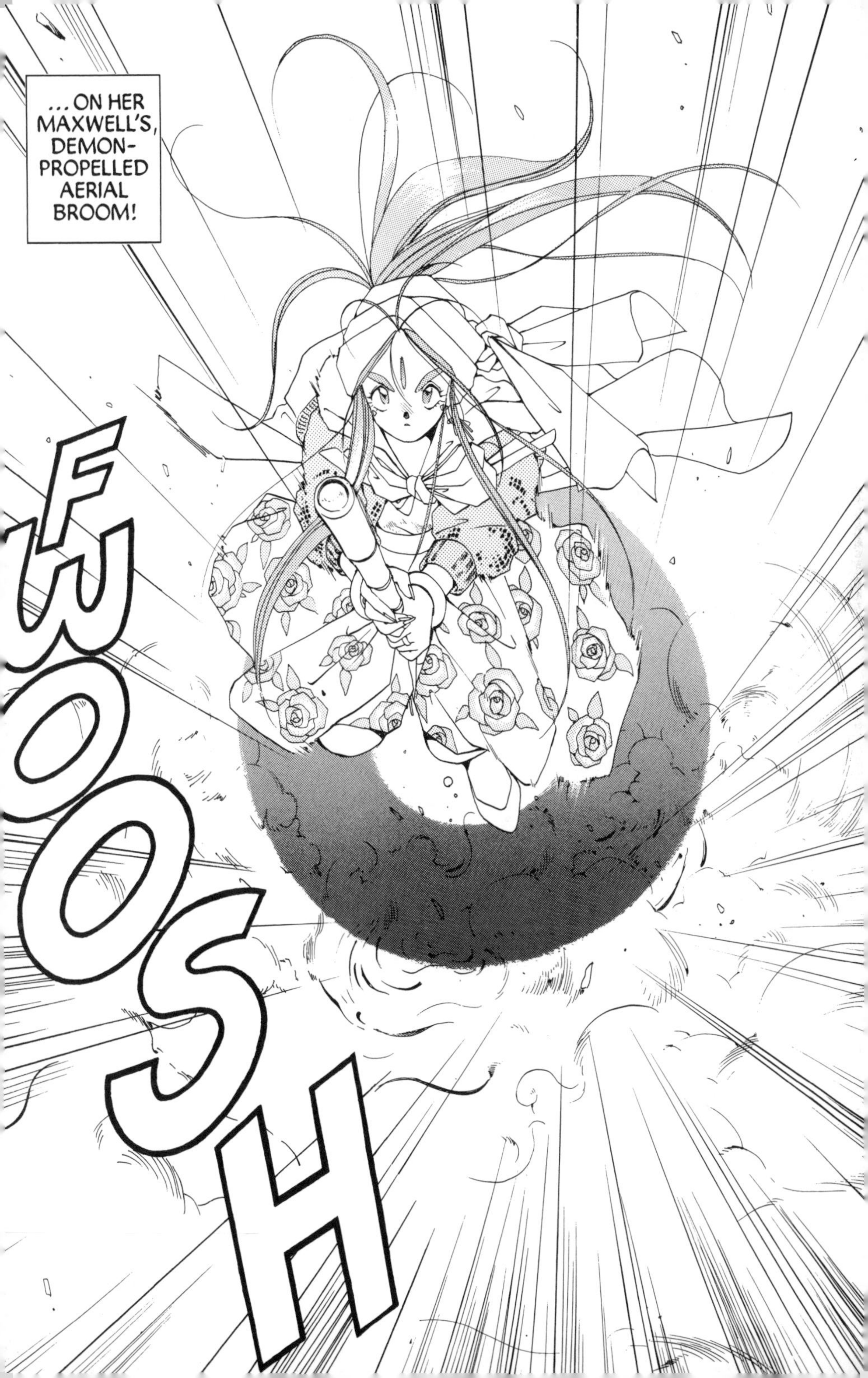
...ON HER MAXWELL'S, DEMON-PROPELLED AERIAL BROOM!
FWOOOSH

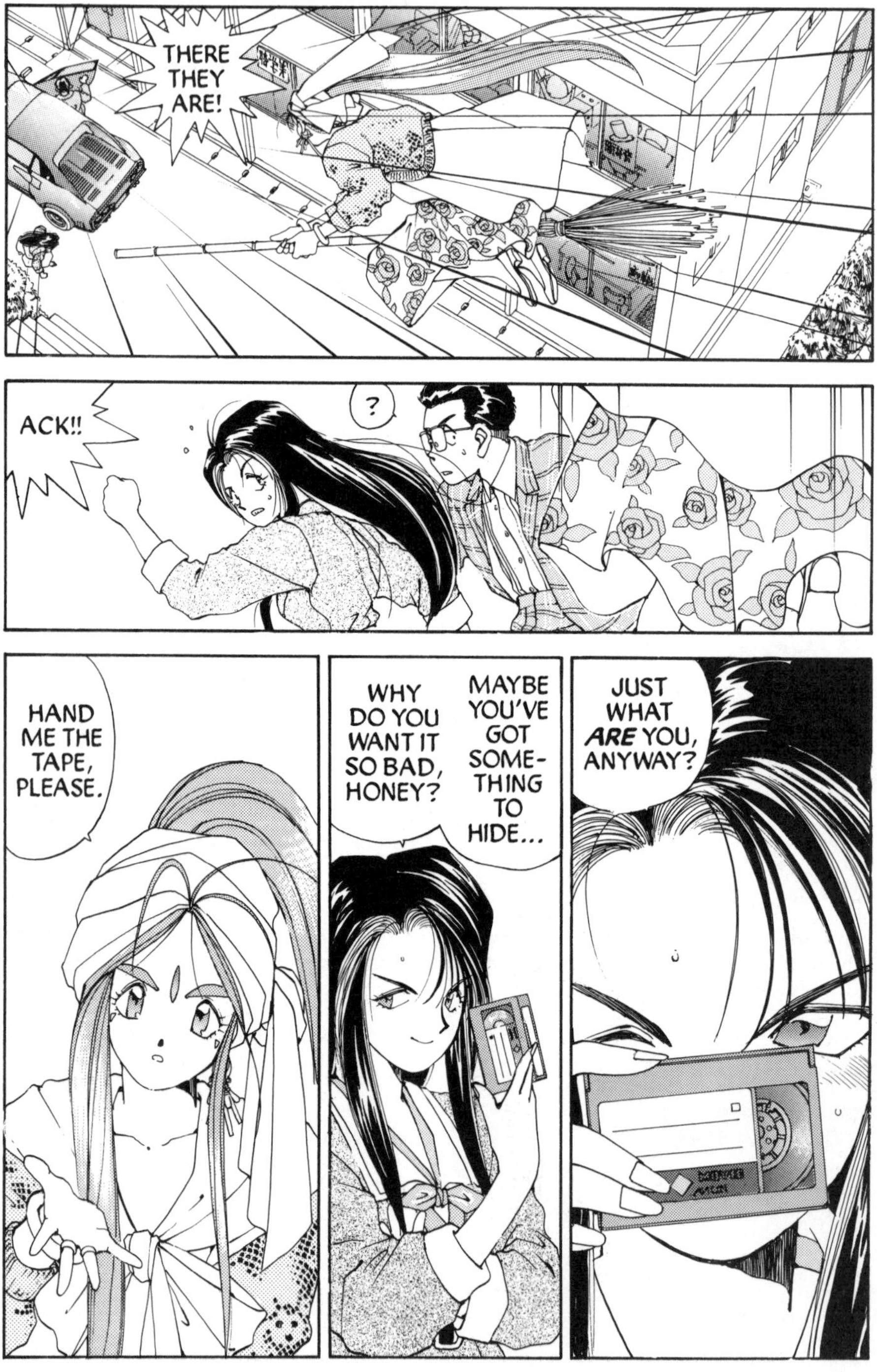
THERE THEY ARE!
ACK!!
?
HAND ME THE TAPE, PLEASE.
WHY DO YOU WANT IT SO BAD, HONEY?
MAYBE YOU'VE GOT SOME- THING TO HIDE...
JUST WHAT *ARE* YOU, ANYWAY?

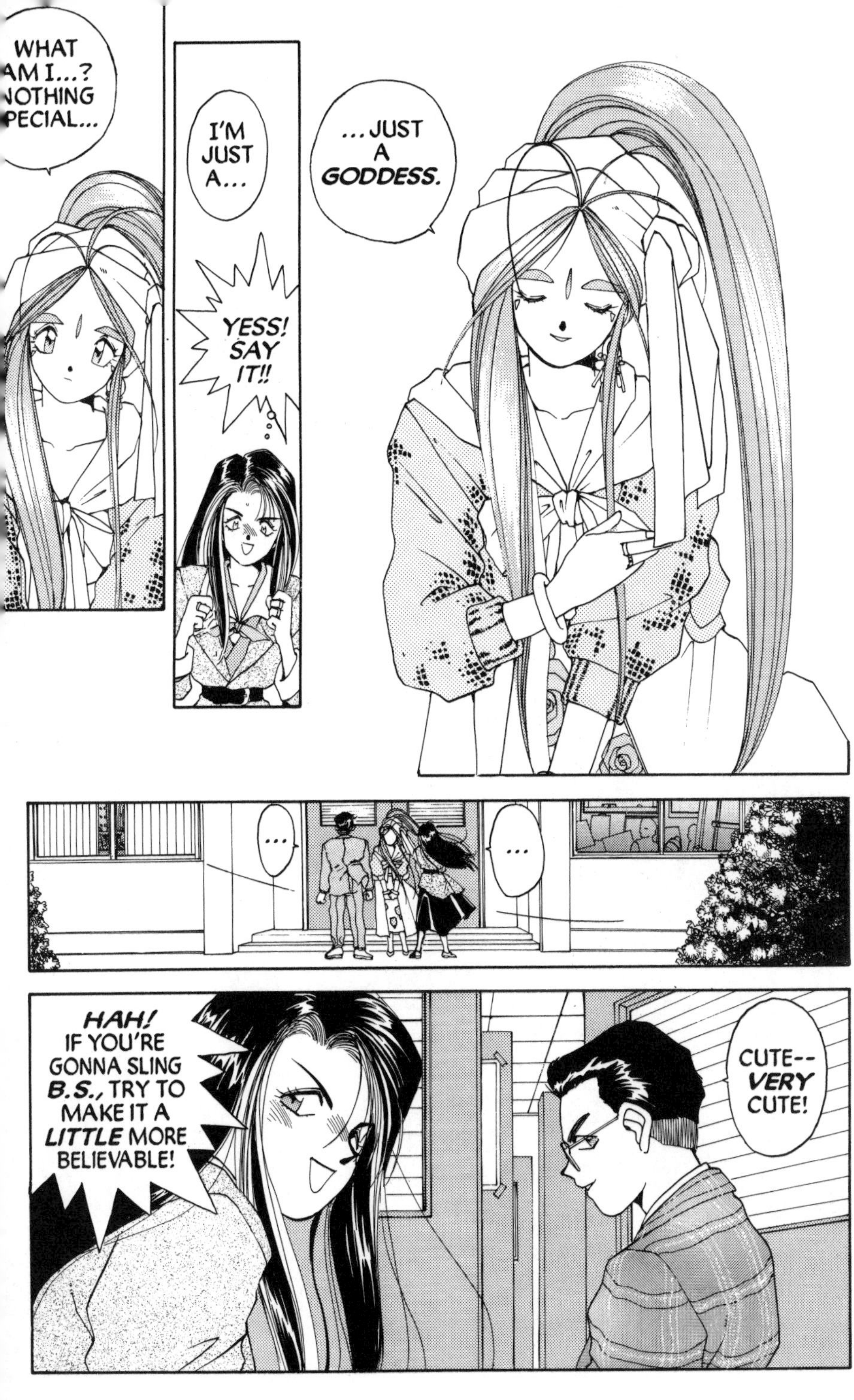
WHAT AM I...? NOTHING PECIAL...
I'M JUST A...
YESS! SAY IT!!
...JUST A GODDESS.
...
...
HAH! IF YOU'RE GONNA SLING B.S., TRY TO MAKE IT A LITTLE MORE BELIEVABLE!
CUTE-- VERY CUTE!

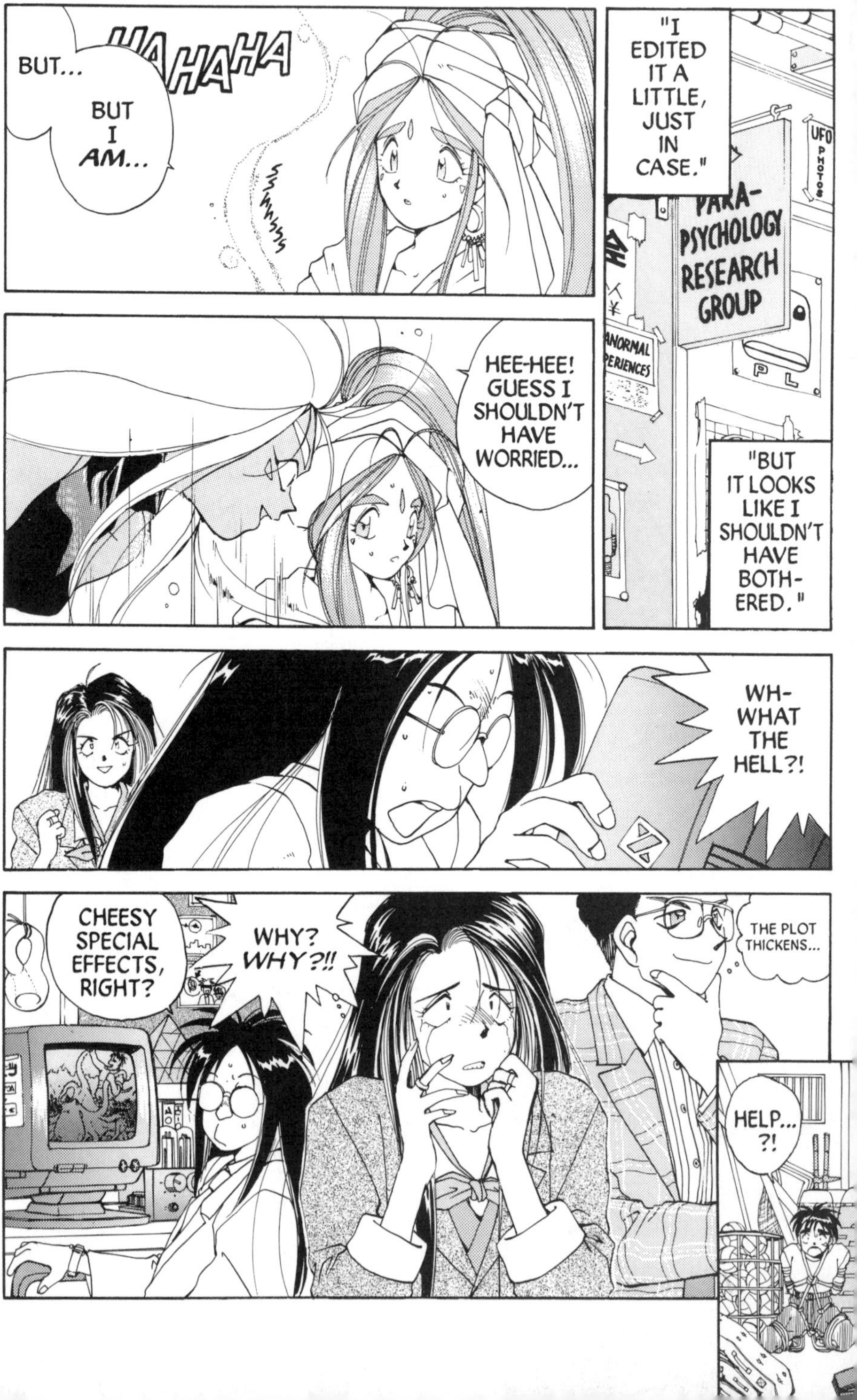
HAHAHA
BUT...
BUT I AM...
SHHHSSS
HEE-HEE! GUESS I SHOULDN'T HAVE WORRIED...
"I EDITED IT A LITTLE, JUST IN CASE."
UFO PHOTOS
PARA-PSYCHOLOGY RESEARCH GROUP
"BUT IT LOOKS LIKE I SHOULDN'T HAVE BOTH-ERED."
WH-WHAT THE HELL?!
CHEESY SPECIAL EFFECTS, RIGHT?
WHY? WHY?!!
THE PLOT THICKENS...
HELP...?!

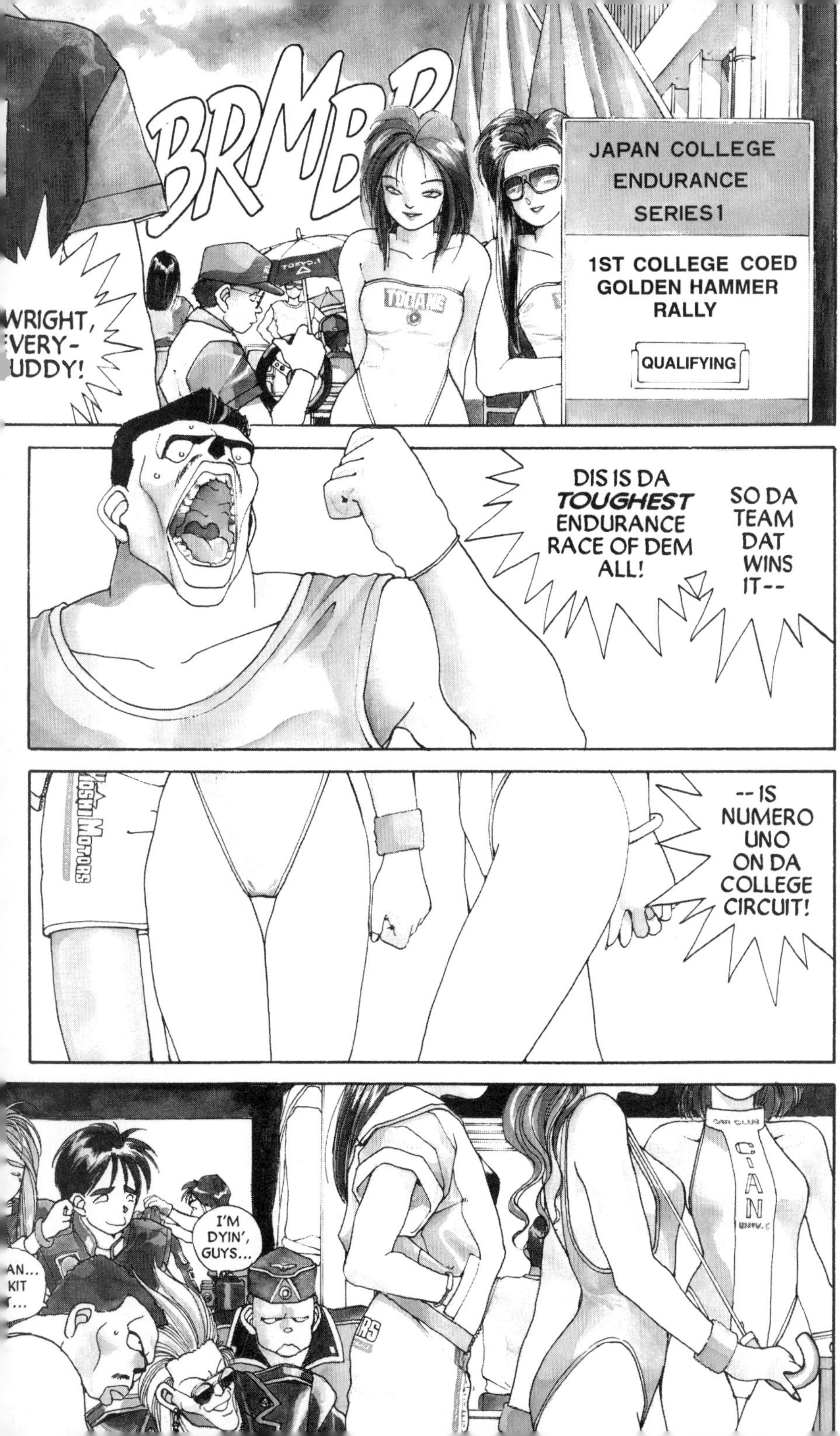

BRMBR
JAPAN COLLEGE ENDURANCE SERIES1
1ST COLLEGE COED GOLDEN HAMMER RALLY
QUALIFYING
WRIGHT, VERY- UDDY!
DIS IS DA *TOUGHEST* ENDURANCE RACE OF DEM ALL!
SO DA TEAM DAT WINS IT--
--IS NUMERO UNO ON DA COLLEGE CIRCUIT!
AN... KIT T...
I'M DYIN', GUYS...
CAR CLUB
CIAN

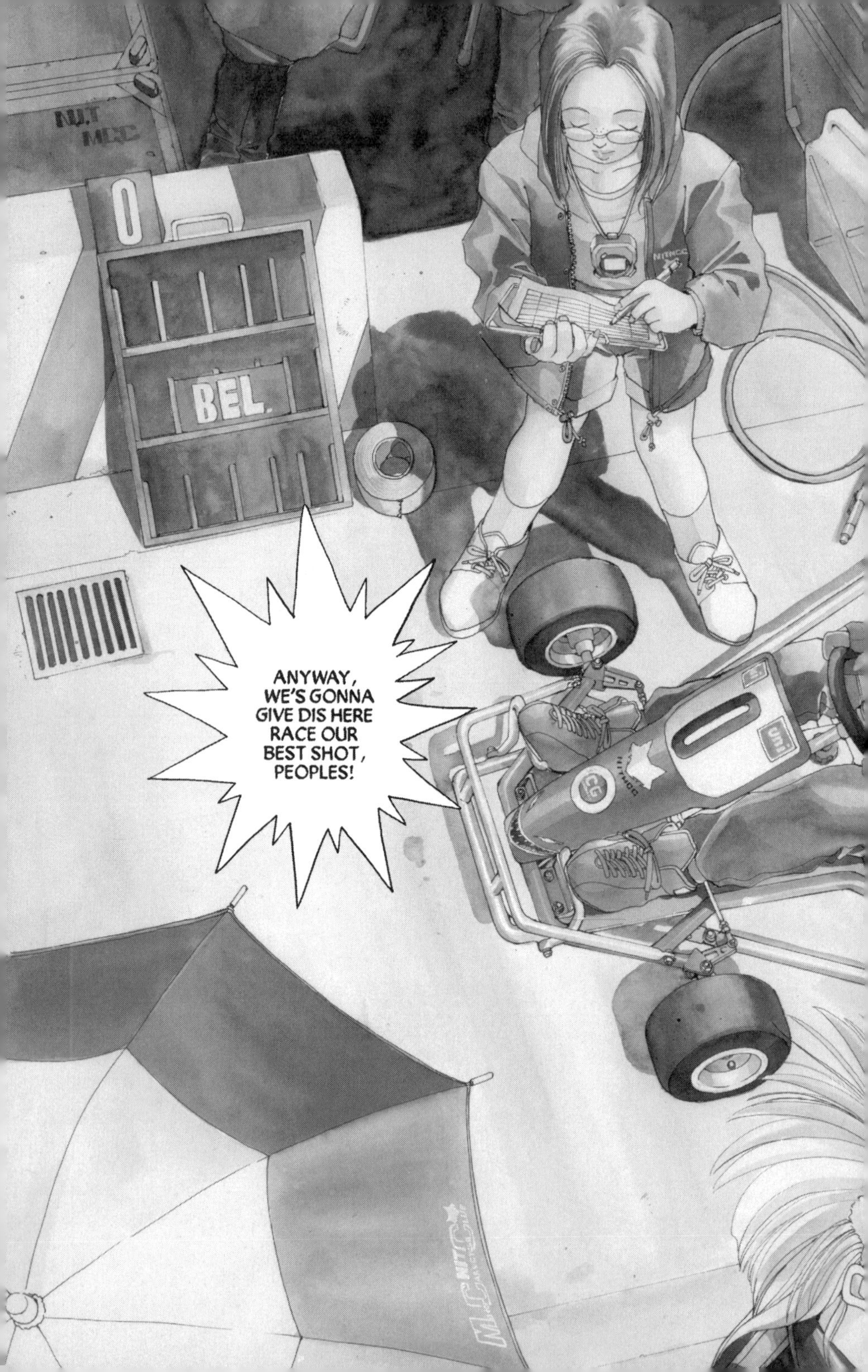
ANYWAY, WE'S GONNA GIVE DIS HERE RACE OUR BEST SHOT, PEOPLES!

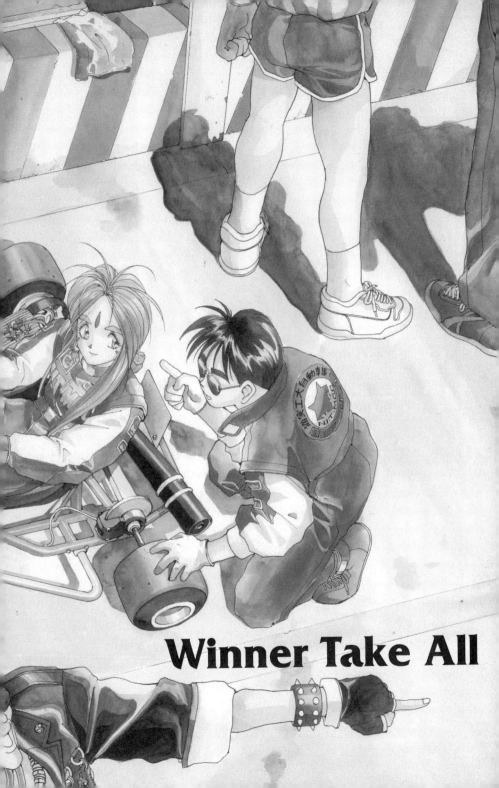

Winner Take All

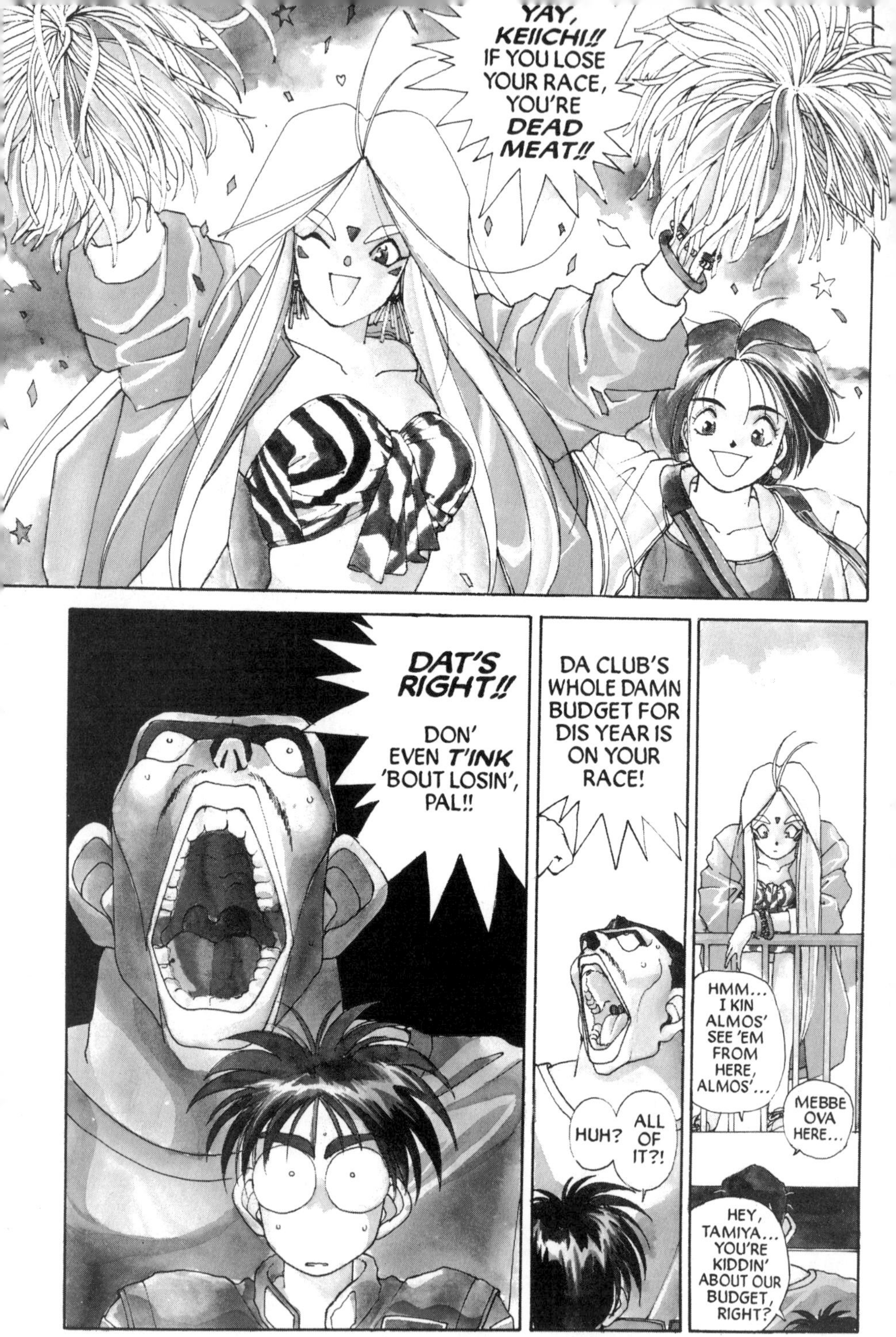
YAY, KEIICHI!! IF YOU LOSE YOUR RACE, YOU'RE DEAD MEAT!!
DAT'S RIGHT!!
DON' EVEN T'INK 'BOUT LOSIN', PAL!!
DA CLUB'S WHOLE DAMN BUDGET FOR DIS YEAR IS ON YOUR RACE!
HUH?
ALL OF IT?!
HMM... I KIN ALMOS' SEE 'EM FROM HERE, ALMOS'...
MEBBE OVA HERE...
HEY, TAMIYA... YOU'RE KIDDIN' ABOUT OUR BUDGET, RIGHT?

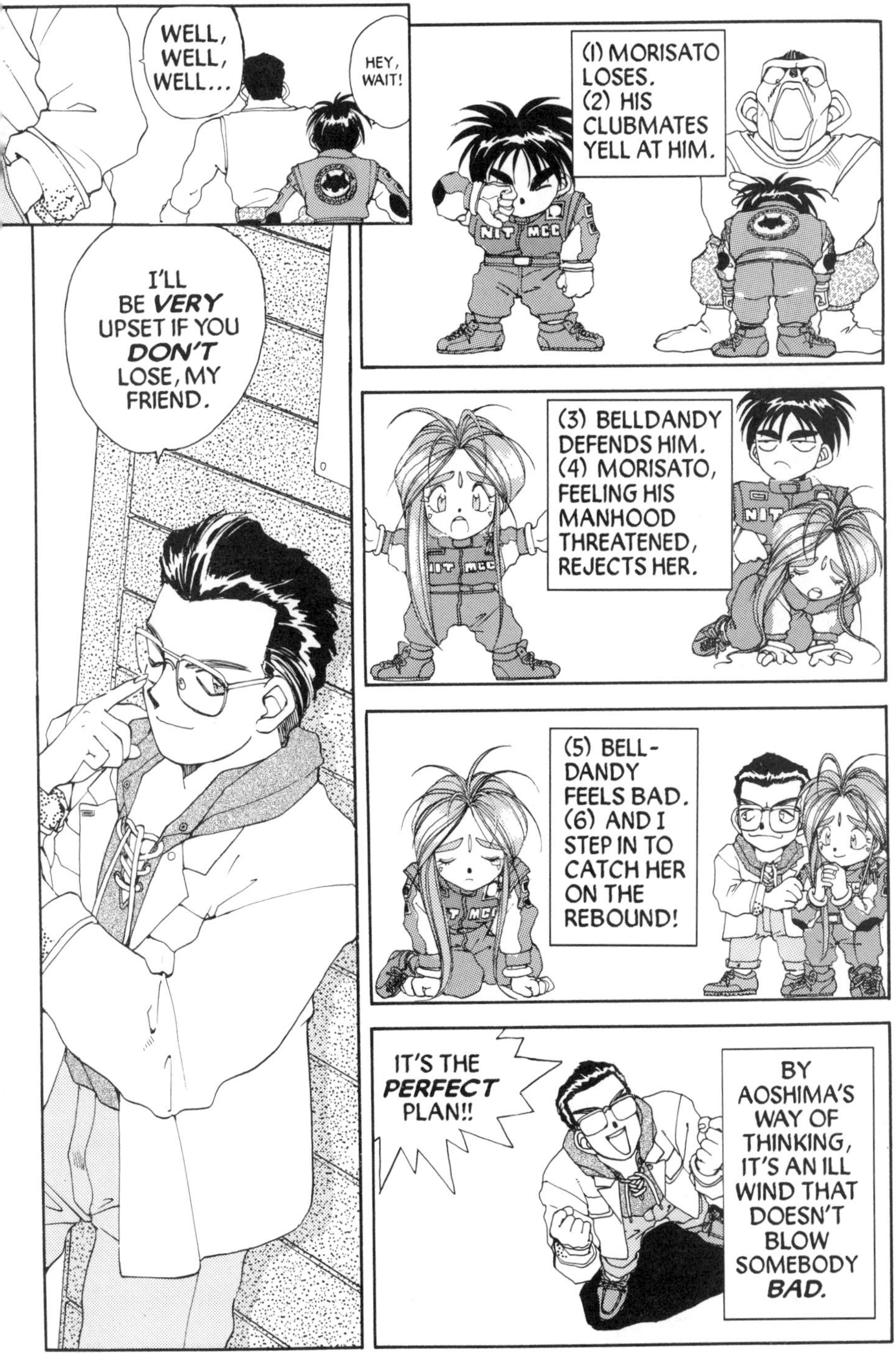
WELL, WELL, WELL...
HEY, WAIT!
I'LL BE ***VERY*** UPSET IF YOU ***DON'T*** LOSE, MY FRIEND.
(1) MORISATO LOSES. (2) HIS CLUBMATES YELL AT HIM.
(3) BELLDANDY DEFENDS HIM. (4) MORISATO, FEELING HIS MANHOOD THREATENED, REJECTS HER.
(5) BELL-DANDY FEELS BAD. (6) AND I STEP IN TO CATCH HER ON THE REBOUND!
IT'S THE ***PERFECT*** PLAN!!
BY AOSHIMA'S WAY OF THINKING, IT'S AN ILL WIND THAT DOESN'T BLOW SOMEBODY ***BAD.***

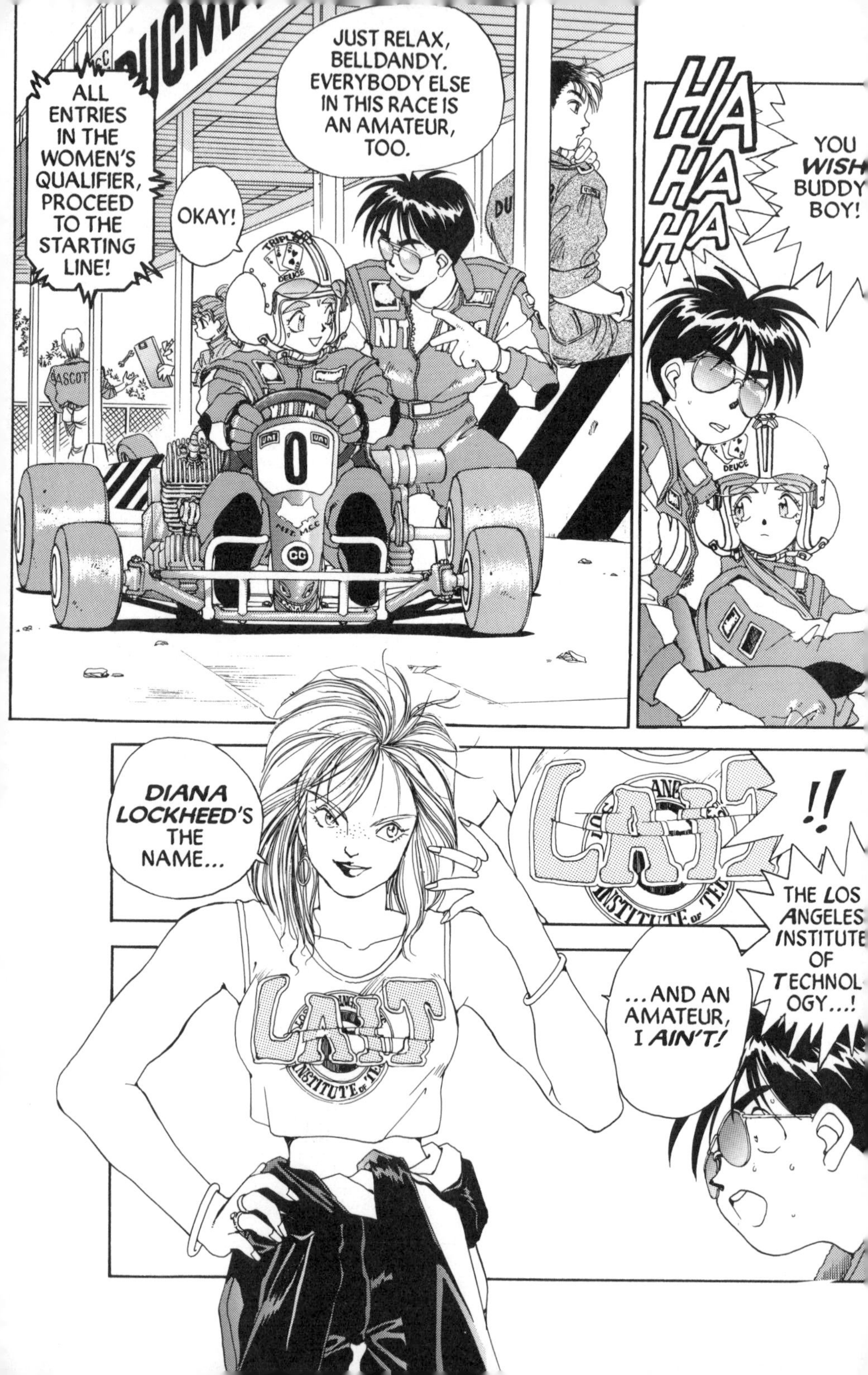
ALL ENTRIES IN THE WOMEN'S QUALIFIER, PROCEED TO THE STARTING LINE!
JUST RELAX, BELLDANDY. EVERYBODY ELSE IN THIS RACE IS AN AMATEUR, TOO.
OKAY!
HA HA HA HA
YOU *WISH* BUDDY BOY!
DIANA LOCKHEED'S THE NAME...
!!
THE LOS ANGELES INSTITUTE OF TECHNOLOGY...!
...AND AN AMATEUR, I *AIN'T!*

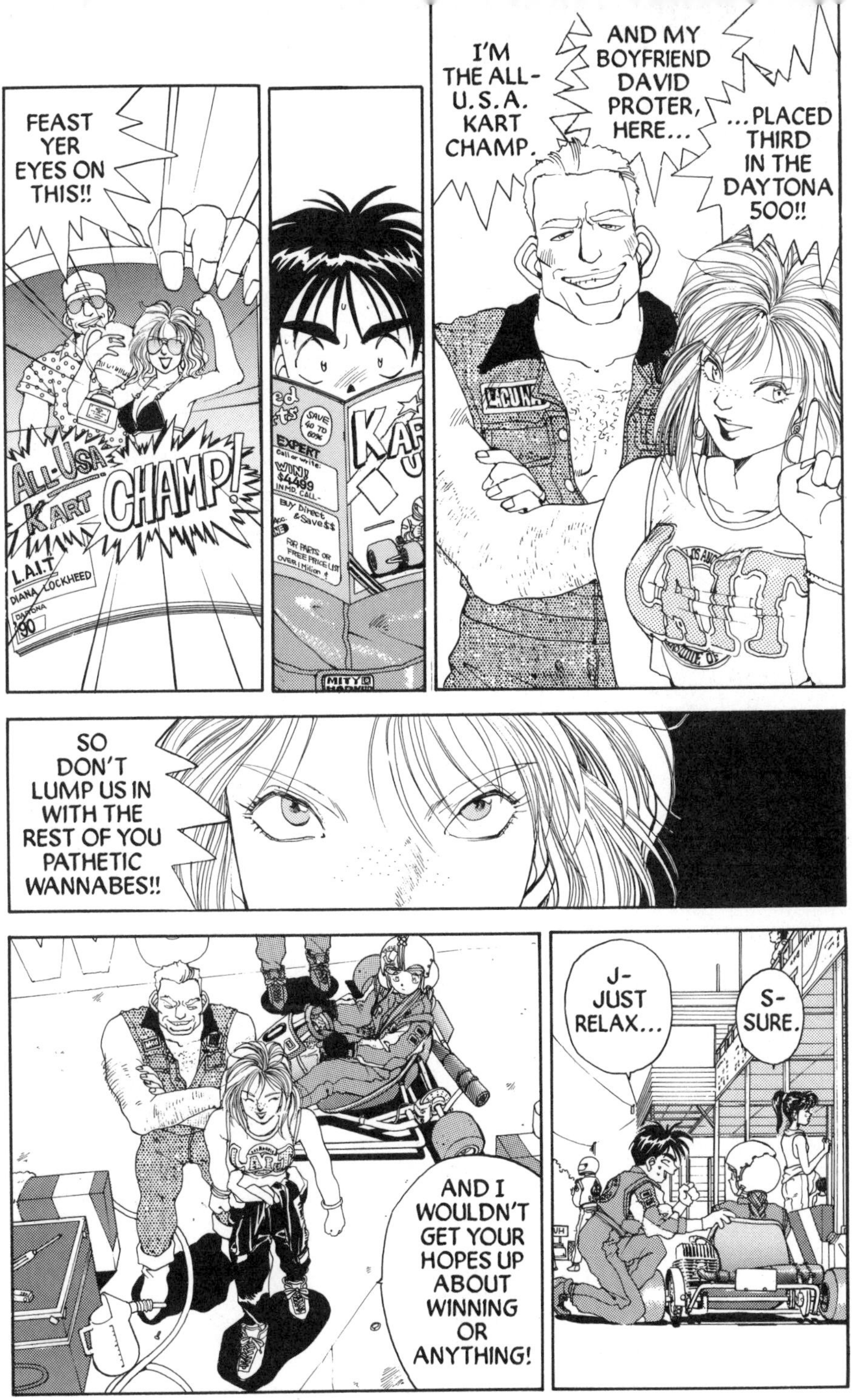
FEAST YER EYES ON THIS!!
ALL-USA KART CHAMP!
L.A.I.T
DIANA LOCKHEED
DAYTONA
90
KART
I'M THE ALL-U.S.A. KART CHAMP.
AND MY BOYFRIEND DAVID PROTER, HERE...
...PLACED THIRD IN THE DAYTONA 500!!
SO DON'T LUMP US IN WITH THE REST OF YOU PATHETIC WANNABES!!
AND I WOULDN'T GET YOUR HOPES UP ABOUT WINNING OR ANYTHING!
J-JUST RELAX...
S-SURE.

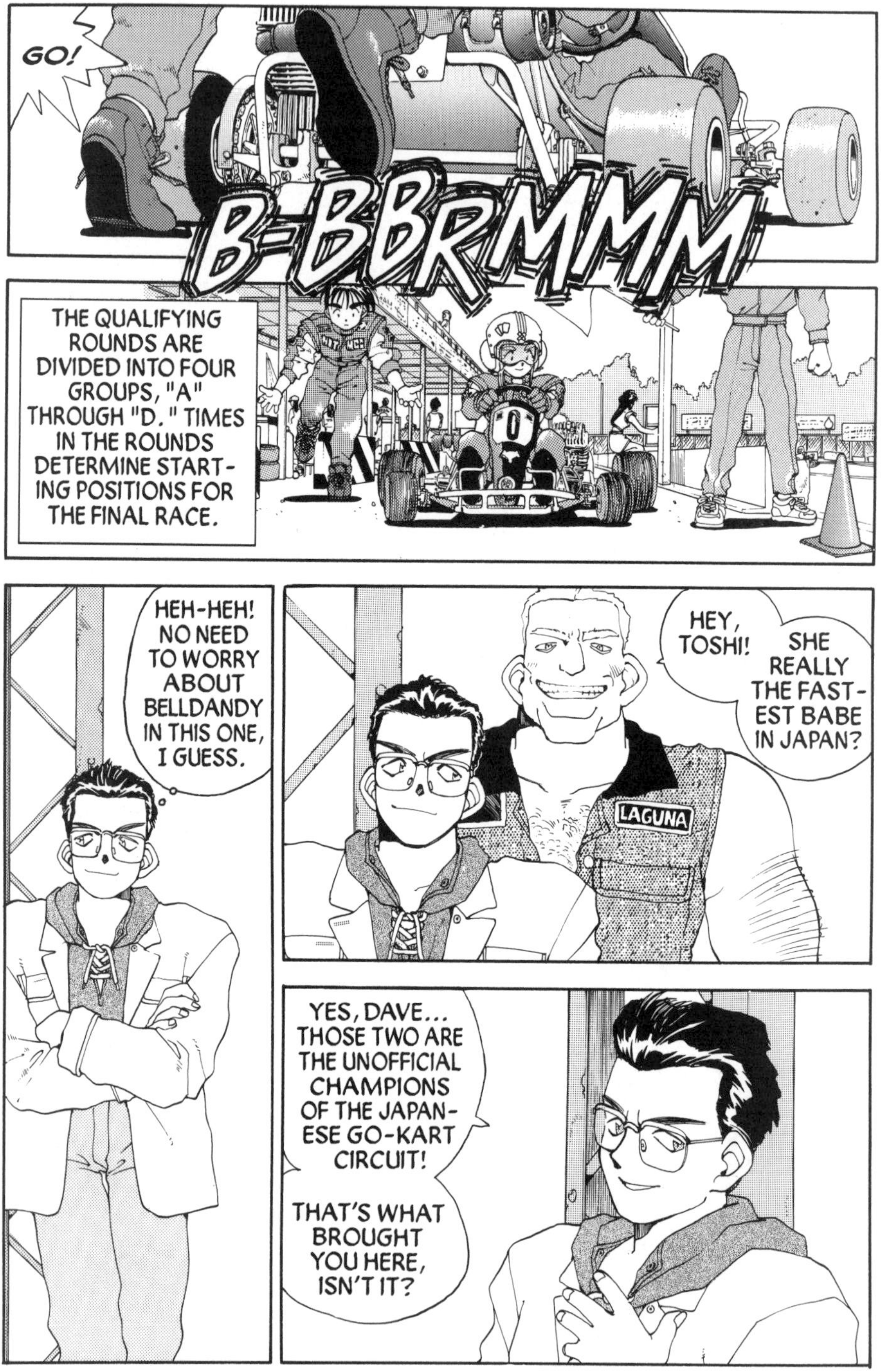
GO!
B-BBRMMMM
THE QUALIFYING ROUNDS ARE DIVIDED INTO FOUR GROUPS, "A" THROUGH "D." TIMES IN THE ROUNDS DETERMINE STARTING POSITIONS FOR THE FINAL RACE.
HEH-HEH! NO NEED TO WORRY ABOUT BELLDANDY IN THIS ONE, I GUESS.
HEY, TOSHI!
SHE REALLY THE FASTEST BABE IN JAPAN?
LAGUNA
YES, DAVE... THOSE TWO ARE THE UNOFFICIAL CHAMPIONS OF THE JAPANESE GO-KART CIRCUIT!
THAT'S WHAT BROUGHT YOU HERE, ISN'T IT?

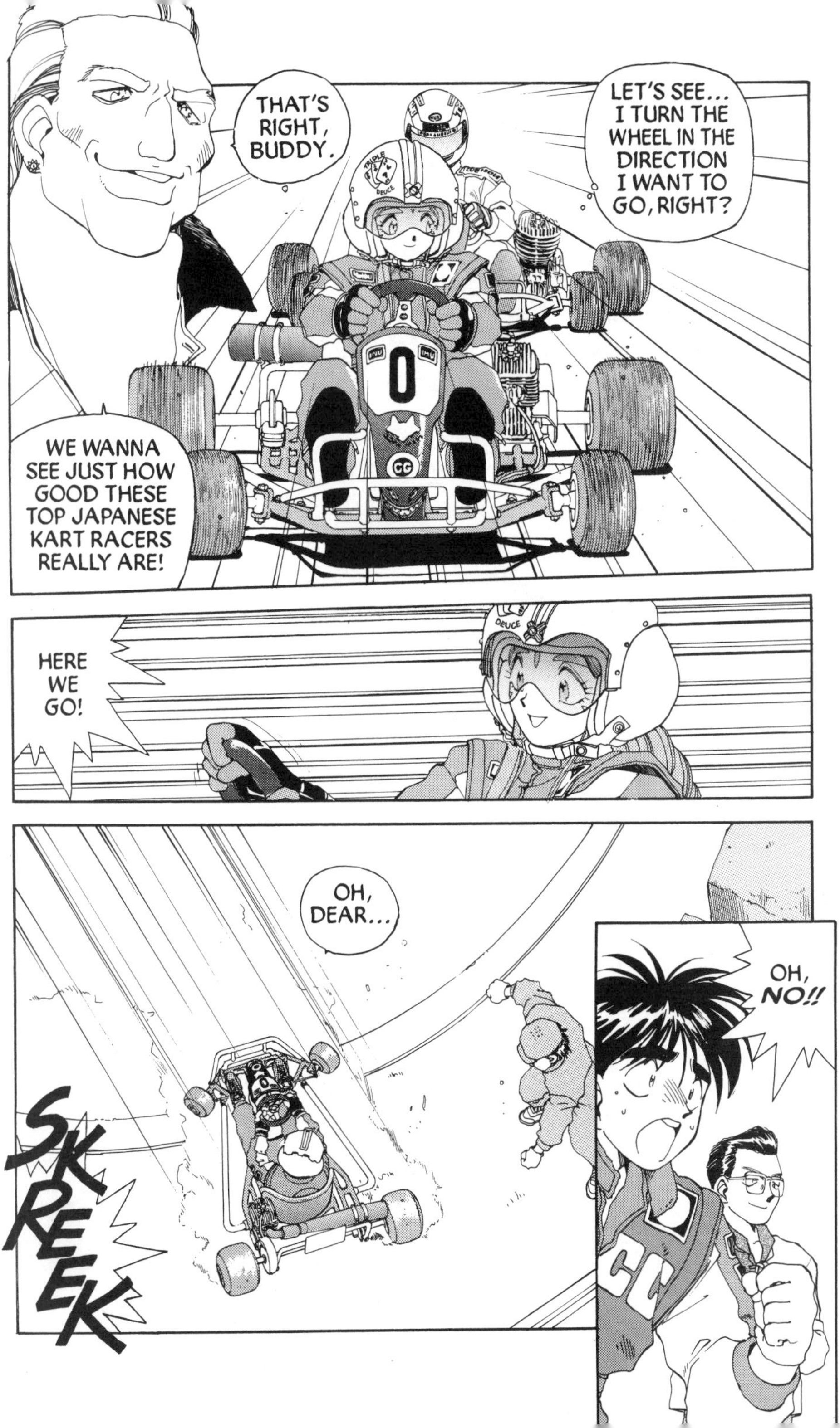
THAT'S RIGHT, BUDDY.
LET'S SEE... I TURN THE WHEEL IN THE DIRECTION I WANT TO GO, RIGHT?
WE WANNA SEE JUST HOW GOOD THESE TOP JAPANESE KART RACERS REALLY ARE!
HERE WE GO!
OH, DEAR...
SKREEK
OH, NO!!

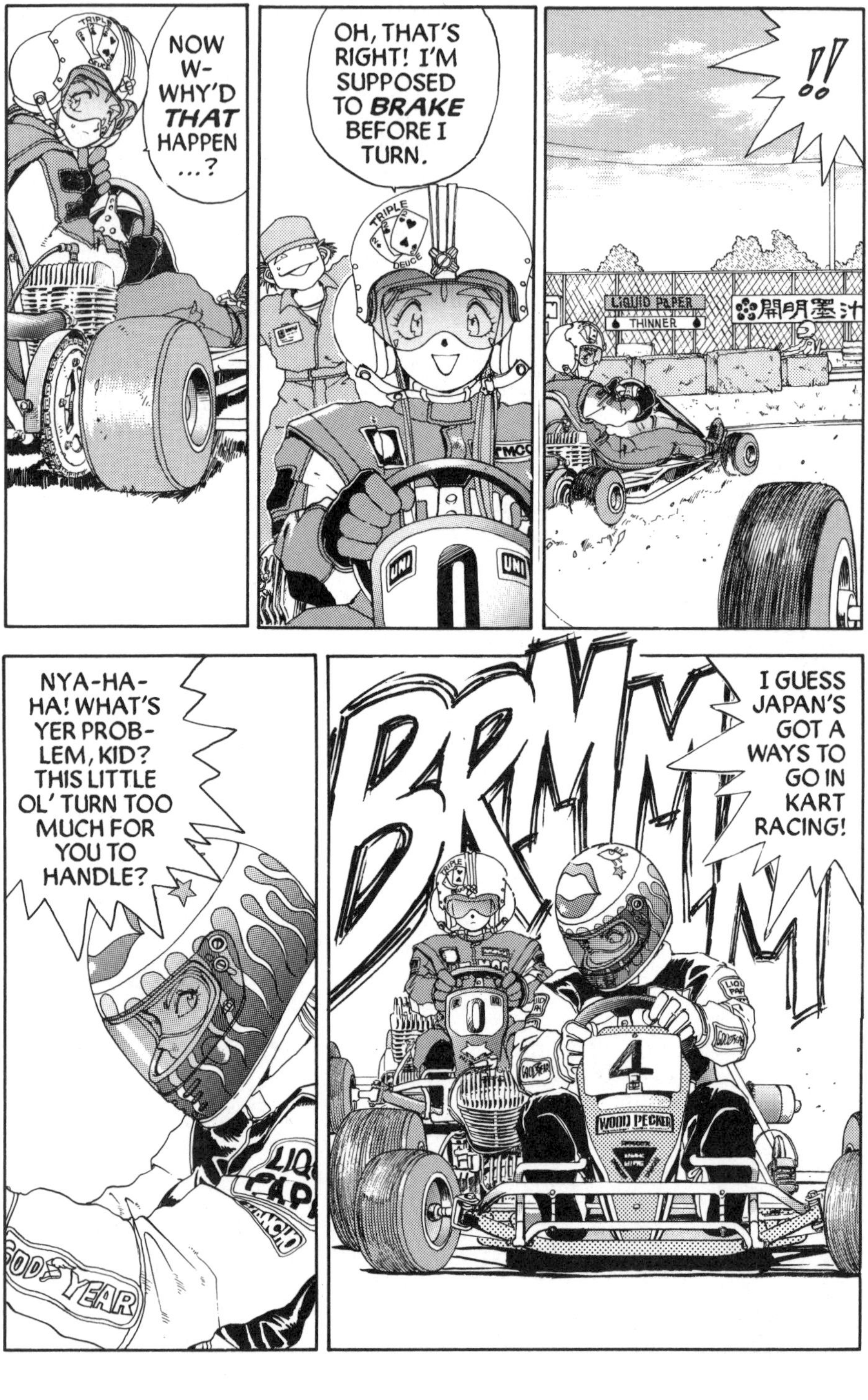
NOW W-WHY'D *THAT* HAPPEN ...?
OH, THAT'S RIGHT! I'M SUPPOSED TO **BRAKE** BEFORE I TURN.
!!
LIQUID PAPER
THINNER
開明墨汁
NYA-HA-HA! WHAT'S YER PROB-LEM, KID? THIS LITTLE OL' TURN TOO MUCH FOR YOU TO HANDLE?
I GUESS JAPAN'S GOT A WAYS TO GO IN KART RACING!
WOOD PECKER

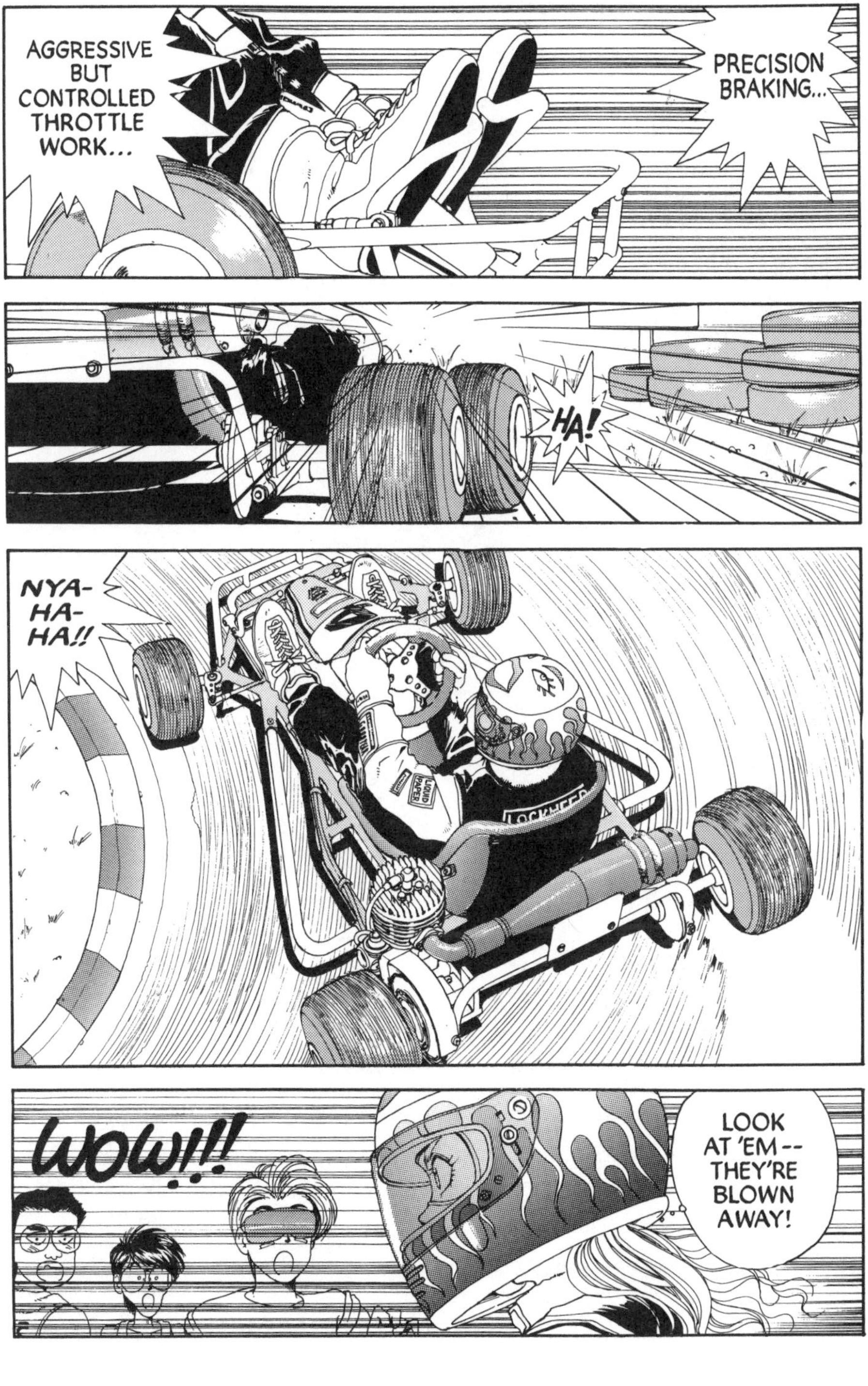
AGGRESSIVE BUT CONTROLLED THROTTLE WORK...
PRECISION BRAKING...
HA!
NYA-HA-HA!!
WOW!!!
LOOK AT 'EM -- THEY'RE BLOWN AWAY!

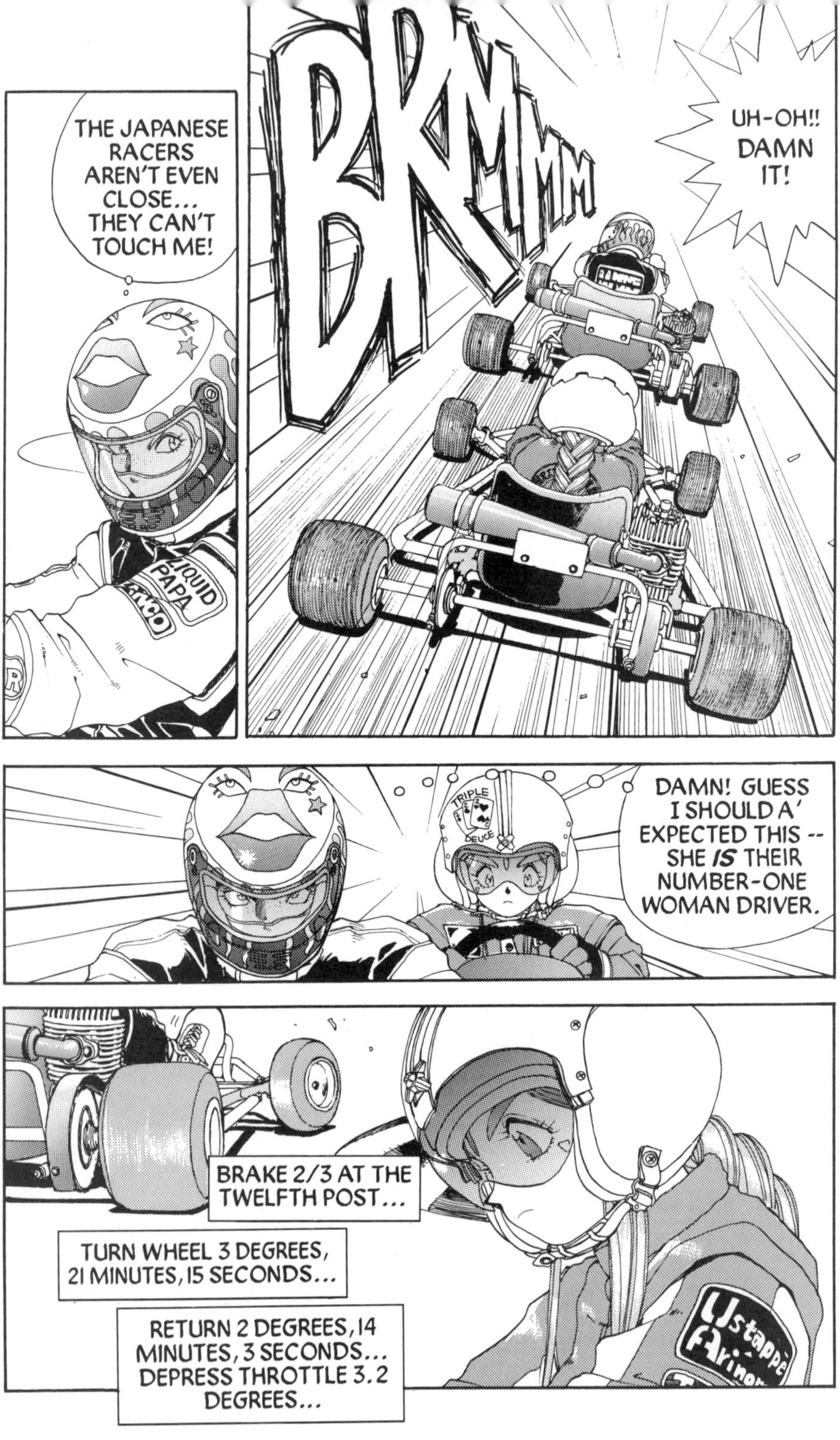
THE JAPANESE RACERS AREN'T EVEN CLOSE... THEY CAN'T TOUCH ME!
UH-OH!! DAMN IT!
DAMN! GUESS I SHOULD A' EXPECTED THIS -- SHE *IS* THEIR NUMBER-ONE WOMAN DRIVER.
BRAKE 2/3 AT THE TWELFTH POST...
TURN WHEEL 3 DEGREES, 21 MINUTES, 15 SECONDS...
RETURN 2 DEGREES, 14 MINUTES, 3 SECONDS... DEPRESS THROTTLE 3.2 DEGREES...

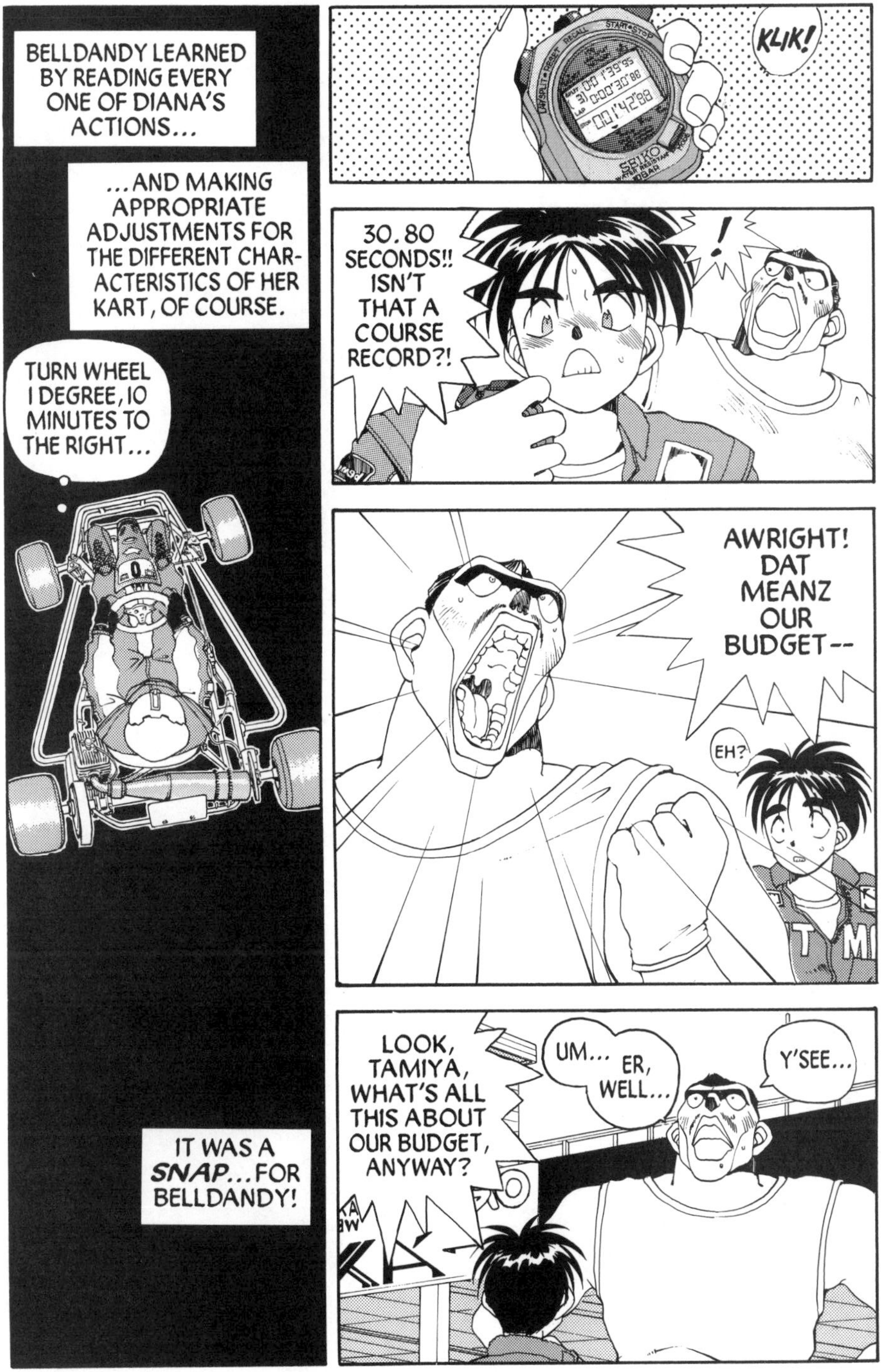

BELLDANDY LEARNED BY READING EVERY ONE OF DIANA'S ACTIONS...
...AND MAKING APPROPRIATE ADJUSTMENTS FOR THE DIFFERENT CHAR-ACTERISTICS OF HER KART, OF COURSE.
TURN WHEEL 1 DEGREE, 10 MINUTES TO THE RIGHT...
IT WAS A *SNAP*...FOR BELLDANDY!
KLIK!
30.80 SECONDS!! ISN'T THAT A COURSE RECORD?!
!
AWRIGHT! DAT MEANZ OUR BUDGET--
EH?
LOOK, TAMIYA, WHAT'S ALL THIS ABOUT OUR BUDGET, ANYWAY?
UM... ER, WELL...
Y'SEE...

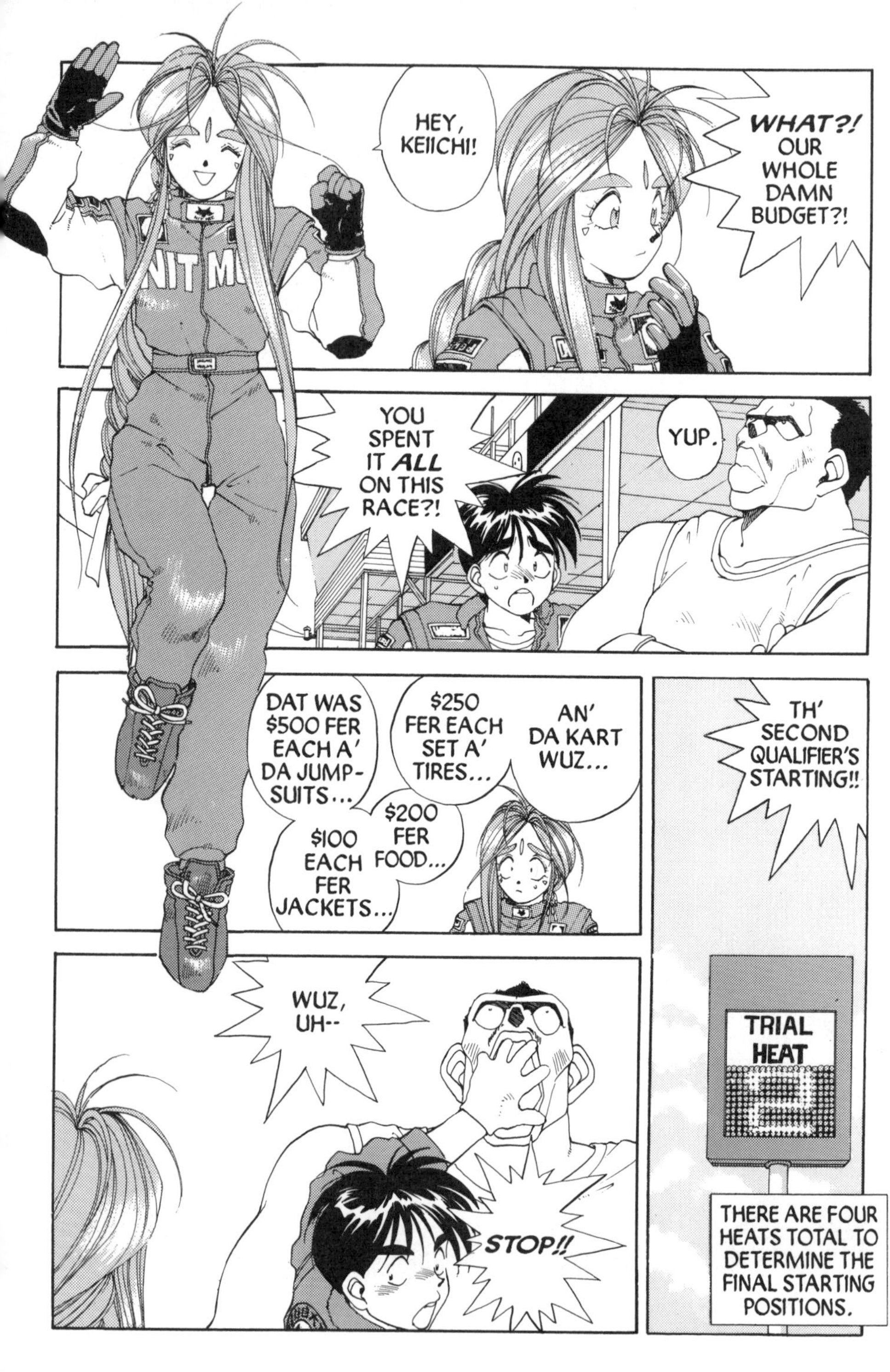
HEY, KEIICHI!
WHAT?! OUR WHOLE DAMN BUDGET?!
YOU SPENT IT ALL ON THIS RACE?!
YUP.
DAT WAS $500 FER EACH A' DA JUMP-SUITS...
$250 FER EACH SET A' TIRES...
AN' DA KART WUZ...
$100 EACH FER JACKETS...
$200 FER FOOD...
WUZ, UH--
STOP!!
TH' SECOND QUALIFIER'S STARTING!!
TRIAL HEAT
THERE ARE FOUR HEATS TOTAL TO DETERMINE THE FINAL STARTING POSITIONS.

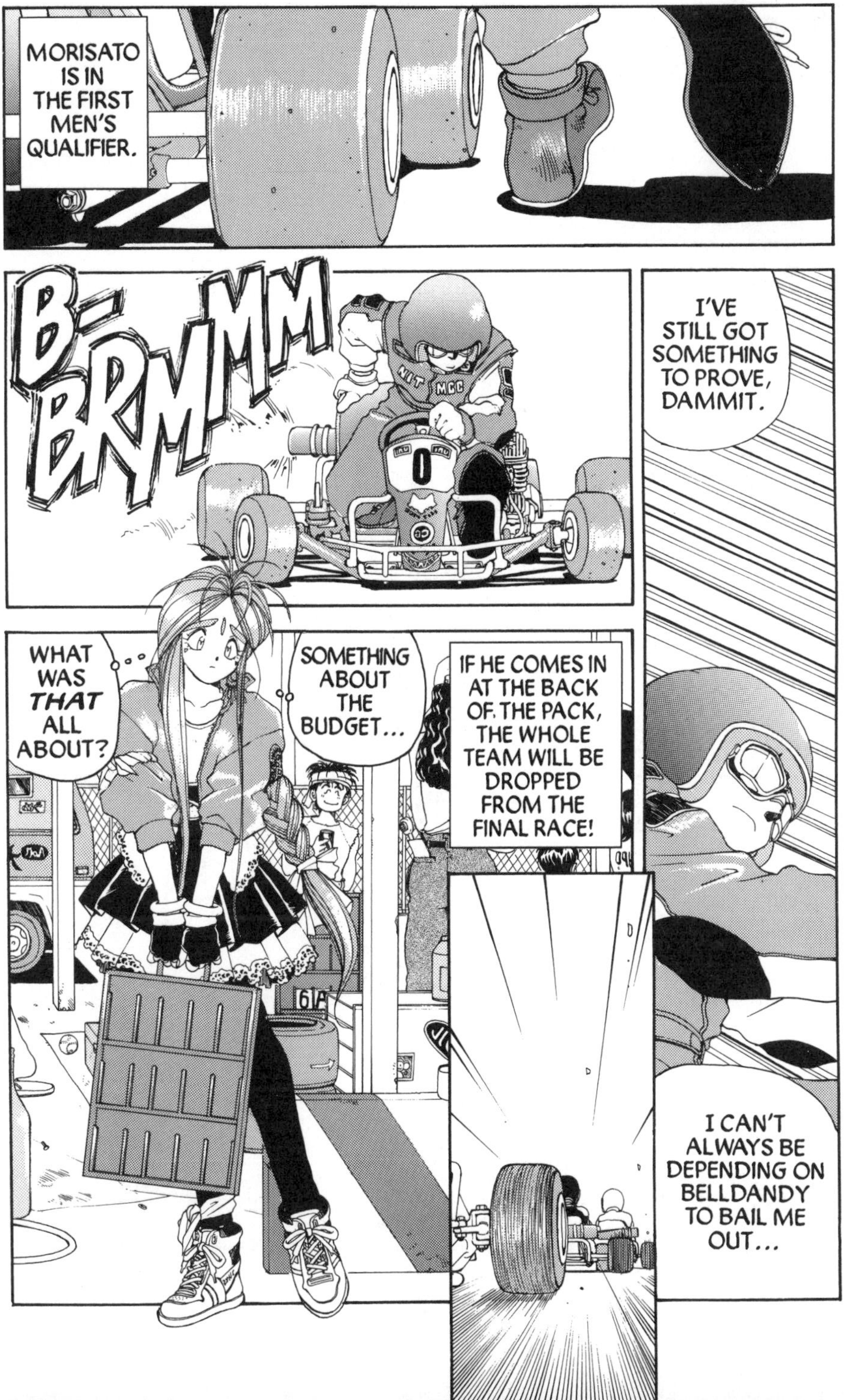
MORISATO IS IN THE FIRST MEN'S QUALIFIER.
B-BRMMM
WHAT WAS *THAT* ALL ABOUT?
SOMETHING ABOUT THE BUDGET...
IF HE COMES IN AT THE BACK OF THE PACK, THE WHOLE TEAM WILL BE DROPPED FROM THE FINAL RACE!
I'VE STILL GOT SOMETHING TO PROVE, DAMMIT.
I CAN'T ALWAYS BE DEPENDING ON BELLDANDY TO BAIL ME OUT...

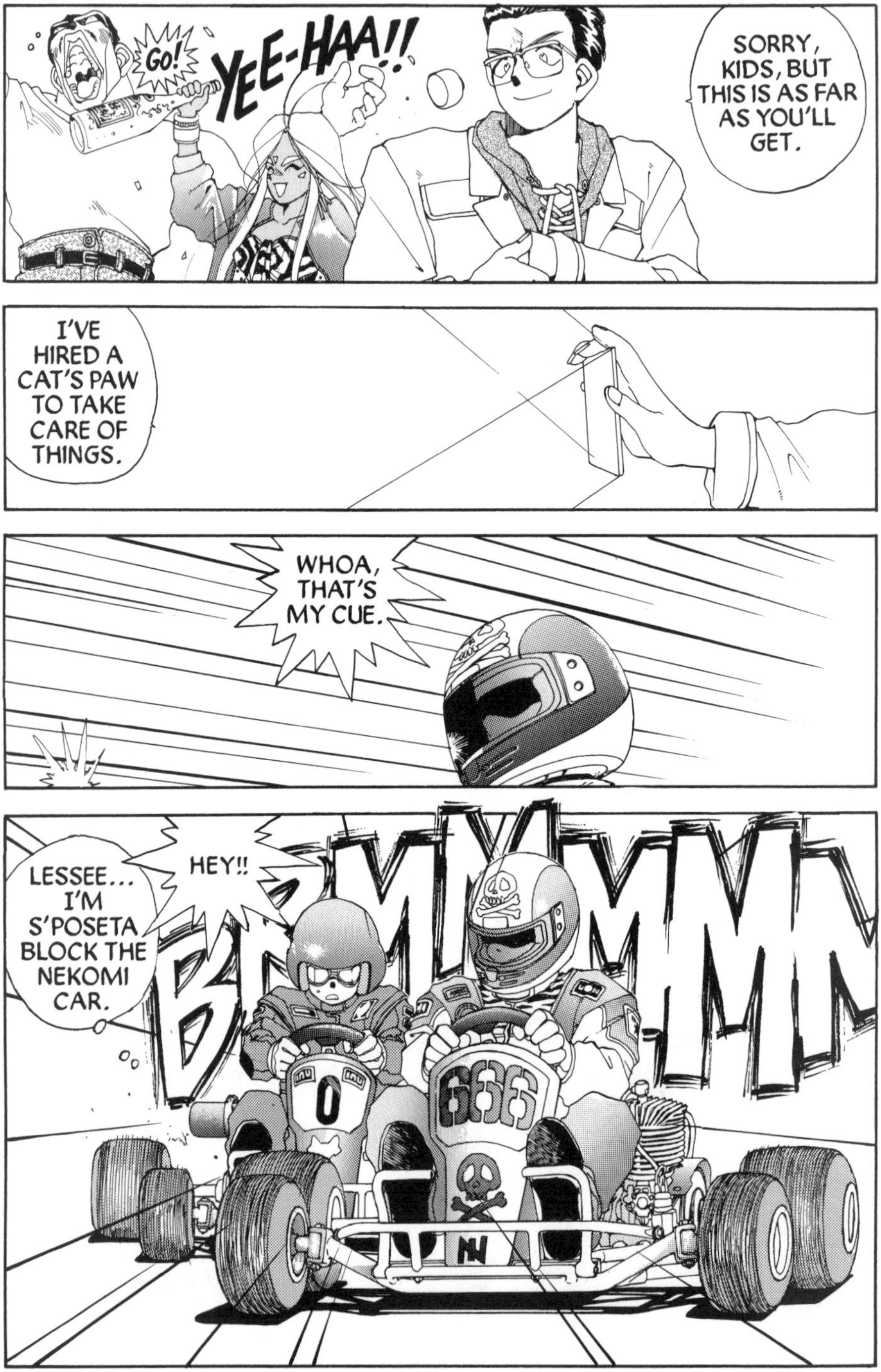
GO!
YEE-HAA!!
SORRY, KIDS, BUT THIS IS AS FAR AS YOU'LL GET.
I'VE HIRED A CAT'S PAW TO TAKE CARE OF THINGS.
WHOA, THAT'S MY CUE.
LESSEE... I'M S'POSETA BLOCK THE NEKOMI CAR.
HEY!!
BMMMMM

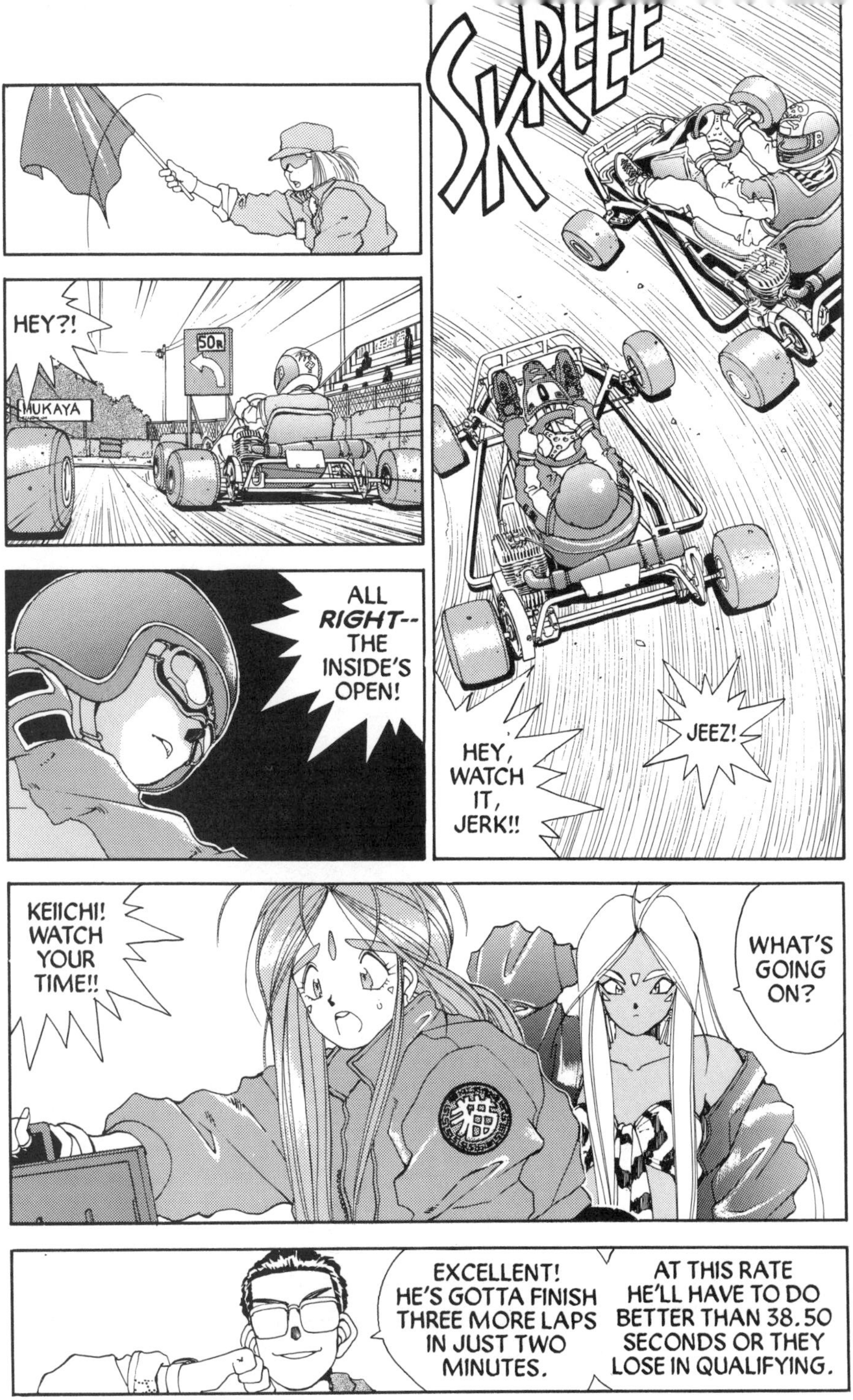
HEY?!
MUKAYA
50R
ALL RIGHT-- THE INSIDE'S OPEN!
SKREEE
HEY, WATCH IT, JERK!!
JEEZ!
KEIICHI! WATCH YOUR TIME!!
WHAT'S GOING ON?
EXCELLENT! HE'S GOTTA FINISH THREE MORE LAPS IN JUST TWO MINUTES.
AT THIS RATE HE'LL HAVE TO DO BETTER THAN 38.50 SECONDS OR THEY LOSE IN QUALIFYING.

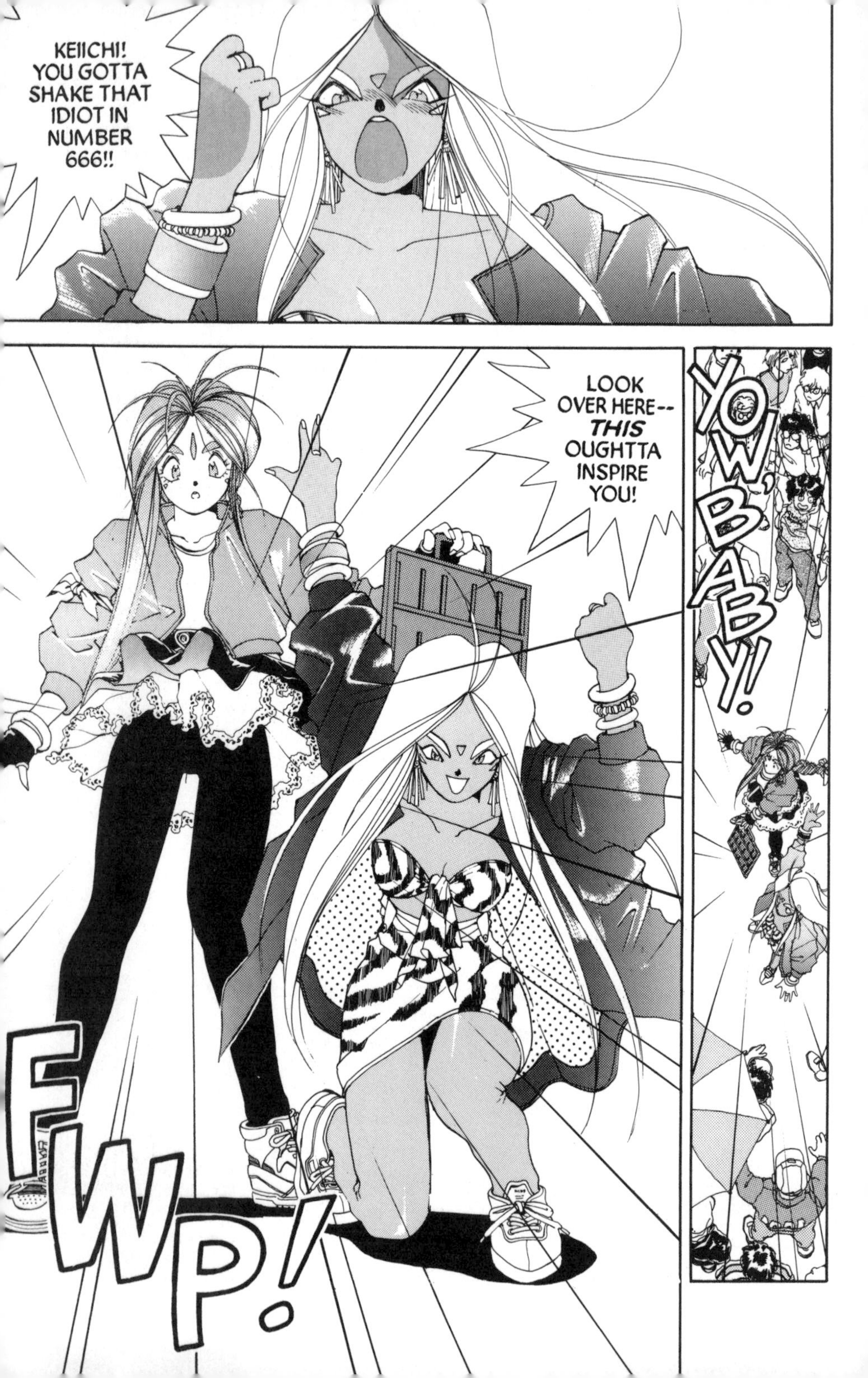
KEIICHI! YOU GOTTA SHAKE THAT IDIOT IN NUMBER 666!!
LOOK OVER HERE-- *THIS* OUGHTTA INSPIRE YOU!
YOW, BABY!
FWP!

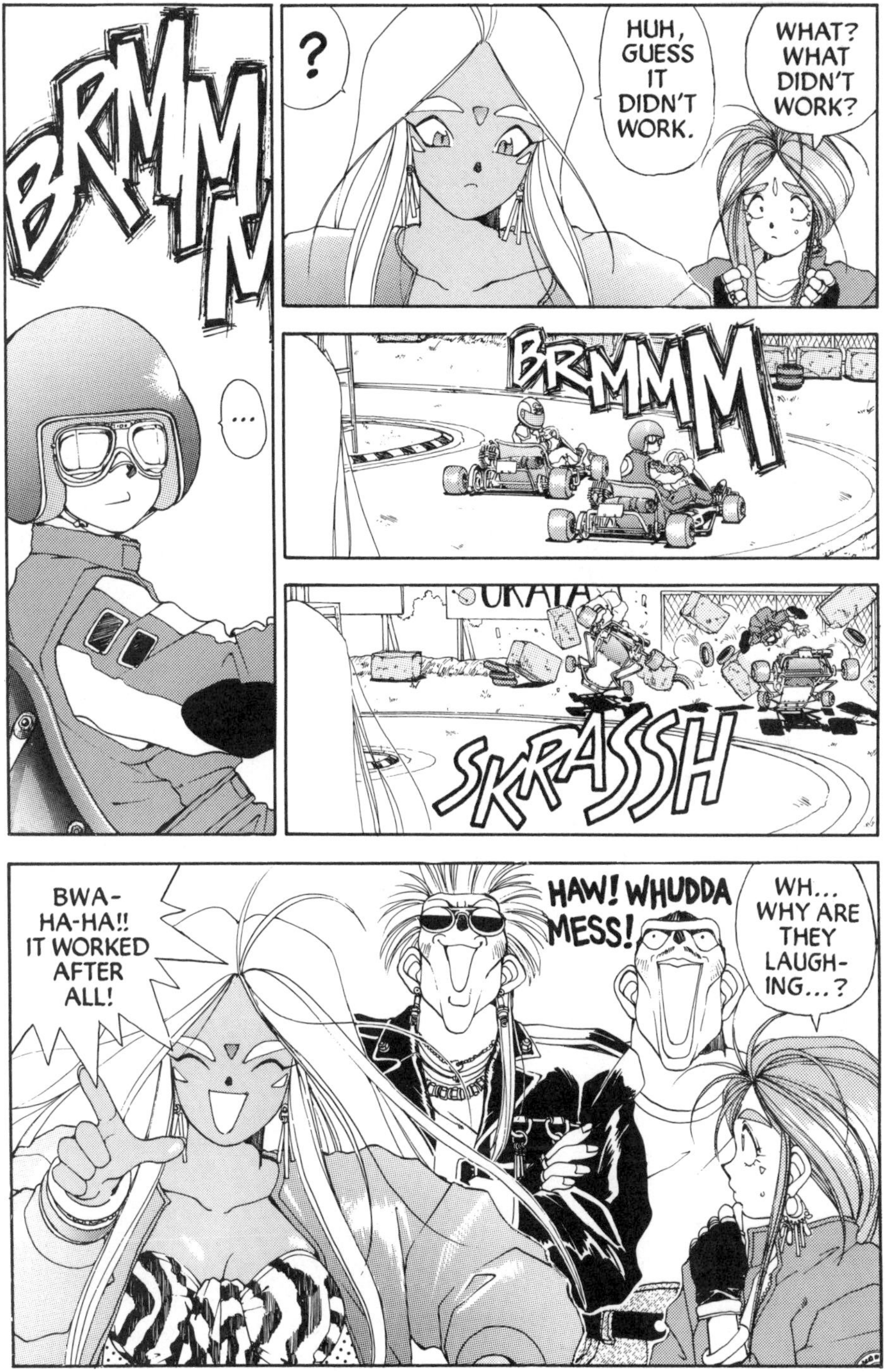
BRMMMM
...
?
HUH, GUESS IT DIDN'T WORK.
WHAT? WHAT DIDN'T WORK?
BRMMM
SKRASSH
BWA-HA-HA!! IT WORKED AFTER ALL!
HAW! WHUDDA MESS!
WH... WHY ARE THEY LAUGHING...?

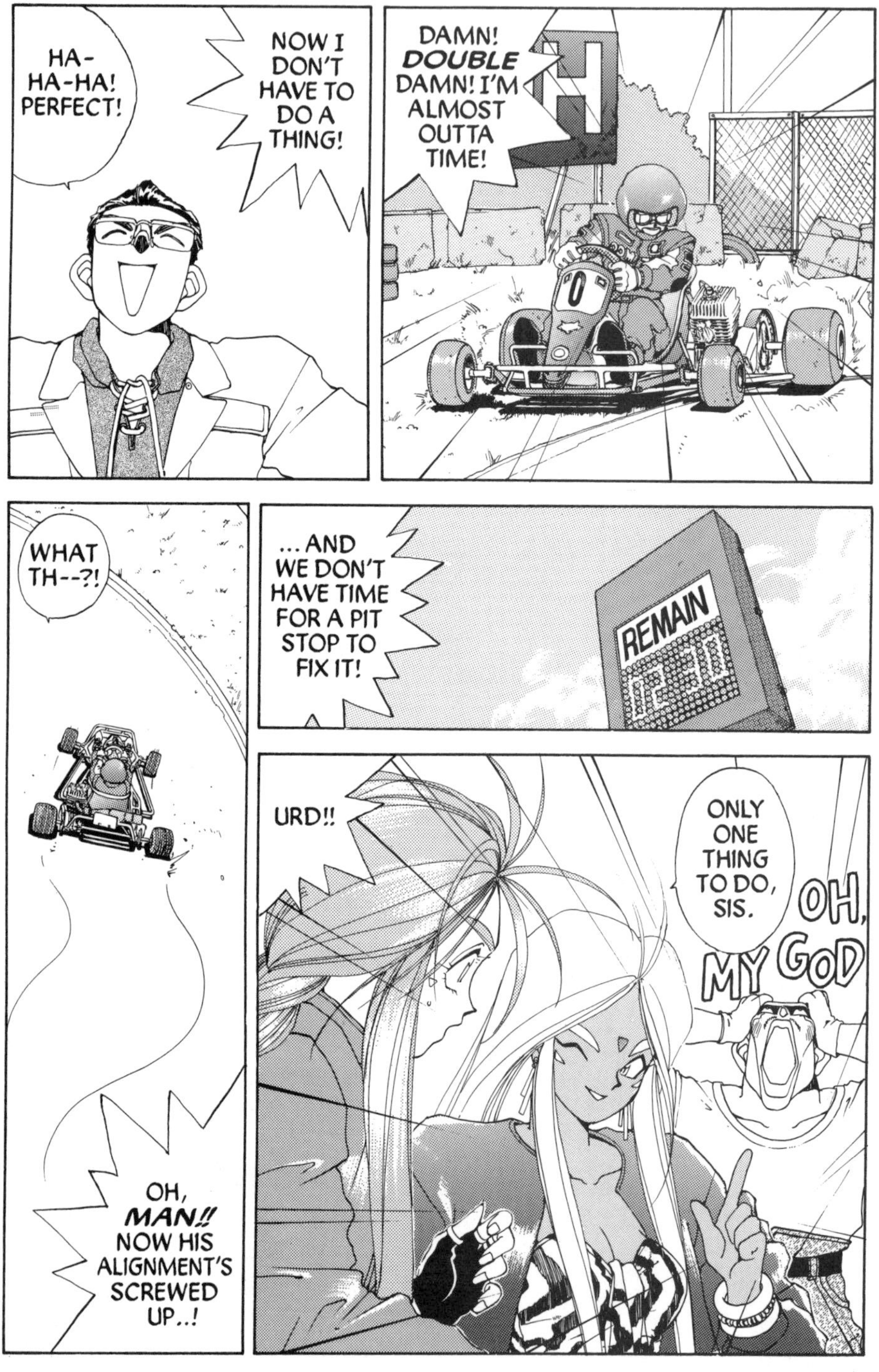
HA-HA-HA! PERFECT!
NOW I DON'T HAVE TO DO A THING!
DAMN! DOUBLE DAMN! I'M ALMOST OUTTA TIME!
H
0
WHAT TH--?!
OH, MAN!! NOW HIS ALIGNMENT'S SCREWED UP..!
...AND WE DON'T HAVE TIME FOR A PIT STOP TO FIX IT!
REMAIN
02:30
URD!!
ONLY ONE THING TO DO, SIS.
OH, MY GOD

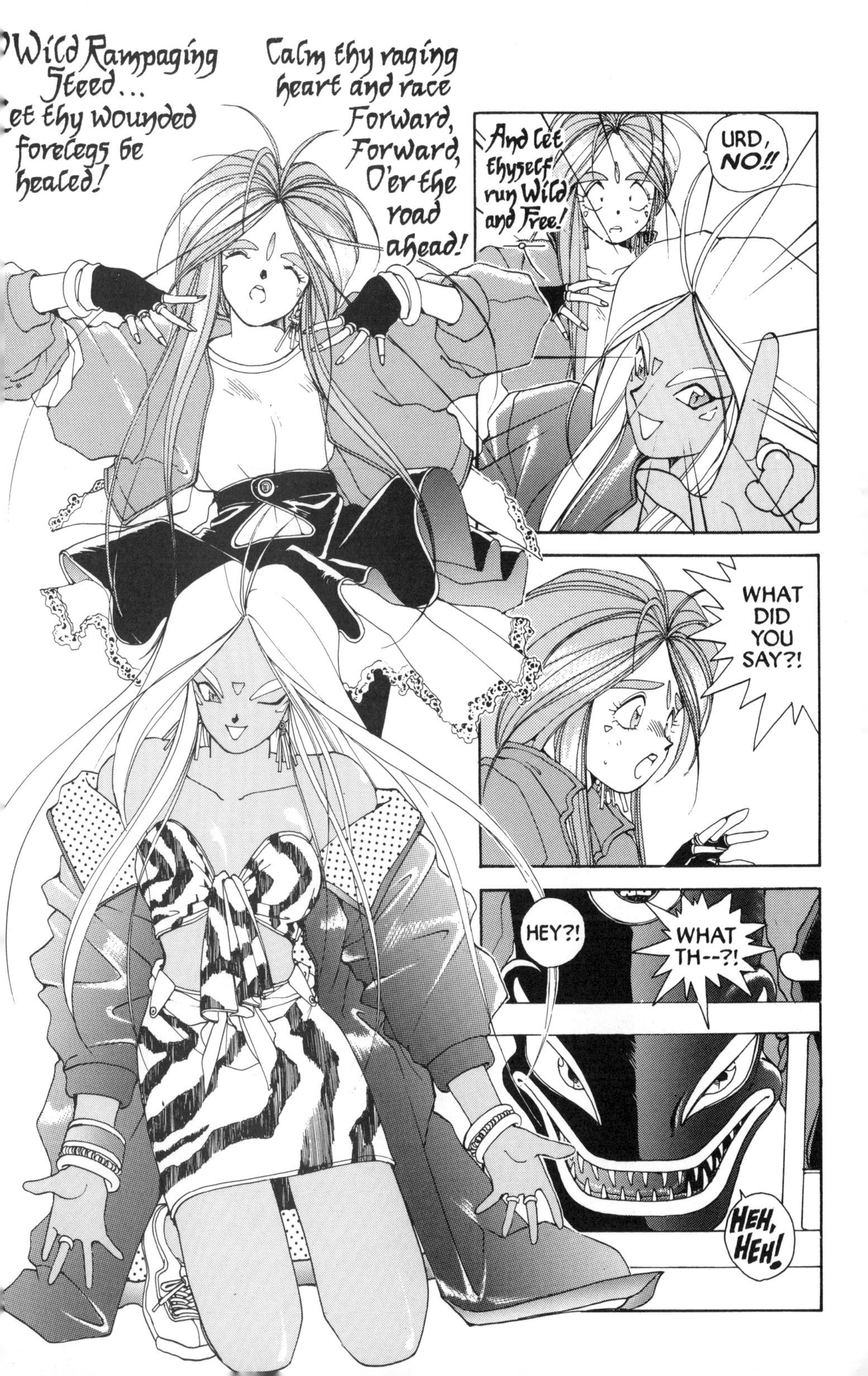
Wild Rampaging Steed...
et thy wounded forelegs be healed!
Calm thy raging heart and race Forward, Forward, O'er the road ahead!
And let thyself run Wild and Free!
URD, NO!!
WHAT DID YOU SAY?!
HEY?!
WHAT TH--?!
HEH, HEH!

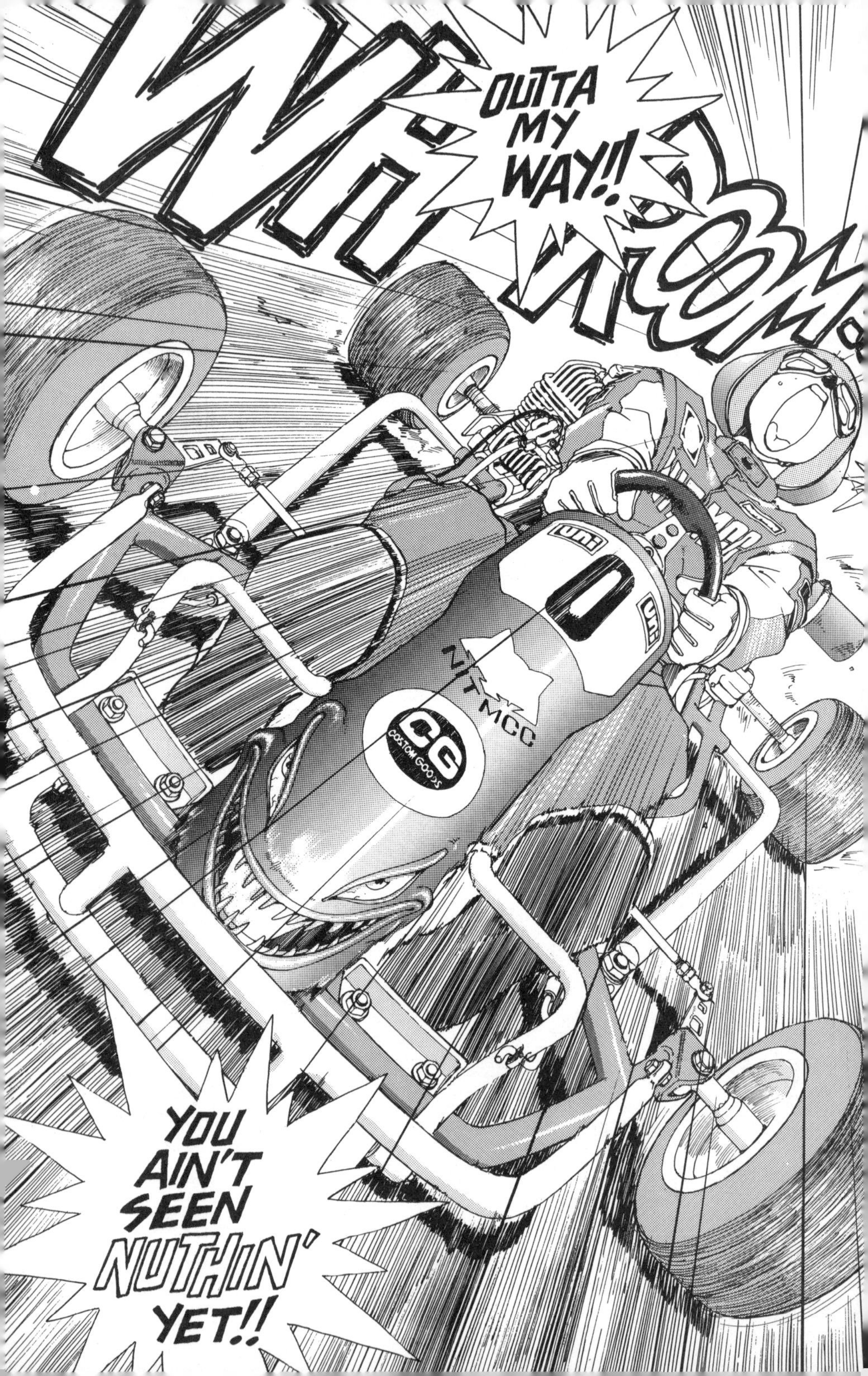
OUTTA MY WAY!!
YOU AIN'T SEEN NUTHIN' YET!!

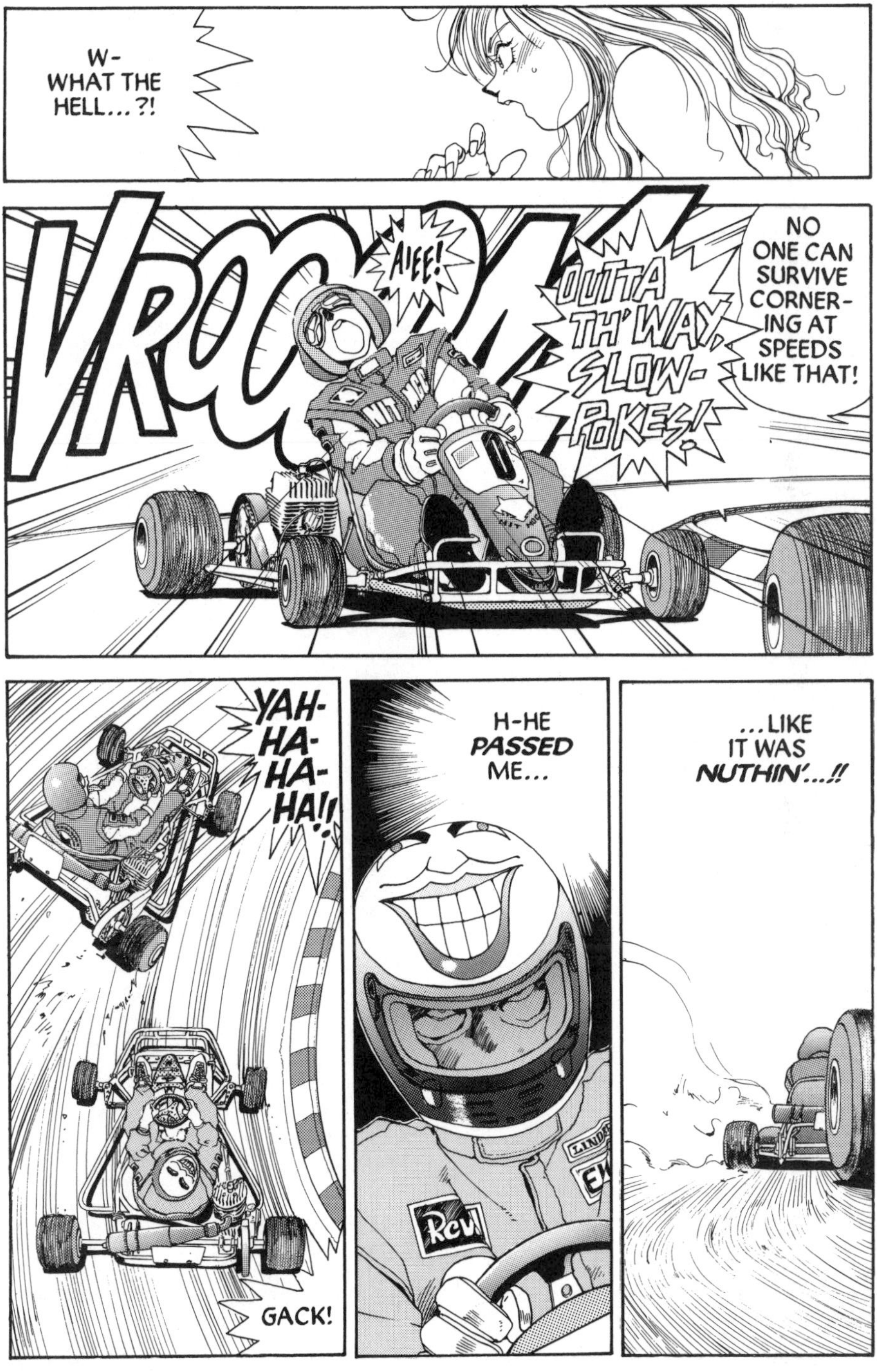
W-
WHAT THE
HELL...?!
VROOOM
AIEE!
OUTTA TH' WAY, SLOW-POKES!
NO ONE CAN SURVIVE CORNER-ING AT SPEEDS LIKE THAT!
YAH-HA-HA-HA!!
GACK!
H-HE PASSED ME...
...LIKE IT WAS NUTHIN'...!!

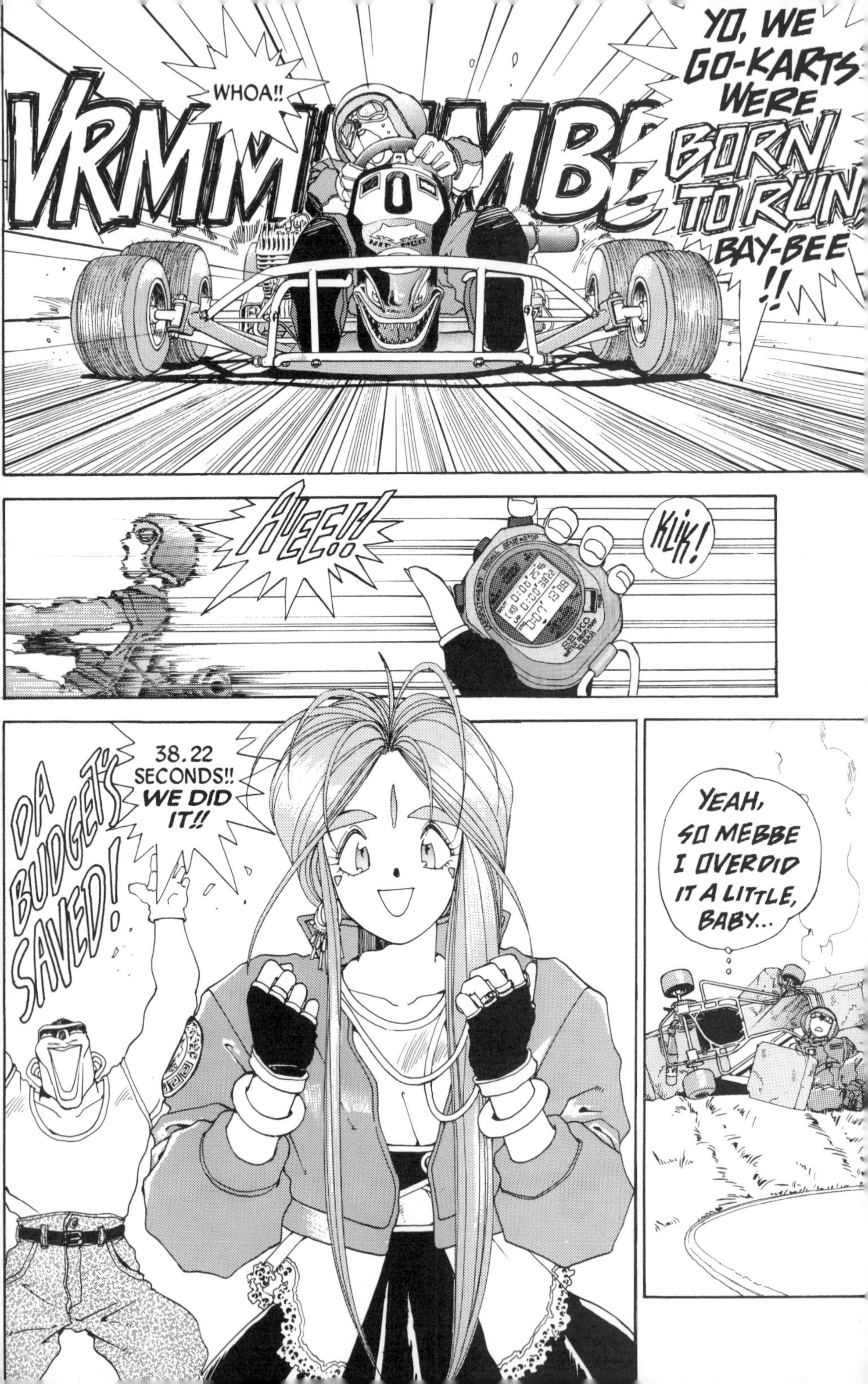
WHOA!!
YO, WE GO-KARTS WERE BORN TO RUN, BAY-BEE!!
HEEE!!
KLIK!
DA BUDGET'S SAVED!
38.22 SECONDS!! WE DID IT!!
YEAH, SO MEBBE I OVERDID IT A LITTLE, BABY...

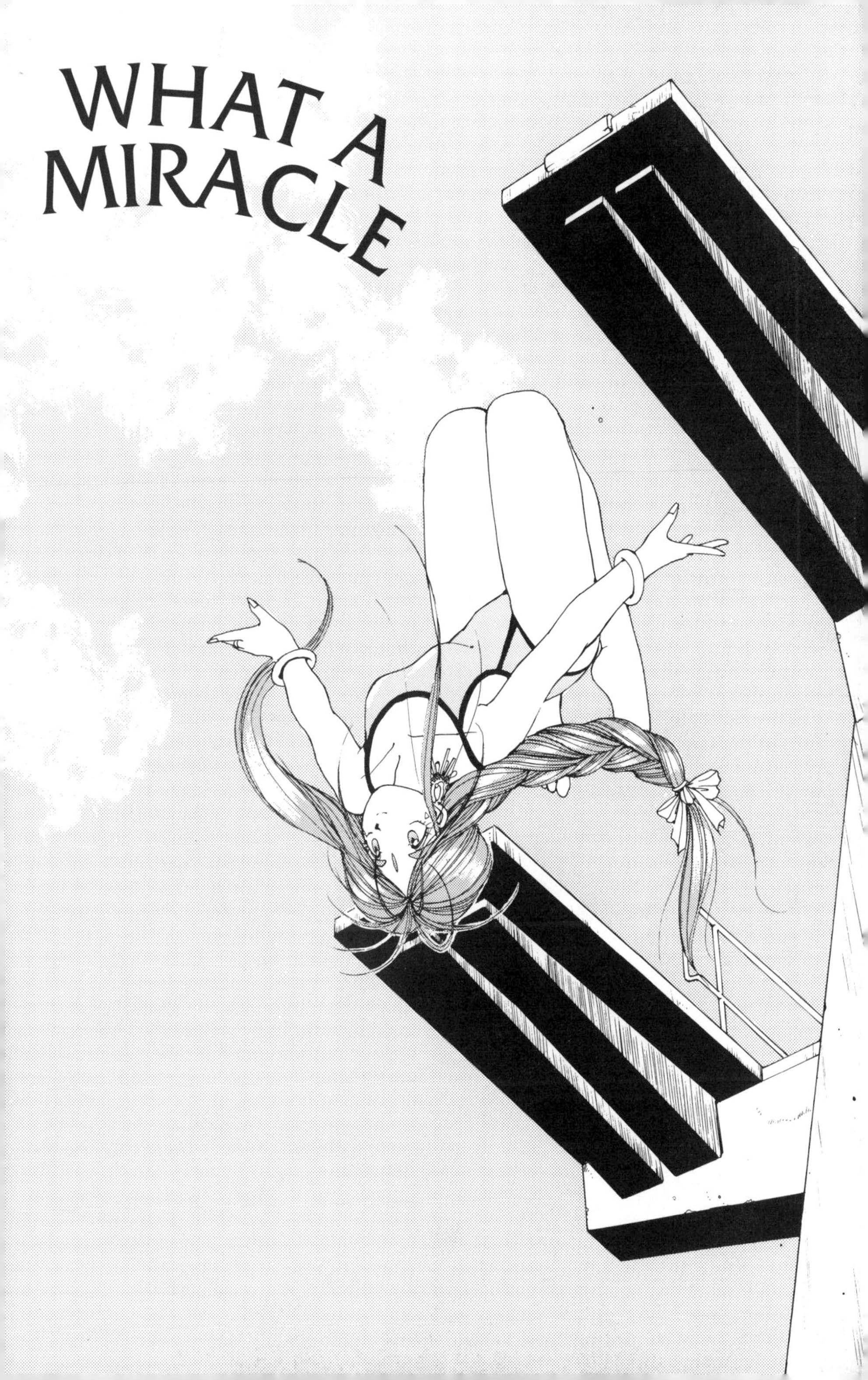
WHAT A
MIRACLE

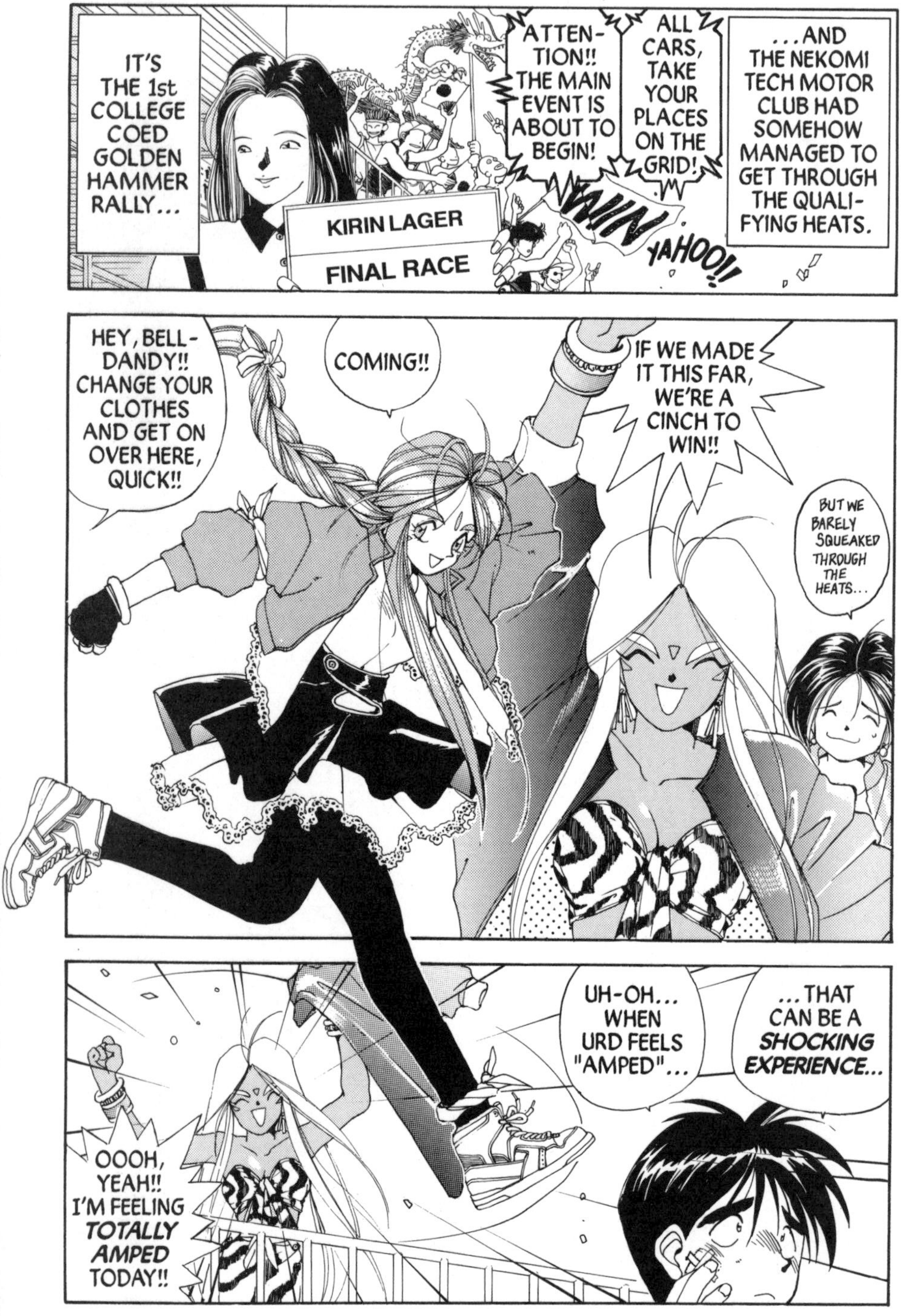
IT'S THE 1st COLLEGE COED GOLDEN HAMMER RALLY...
KIRIN LAGER
FINAL RACE
ATTEN-TION!! THE MAIN EVENT IS ABOUT TO BEGIN!
ALL CARS, TAKE YOUR PLACES ON THE GRID!
VAIIIN
YAHOO!!
...AND THE NEKOMI TECH MOTOR CLUB HAD SOMEHOW MANAGED TO GET THROUGH THE QUALI-FYING HEATS.
HEY, BELL-DANDY!! CHANGE YOUR CLOTHES AND GET ON OVER HERE, QUICK!!
COMING!!
IF WE MADE IT THIS FAR, WE'RE A CINCH TO WIN!!
BUT WE BARELY SQUEAKED THROUGH THE HEATS...
OOOH, YEAH!! I'M FEELING TOTALLY AMPED TODAY!!
UH-OH... WHEN URD FEELS "AMPED"...
...THAT CAN BE A SHOCKING EXPERIENCE...

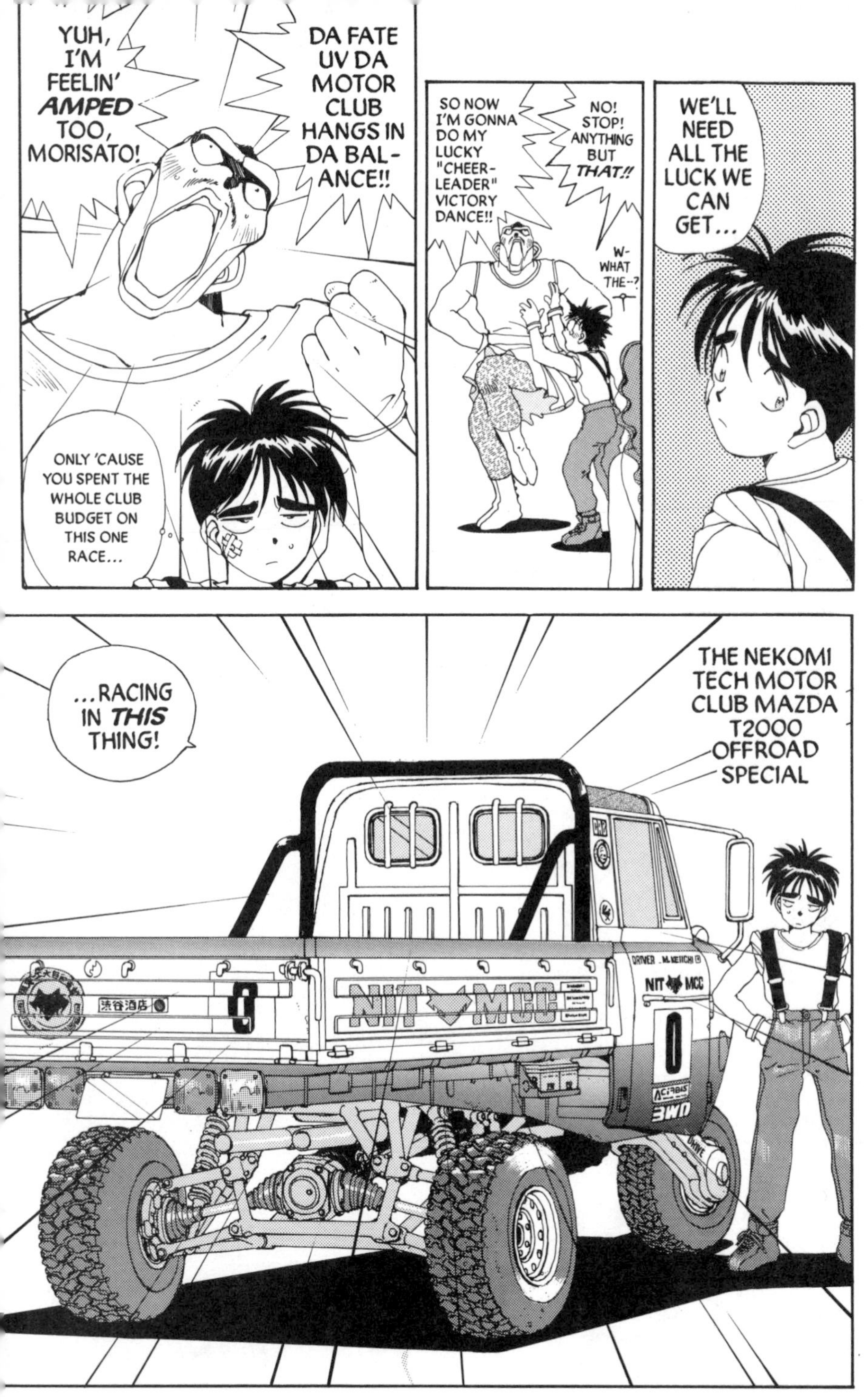
YUH, I'M FEELIN' *AMPED* TOO, MORISATO!
DA FATE UV DA MOTOR CLUB HANGS IN DA BAL-ANCE!!
ONLY 'CAUSE YOU SPENT THE WHOLE CLUB BUDGET ON THIS ONE RACE...
SO NOW I'M GONNA DO MY LUCKY "CHEER-LEADER" VICTORY DANCE!!
NO! STOP! ANYTHING BUT *THAT!!*
W-WHAT THE--?
WE'LL NEED ALL THE LUCK WE CAN GET...
...RACING IN *THIS* THING!
THE NEKOMI TECH MOTOR CLUB MAZDA T2000 OFFROAD SPECIAL
NIT MCC

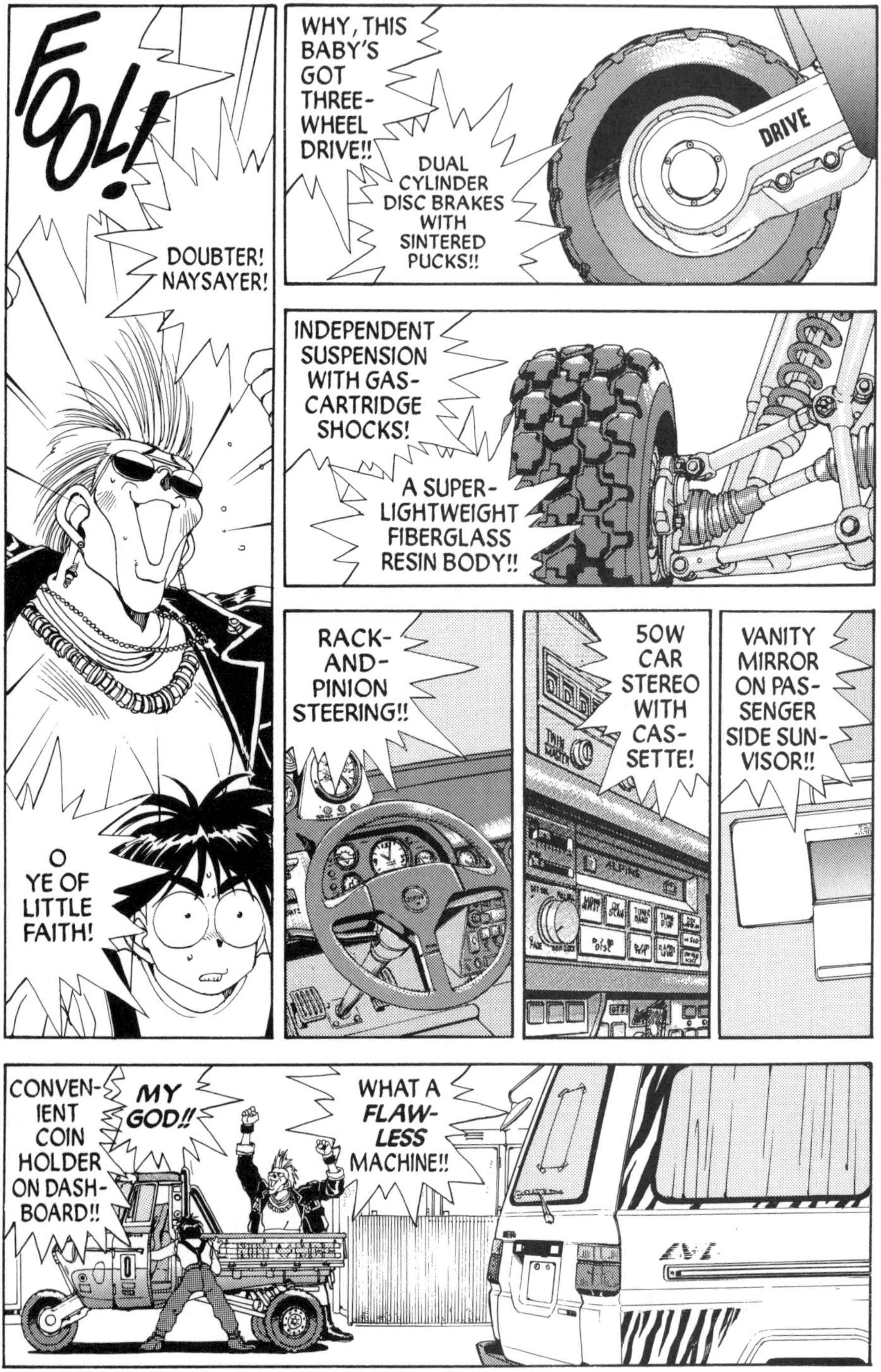
FOOL!
DOUBTER! NAYSAYER!
O YE OF LITTLE FAITH!
WHY, THIS BABY'S GOT THREE-WHEEL DRIVE!!
DRIVE
DUAL CYLINDER DISC BRAKES WITH SINTERED PUCKS!!
INDEPENDENT SUSPENSION WITH GAS-CARTRIDGE SHOCKS!
A SUPER-LIGHTWEIGHT FIBERGLASS RESIN BODY!!
RACK-AND-PINION STEERING!!
50W CAR STEREO WITH CAS-SETTE!
ALPINE
VANITY MIRROR ON PAS-SENGER SIDE SUN-VISOR!!
CONVEN-IENT COIN HOLDER ON DASH-BOARD!!
MY GOD!!
WHAT A FLAWLESS MACHINE!!

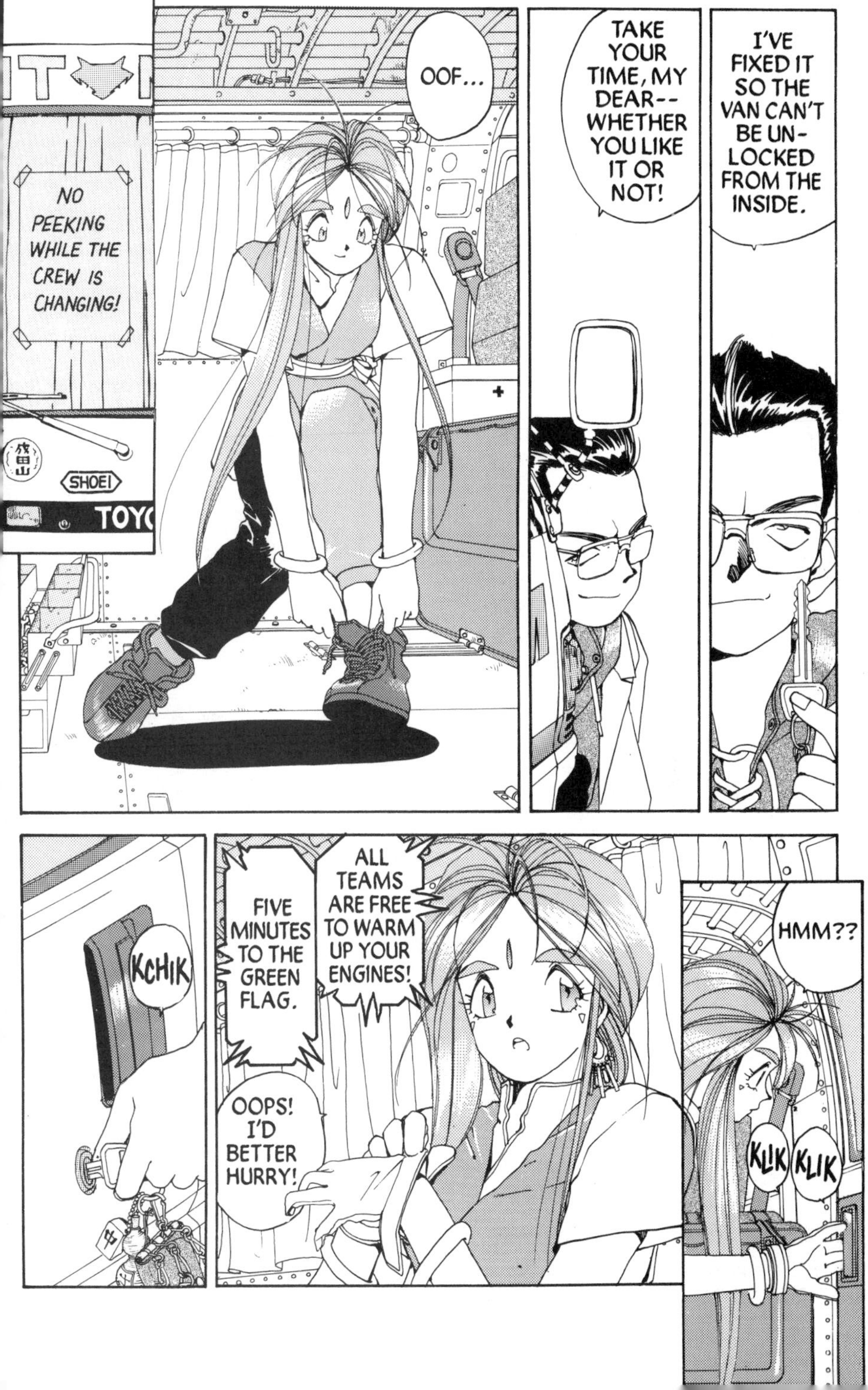

NO PEEKING WHILE THE CREW IS CHANGING!
SHOEI
TOYO
OOF...
TAKE YOUR TIME, MY DEAR-- WHETHER YOU LIKE IT OR NOT!
I'VE FIXED IT SO THE VAN CAN'T BE UN-LOCKED FROM THE INSIDE.
KCHIK
FIVE MINUTES TO THE GREEN FLAG.
ALL TEAMS ARE FREE TO WARM UP YOUR ENGINES!
OOPS! I'D BETTER HURRY!
HMM??
KLIK
KLIK

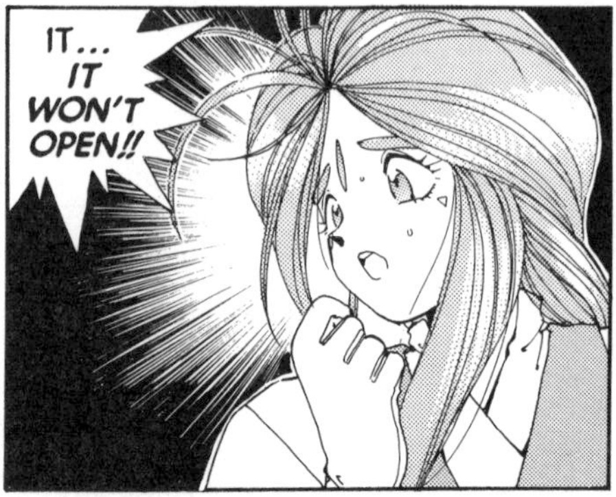
IT... *IT WON'T OPEN!!*

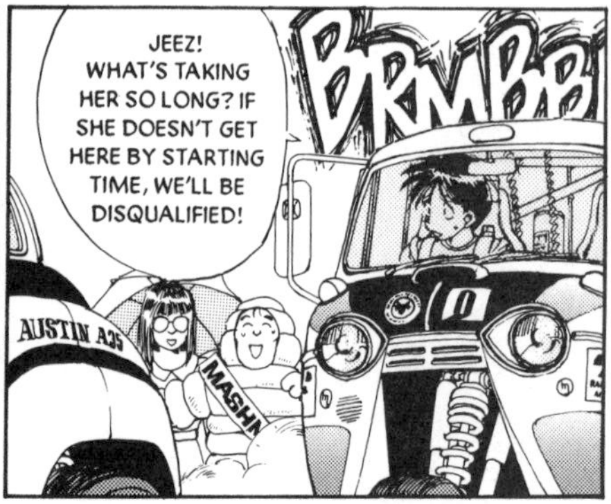
JEEZ! WHAT'S TAKING HER SO LONG? IF SHE DOESN'T GET HERE BY STARTING TIME, WE'LL BE DISQUALIFIED!
AUSTIN A35

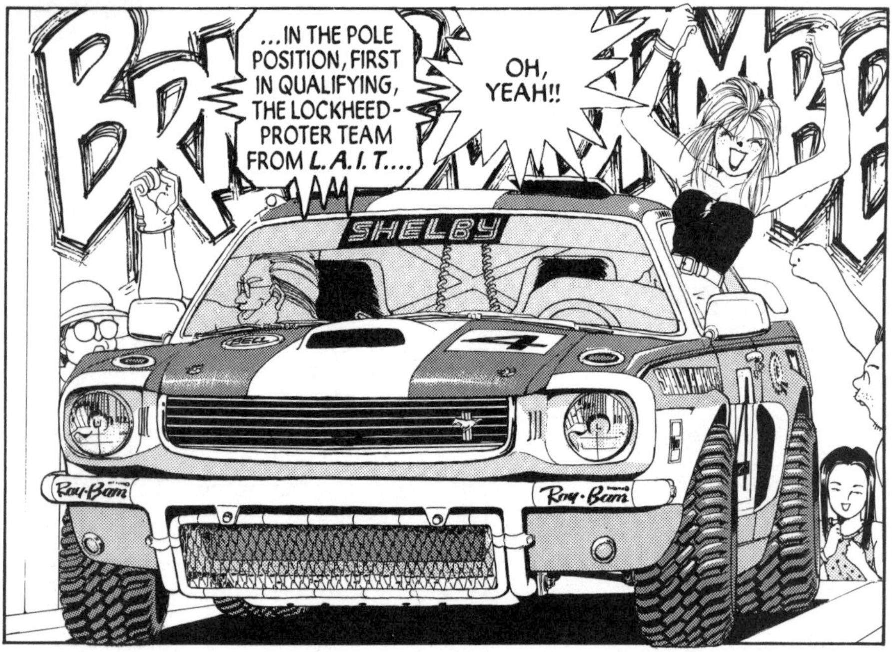
...IN THE POLE POSITION, FIRST IN QUALIFYING, THE LOCKHEED-PROTER TEAM FROM *L.A.I.T.*...
OH, YEAH!!
SHELBY
Ray-Bam
Ray-Bam

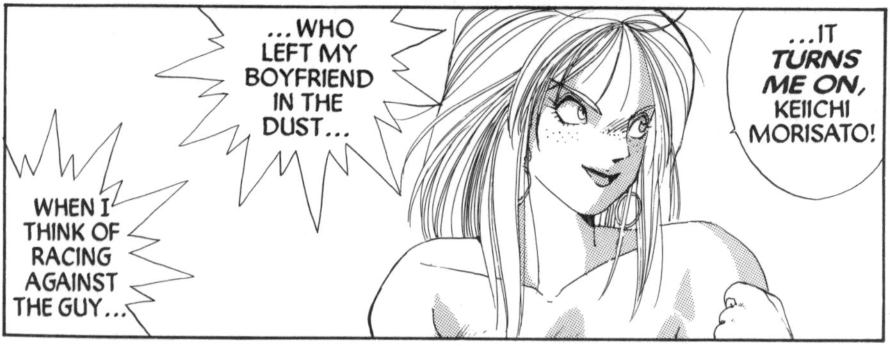
WHEN I THINK OF RACING AGAINST THE GUY...
...WHO LEFT MY BOYFRIEND IN THE DUST...
...IT *TURNS ME ON,* KEIICHI MORISATO!

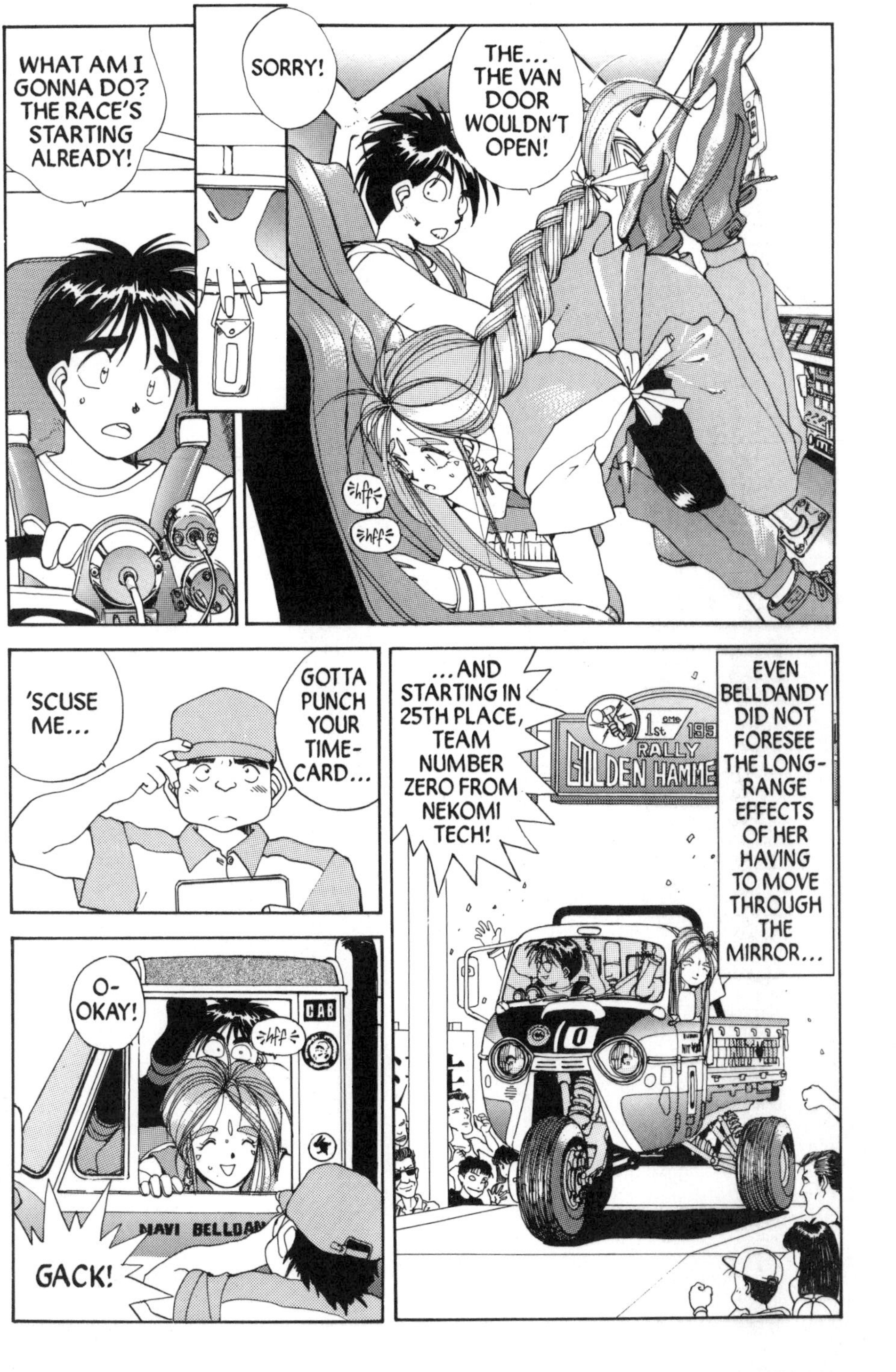
WHAT AM I GONNA DO? THE RACE'S STARTING ALREADY!
SORRY!
THE... THE VAN DOOR WOULDN'T OPEN!
hff
hff
'SCUSE ME...
GOTTA PUNCH YOUR TIME-CARD...
O-OKAY!
CAB
hff
NAVI BELLDAN
GACK!
...AND STARTING IN 25TH PLACE, TEAM NUMBER ZERO FROM NEKOMI TECH!
1st
RALLY
GOLDEN HAMME
EVEN BELLDANDY DID NOT FORESEE THE LONG-RANGE EFFECTS OF HER HAVING TO MOVE THROUGH THE MIRROR...
0

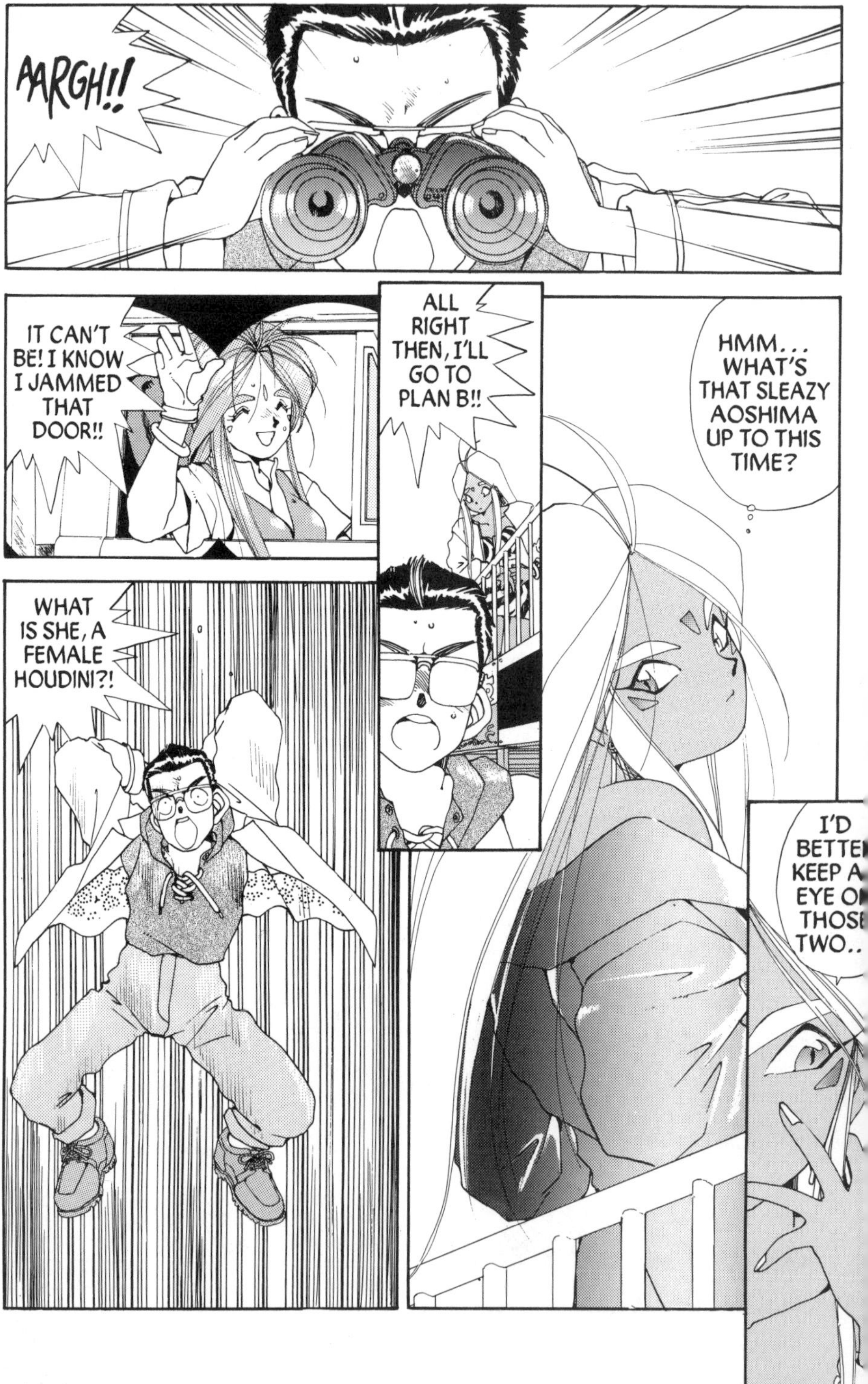
AARGH!!
IT CAN'T BE! I KNOW I JAMMED THAT DOOR!!
WHAT IS SHE, A FEMALE HOUDINI?!
ALL RIGHT THEN, I'LL GO TO PLAN B!!
HMM... WHAT'S THAT SLEAZY AOSHIMA UP TO THIS TIME?
I'D BETTE KEEP A EYE O THOSE TWO..

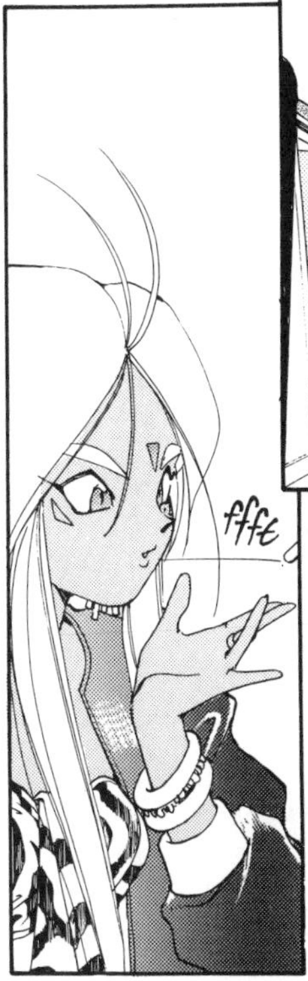
fffe

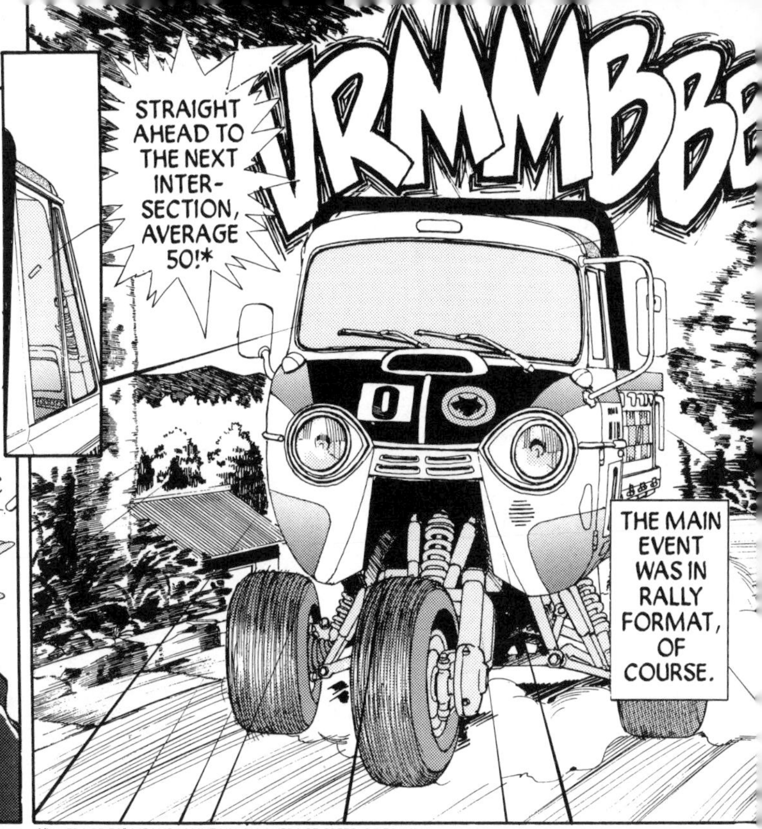
STRAIGHT AHEAD TO THE NEXT INTER-SECTION, AVERAGE 50!*
JRMMBB
THE MAIN EVENT WAS IN RALLY FORMAT, OF COURSE.

*"AVERAGE 50" MEANS MAINTAIN AN AVERAGE SPEED OF 50 MPH.

A RALLY IS NOTA CONTEST OF PURE SPEED. INSTEAD, YOU FOLLOW A MAP THAT SHOWS AVERAGE SPEEDS BETWEEN POINTS.

30 MILES FROM POINT A TO POINT B AT A DESIGNATED AVERAGE SPEED OF 40MPH-- ARRIVAL TIME WOULD BE 45 MINUTES AFTER DEPARTURE.

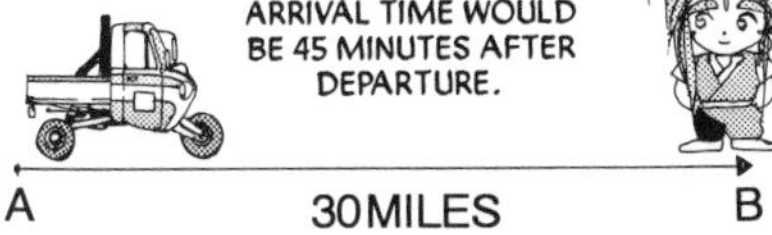
A
30MILES
B

THE CHAL-LENGE IS TO REACH EACH CHECKPOINT EXACTLY AT THE DESIGNATED TIME.

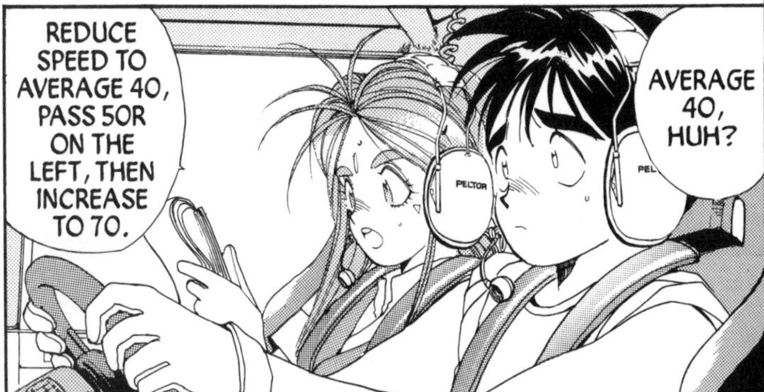
REDUCE SPEED TO AVERAGE 40, PASS 5OR ON THE LEFT, THEN INCREASE TO 70.
AVERAGE 40, HUH?
PELTOR

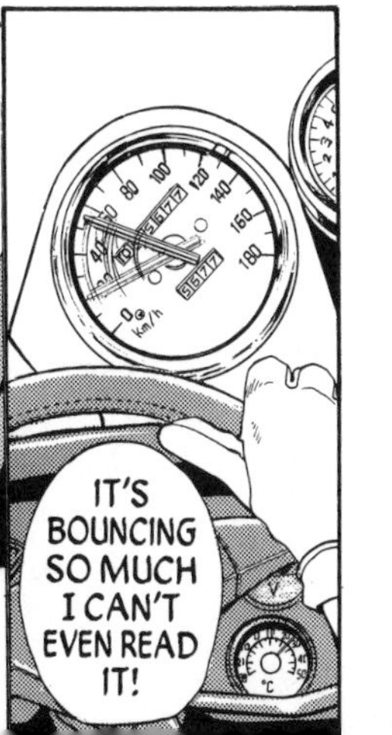
IT'S BOUNCING SO MUCH I CAN'T EVEN READ IT!

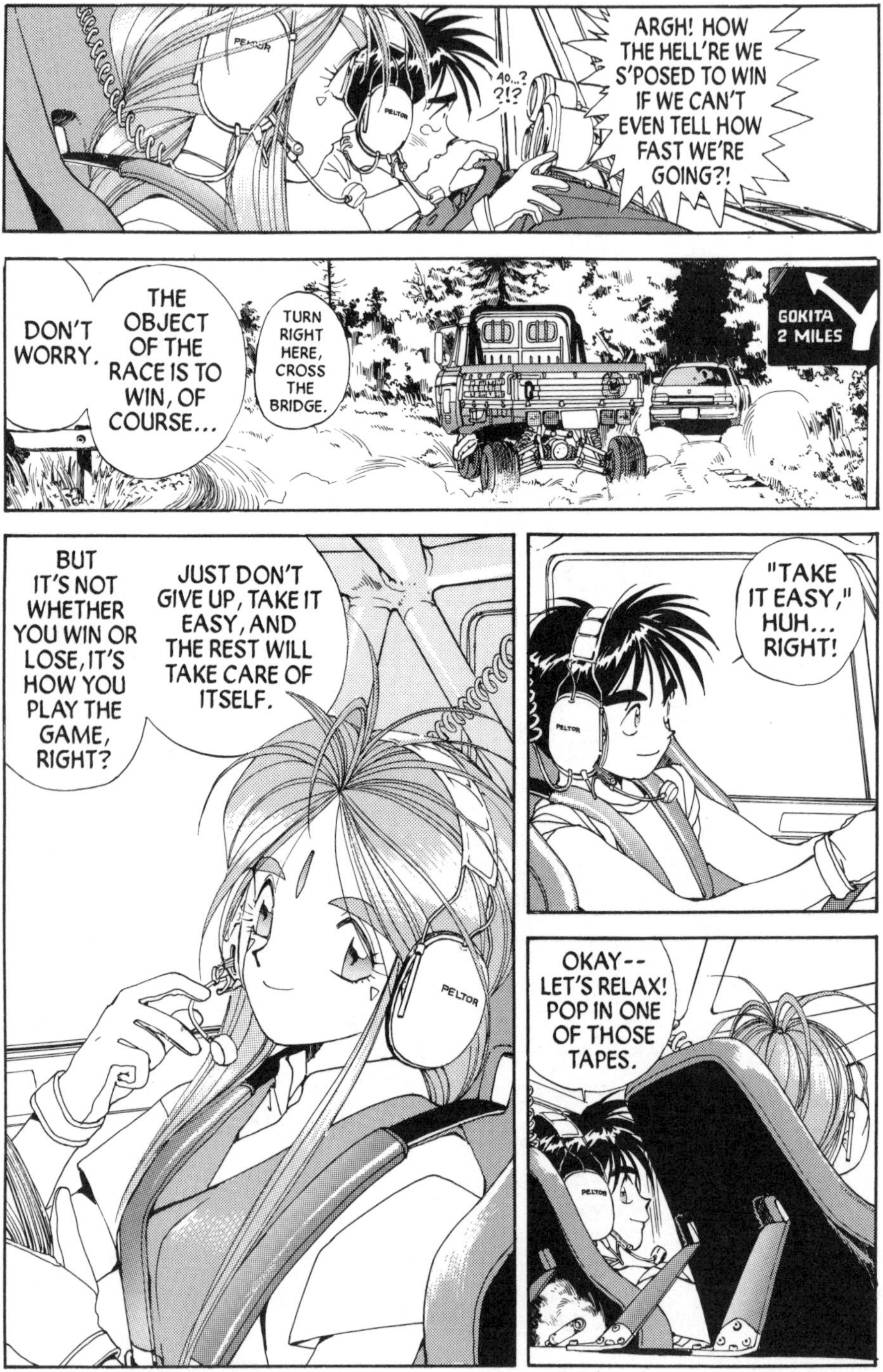
40...?
?!?
ARGH! HOW THE HELL'RE WE S'POSED TO WIN IF WE CAN'T EVEN TELL HOW FAST WE'RE GOING?!
DON'T WORRY.
THE OBJECT OF THE RACE IS TO WIN, OF COURSE...
TURN RIGHT HERE, CROSS THE BRIDGE.
GOKITA 2 MILES
BUT IT'S NOT WHETHER YOU WIN OR LOSE, IT'S HOW YOU PLAY THE GAME, RIGHT?
JUST DON'T GIVE UP, TAKE IT EASY, AND THE REST WILL TAKE CARE OF ITSELF.
"TAKE IT EASY," HUH... RIGHT!
OKAY-- LET'S RELAX! POP IN ONE OF THOSE TAPES.

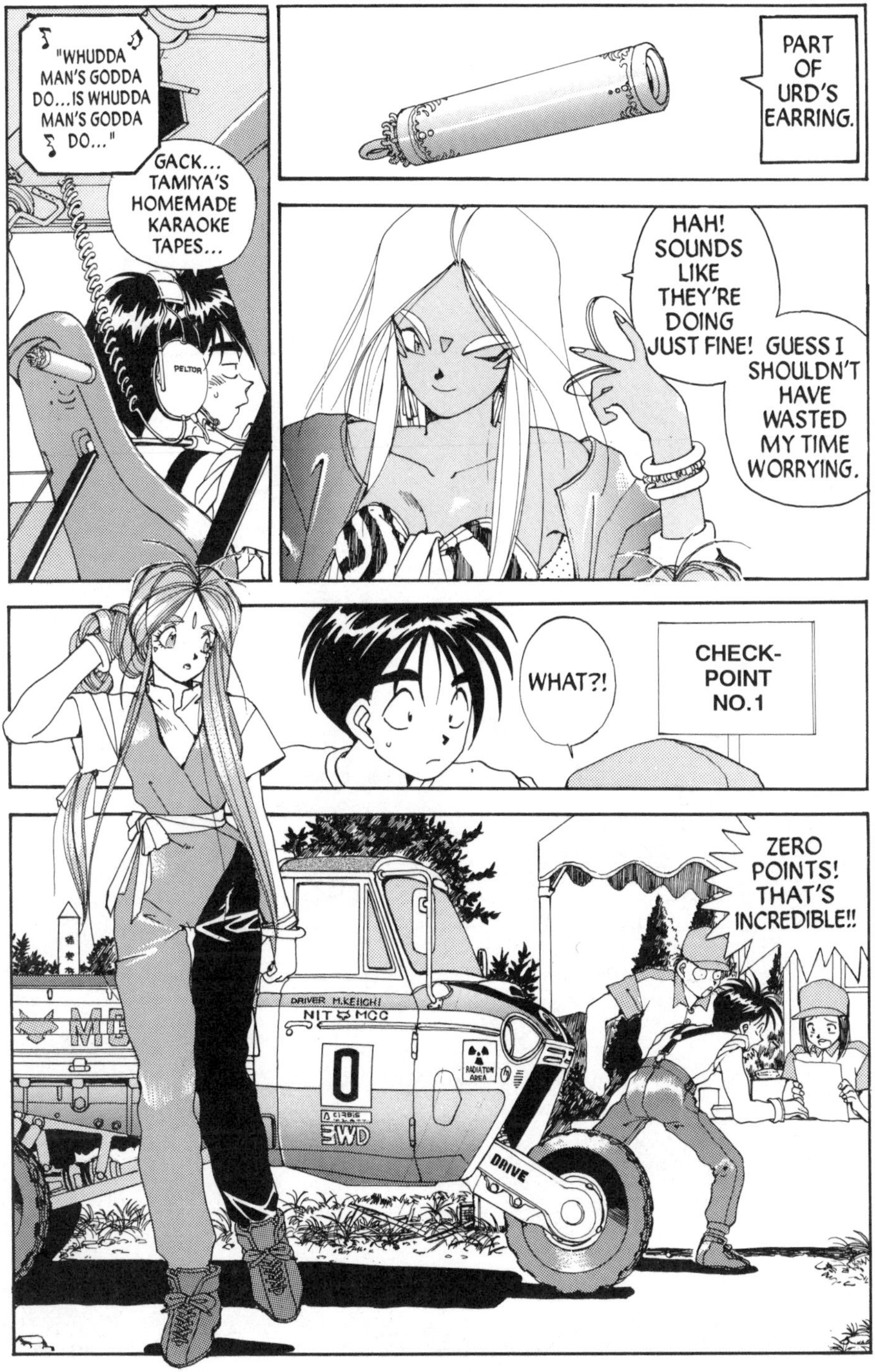
"WHUDDA MAN'S GODDA DO...IS WHUDDA MAN'S GODDA DO..."
GACK... TAMIYA'S HOMEMADE KARAOKE TAPES...
PELTOR
PART OF URD'S EARRING.
HAH! SOUNDS LIKE THEY'RE DOING JUST FINE!
GUESS I SHOULDN'T HAVE WASTED MY TIME WORRYING.
WHAT?!
CHECK-POINT NO.1
ZERO POINTS! THAT'S INCREDIBLE!!
DRIVER M.KEIICHI
NIT MCC
0
RADIATION AREA
DRIVE

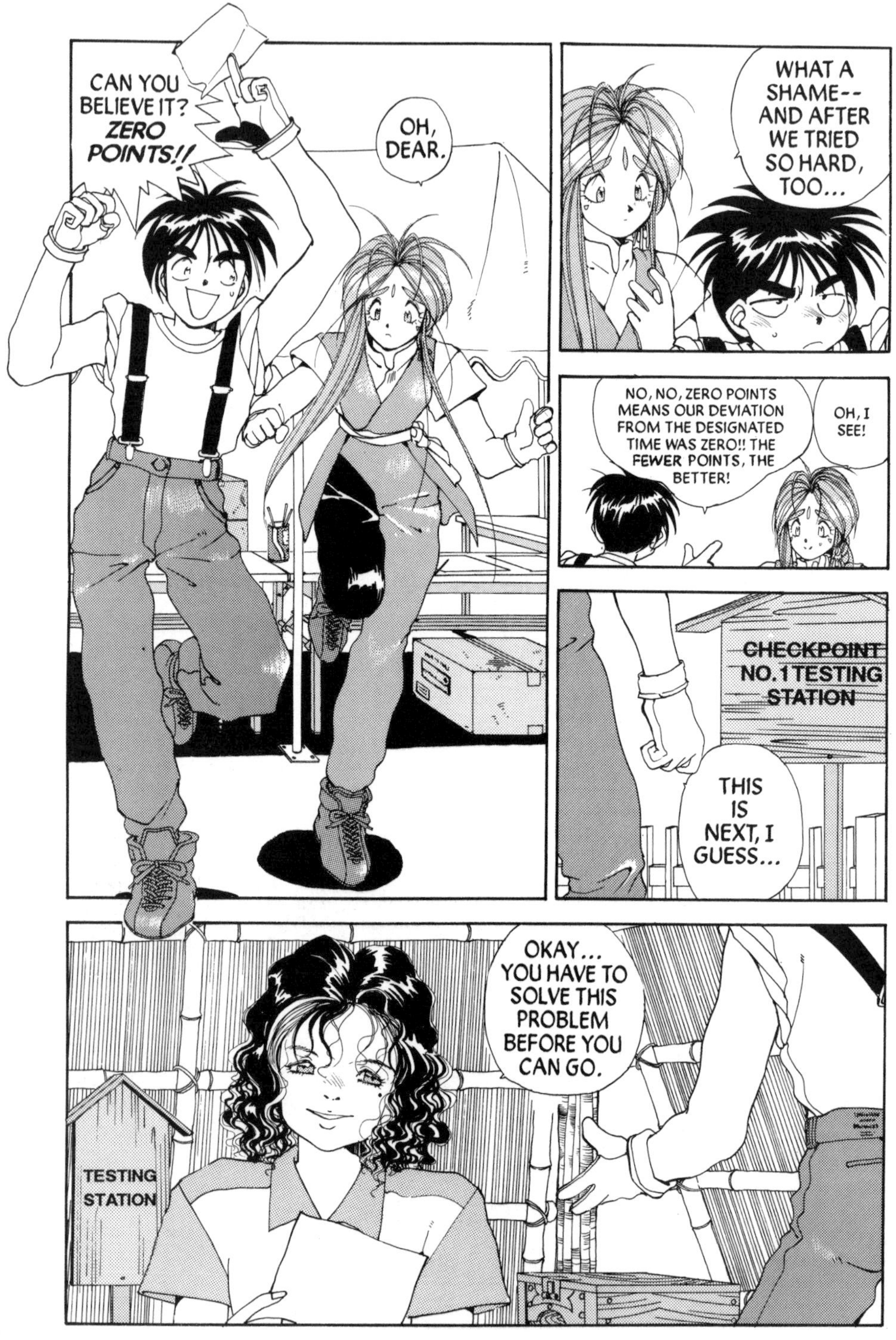
CAN YOU BELIEVE IT? ZERO POINTS!!
OH, DEAR.
WHAT A SHAME-- AND AFTER WE TRIED SO HARD, TOO...
NO, NO, ZERO POINTS MEANS OUR DEVIATION FROM THE DESIGNATED TIME WAS ZERO!! THE FEWER POINTS, THE BETTER!
OH, I SEE!
CHECKPOINT NO.1 TESTING STATION
THIS IS NEXT, I GUESS...
TESTING STATION
OKAY... YOU HAVE TO SOLVE THIS PROBLEM BEFORE YOU CAN GO.

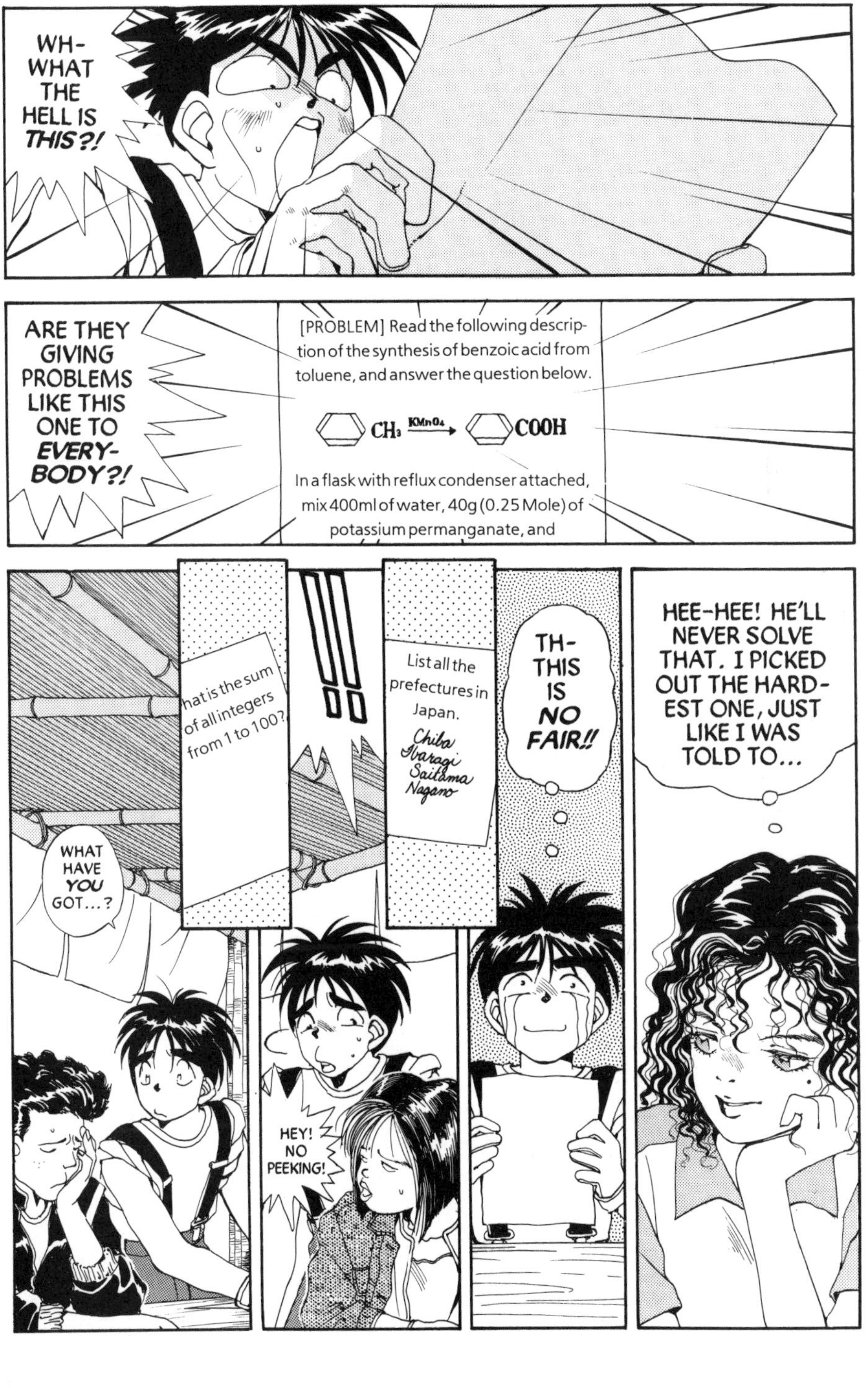
WH- WHAT THE HELL IS THIS?!
ARE THEY GIVING PROBLEMS LIKE THIS ONE TO EVERY-BODY?!
[PROBLEM] Read the following description of the synthesis of benzoic acid from toluene, and answer the question below.
CH3 KMnO4 COOH
In a flask with reflux condenser attached, mix 400ml of water, 40g (0.25 Mole) of potassium permanganate, and
WHAT HAVE YOU GOT...?
hat is the sum of all integers from 1 to 100?
!!
HEY! NO PEEKING!
List all the prefectures in Japan.
Chiba Ibaragi Saitama Nagano
TH- THIS IS NO FAIR!!
HEE-HEE! HE'LL NEVER SOLVE THAT. I PICKED OUT THE HARD-EST ONE, JUST LIKE I WAS TOLD TO...

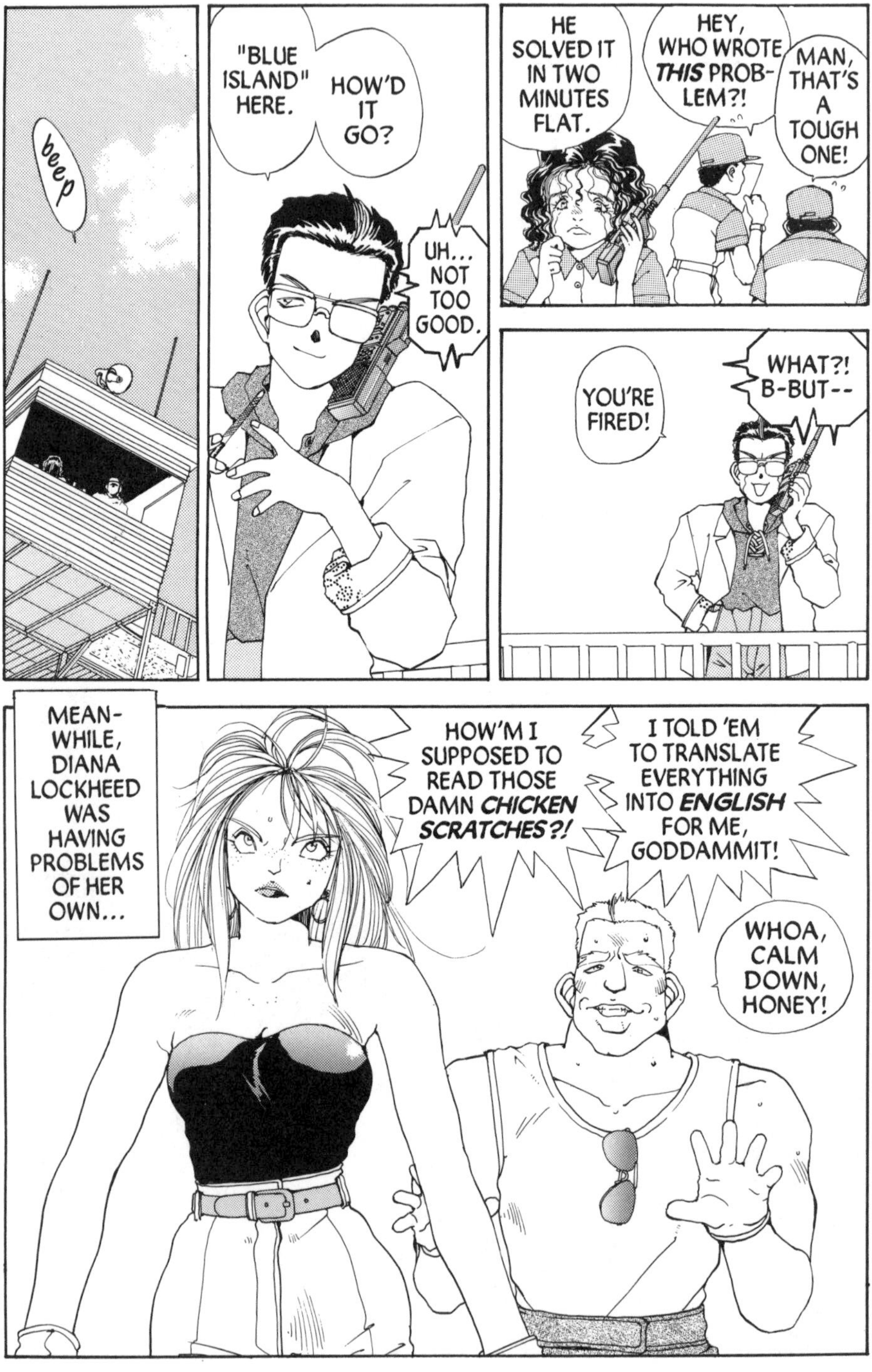
beep
"BLUE ISLAND" HERE.
HOW'D IT GO?
UH... NOT TOO GOOD.
HE SOLVED IT IN TWO MINUTES FLAT.
HEY, WHO WROTE *THIS* PROB-LEM?!
MAN, THAT'S A TOUGH ONE!
YOU'RE FIRED!
WHAT?! B-BUT--
MEAN-WHILE, DIANA LOCKHEED WAS HAVING PROBLEMS OF HER OWN...
HOW'M I SUPPOSED TO READ THOSE DAMN *CHICKEN SCRATCHES?!*
I TOLD 'EM TO TRANSLATE EVERYTHING INTO *ENGLISH* FOR ME, GODDAMMIT!
WHOA, CALM DOWN, HONEY!

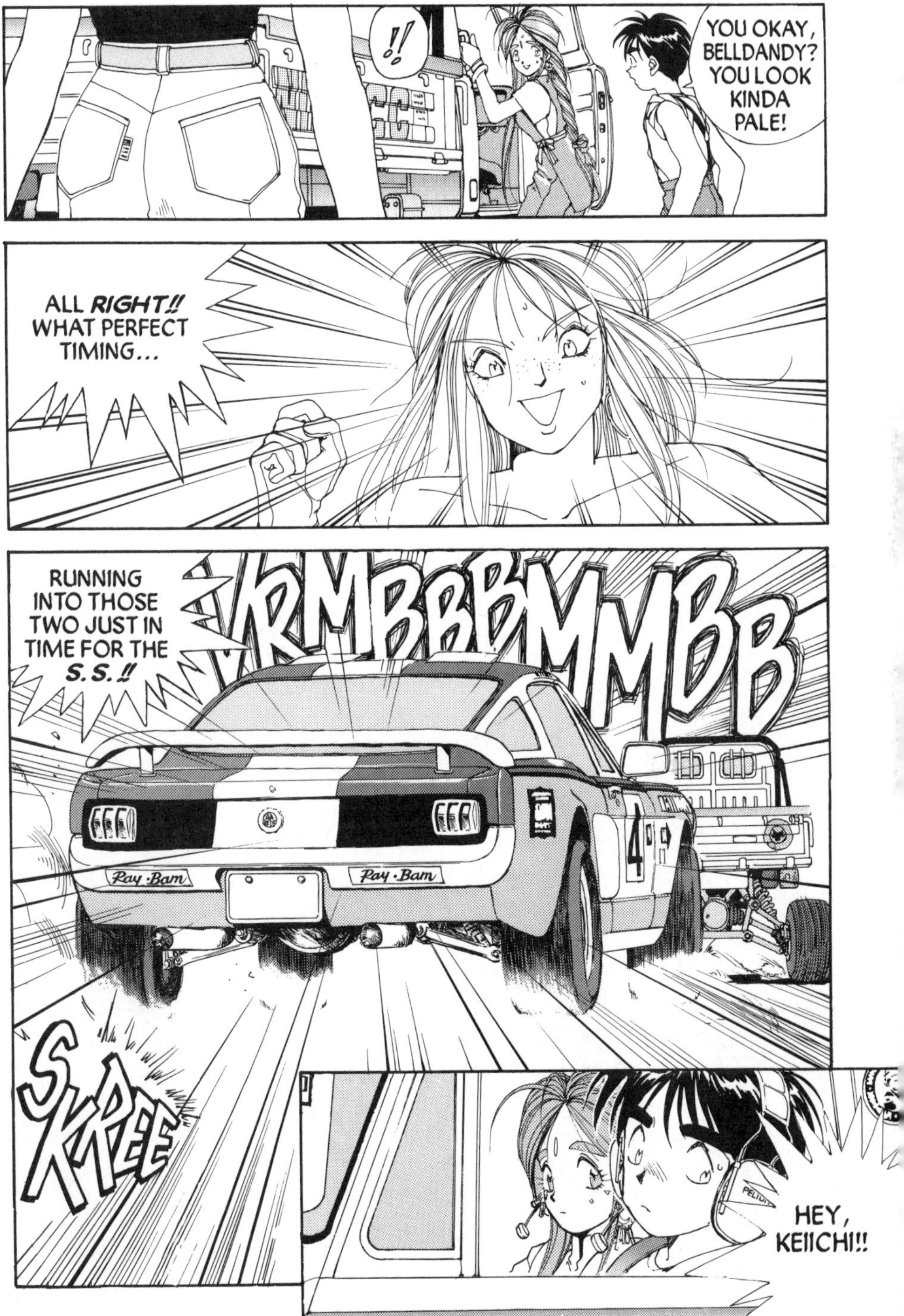
!!
YOU OKAY, BELLDANDY? YOU LOOK KINDA PALE!
ALL RIGHT!! WHAT PERFECT TIMING...
RUNNING INTO THOSE TWO JUST IN TIME FOR THE S.S.!!
VRMBBBMMMBB
Ray·Bam
Ray·Bam
SKREE
HEY, KEIICHI!!

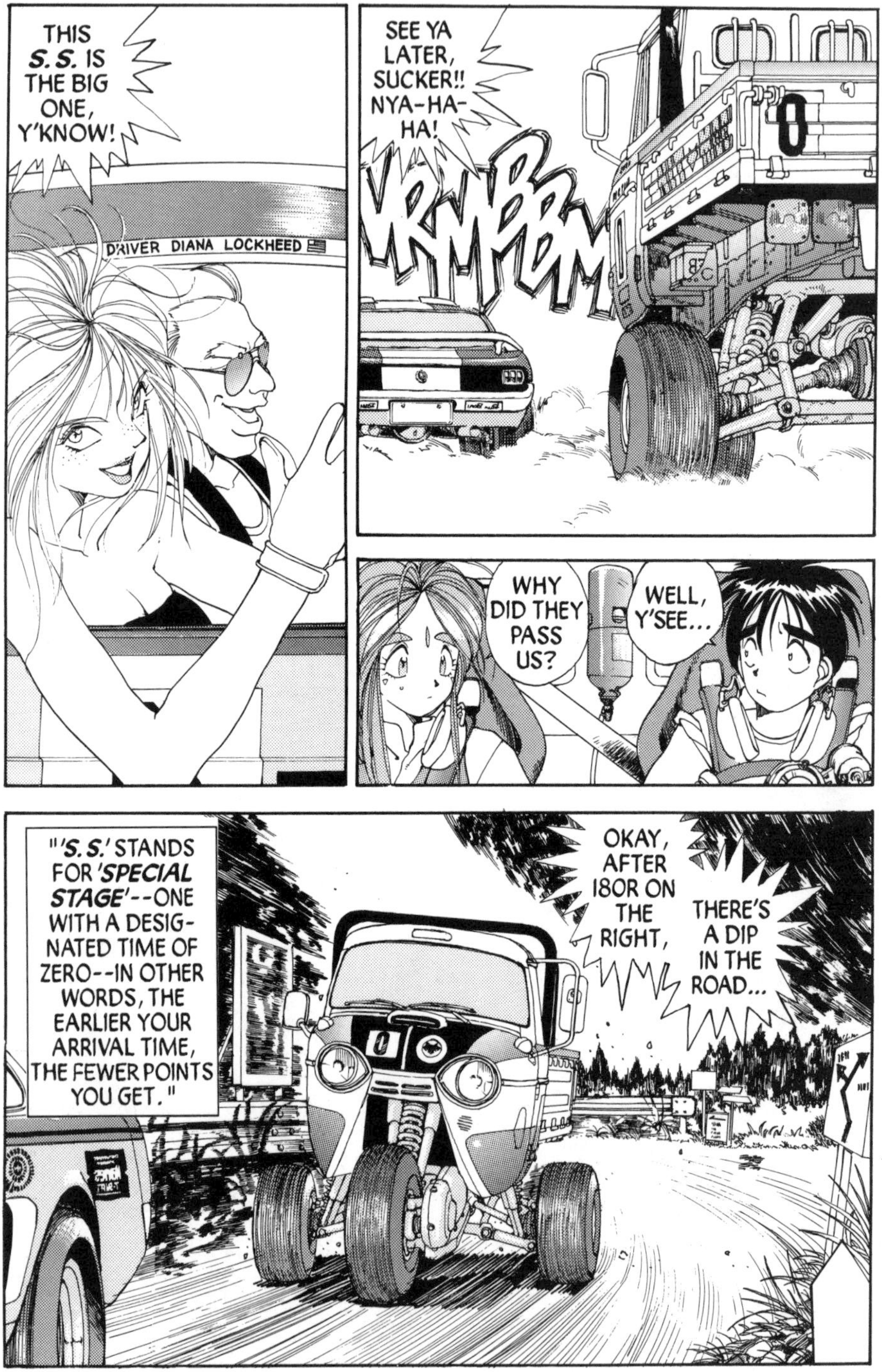
THIS S.S. IS THE BIG ONE, Y'KNOW!
DRIVER DIANA LOCKHEED
SEE YA LATER, SUCKER!! NYA-HA-HA!
VRMBRMBM
WHY DID THEY PASS US?
WELL, Y'SEE...
"'S.S.' STANDS FOR 'SPECIAL STAGE'--ONE WITH A DESIGNATED TIME OF ZERO--IN OTHER WORDS, THE EARLIER YOUR ARRIVAL TIME, THE FEWER POINTS YOU GET."
OKAY, AFTER 180R ON THE RIGHT,
THERE'S A DIP IN THE ROAD...

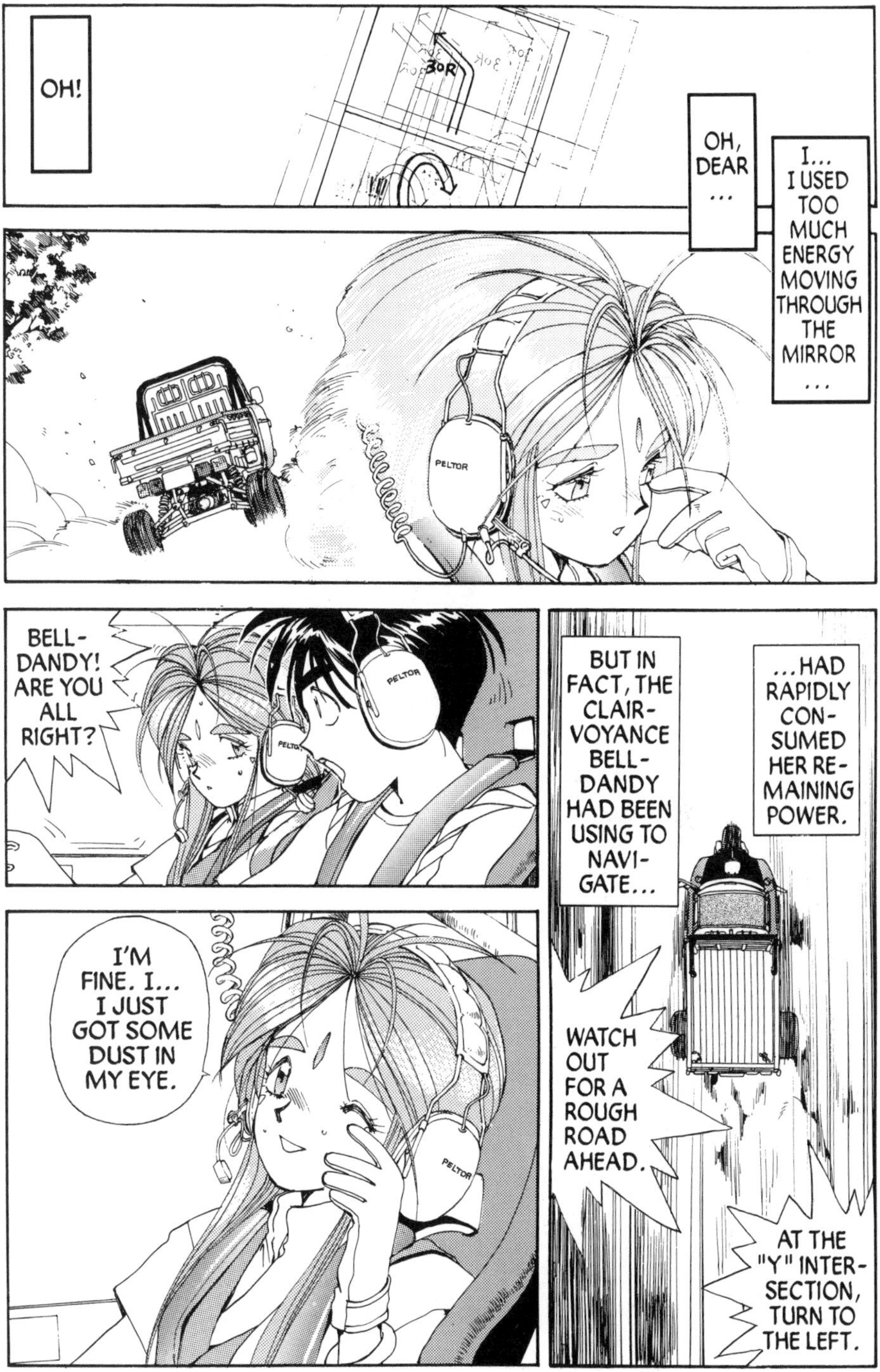
OH!
OH, DEAR ...
I... I USED TOO MUCH ENERGY MOVING THROUGH THE MIRROR ...
BELL-DANDY! ARE YOU ALL RIGHT?
I'M FINE. I... I JUST GOT SOME DUST IN MY EYE.
BUT IN FACT, THE CLAIR-VOYANCE BELL-DANDY HAD BEEN USING TO NAVI-GATE...
...HAD RAPIDLY CON-SUMED HER RE-MAINING POWER.
WATCH OUT FOR A ROUGH ROAD AHEAD.
AT THE "Y" INTER-SECTION, TURN TO THE LEFT.

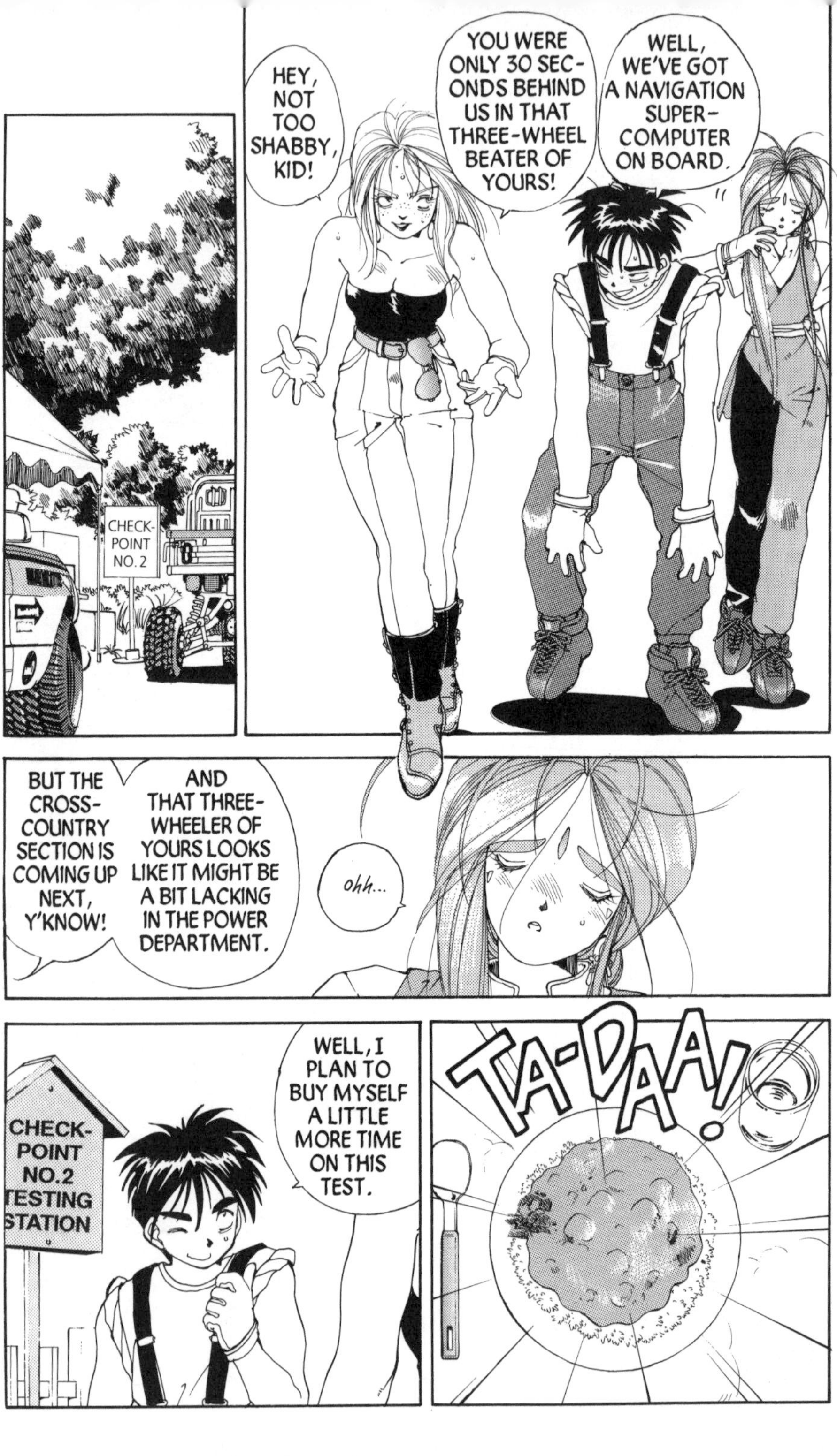
CHECK-POINT NO. 2
HEY, NOT TOO SHABBY, KID!
YOU WERE ONLY 30 SEC-ONDS BEHIND US IN THAT THREE-WHEEL BEATER OF YOURS!
WELL, WE'VE GOT A NAVIGATION SUPER-COMPUTER ON BOARD.
BUT THE CROSS-COUNTRY SECTION IS COMING UP NEXT, Y'KNOW!
AND THAT THREE-WHEELER OF YOURS LOOKS LIKE IT MIGHT BE A BIT LACKING IN THE POWER DEPARTMENT.
ohh...
CHECK-POINT NO.2 TESTING STATION
WELL, I PLAN TO BUY MYSELF A LITTLE MORE TIME ON THIS TEST.
TA-DAA!

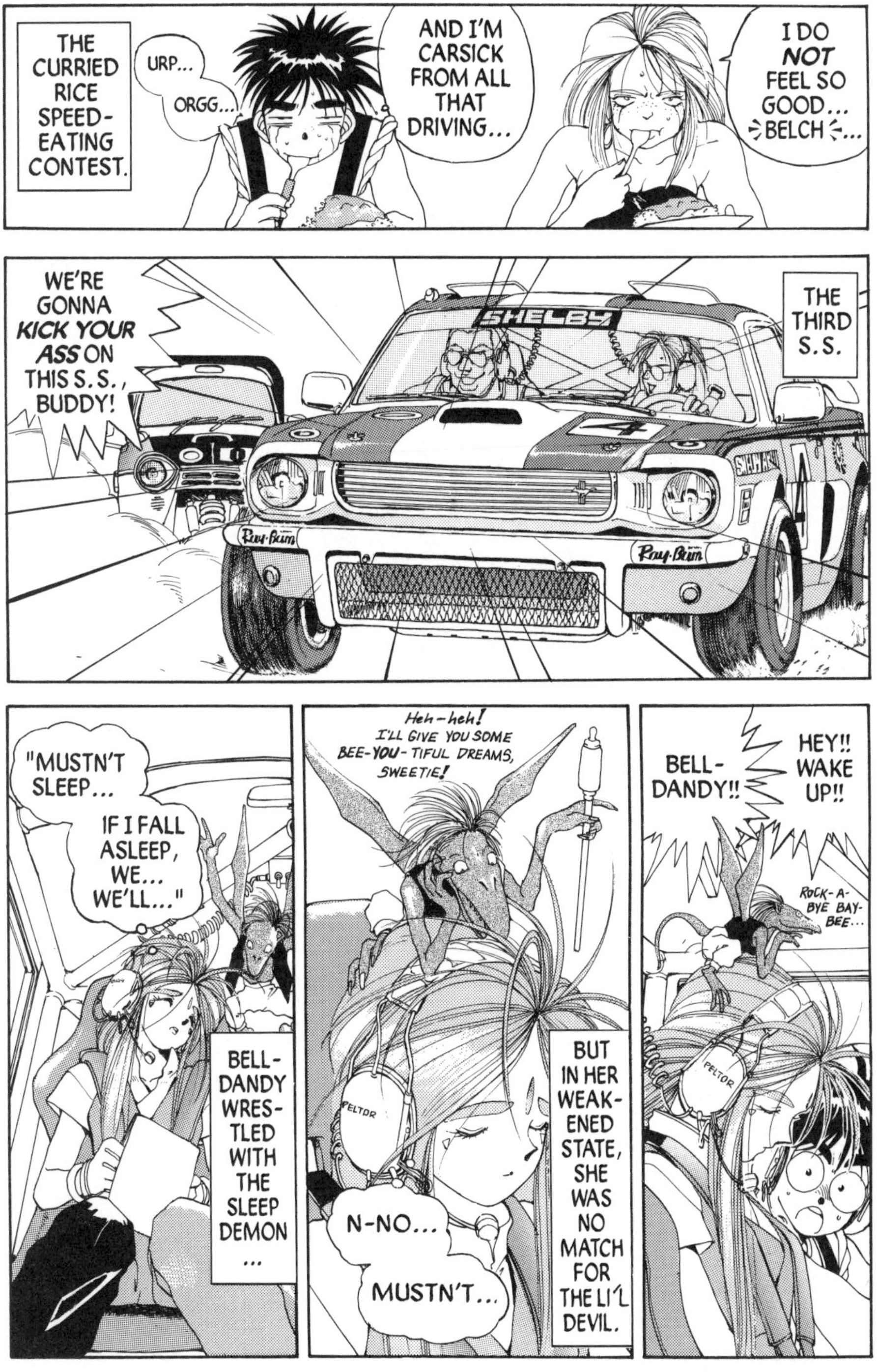
THE CURRIED RICE SPEED-EATING CONTEST.
URP...
ORGG...
AND I'M CARSICK FROM ALL THAT DRIVING...
I DO **NOT** FEEL SO GOOD... BELCH...
WE'RE GONNA **KICK YOUR ASS** ON THIS S.S., BUDDY!
SHELBY
THE THIRD S.S.
"MUSTN'T SLEEP...
IF I FALL ASLEEP, WE... WE'LL..."
BELL-DANDY WRES-TLED WITH THE SLEEP DEMON ...
Heh-heh! I'LL GIVE YOU SOME BEE-YOU-TIFUL DREAMS, SWEETIE!
PELTOR
N-NO...
MUSTN'T...
BUT IN HER WEAK-ENED STATE, SHE WAS NO MATCH FOR THE LI'L DEVIL.
BELL-DANDY!!
HEY!! WAKE UP!!
ROCK-A-BYE BAY-BEE...
PELTOR

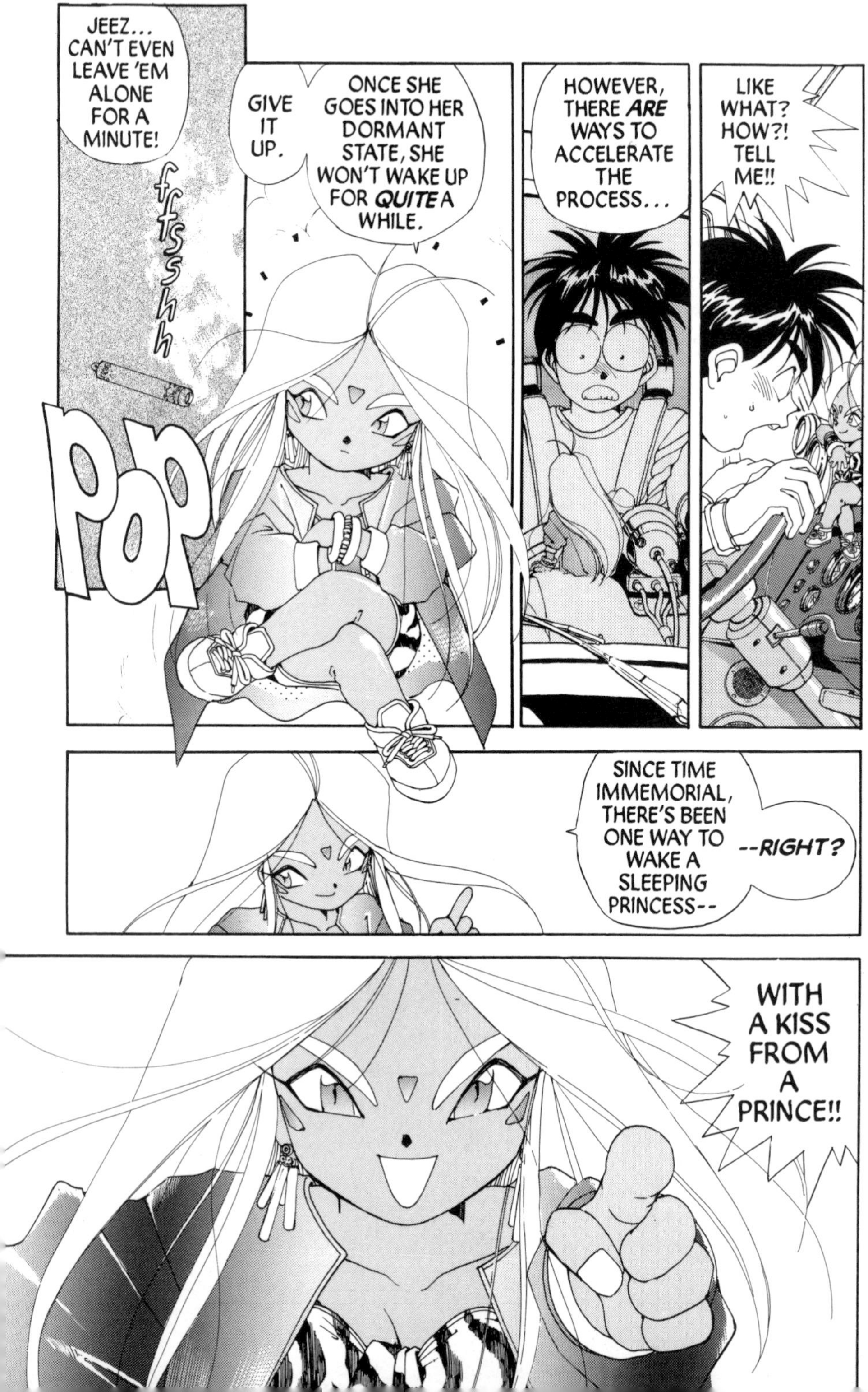

JEEZ... CAN'T EVEN LEAVE 'EM ALONE FOR A MINUTE!
ffsshh
POP
GIVE IT UP.
ONCE SHE GOES INTO HER DORMANT STATE, SHE WON'T WAKE UP FOR QUITE A WHILE.
HOWEVER, THERE ARE WAYS TO ACCELERATE THE PROCESS...
LIKE WHAT? HOW?! TELL ME!!
SINCE TIME IMMEMORIAL, THERE'S BEEN ONE WAY TO WAKE A SLEEPING PRINCESS--
--RIGHT?
WITH A KISS FROM A PRINCE!!

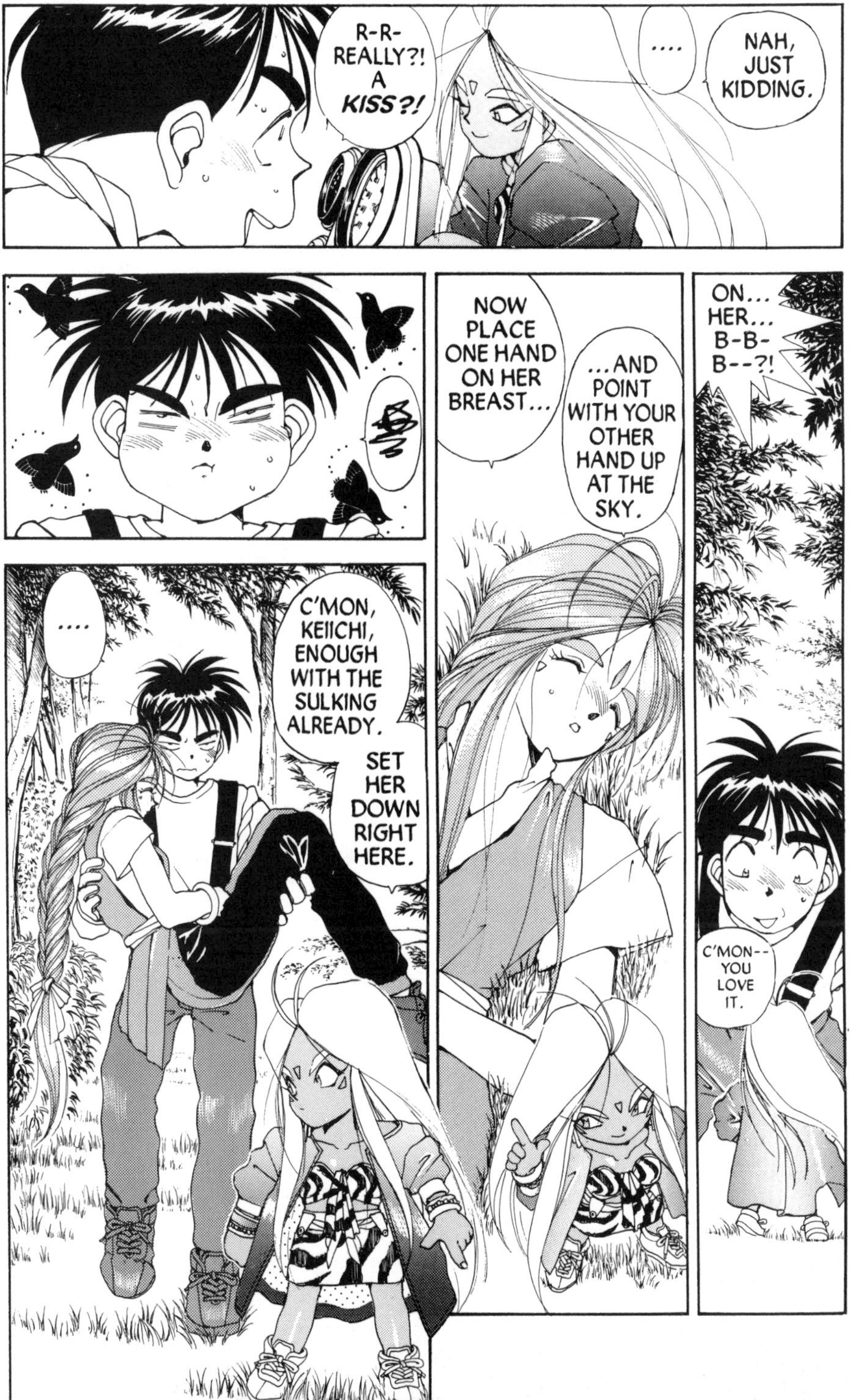
R-R-REALLY?! A KISS?!
....
NAH, JUST KIDDING.
....
C'MON, KEIICHI, ENOUGH WITH THE SULKING ALREADY.
SET HER DOWN RIGHT HERE.
NOW PLACE ONE HAND ON HER BREAST...
...AND POINT WITH YOUR OTHER HAND UP AT THE SKY.
ON... HER... B-B-B--?!
C'MON-- YOU LOVE IT.

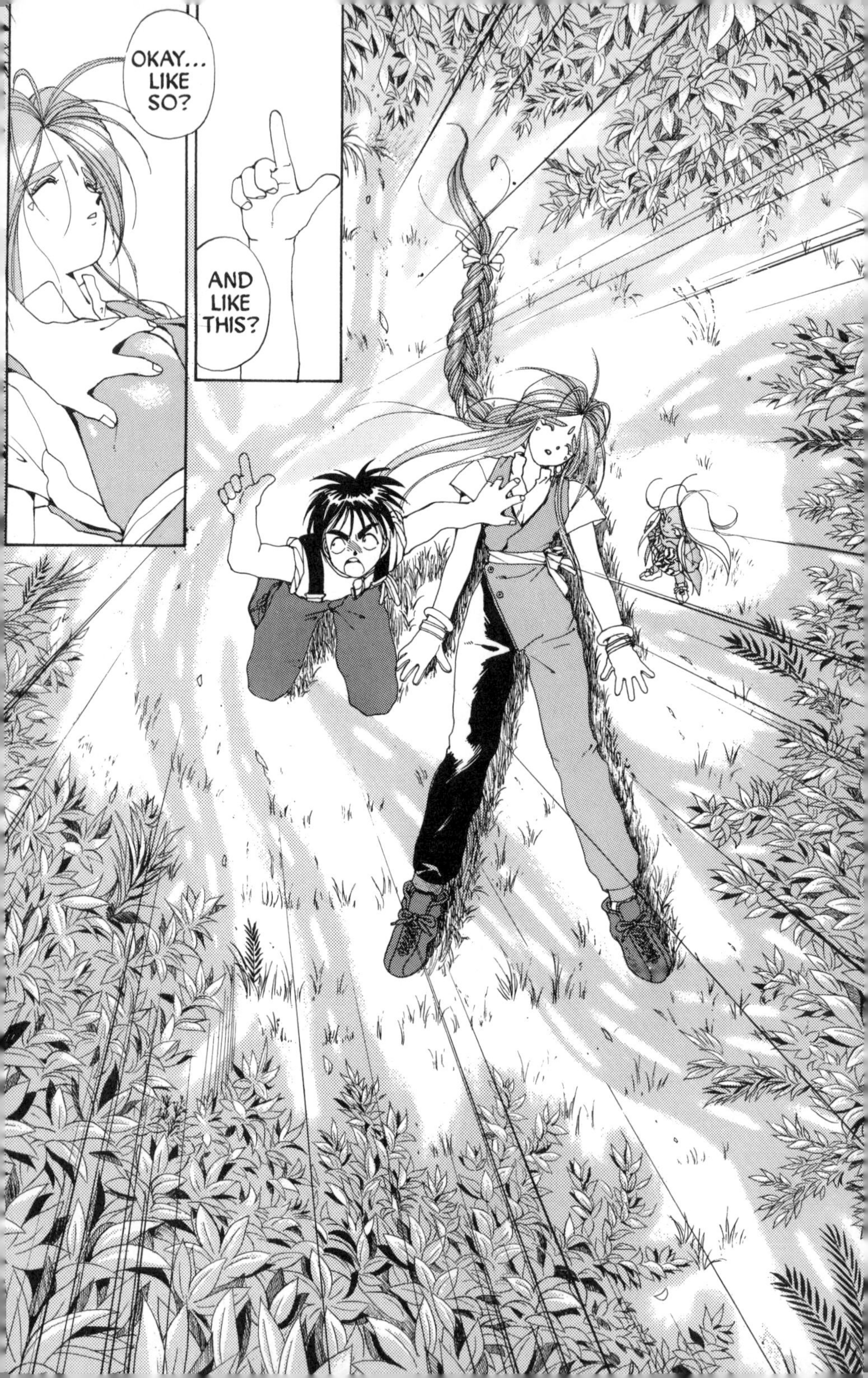
OKAY... LIKE SO?
AND LIKE THIS?

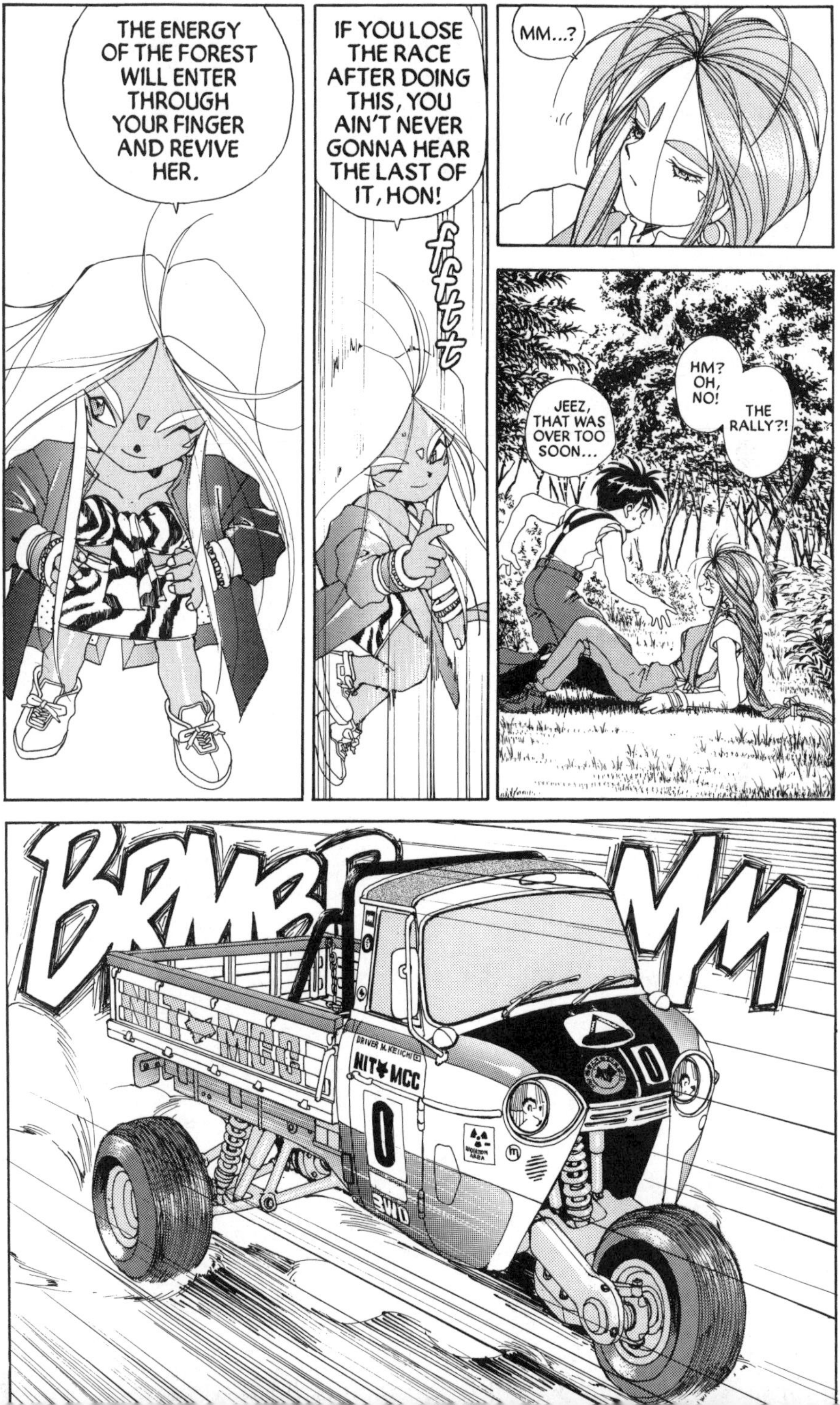
THE ENERGY OF THE FOREST WILL ENTER THROUGH YOUR FINGER AND REVIVE HER.
IF YOU LOSE THE RACE AFTER DOING THIS, YOU AIN'T NEVER GONNA HEAR THE LAST OF IT, HON!
fftt
MM...?
JEEZ, THAT WAS OVER TOO SOON...
HM? OH, NO!
THE RALLY?!
BRMB
MM
NIT MCC
DRIVER M. KEIICHI
NIT MCC
0
3WD

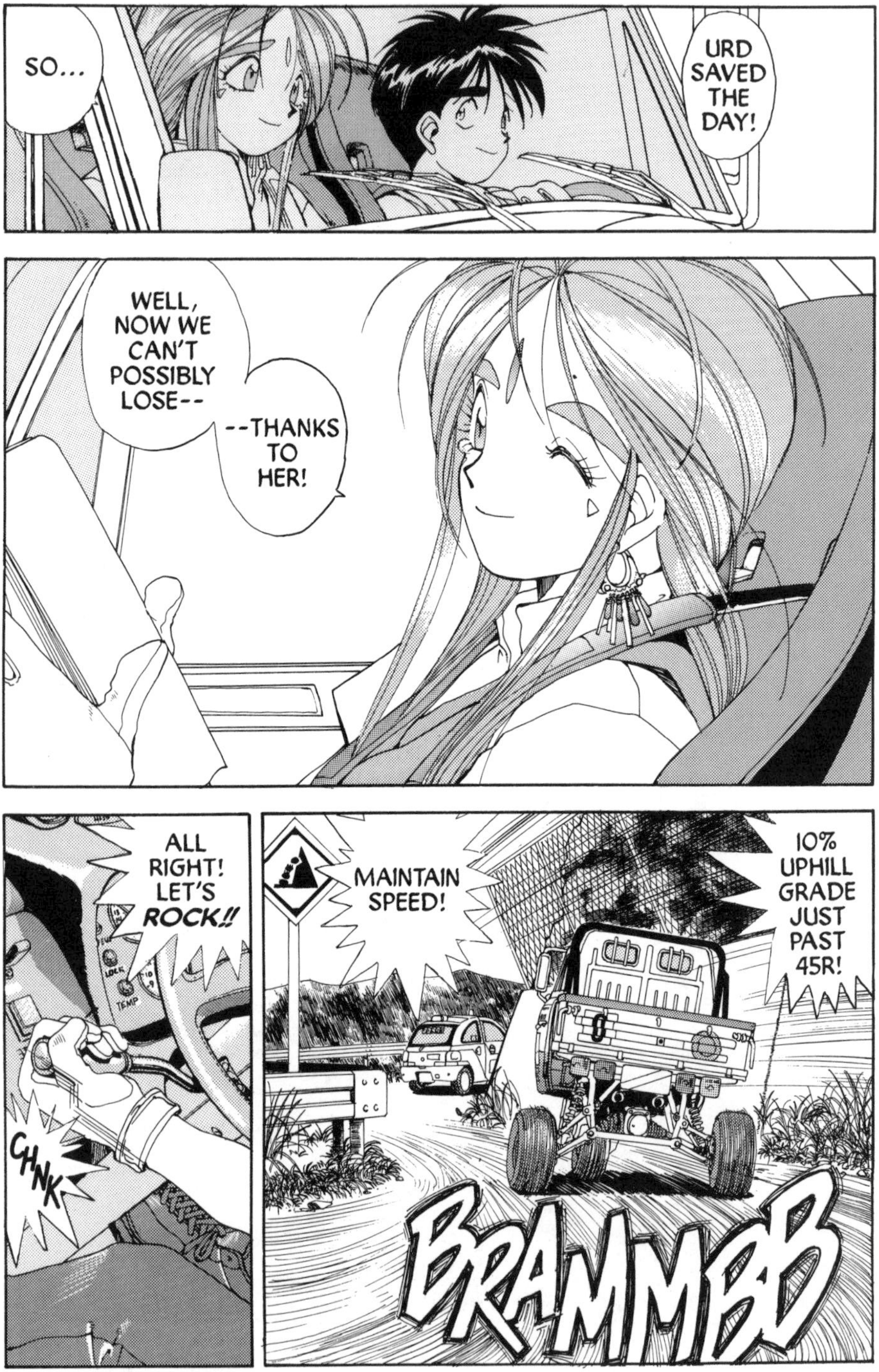
SO...
URD SAVED THE DAY!
WELL, NOW WE CAN'T POSSIBLY LOSE--
--THANKS TO HER!
ALL RIGHT! LET'S ROCK!!
CHNK
MAINTAIN SPEED!
10% UPHILL GRADE JUST PAST 45R!
BRAMMBB

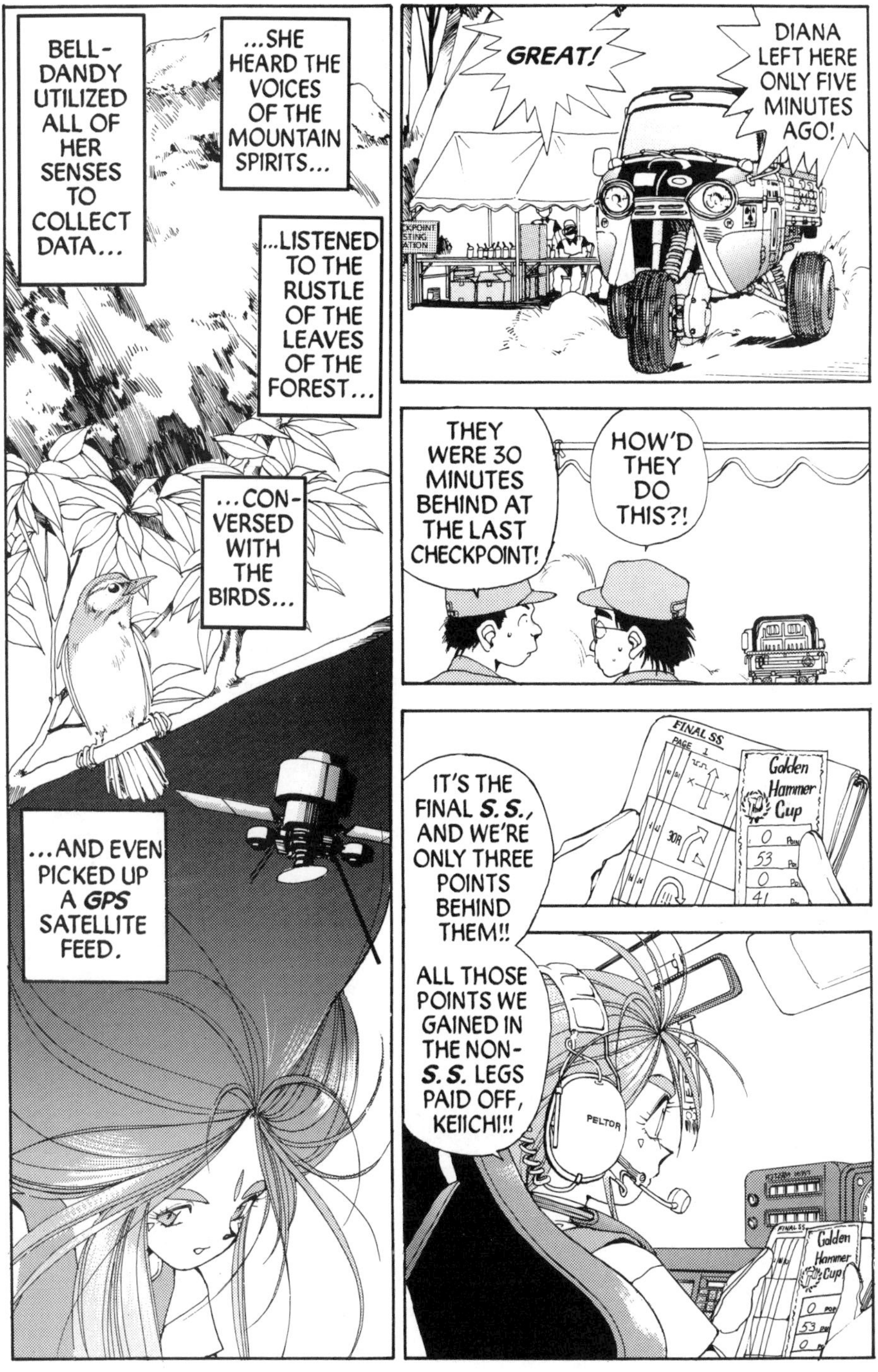
BELL-DANDY UTILIZED ALL OF HER SENSES TO COLLECT DATA...
...SHE HEARD THE VOICES OF THE MOUNTAIN SPIRITS...
...LISTENED TO THE RUSTLE OF THE LEAVES OF THE FOREST...
...CONVERSED WITH THE BIRDS...
...AND EVEN PICKED UP A GPS SATELLITE FEED.
GREAT!
DIANA LEFT HERE ONLY FIVE MINUTES AGO!
THEY WERE 30 MINUTES BEHIND AT THE LAST CHECKPOINT!
HOW'D THEY DO THIS?!
FINAL SS
PAGE 1
Golden Hammer Cup
IT'S THE FINAL S.S., AND WE'RE ONLY THREE POINTS BEHIND THEM!!
ALL THOSE POINTS WE GAINED IN THE NON-S.S. LEGS PAID OFF, KEIICHI!!
PELTOR
FINAL SS
Golden Hammer Cup

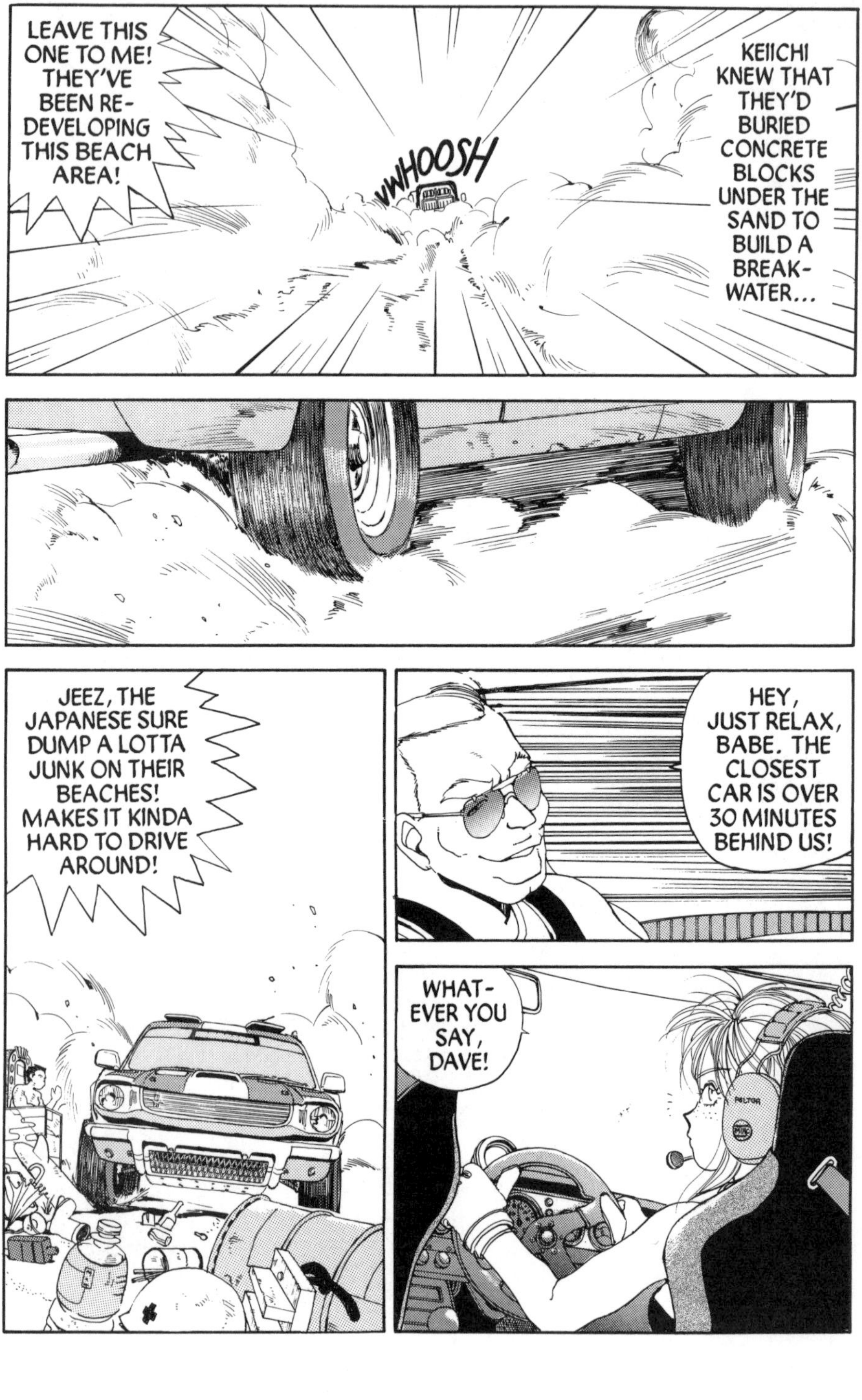
LEAVE THIS ONE TO ME! THEY'VE BEEN RE-DEVELOPING THIS BEACH AREA!
VWHOOSH
KEIICHI KNEW THAT THEY'D BURIED CONCRETE BLOCKS UNDER THE SAND TO BUILD A BREAK-WATER...
JEEZ, THE JAPANESE SURE DUMP A LOTTA JUNK ON THEIR BEACHES! MAKES IT KINDA HARD TO DRIVE AROUND!
HEY, JUST RELAX, BABE. THE CLOSEST CAR IS OVER 30 MINUTES BEHIND US!
WHAT-EVER YOU SAY, DAVE!

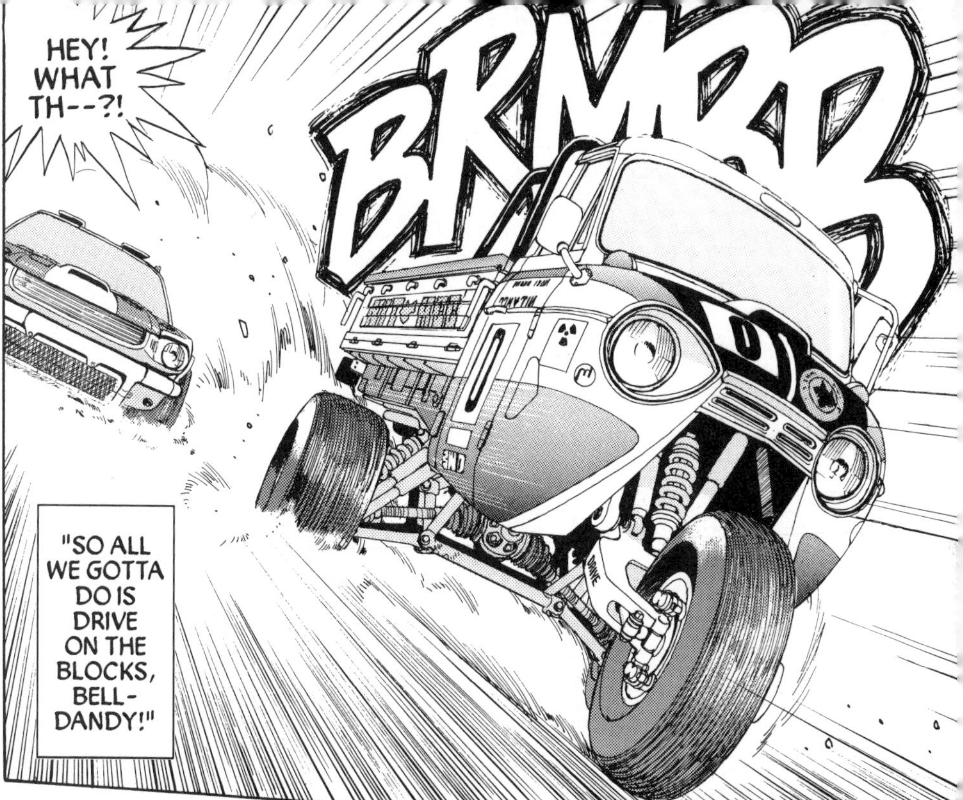
HEY! WHAT TH--?!
"SO ALL WE GOTTA DO IS DRIVE ON THE BLOCKS, BELL-DANDY!"
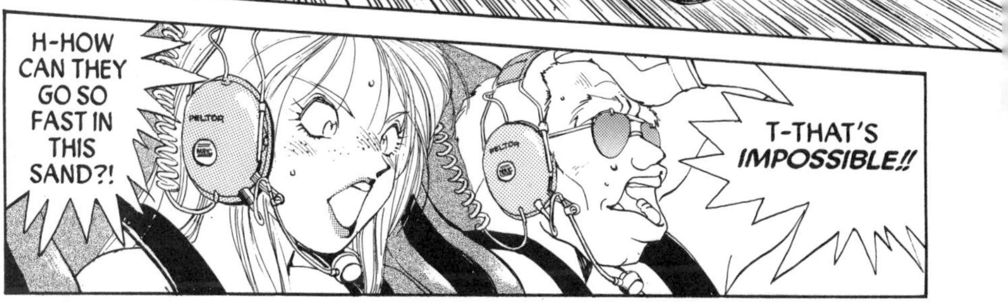
H-HOW CAN THEY GO SO FAST IN THIS SAND?!
T-THAT'S *IMPOSSIBLE!!*
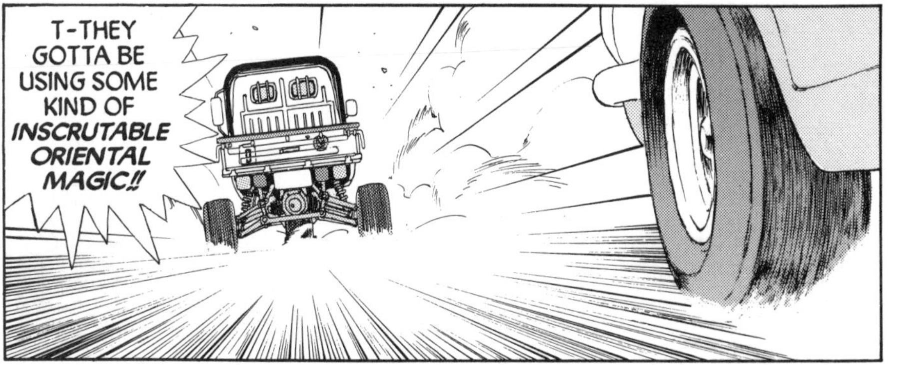
T-THEY GOTTA BE USING SOME KIND OF *INSCRUTABLE ORIENTAL MAGIC!!*

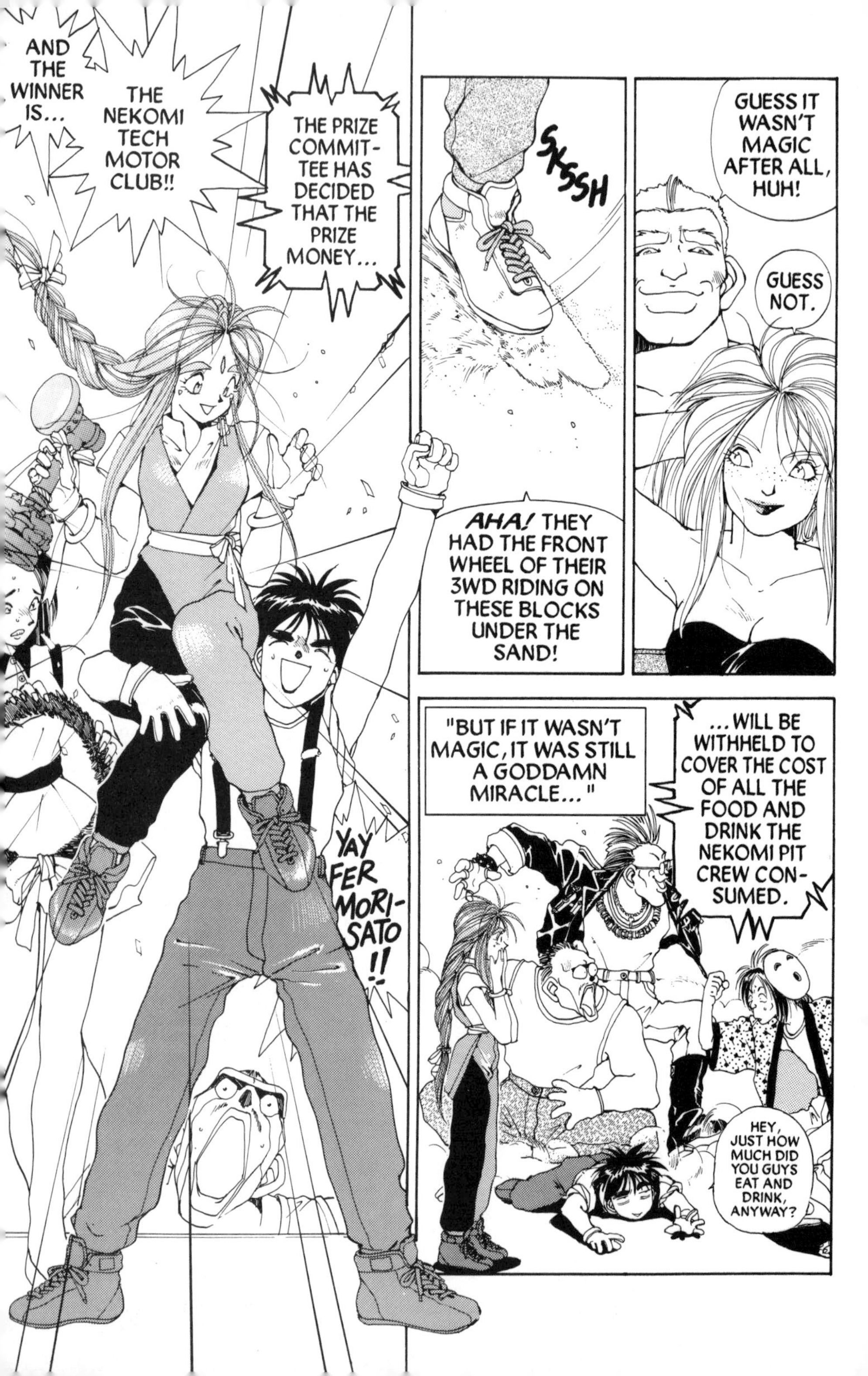
AND THE WINNER IS...
THE NEKOMI TECH MOTOR CLUB!!
THE PRIZE COMMIT-TEE HAS DECIDED THAT THE PRIZE MONEY...
YAY FER MORI-SATO!!
SKSSH
AHA! THEY HAD THE FRONT WHEEL OF THEIR 3WD RIDING ON THESE BLOCKS UNDER THE SAND!
GUESS IT WASN'T MAGIC AFTER ALL, HUH!
GUESS NOT.
"BUT IF IT WASN'T MAGIC, IT WAS STILL A GODDAMN MIRACLE..."
...WILL BE WITHHELD TO COVER THE COST OF ALL THE FOOD AND DRINK THE NEKOMI PIT CREW CON-SUMED.
HEY, JUST HOW MUCH DID YOU GUYS EAT AND DRINK, ANYWAY?

On a Wing and a Prayer

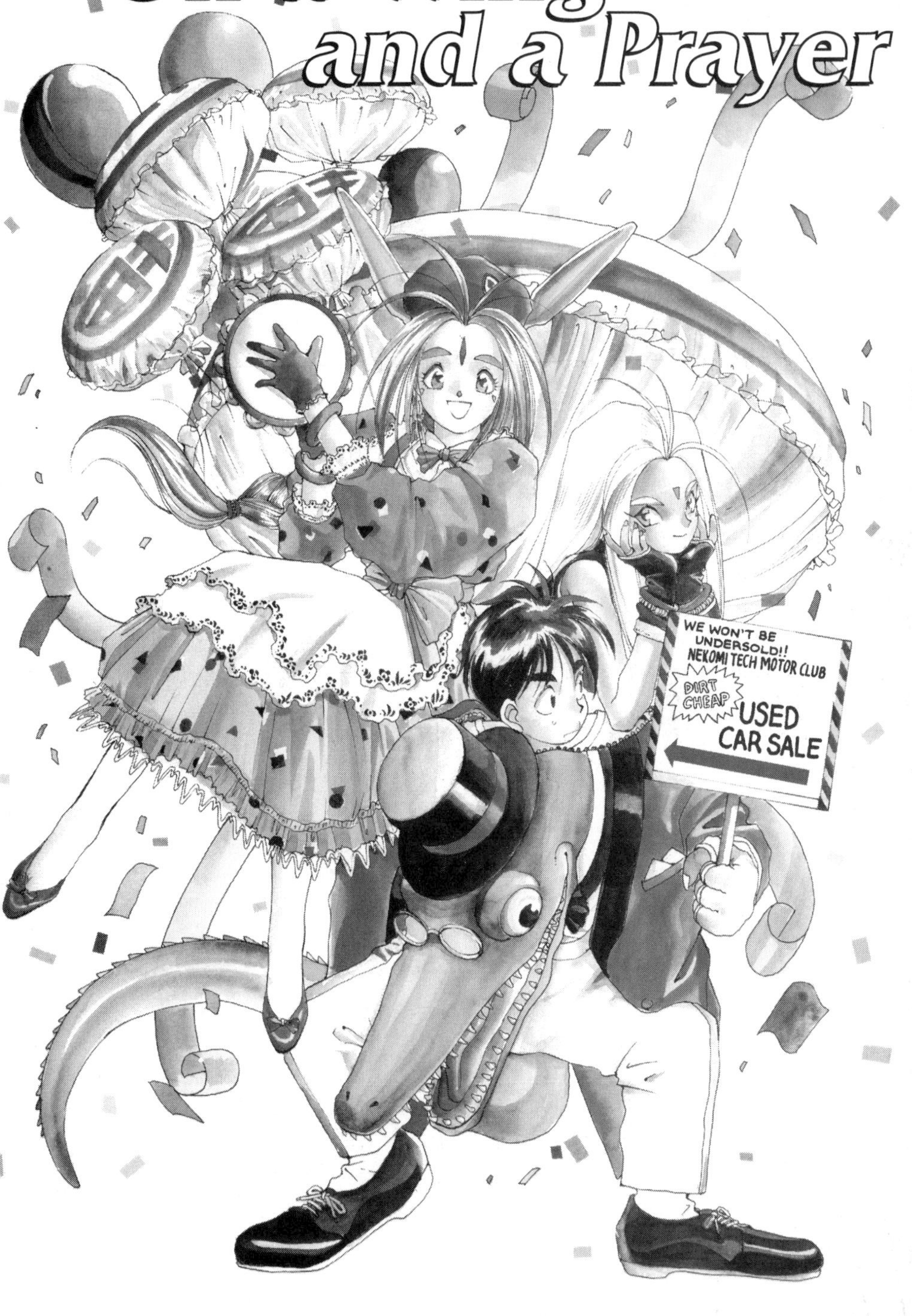
WE WON'T BE UNDERSOLD!!
NEKOMI TECH MOTOR CLUB
DIRT CHEAP
USED CAR SALE

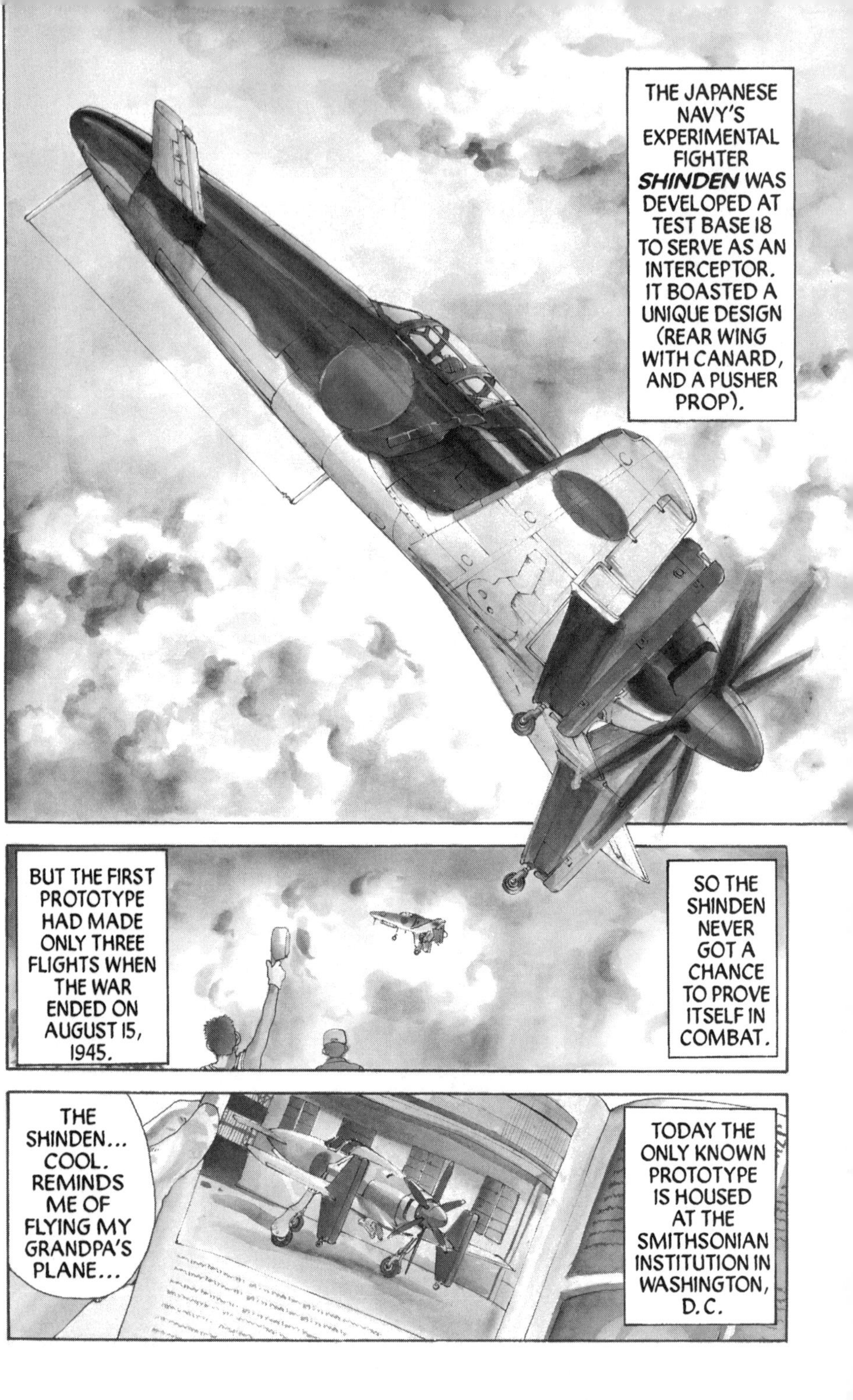
THE JAPANESE NAVY'S EXPERIMENTAL FIGHTER *SHINDEN* WAS DEVELOPED AT TEST BASE 18 TO SERVE AS AN INTERCEPTOR. IT BOASTED A UNIQUE DESIGN (REAR WING WITH CANARD, AND A PUSHER PROP).
BUT THE FIRST PROTOTYPE HAD MADE ONLY THREE FLIGHTS WHEN THE WAR ENDED ON AUGUST 15, 1945.
SO THE SHINDEN NEVER GOT A CHANCE TO PROVE ITSELF IN COMBAT.
THE SHINDEN... COOL. REMINDS ME OF FLYING MY GRANDPA'S PLANE...
TODAY THE ONLY KNOWN PROTOTYPE IS HOUSED AT THE SMITHSONIAN INSTITUTION IN WASHINGTON, D.C.

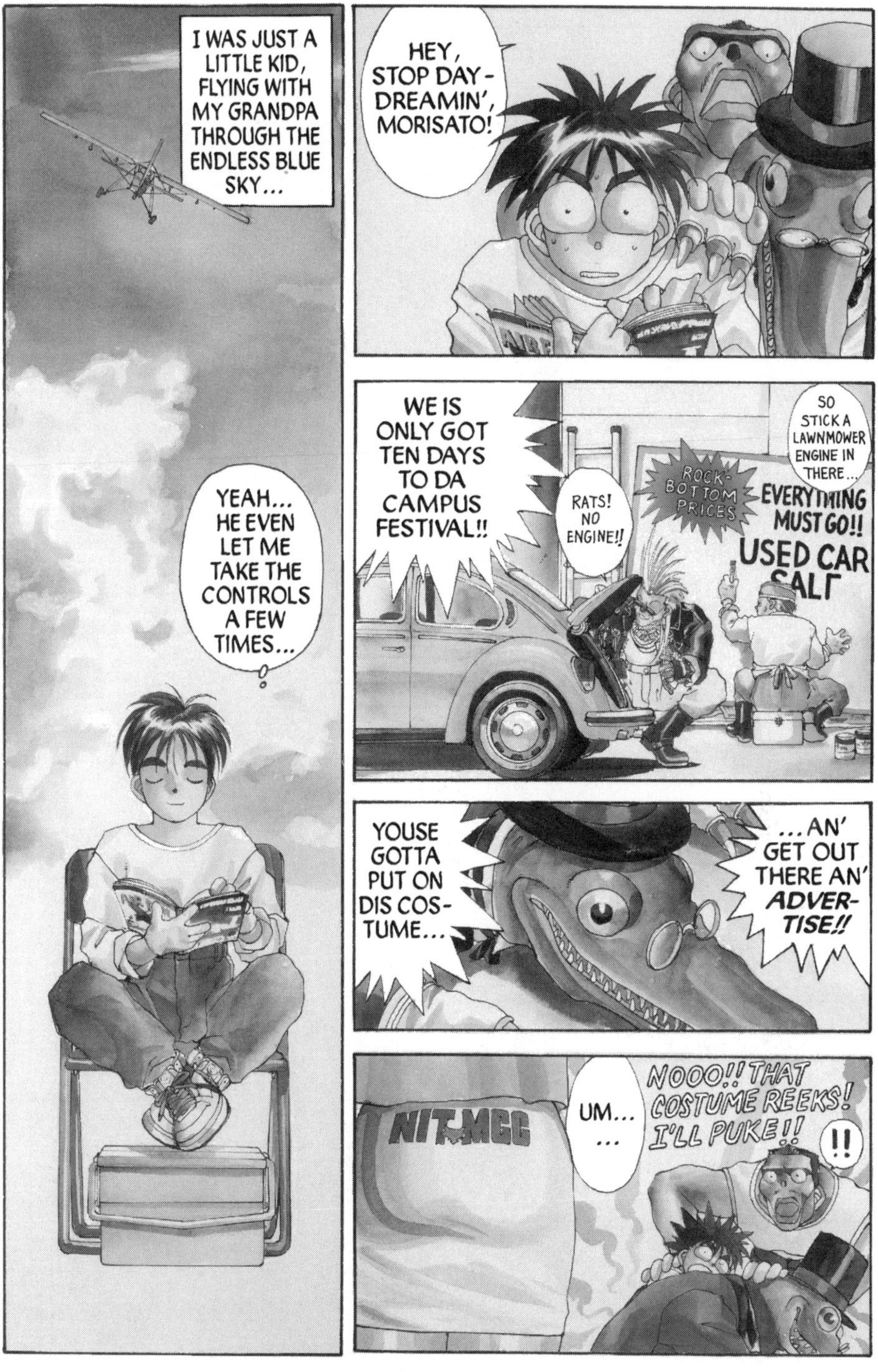
I WAS JUST A LITTLE KID, FLYING WITH MY GRANDPA THROUGH THE ENDLESS BLUE SKY...
YEAH... HE EVEN LET ME TAKE THE CONTROLS A FEW TIMES...
HEY, STOP DAY-DREAMIN', MORISATO!
WE IS ONLY GOT TEN DAYS TO DA CAMPUS FESTIVAL!!
RATS! NO ENGINE!!
ROCK-BOTTOM PRICES
EVERYTHING MUST GO!!
USED CAR SAL
SO STICK A LAWNMOWER ENGINE IN THERE...
YOUSE GOTTA PUT ON DIS COSTUME...
...AN' GET OUT THERE AN' *ADVERTISE!!*
NIT-MCC
UM... ...
NOOO!! THAT COSTUME REEKS! I'LL PUKE!!
!!

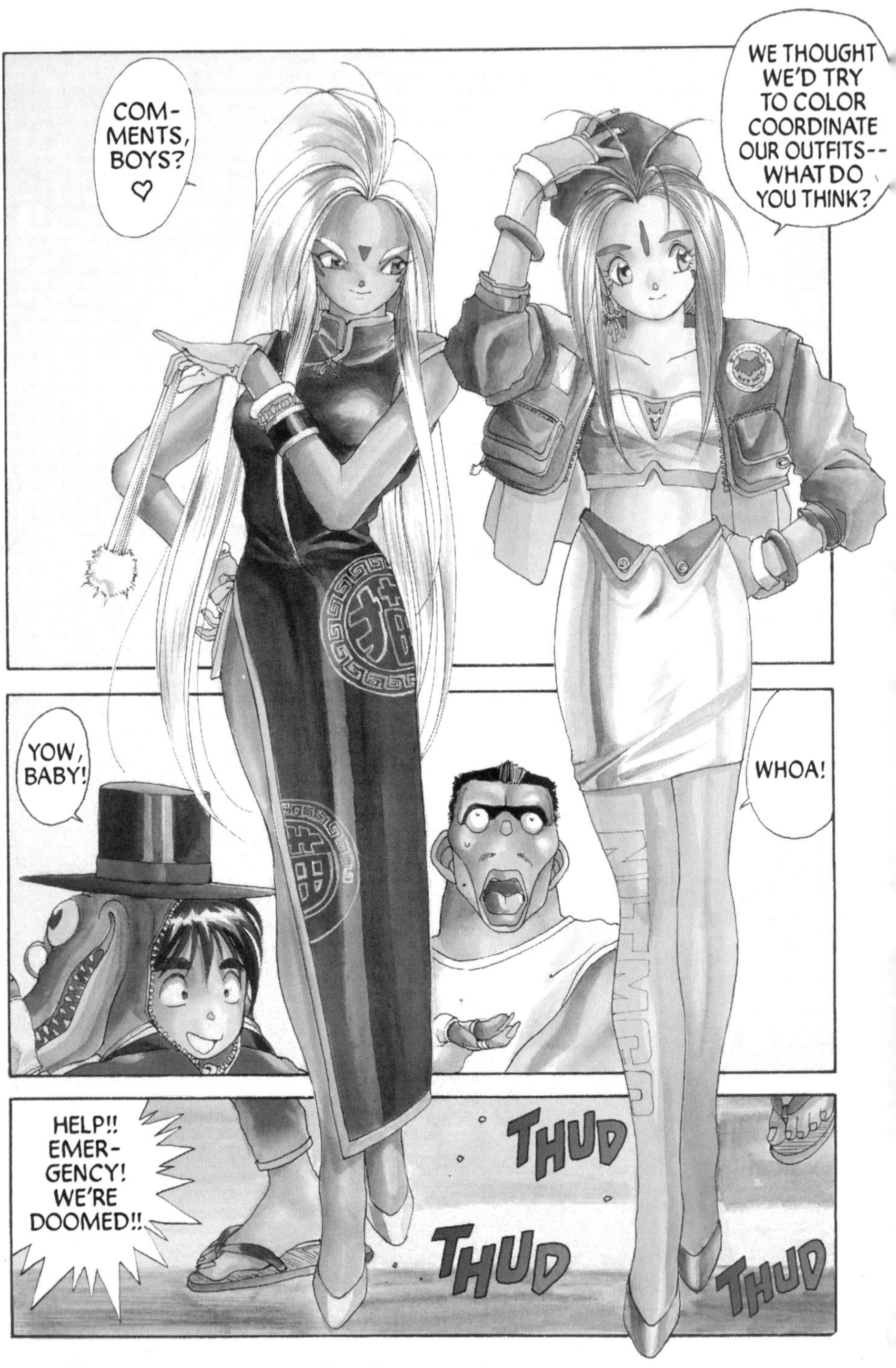
COM-MENTS, BOYS? ♡
WE THOUGHT WE'D TRY TO COLOR COORDINATE OUR OUTFITS-- WHAT DO YOU THINK?
YOW, BABY!
WHOA!
HELP!! EMER-GENCY! WE'RE DOOMED!!
THUD
THUD
THUD

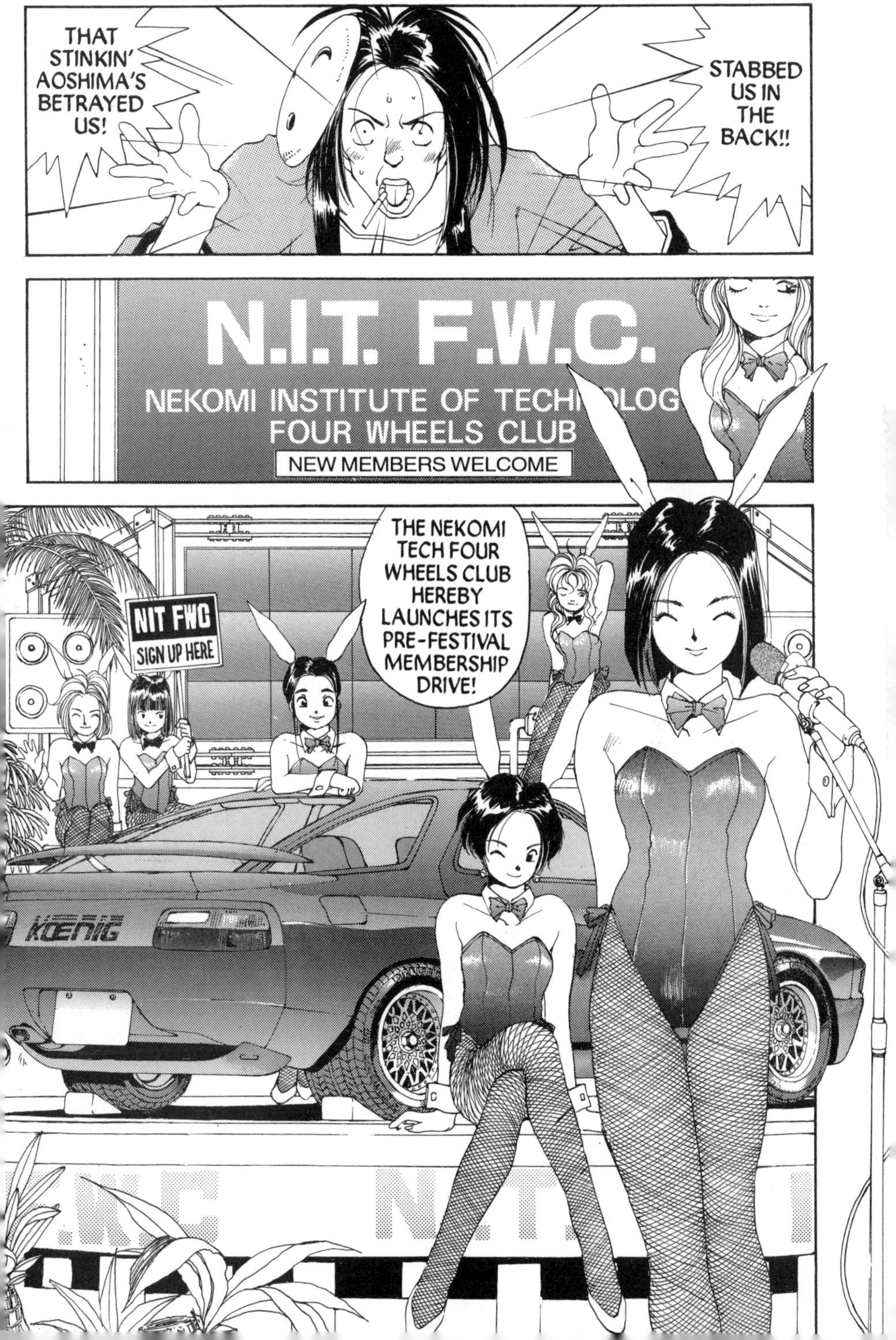
THAT STINKIN' AOSHIMA'S BETRAYED US!
STABBED US IN THE BACK!!
N.I.T. F.W.C.
NEKOMI INSTITUTE OF TECH OLOG
FOUR WHEELS CLUB
NEW MEMBERS WELCOME
NIT FWC
SIGN UP HERE
THE NEKOMI TECH FOUR WHEELS CLUB HEREBY LAUNCHES ITS PRE-FESTIVAL MEMBERSHIP DRIVE!
KOENIG

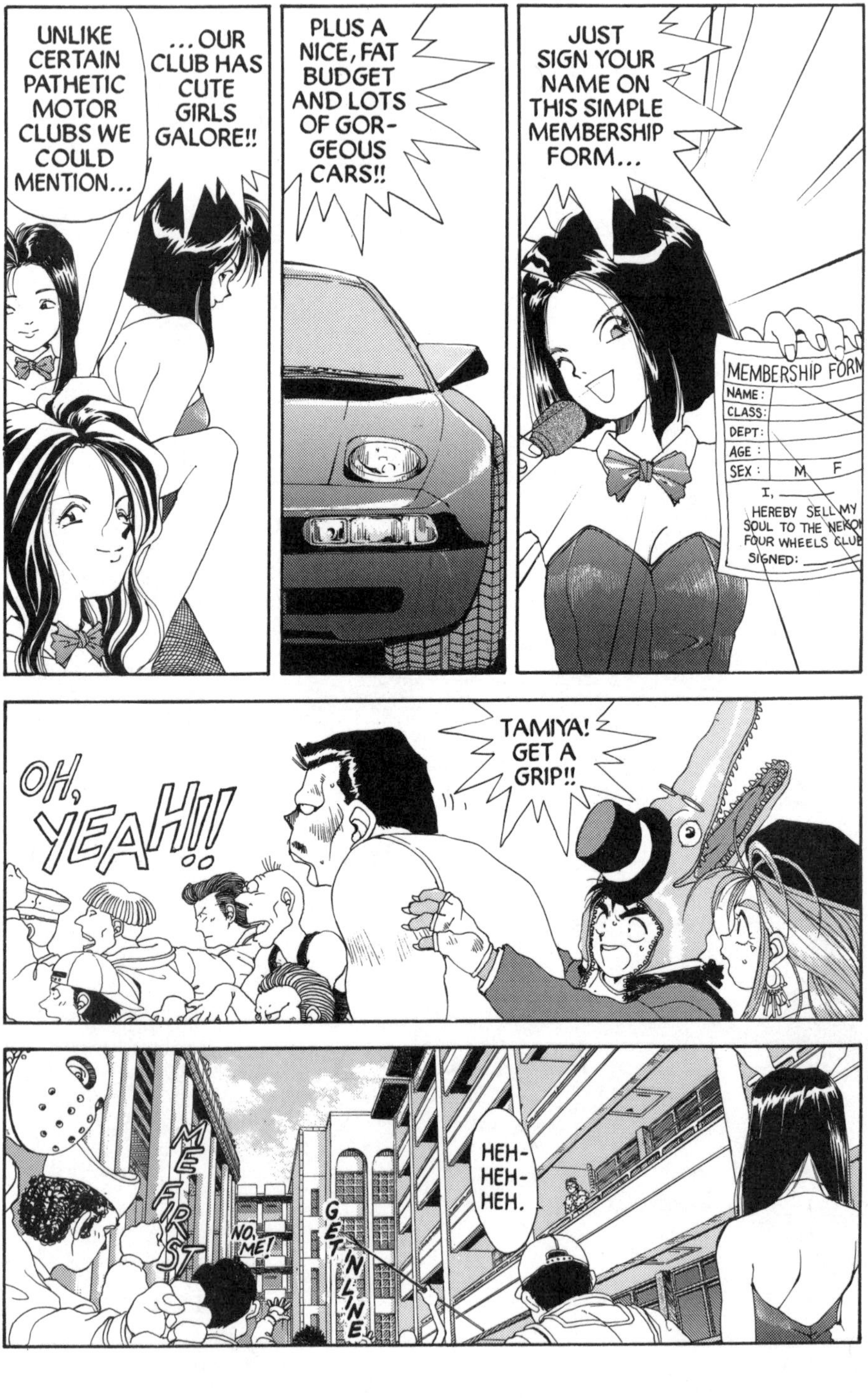
UNLIKE CERTAIN PATHETIC MOTOR CLUBS WE COULD MENTION...
...OUR CLUB HAS CUTE GIRLS GALORE!!
PLUS A NICE, FAT BUDGET AND LOTS OF GOR-GEOUS CARS!!
JUST SIGN YOUR NAME ON THIS SIMPLE MEMBERSHIP FORM...
MEMBERSHIP FORM
NAME:
CLASS:
DEPT:
AGE:
SEX: M F
I, ______ HEREBY SELL MY SOUL TO THE NEKO FOUR WHEELS CLUB
SIGNED: ______
OH, YEAH!!
TAMIYA! GET A GRIP!!
ME FIRST
NO, ME!
GET IN LINE
HEH-HEH-HEH.

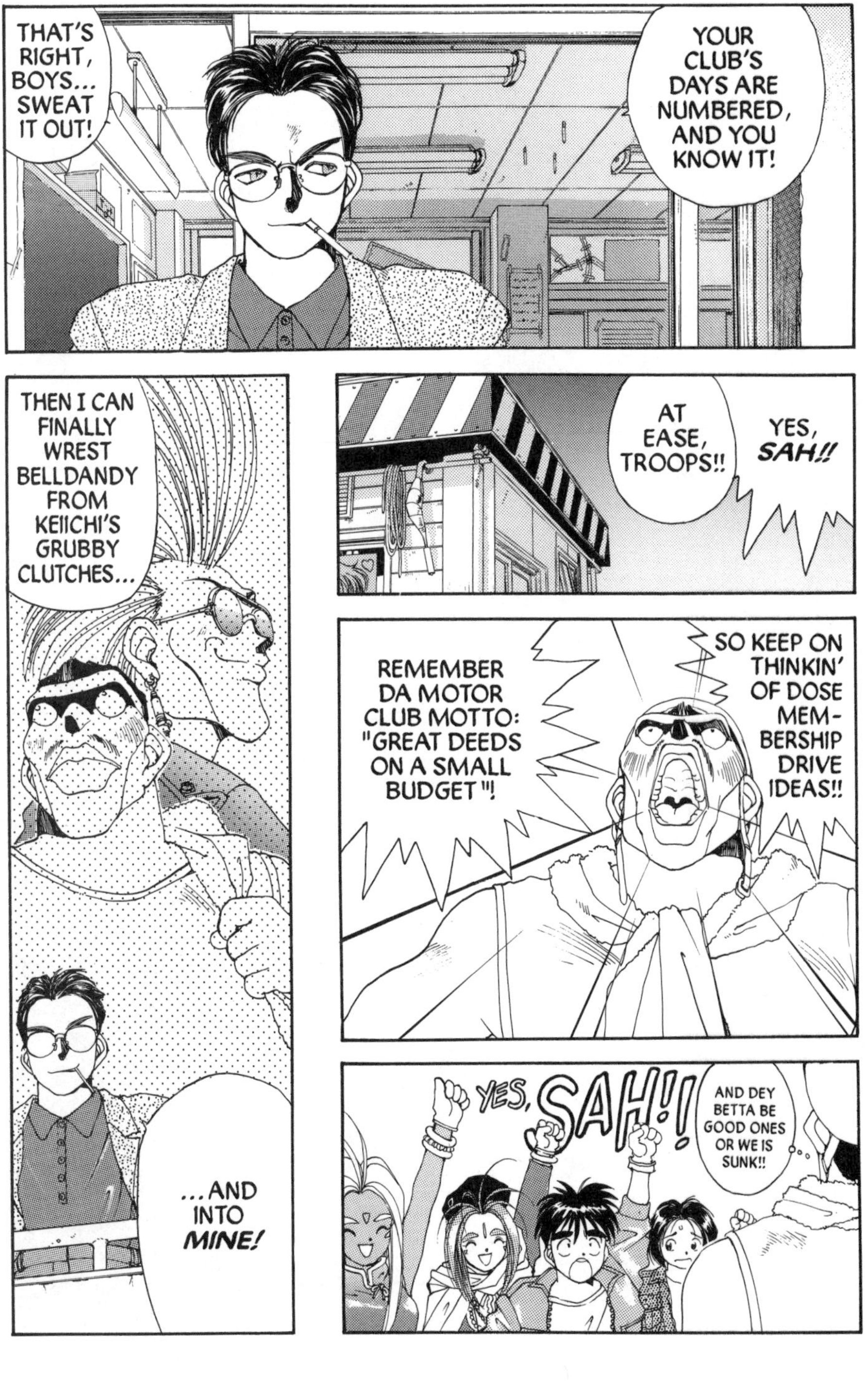
THAT'S RIGHT, BOYS... SWEAT IT OUT!
YOUR CLUB'S DAYS ARE NUMBERED, AND YOU KNOW IT!
THEN I CAN FINALLY WREST BELLDANDY FROM KEIICHI'S GRUBBY CLUTCHES...
...AND INTO *MINE!*
AT EASE, TROOPS!!
YES, *SAH!!*
REMEMBER DA MOTOR CLUB MOTTO: "GREAT DEEDS ON A SMALL BUDGET"!
SO KEEP ON THINKIN' OF DOSE MEM-BERSHIP DRIVE IDEAS!!
YES, SAH!!
AND DEY BETTA BE GOOD ONES OR WE IS SUNK!!

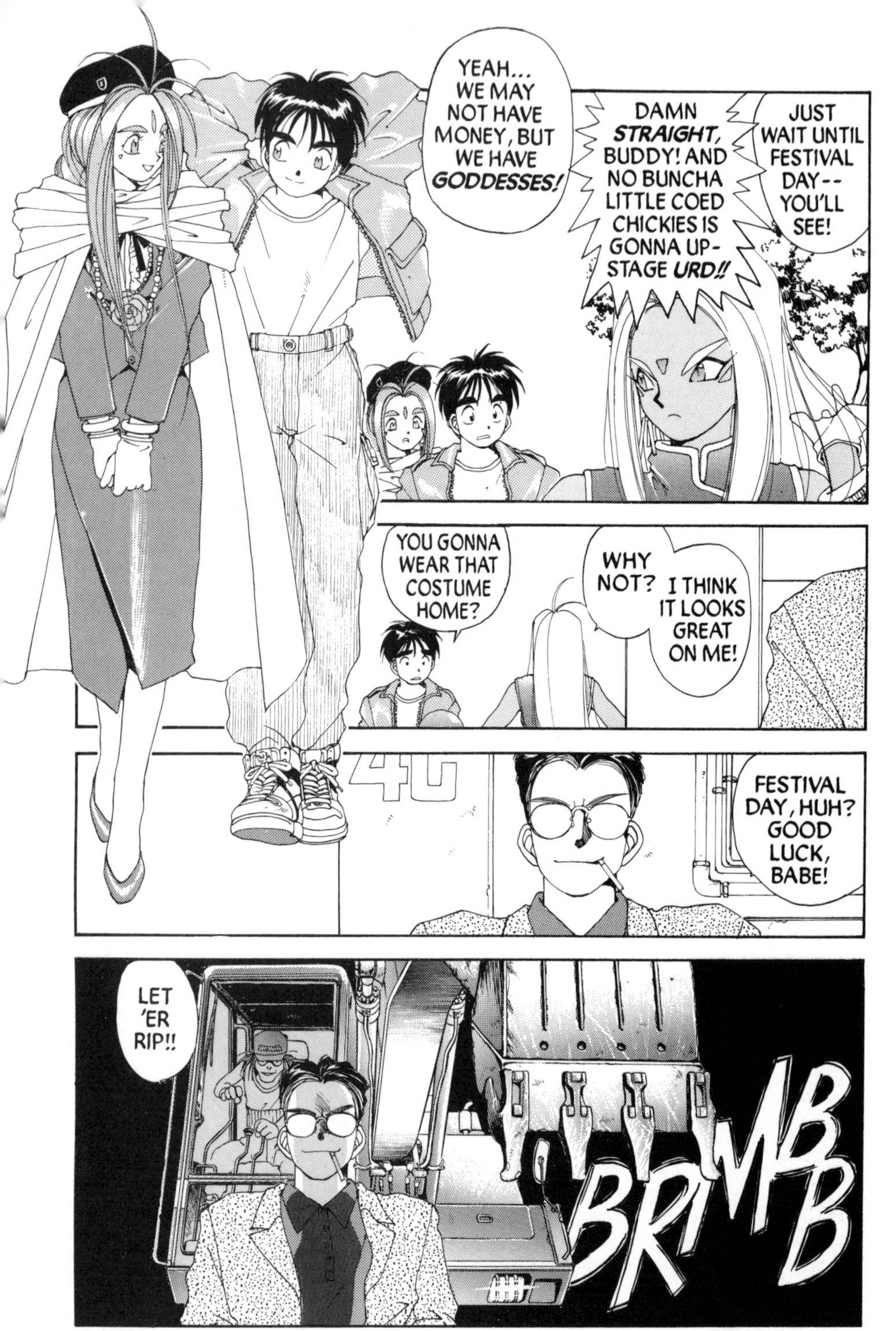
YEAH... WE MAY NOT HAVE MONEY, BUT WE HAVE GODDESSES!
DAMN STRAIGHT, BUDDY! AND NO BUNCHA LITTLE COED CHICKIES IS GONNA UP-STAGE URD!!
JUST WAIT UNTIL FESTIVAL DAY-- YOU'LL SEE!
YOU GONNA WEAR THAT COSTUME HOME?
WHY NOT?
I THINK IT LOOKS GREAT ON ME!
FESTIVAL DAY, HUH? GOOD LUCK, BABE!
LET 'ER RIP!!
BRMB BRMB

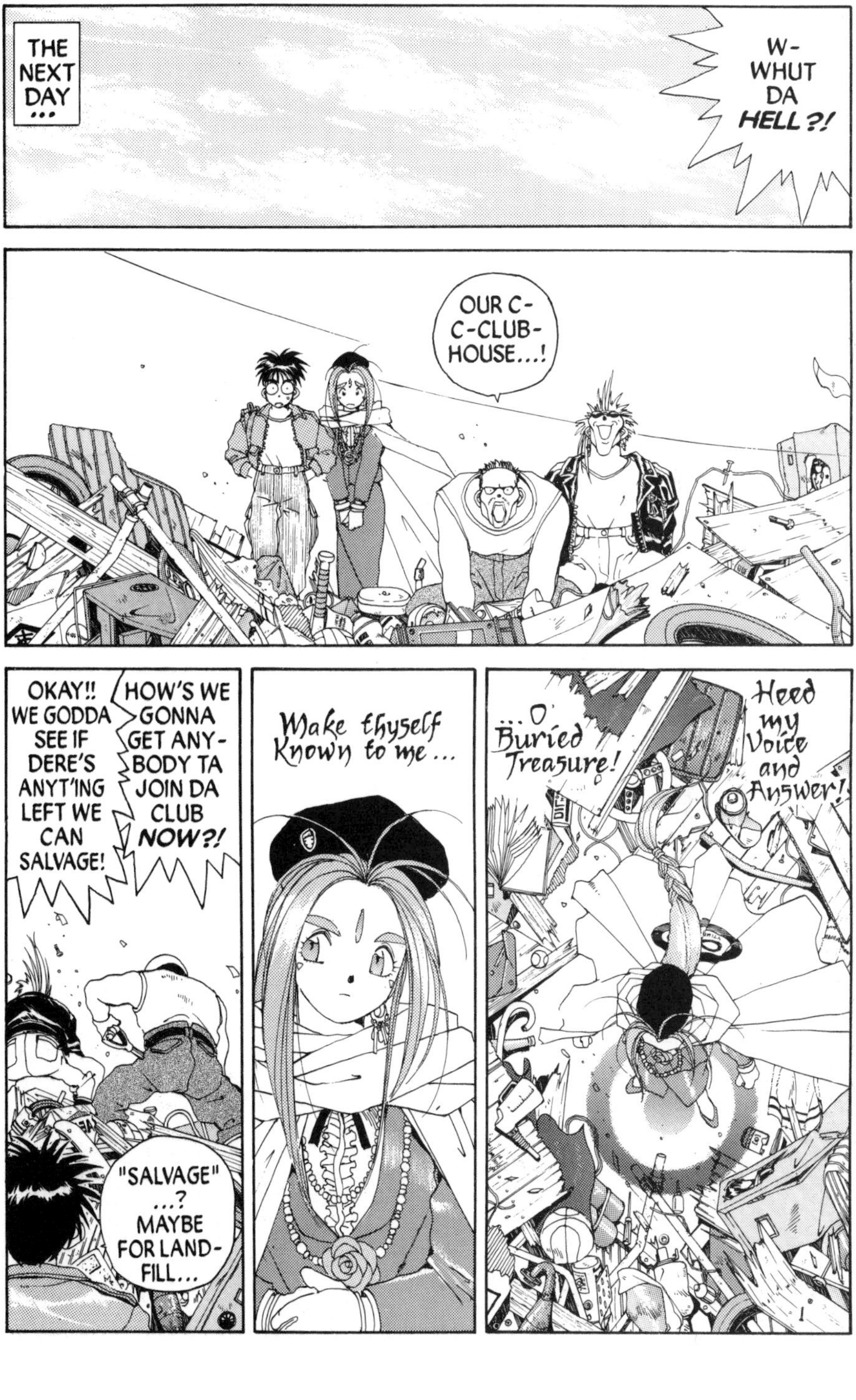
THE NEXT DAY ...
W- WHUT DA HELL ?!
OUR C- C-CLUB-HOUSE...!
OKAY!! WE GODDA SEE IF DERE'S ANYT'ING LEFT WE CAN SALVAGE!
HOW'S WE GONNA GET ANY-BODY TA JOIN DA CLUB NOW?!
"SALVAGE" ...? MAYBE FOR LAND-FILL...
Make thyself Known to me...
...O Buried Treasure!
Heed my Voice and Answer!

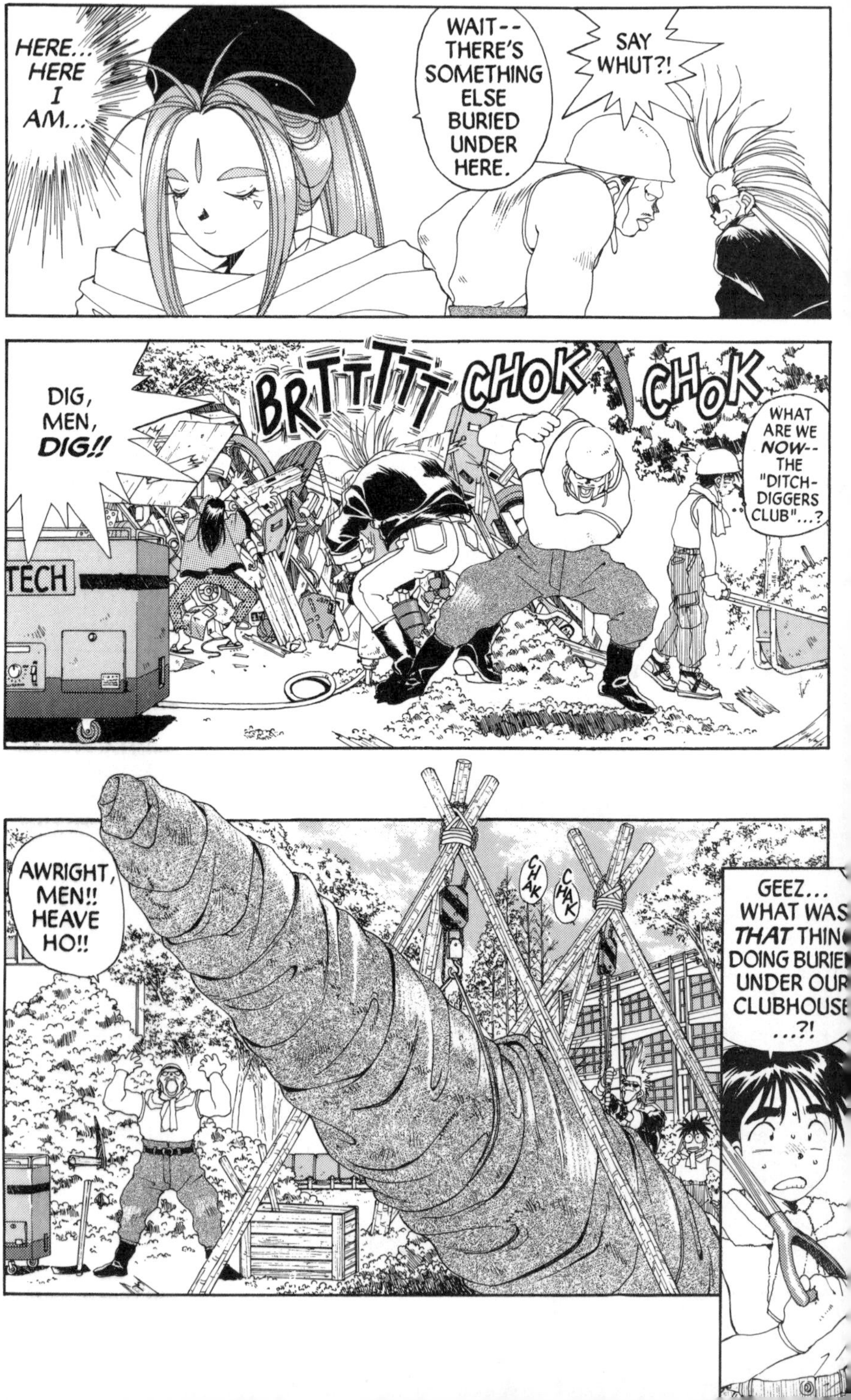
HERE... HERE I AM...
WAIT-- THERE'S SOMETHING ELSE BURIED UNDER HERE.
SAY WHUT?!
DIG, MEN, DIG!!
BRTTTTTT
CHOK
CHOK
TECH
WHAT ARE WE NOW-- THE "DITCH-DIGGERS CLUB"...?
AWRIGHT, MEN!! HEAVE HO!!
CHAK
CHAK
GEEZ... WHAT WAS THAT THIN DOING BURIE UNDER OUR CLUBHOUS ...?!

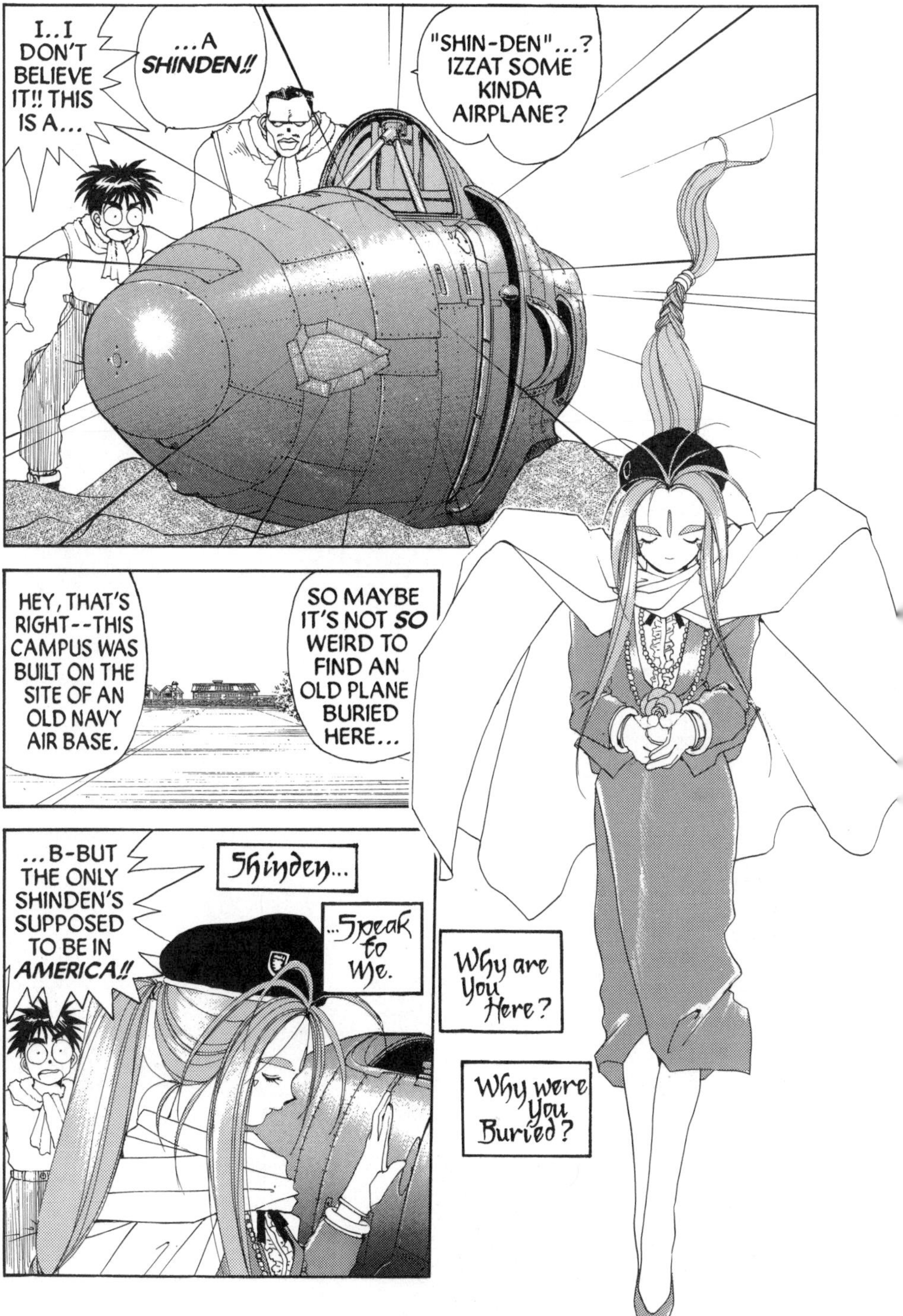
I..I DON'T BELIEVE IT!! THIS IS A...
...A *SHINDEN!!*
"SHIN-DEN"...? IZZAT SOME KINDA AIRPLANE?
HEY, THAT'S RIGHT--THIS CAMPUS WAS BUILT ON THE SITE OF AN OLD NAVY AIR BASE.
SO MAYBE IT'S NOT *SO* WEIRD TO FIND AN OLD PLANE BURIED HERE...
...B-BUT THE ONLY SHINDEN'S SUPPOSED TO BE IN *AMERICA!!*
Shinden...
...Speak to Me.
Why are You Here?
Why were You Buried?

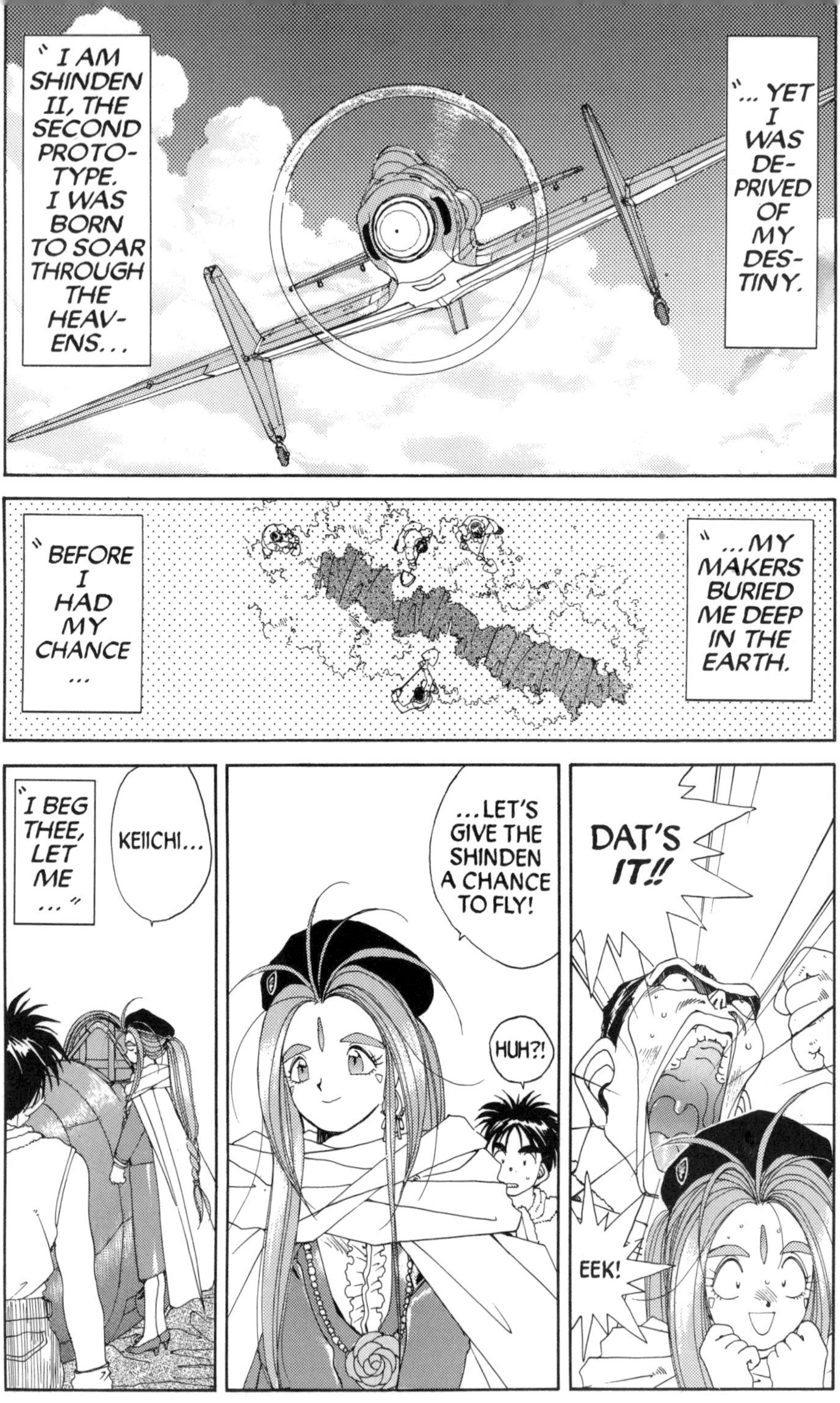
"I AM SHINDEN II, THE SECOND PROTO-TYPE. I WAS BORN TO SOAR THROUGH THE HEAV-ENS...
"...YET I WAS DE-PRIVED OF MY DES-TINY.
"BEFORE I HAD MY CHANCE ...
"...MY MAKERS BURIED ME DEEP IN THE EARTH.
"I BEG THEE, LET ME ..."
KEIICHI...
...LET'S GIVE THE SHINDEN A CHANCE TO FLY!
HUH?!
DAT'S IT!!
EEK!

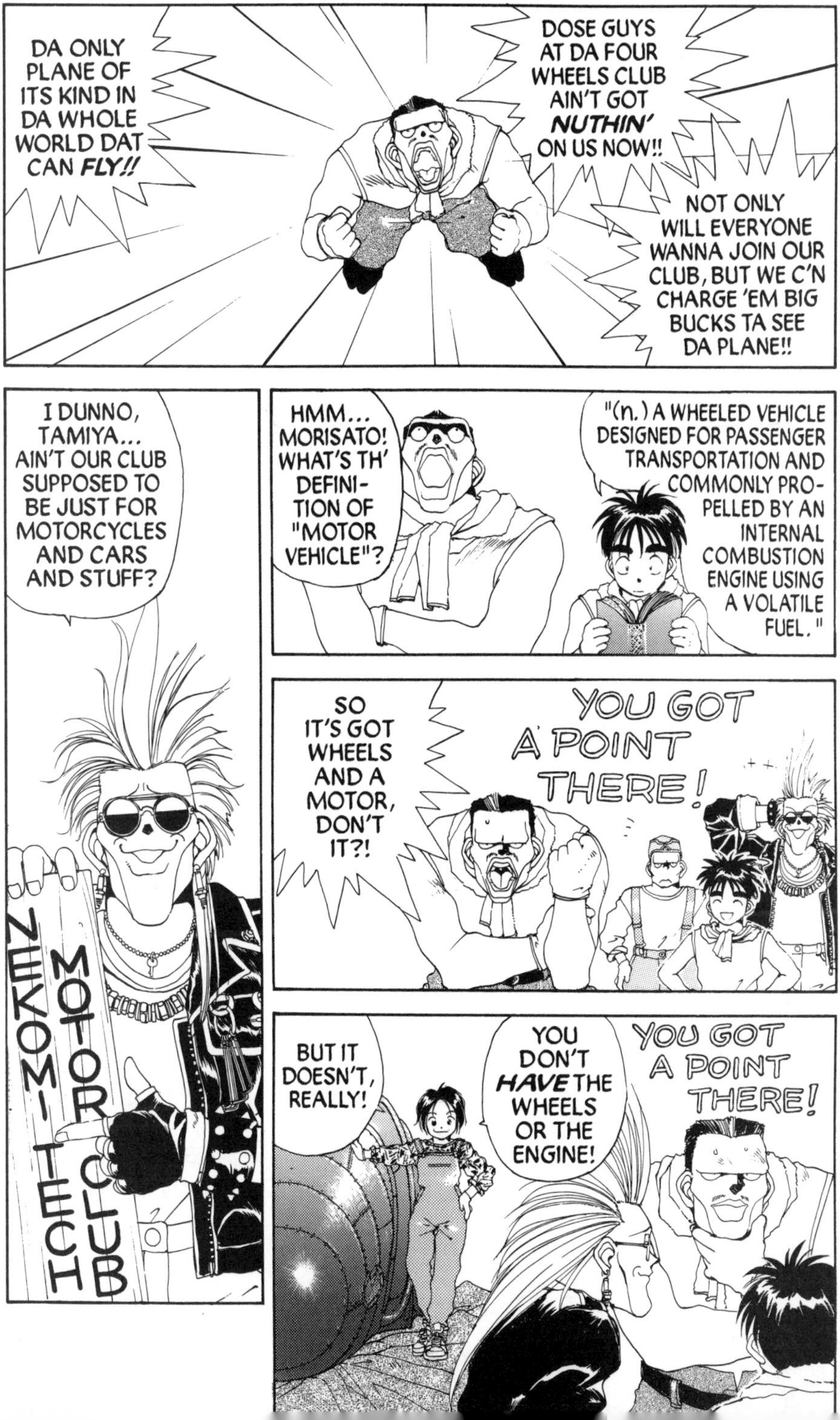
DA ONLY PLANE OF ITS KIND IN DA WHOLE WORLD DAT CAN *FLY!!*
DOSE GUYS AT DA FOUR WHEELS CLUB AIN'T GOT *NUTHIN'* ON US NOW!!
NOT ONLY WILL EVERYONE WANNA JOIN OUR CLUB, BUT WE C'N CHARGE 'EM BIG BUCKS TA SEE DA PLANE!!
I DUNNO, TAMIYA... AIN'T OUR CLUB SUPPOSED TO BE JUST FOR MOTORCYCLES AND CARS AND STUFF?
NEKOMI TECH MOTOR CLUB
HMM... MORISATO! WHAT'S TH' DEFINI-TION OF "MOTOR VEHICLE"?
"(n.) A WHEELED VEHICLE DESIGNED FOR PASSENGER TRANSPORTATION AND COMMONLY PRO-PELLED BY AN INTERNAL COMBUSTION ENGINE USING A VOLATILE FUEL."
SO IT'S GOT WHEELS AND A MOTOR, DON'T IT?!
YOU GOT A POINT THERE!
BUT IT DOESN'T, REALLY!
YOU DON'T *HAVE* THE WHEELS OR THE ENGINE!
YOU GOT A POINT THERE!

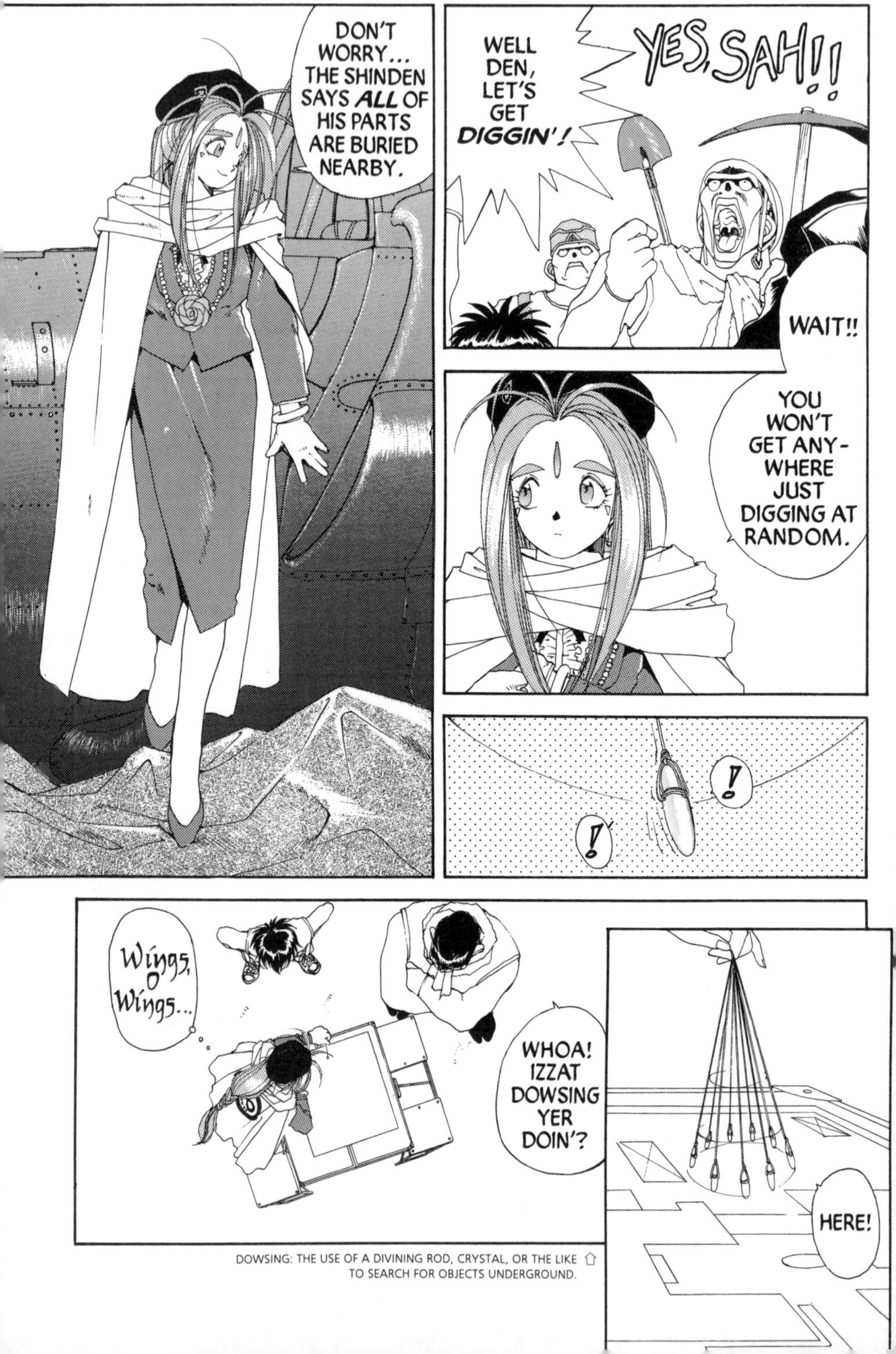
DON'T WORRY... THE SHINDEN SAYS ALL OF HIS PARTS ARE BURIED NEARBY.
WELL DEN, LET'S GET DIGGIN'!
YES, SAH!!
WAIT!!
YOU WON'T GET ANY-WHERE JUST DIGGING AT RANDOM.
!
!
Wings, O Wings...
WHOA! IZZAT DOWSING YER DOIN'?
HERE!

DOWSING: THE USE OF A DIVINING ROD, CRYSTAL, OR THE LIKE ⇧
TO SEARCH FOR OBJECTS UNDERGROUND.

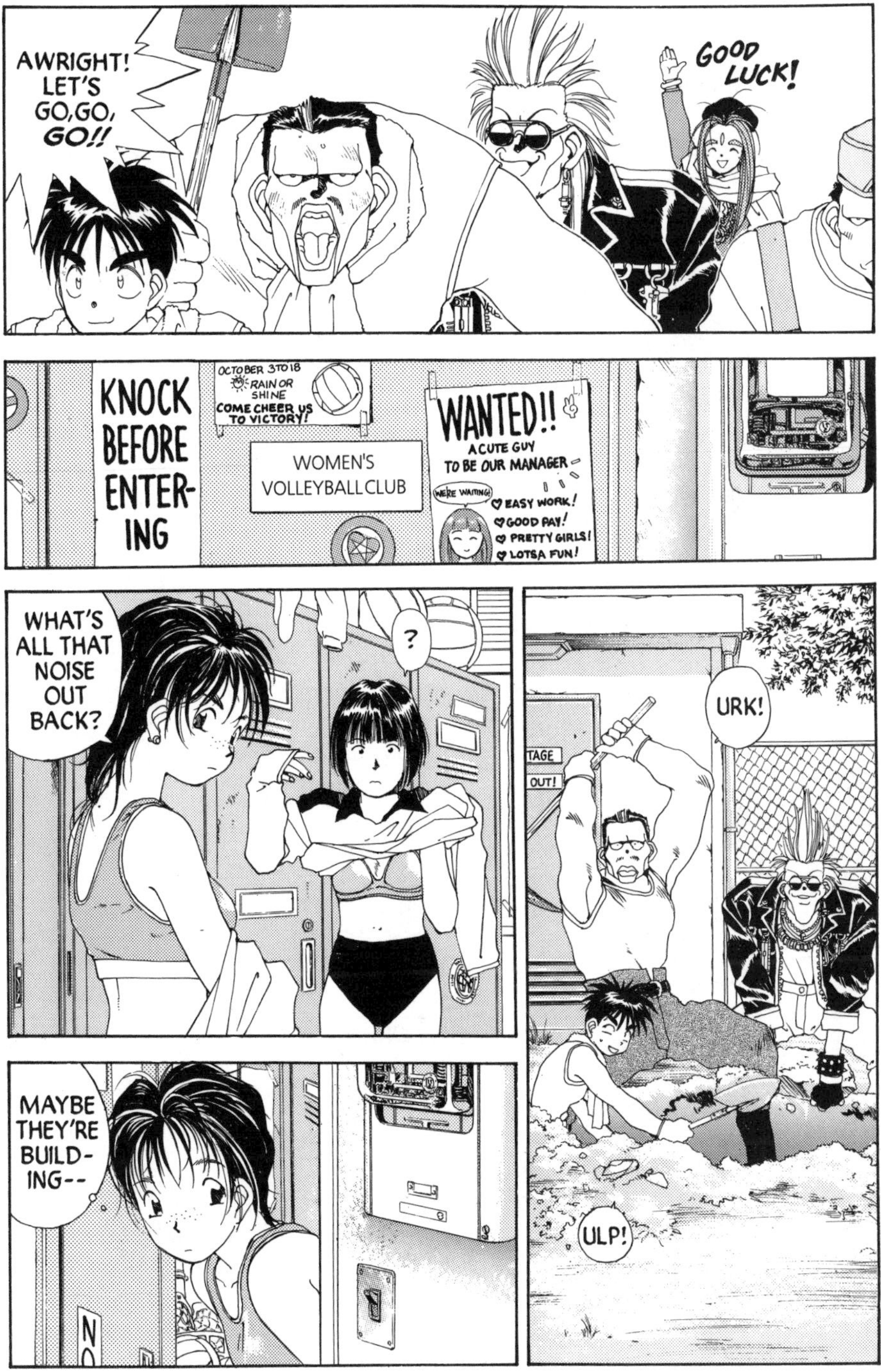
AWRIGHT! LET'S GO, GO, GO!!
GOOD LUCK!
KNOCK BEFORE ENTER-ING
OCTOBER 3TO18
RAIN OR SHINE
COME CHEER US TO VICTORY!
WOMEN'S VOLLEYBALL CLUB
WANTED!!
A CUTE GUY TO BE OUR MANAGER
WE'RE WAITING!
EASY WORK!
GOOD PAY!
PRETTY GIRLS!
LOTSA FUN!
WHAT'S ALL THAT NOISE OUT BACK?
?
MAYBE THEY'RE BUILD-ING--
URK!
ULP!

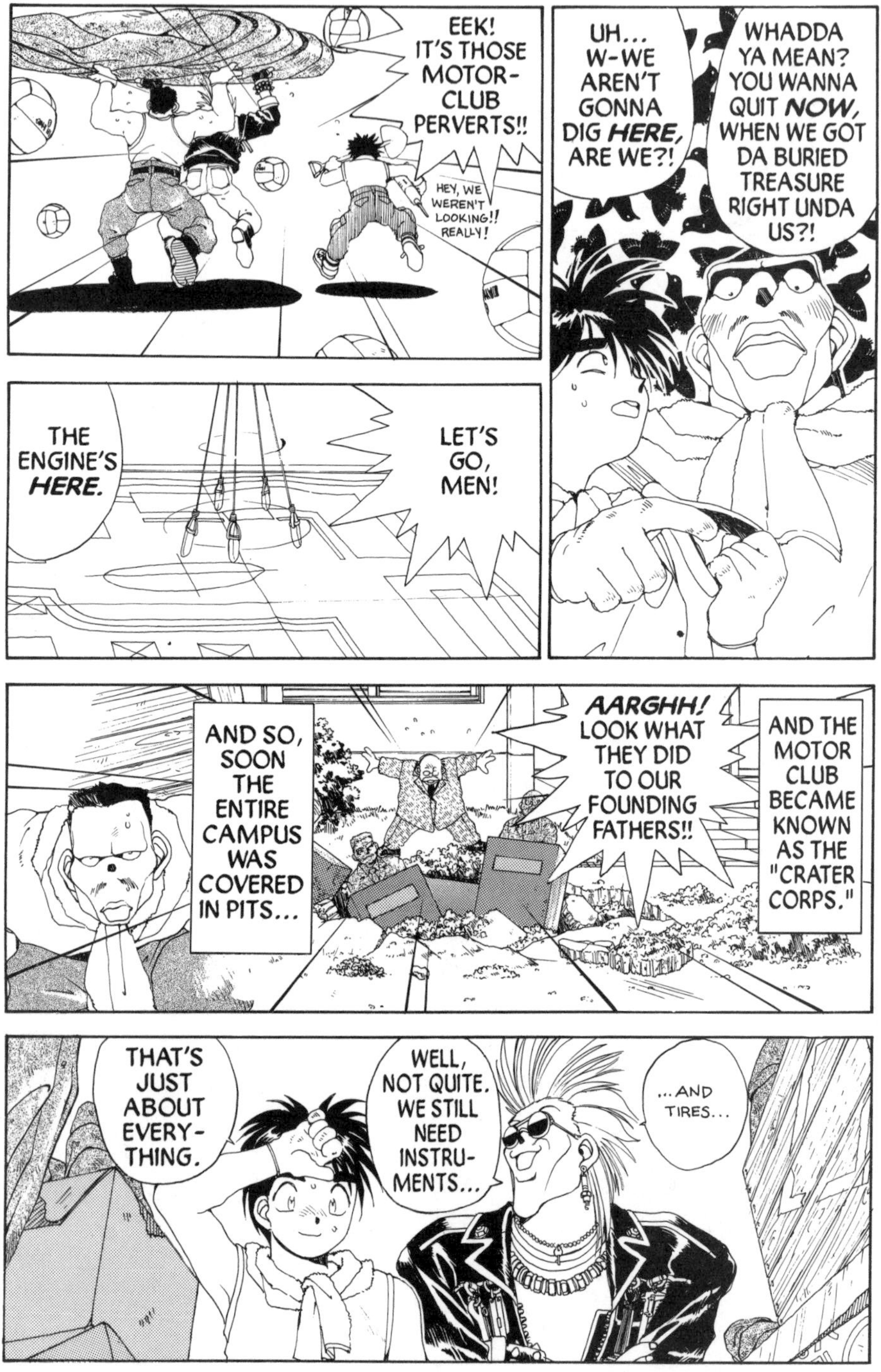
EEK! IT'S THOSE MOTOR-CLUB PERVERTS!!
HEY, WE WEREN'T LOOKING!! REALLY!
UH... W-WE AREN'T GONNA DIG HERE, ARE WE?!
WHADDA YA MEAN? YOU WANNA QUIT NOW, WHEN WE GOT DA BURIED TREASURE RIGHT UNDA US?!
THE ENGINE'S HERE.
LET'S GO, MEN!
AND SO, SOON THE ENTIRE CAMPUS WAS COVERED IN PITS...
AARGHH! LOOK WHAT THEY DID TO OUR FOUNDING FATHERS!!
AND THE MOTOR CLUB BECAME KNOWN AS THE "CRATER CORPS."
THAT'S JUST ABOUT EVERY-THING.
WELL, NOT QUITE. WE STILL NEED INSTRU-MENTS...
...AND TIRES...

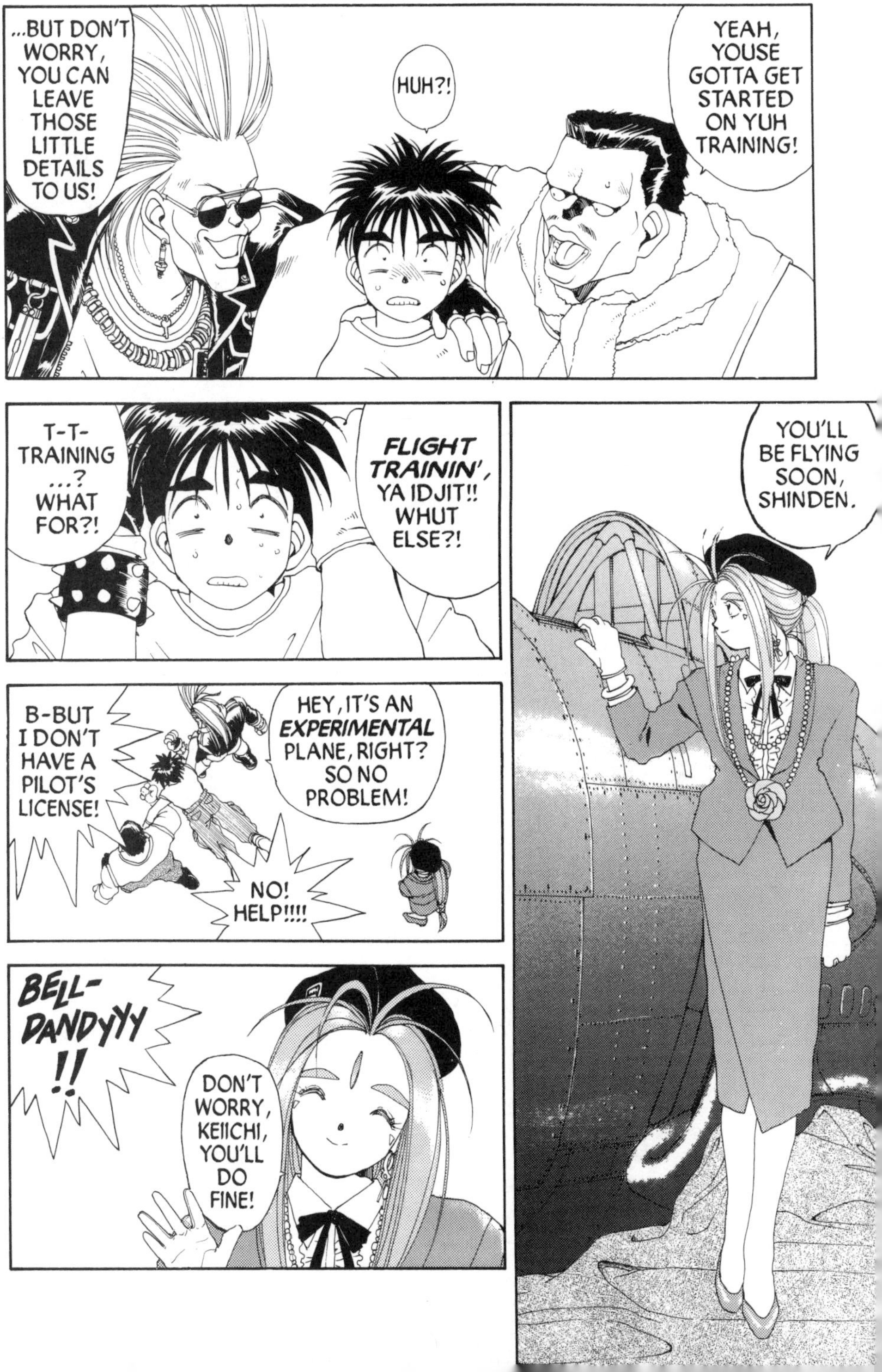
...BUT DON'T WORRY, YOU CAN LEAVE THOSE LITTLE DETAILS TO US!
HUH?!
YEAH, YOUSE GOTTA GET STARTED ON YUH TRAINING!
T-T-TRAINING ...? WHAT FOR?!
FLIGHT TRAININ', YA IDJIT!! WHUT ELSE?!
B-BUT I DON'T HAVE A PILOT'S LICENSE!
HEY, IT'S AN EXPERIMENTAL PLANE, RIGHT? SO NO PROBLEM!
NO! HELP!!!!
BELL-DANDYYY!!
DON'T WORRY, KEIICHI, YOU'LL DO FINE!
YOU'LL BE FLYING SOON, SHINDEN.

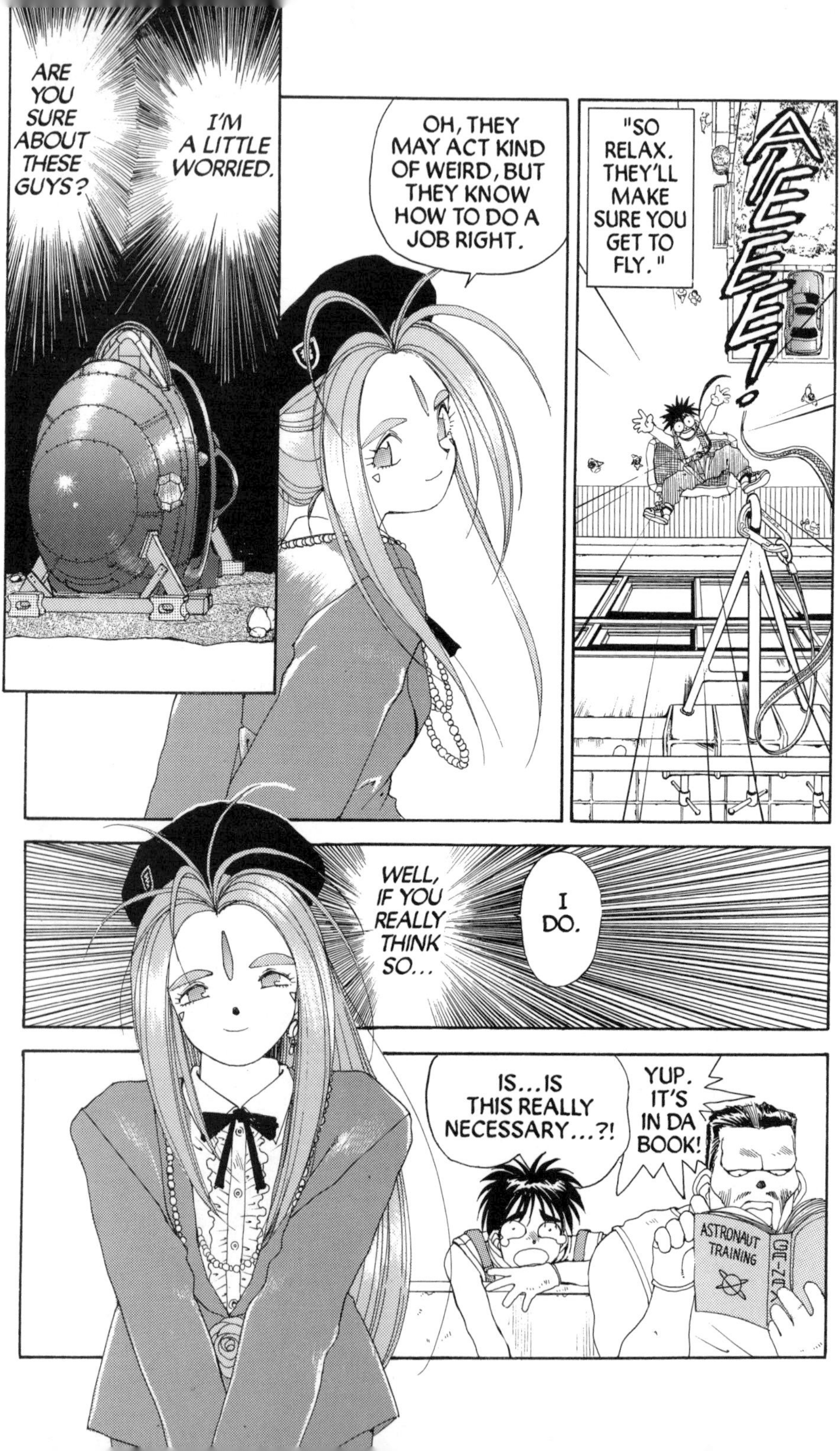
ARE YOU SURE ABOUT THESE GUYS?
I'M A LITTLE WORRIED.
OH, THEY MAY ACT KIND OF WEIRD, BUT THEY KNOW HOW TO DO A JOB RIGHT.
"SO RELAX. THEY'LL MAKE SURE YOU GET TO FLY."
AIEEEE!
WELL, IF YOU REALLY THINK SO...
I DO.
IS...IS THIS REALLY NECESSARY...?!
YUP. IT'S IN DA BOOK!
ASTRONAUT TRAINING

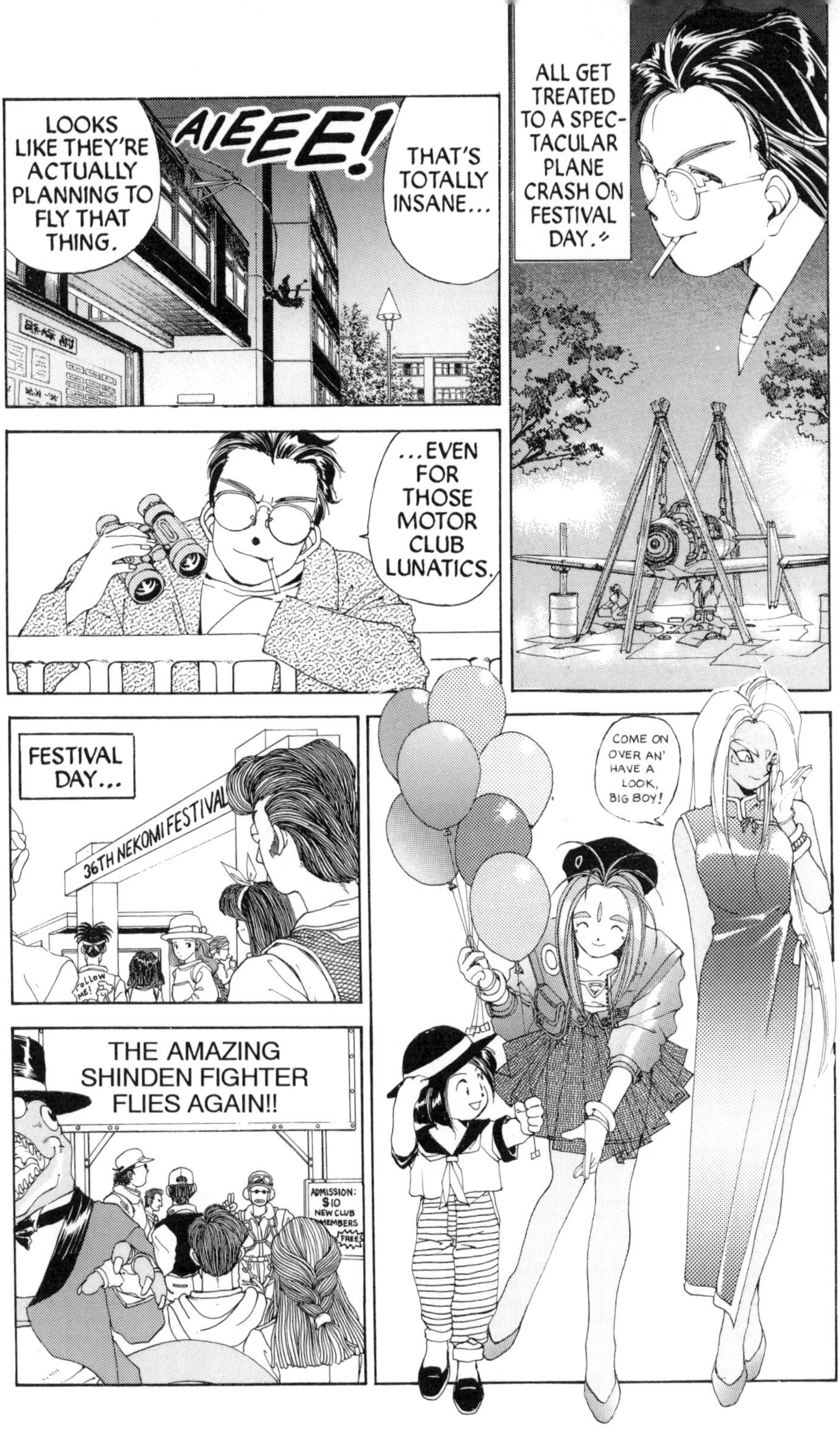
LOOKS LIKE THEY'RE ACTUALLY PLANNING TO FLY THAT THING.
AIEEE!
THAT'S TOTALLY INSANE...
...EVEN FOR THOSE MOTOR CLUB LUNATICS.
ALL GET TREATED TO A SPECTACULAR PLANE CRASH ON FESTIVAL DAY.
FESTIVAL DAY...
36TH NEKOMI FESTIVAL
FOLLOW ME!
THE AMAZING SHINDEN FIGHTER FLIES AGAIN!!
ADMISSION: $10
NEW CLUB
FREE
COME ON OVER AN' HAVE A LOOK, BIG BOY!

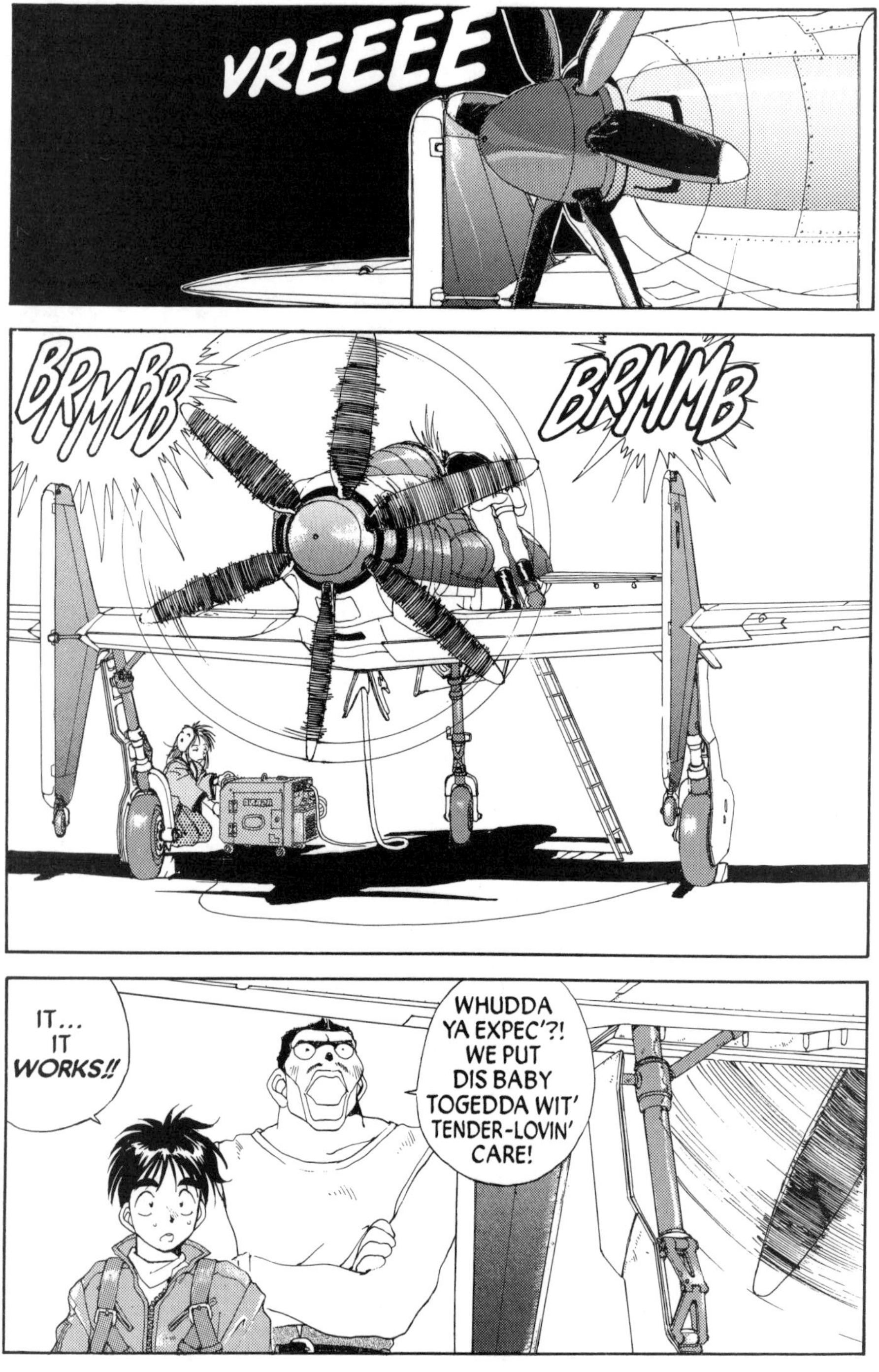
VREEEE
BRMBB
BRMMB
IT... IT **WORKS!!**
WHUDDA YA EXPEC'?! WE PUT DIS BABY TOGEDDA WIT' TENDER-LOVIN' CARE!

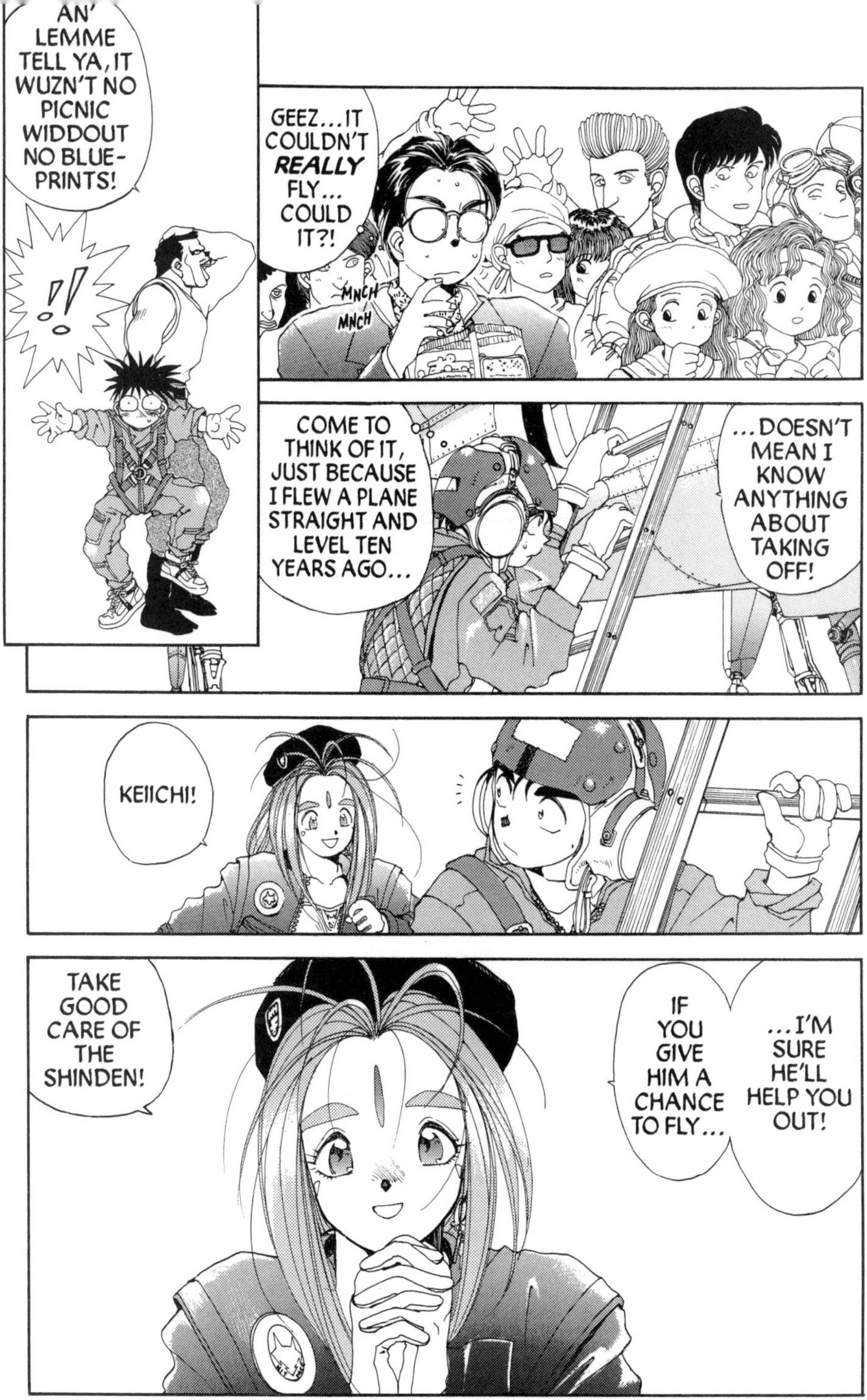
AN' LEMME TELL YA, IT WUZN'T NO PICNIC WIDDOUT NO BLUE-PRINTS!
!!
GEEZ... IT COULDN'T **REALLY** FLY... COULD IT?!
MNCH
MNCH
COME TO THINK OF IT, JUST BECAUSE I FLEW A PLANE STRAIGHT AND LEVEL TEN YEARS AGO...
...DOESN'T MEAN I KNOW ANYTHING ABOUT TAKING OFF!
KEIICHI!
TAKE GOOD CARE OF THE SHINDEN!
IF YOU GIVE HIM A CHANCE TO FLY...
...I'M SURE HE'LL HELP YOU OUT!

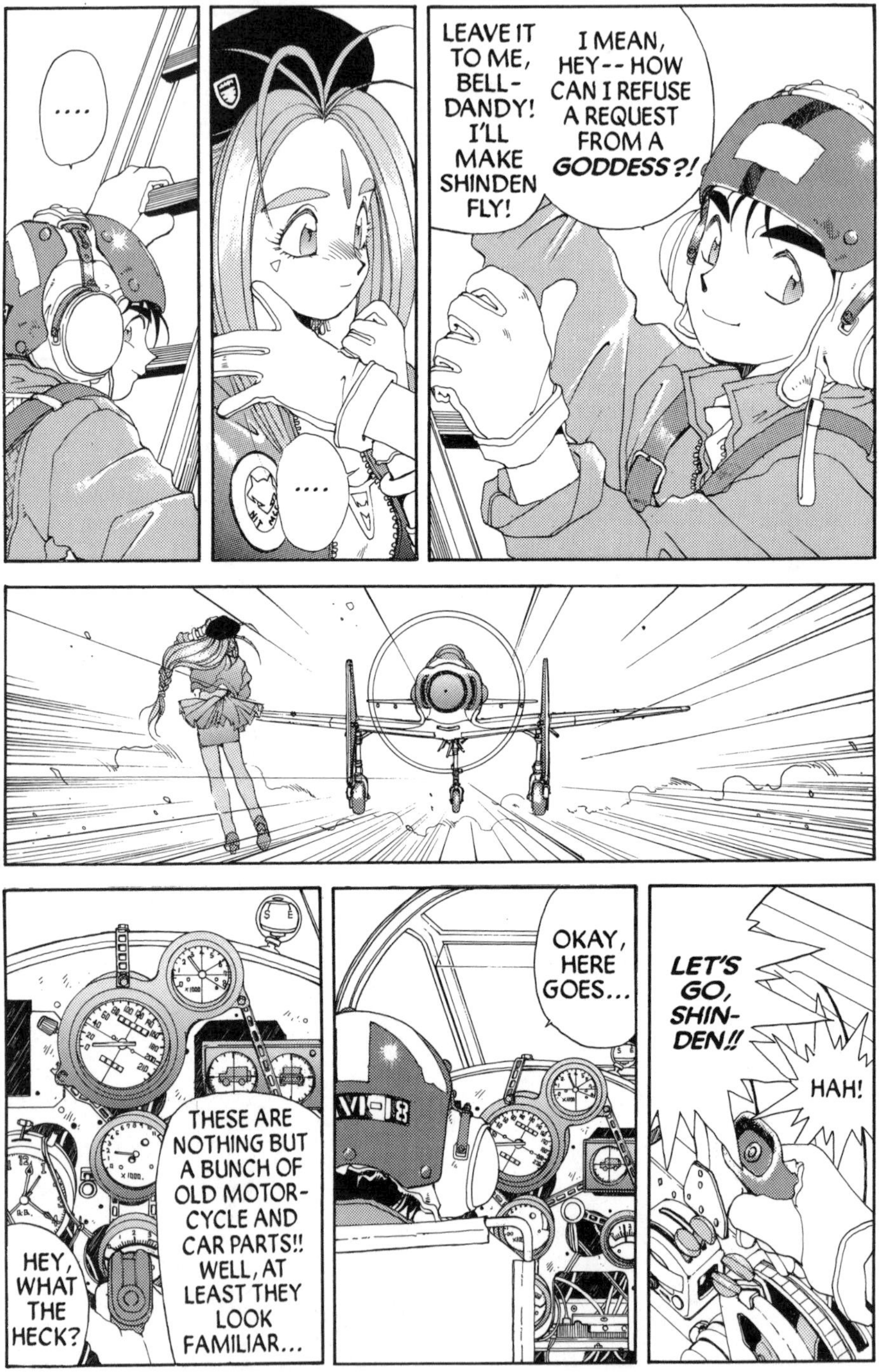
....
....
LEAVE IT TO ME, BELL-DANDY! I'LL MAKE SHINDEN FLY!
I MEAN, HEY-- HOW CAN I REFUSE A REQUEST FROM A *GODDESS?!*
HEY, WHAT THE HECK?
THESE ARE NOTHING BUT A BUNCH OF OLD MOTOR-CYCLE AND CAR PARTS!! WELL, AT LEAST THEY LOOK FAMILIAR...
OKAY, HERE GOES...
LET'S GO, SHIN-DEN!!
HAH!

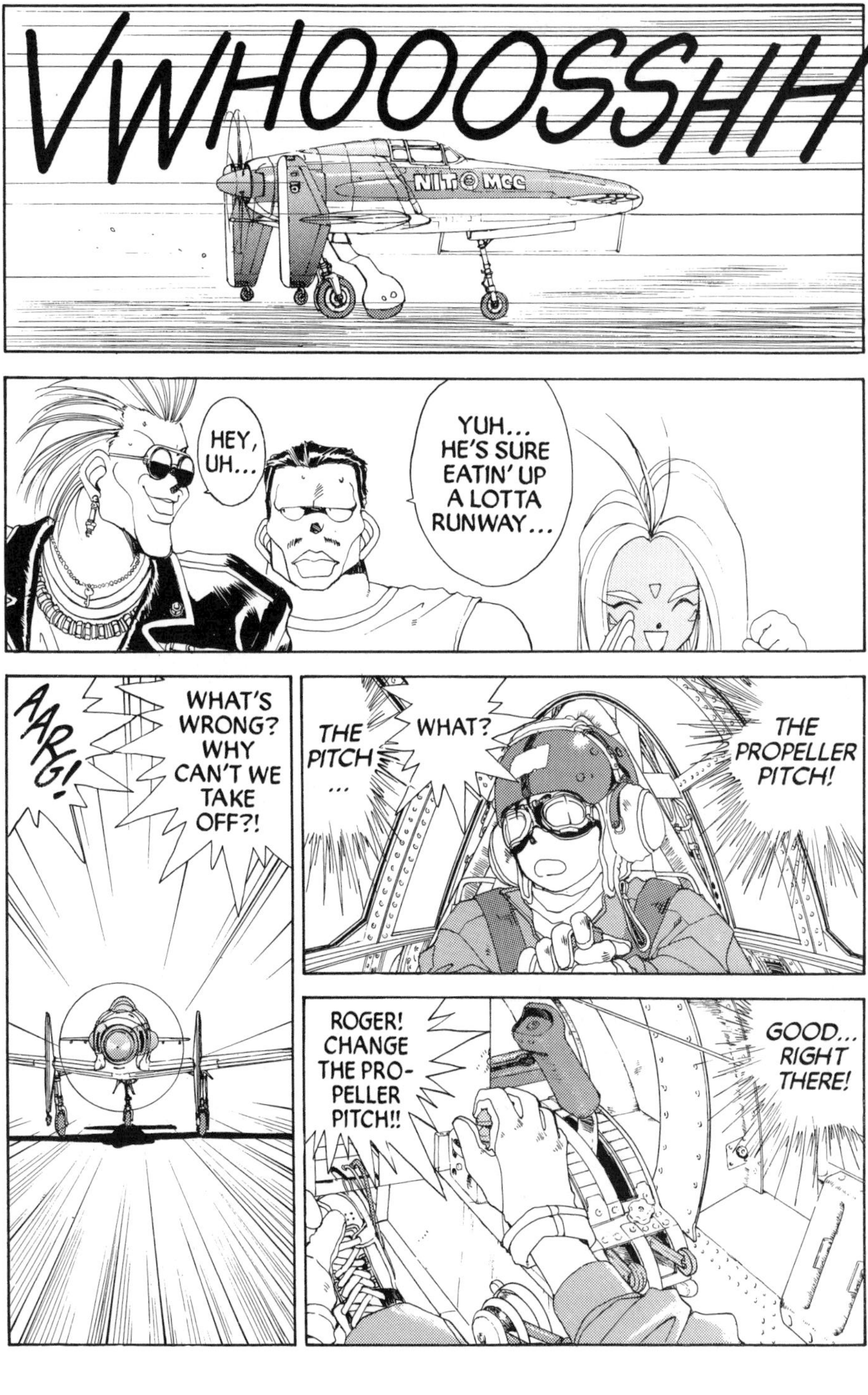
VWHOOOSSHH
NIT MCC
HEY, UH...
YUH... HE'S SURE EATIN' UP A LOTTA RUNWAY...
AARG!
WHAT'S WRONG? WHY CAN'T WE TAKE OFF?!
THE PITCH ...
WHAT?
THE PROPELLER PITCH!
ROGER! CHANGE THE PRO-PELLER PITCH!!
GOOD... RIGHT THERE!

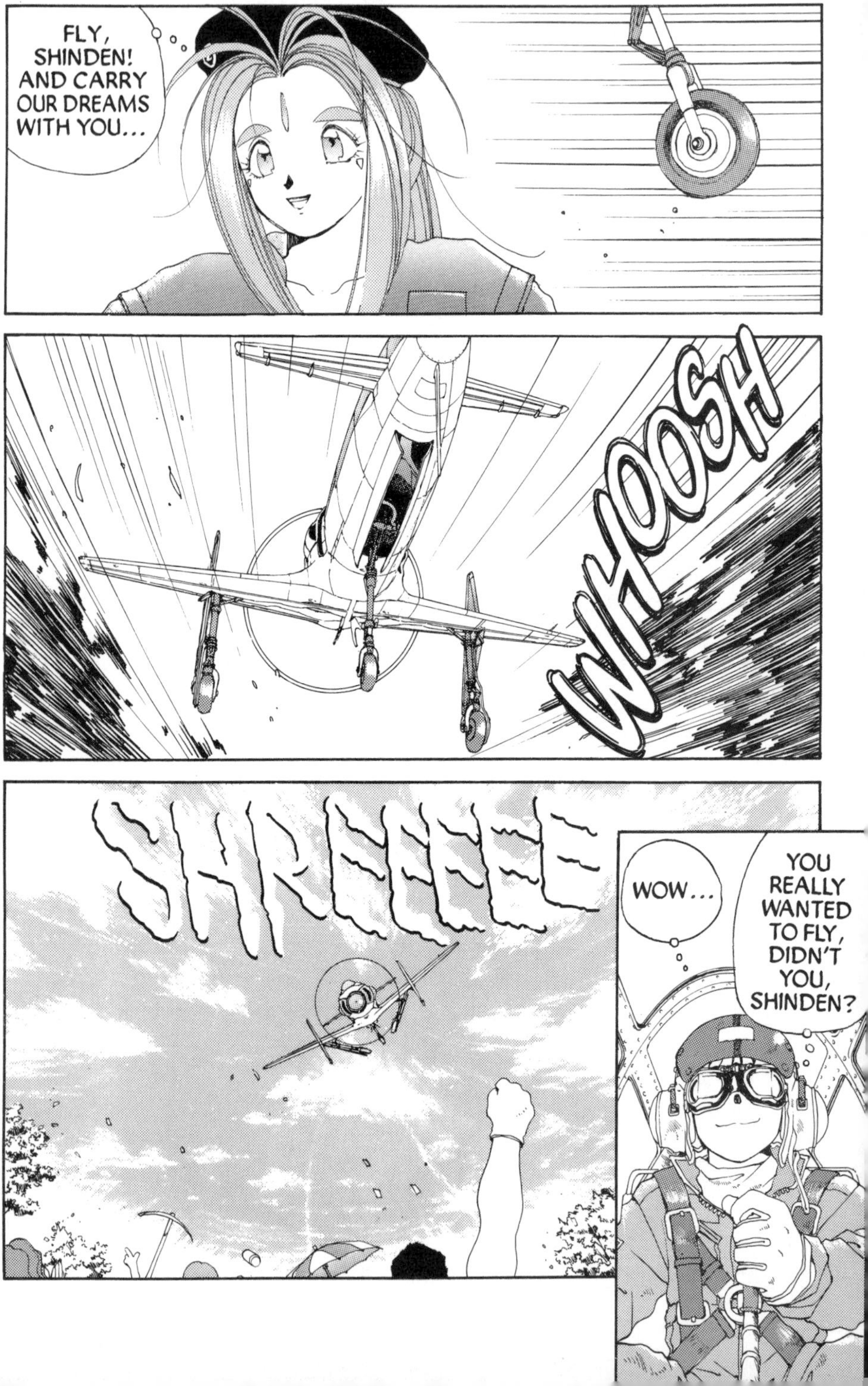
FLY, SHINDEN! AND CARRY OUR DREAMS WITH YOU...
WHOOSH
SHREEEEE
WOW...
YOU REALLY WANTED TO FLY, DIDN'T YOU, SHINDEN?

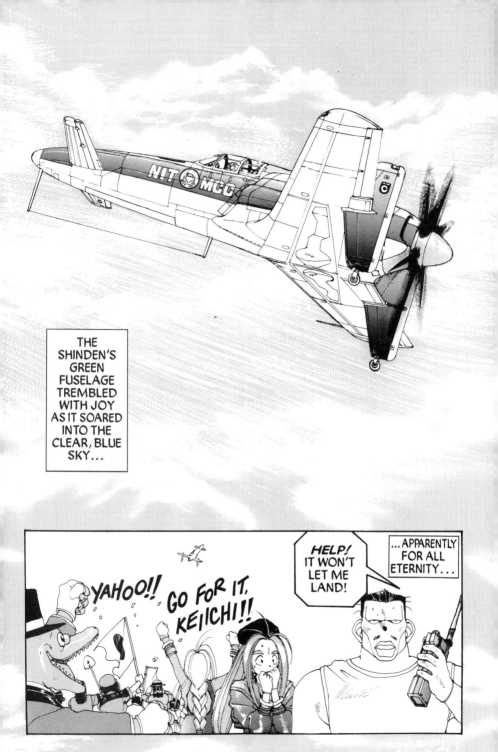

THE SHINDEN'S GREEN FUSELAGE TREMBLED WITH JOY AS IT SOARED INTO THE CLEAR, BLUE SKY...

YAHOO!!

GO FOR IT, KEIICHI!!

HELP! IT WON'T LET ME LAND!

...APPARENTLY FOR ALL ETERNITY...

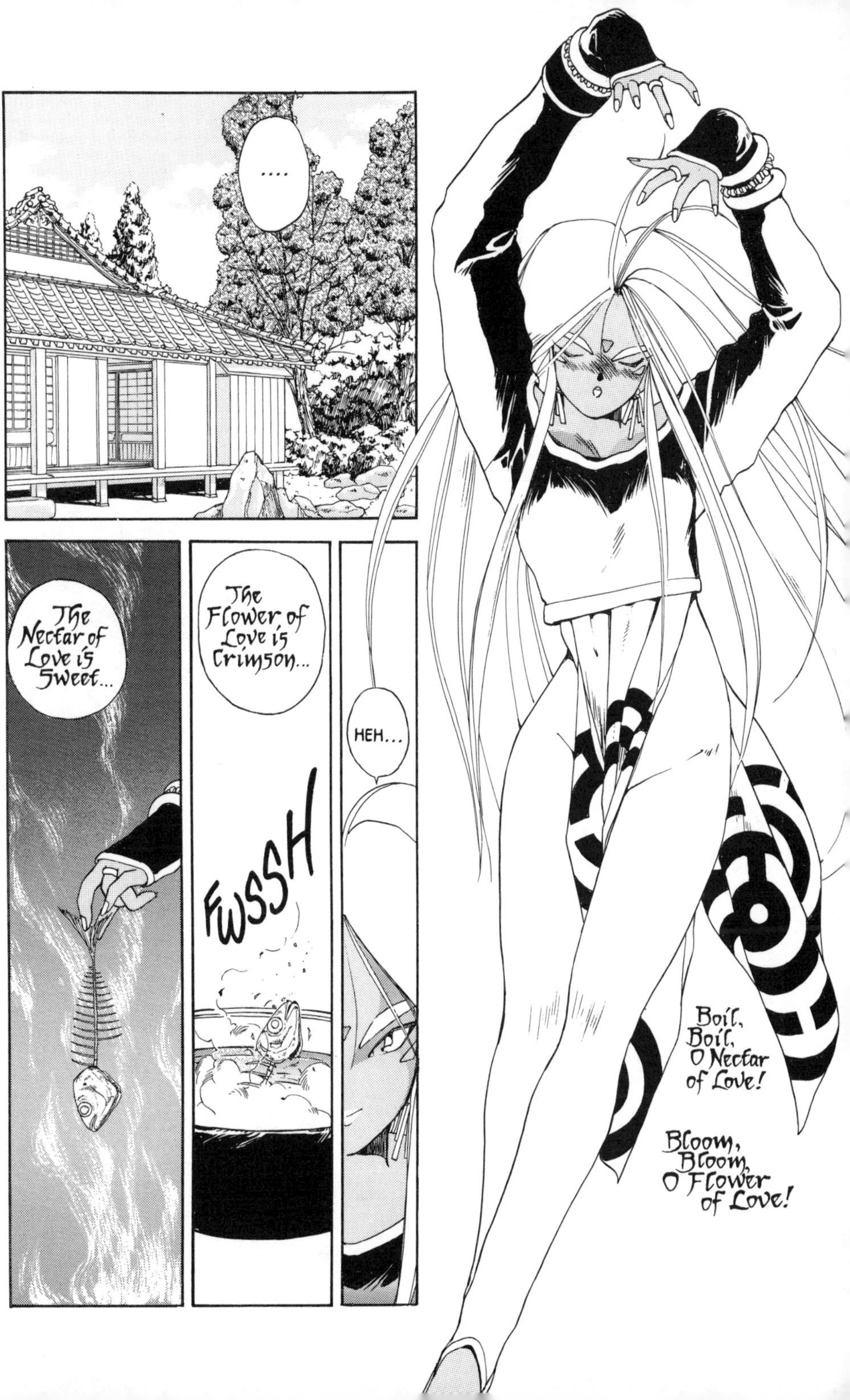
....
The Nectar of Love is Sweet...
The Flower of Love is Crimson...
FWSSH
HEH...
Boil, Boil, O Nectar of Love!
Bloom, Bloom, O Flower of Love!

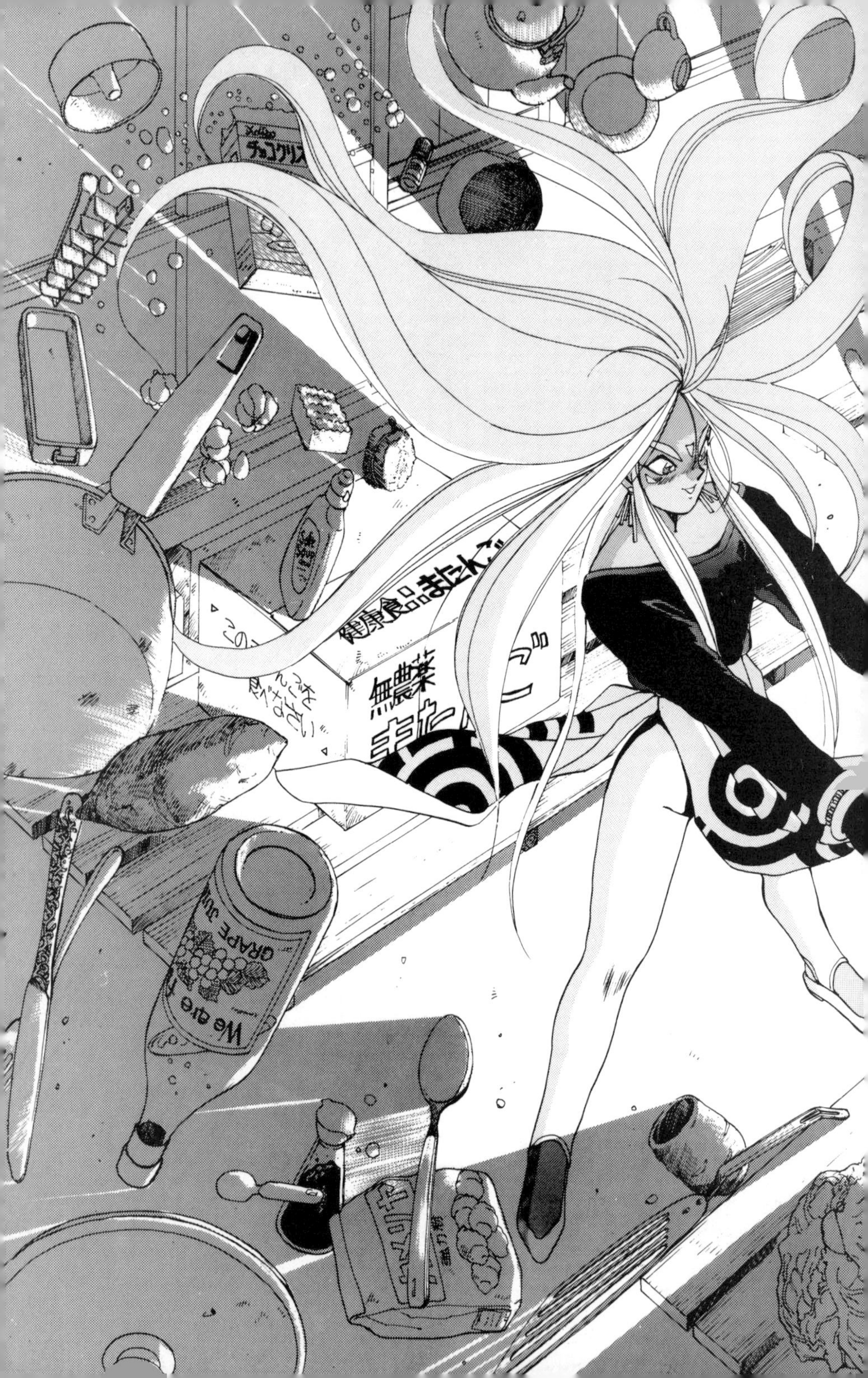
健康食品まにんご
無農薬
GRAPE

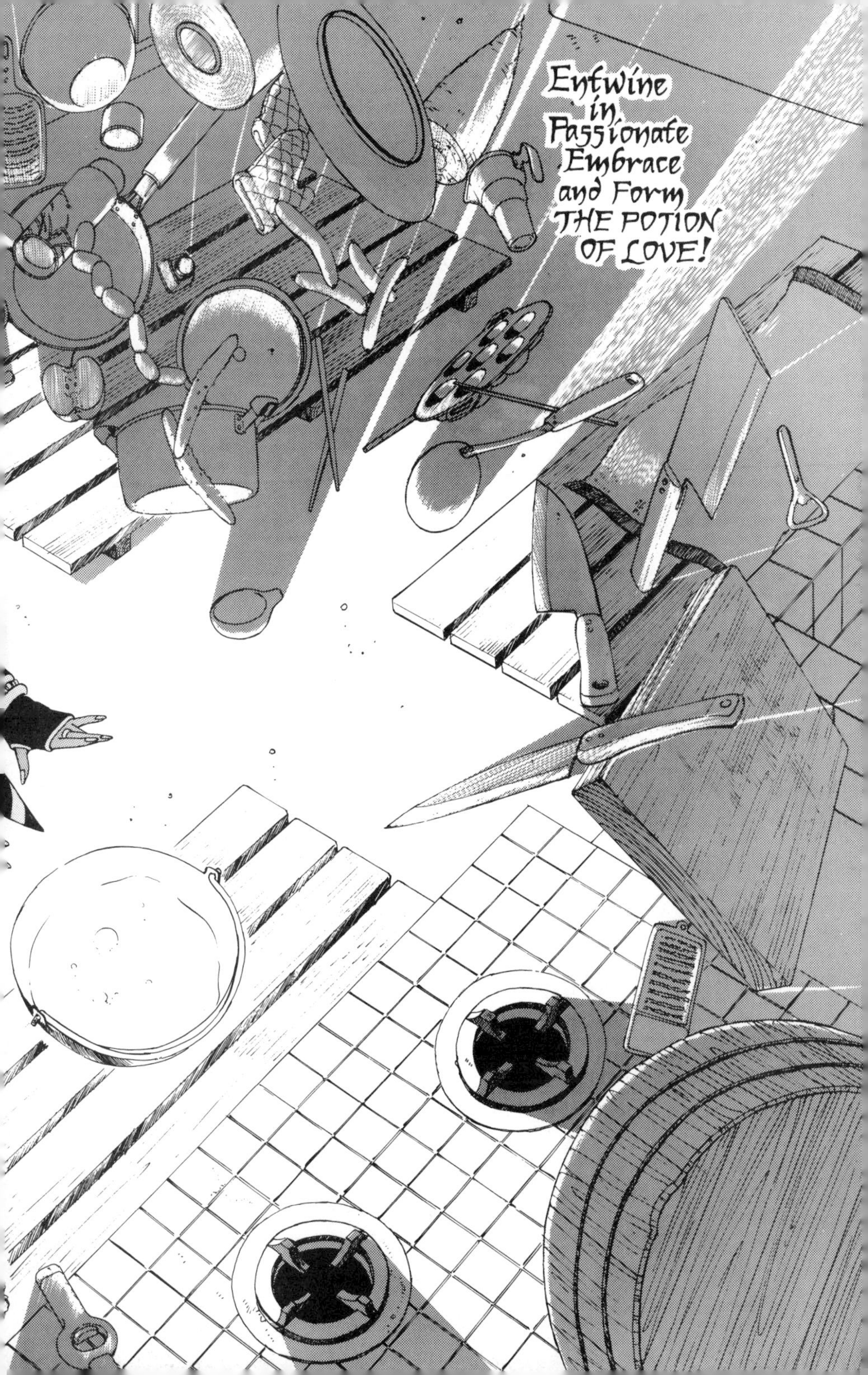
Entwine in Passionate Embrace and Form THE POTION OF LOVE!

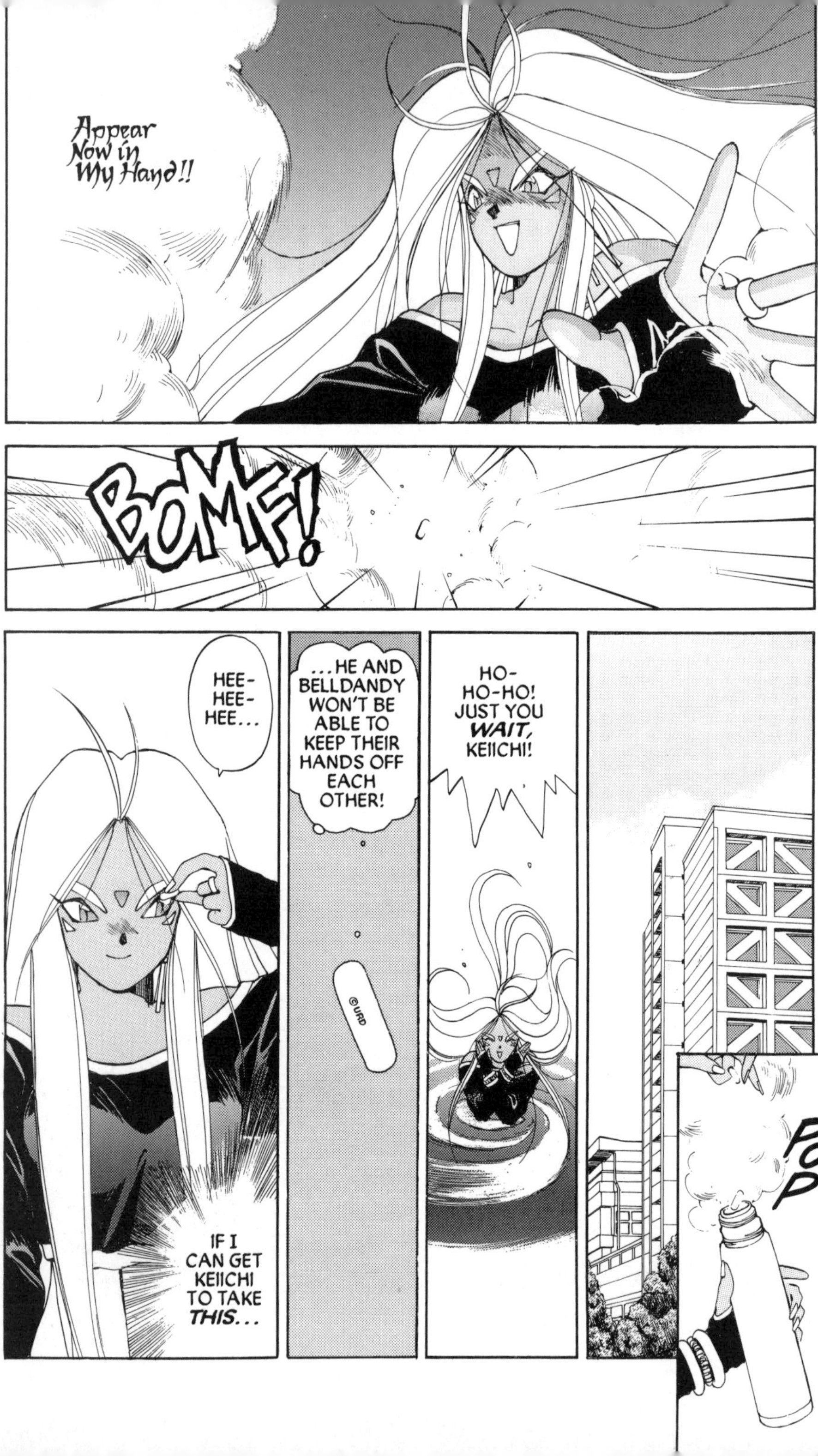
Appear Now in My Hand!!
BOMF!
HEE-HEE-HEE...
IF I CAN GET KEIICHI TO TAKE *THIS*...
...HE AND BELLDANDY WON'T BE ABLE TO KEEP THEIR HANDS OFF EACH OTHER!
HO-HO-HO! JUST YOU *WAIT,* KEIICHI!
POP

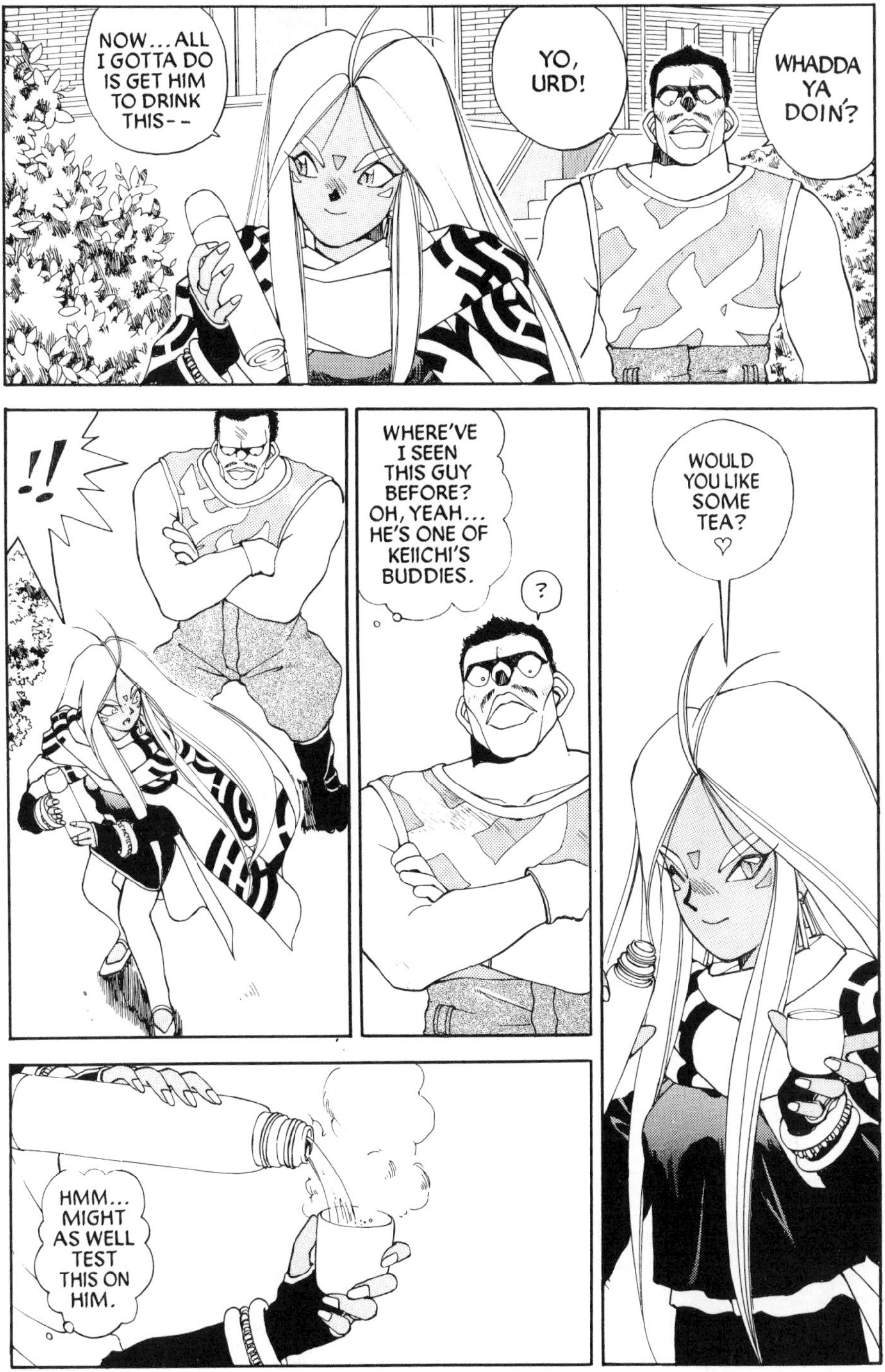
NOW... ALL I GOTTA DO IS GET HIM TO DRINK THIS--
YO, URD!
WHADDA YA DOIN'?
!!
WHERE'VE I SEEN THIS GUY BEFORE? OH, YEAH... HE'S ONE OF KEIICHI'S BUDDIES.
?
HMM... MIGHT AS WELL TEST THIS ON HIM.
WOULD YOU LIKE SOME TEA? ♡

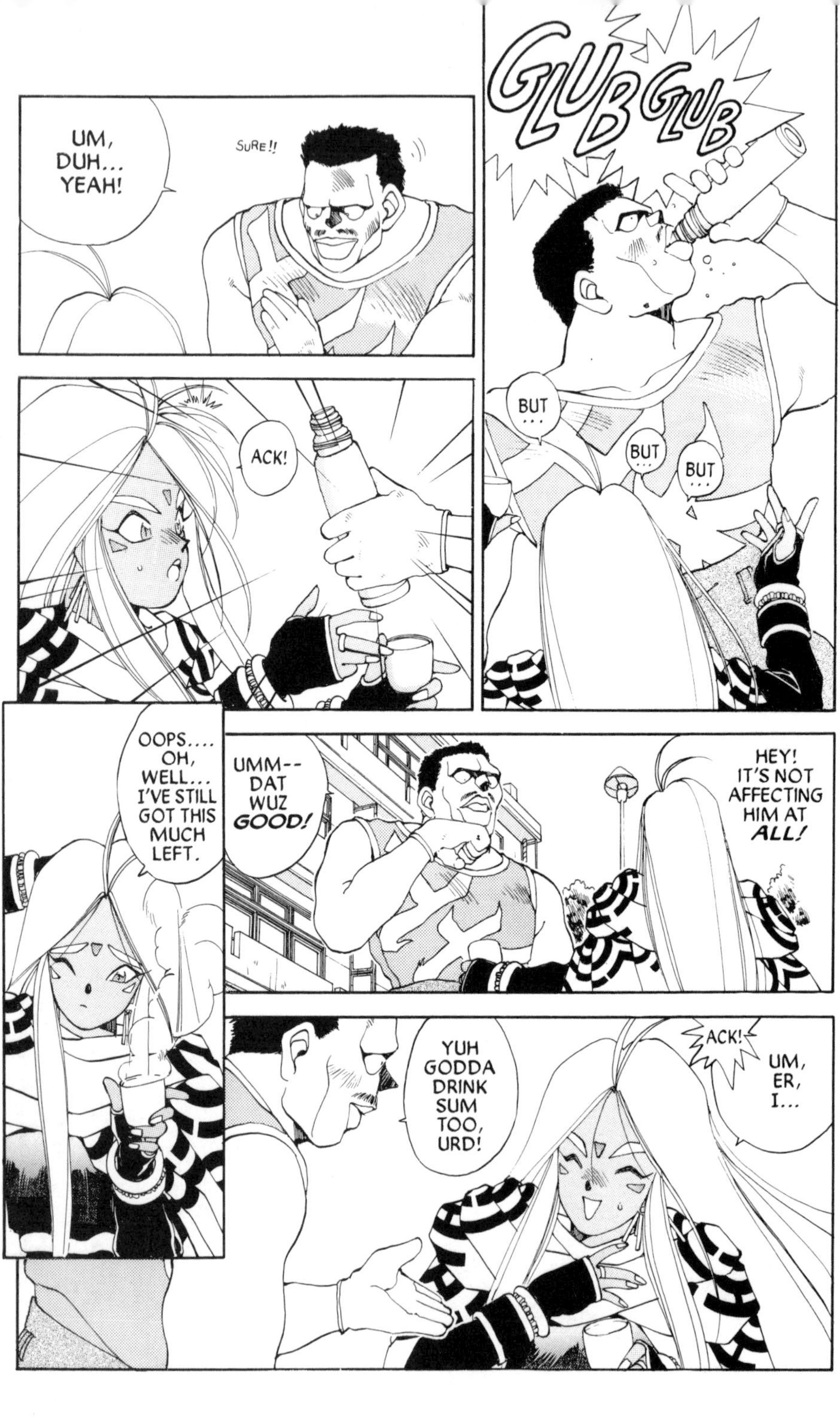
UM, DUH... YEAH!
SURE!!
ACK!
GLUB GLUB
BUT...
BUT...
BUT...
OOPS.... OH, WELL... I'VE STILL GOT THIS MUCH LEFT.
UMM-- DAT WUZ *GOOD!*
HEY! IT'S NOT AFFECTING HIM AT *ALL!*
YUH GODDA DRINK SUM TOO, URD!
ACK!
UM, ER, I...

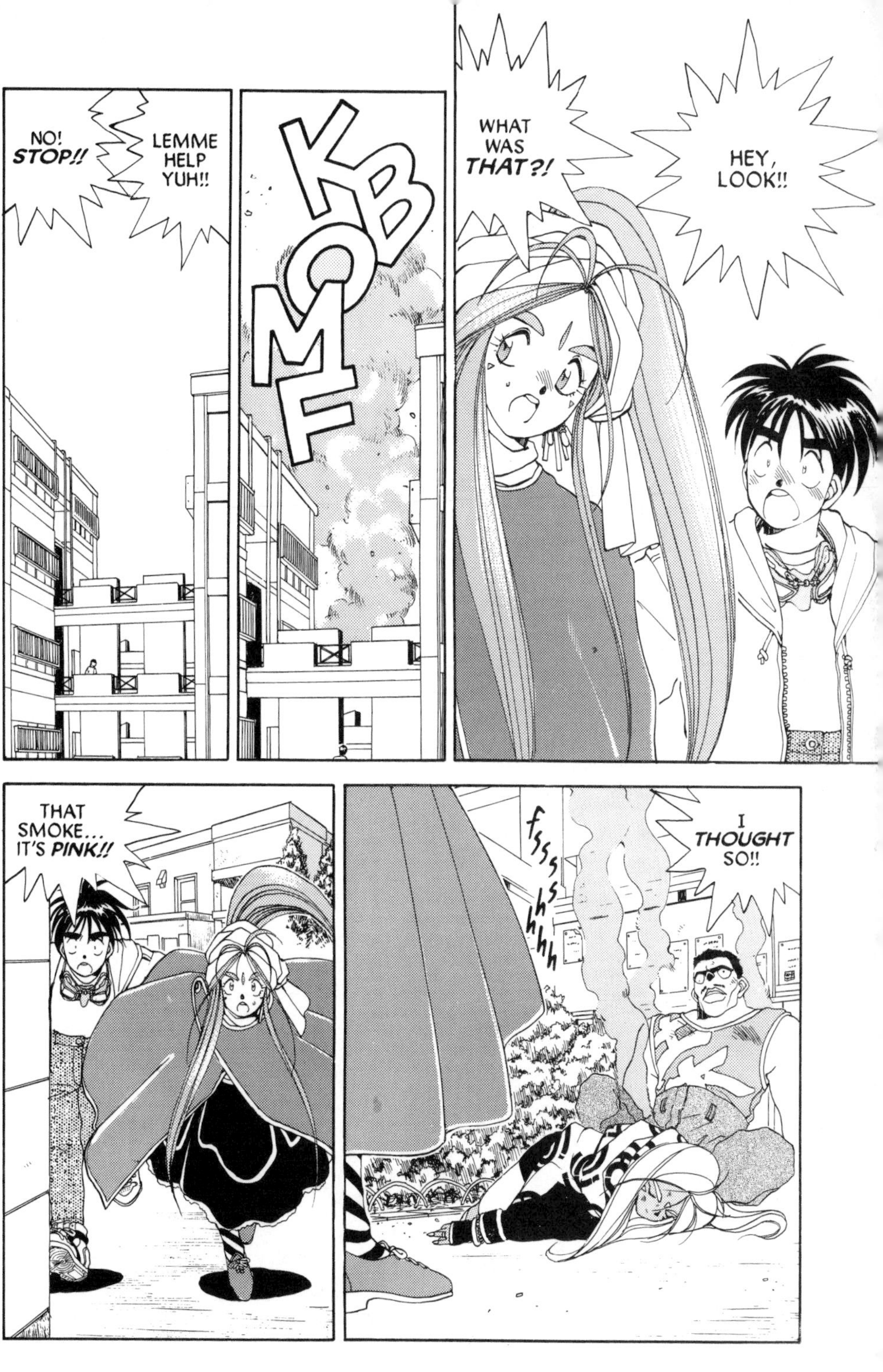

NO! STOP!!
LEMME HELP YUH!!
KBOOMF
WHAT WAS THAT?!
HEY, LOOK!!
THAT SMOKE... IT'S PINK!!
fssssshhhh
I THOUGHT SO!!

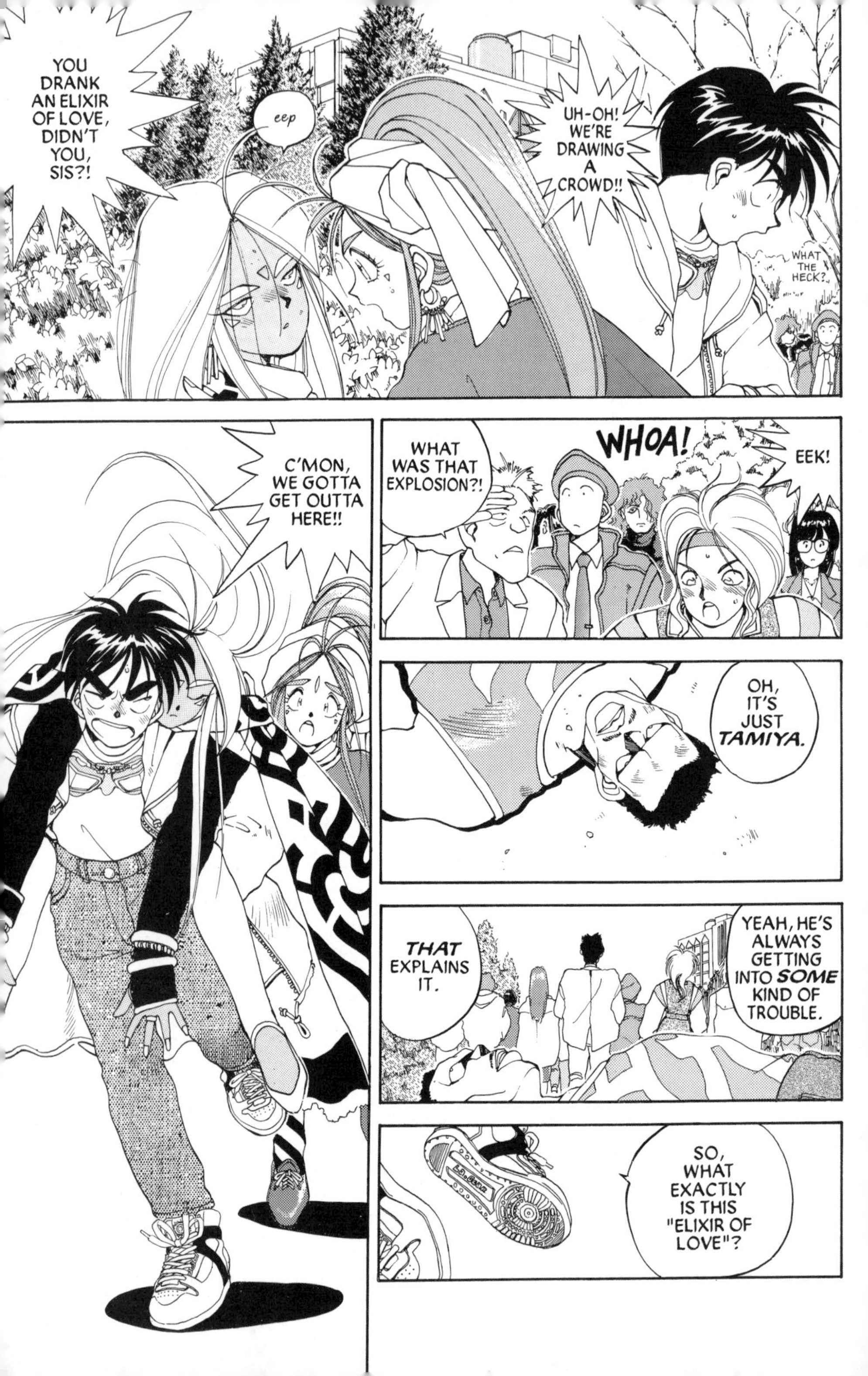
YOU DRANK AN ELIXIR OF LOVE, DIDN'T YOU, SIS?!
eep
UH-OH! WE'RE DRAWING A CROWD!!
WHAT THE HECK?
C'MON, WE GOTTA GET OUTTA HERE!!
WHAT WAS THAT EXPLOSION?!
WHOA!
EEK!
OH, IT'S JUST TAMIYA.
THAT EXPLAINS IT.
YEAH, HE'S ALWAYS GETTING INTO SOME KIND OF TROUBLE.
SO, WHAT EXACTLY IS THIS "ELIXIR OF LOVE"?

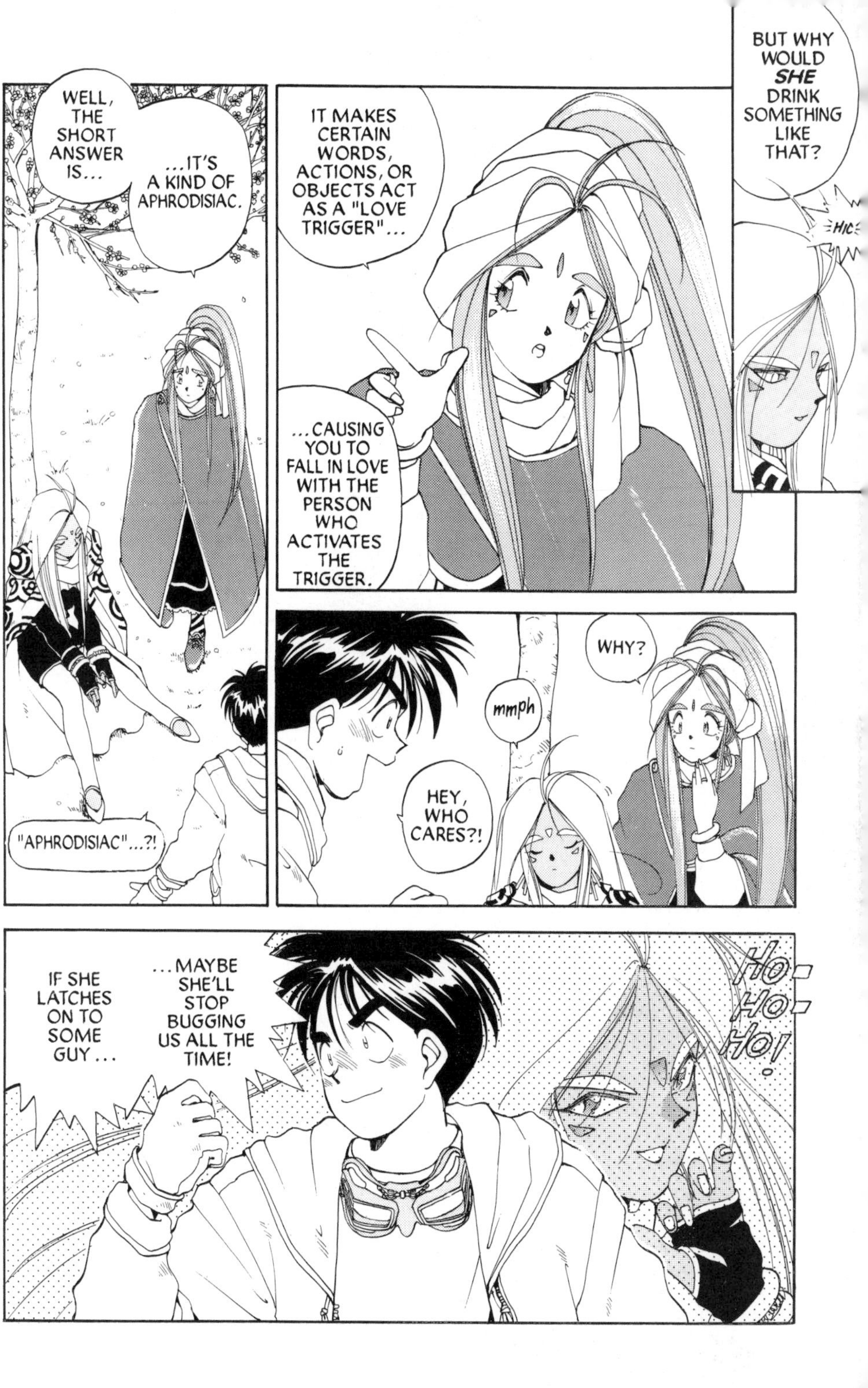
WELL, THE SHORT ANSWER IS...
...IT'S A KIND OF APHRODISIAC.
"APHRODISIAC"...?!
IT MAKES CERTAIN WORDS, ACTIONS, OR OBJECTS ACT AS A "LOVE TRIGGER"...
...CAUSING YOU TO FALL IN LOVE WITH THE PERSON WHO ACTIVATES THE TRIGGER.
BUT WHY WOULD ***SHE*** DRINK SOMETHING LIKE THAT?
HIC
WHY?
mmph
HEY, WHO CARES?!
IF SHE LATCHES ON TO SOME GUY...
...MAYBE SHE'LL STOP BUGGING US ALL THE TIME!
HO-HO-HO!

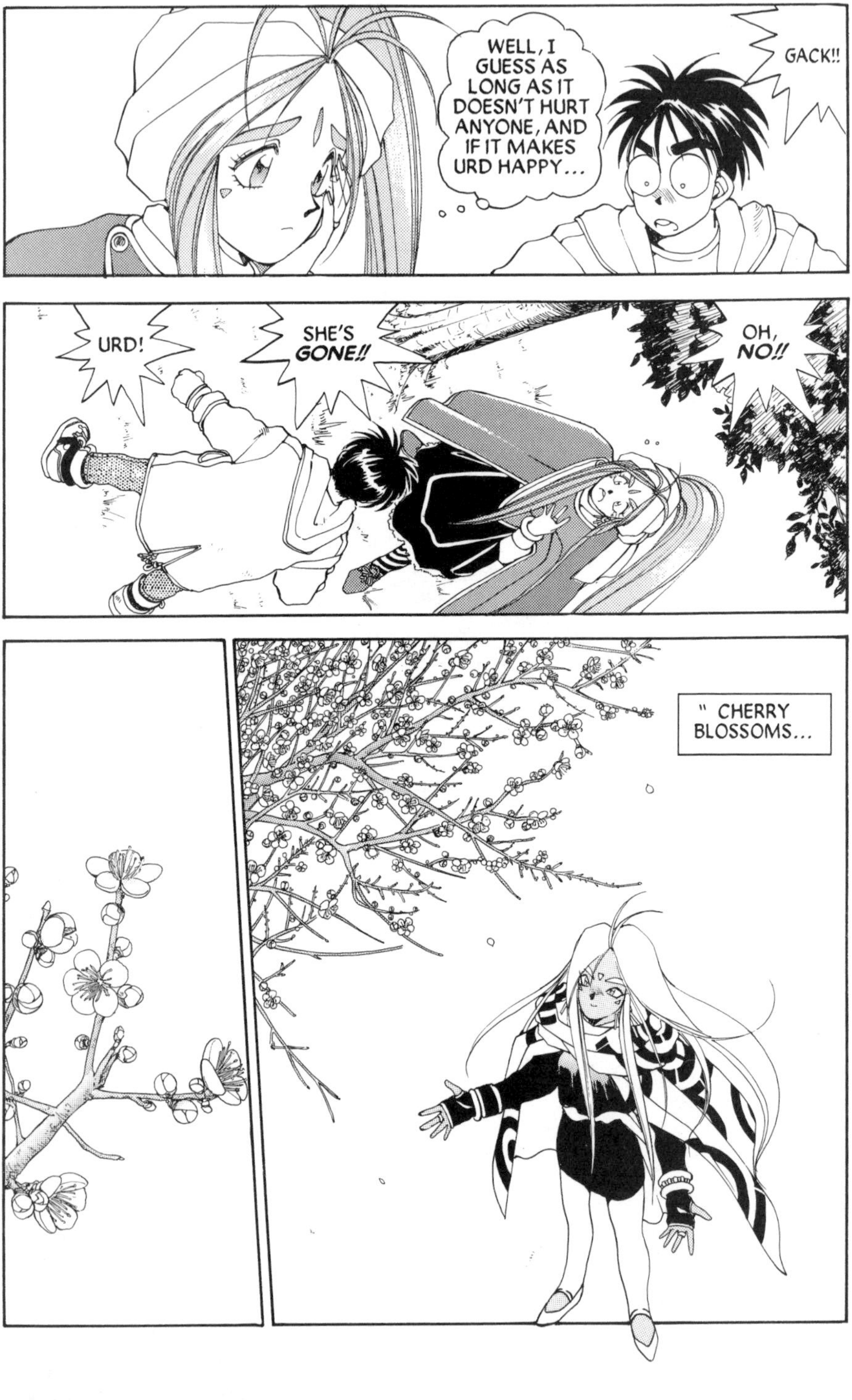
WELL, I GUESS AS LONG AS IT DOESN'T HURT ANYONE, AND IF IT MAKES URD HAPPY...
GACK!!
URD!
SHE'S GONE!!
OH, NO!!
" CHERRY BLOSSOMS...

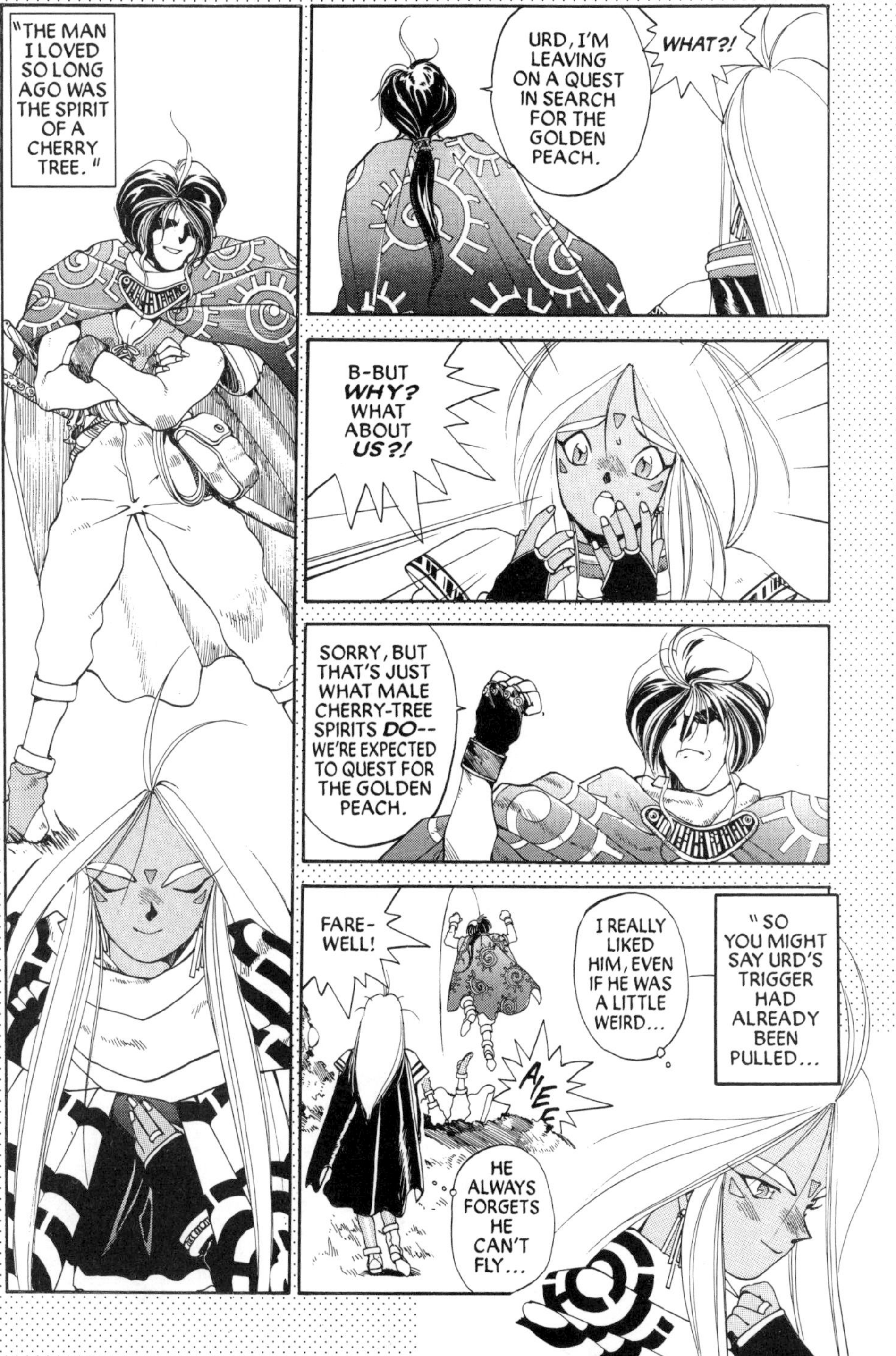
"THE MAN I LOVED SO LONG AGO WAS THE SPIRIT OF A CHERRY TREE."
URD, I'M LEAVING ON A QUEST IN SEARCH FOR THE GOLDEN PEACH.
WHAT?!
B-BUT WHY? WHAT ABOUT US?!
SORRY, BUT THAT'S JUST WHAT MALE CHERRY-TREE SPIRITS DO-- WE'RE EXPECTED TO QUEST FOR THE GOLDEN PEACH.
FARE-WELL!
I REALLY LIKED HIM, EVEN IF HE WAS A LITTLE WEIRD...
"SO YOU MIGHT SAY URD'S TRIGGER HAD ALREADY BEEN PULLED..."
AIEE
HE ALWAYS FORGETS HE CAN'T FLY...

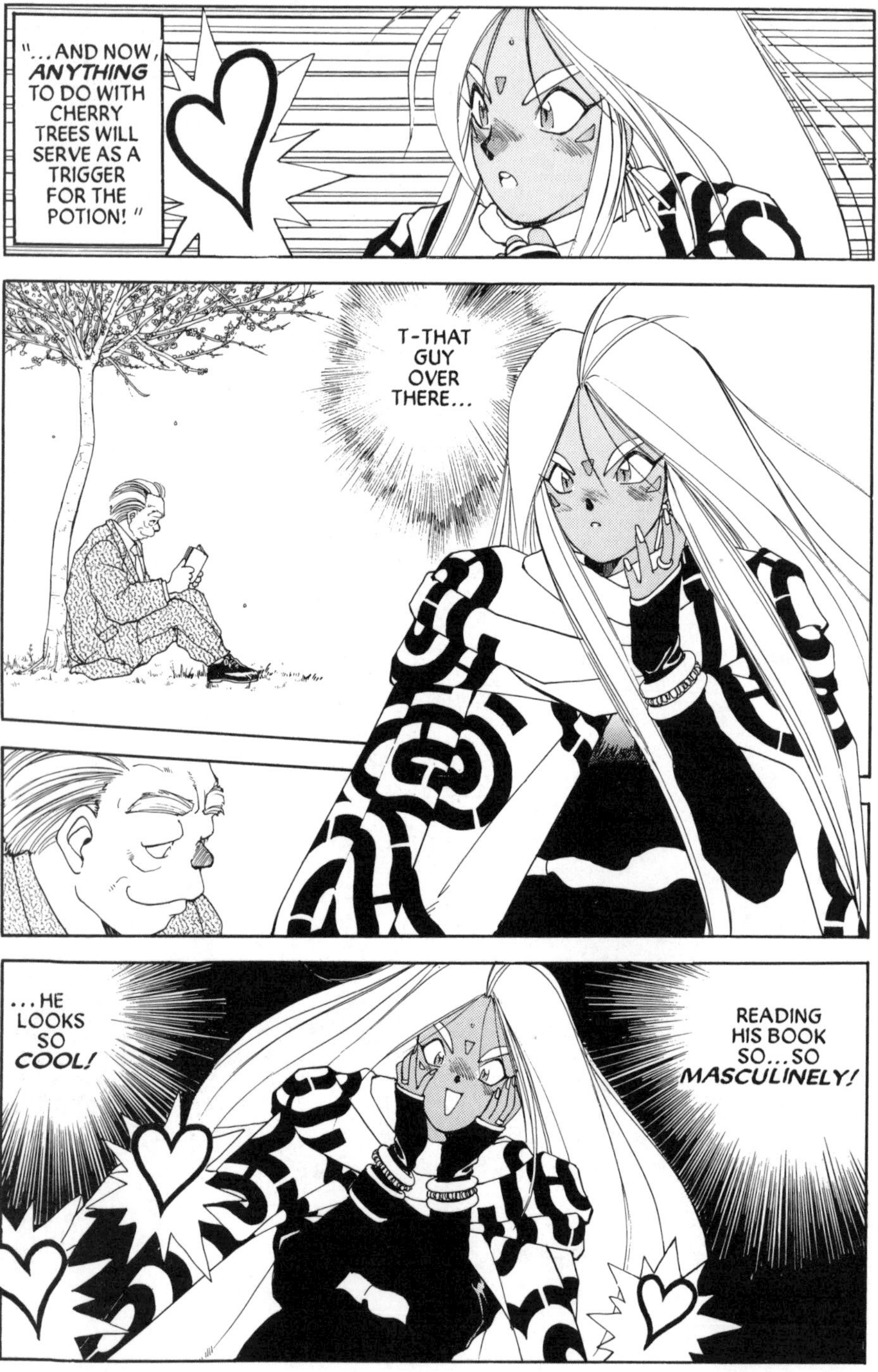
"...AND NOW, ***ANYTHING*** TO DO WITH CHERRY TREES WILL SERVE AS A TRIGGER FOR THE POTION!"
T-THAT GUY OVER THERE...
...HE LOOKS SO ***COOL!***
READING HIS BOOK SO...SO ***MASCULINELY!***

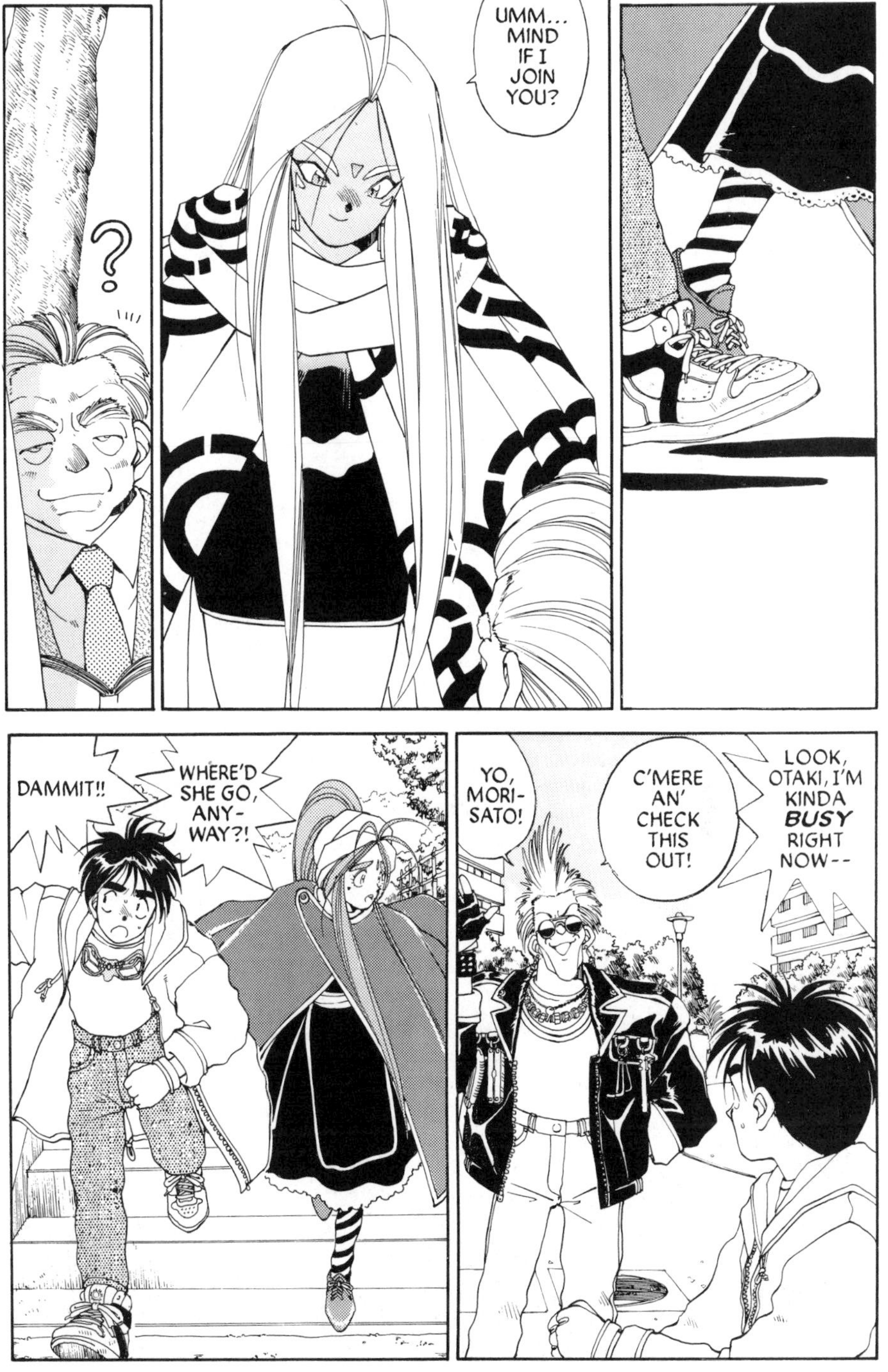
?
UMM... MIND IF I JOIN YOU?
DAMMIT!!
WHERE'D SHE GO, ANY-WAY?!
YO, MORI-SATO!
C'MERE AN' CHECK THIS OUT!
LOOK, OTAKI, I'M KINDA ***BUSY*** RIGHT NOW--

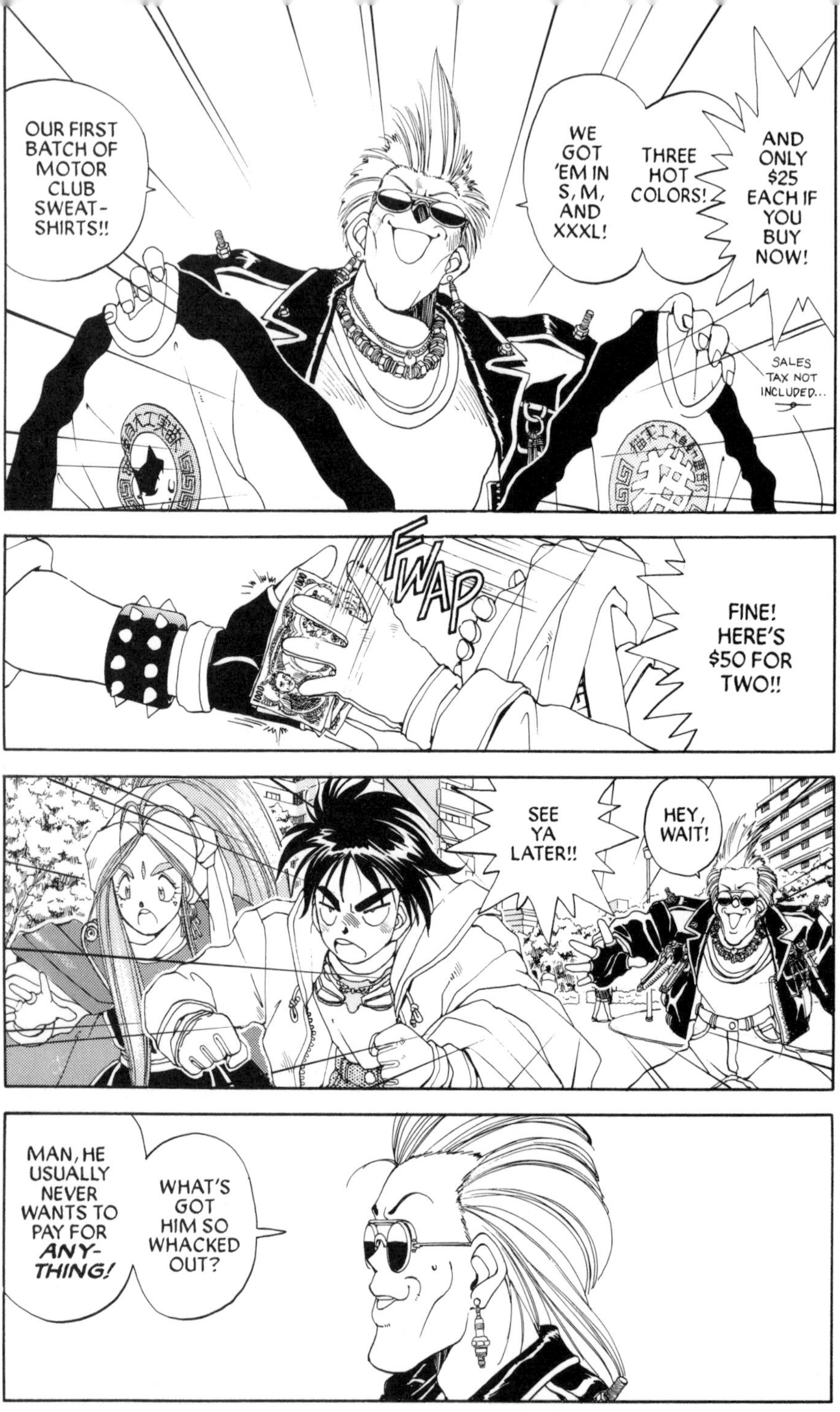
OUR FIRST BATCH OF MOTOR CLUB SWEAT-SHIRTS!!
WE GOT 'EM IN S, M, AND XXXL!
THREE HOT COLORS!
AND ONLY $25 EACH IF YOU BUY NOW!
SALES TAX NOT INCLUDED...
FWAP
FINE! HERE'S $50 FOR TWO!!
SEE YA LATER!!
HEY, WAIT!
MAN, HE USUALLY NEVER WANTS TO PAY FOR *ANY-THING!*
WHAT'S GOT HIM SO WHACKED OUT?

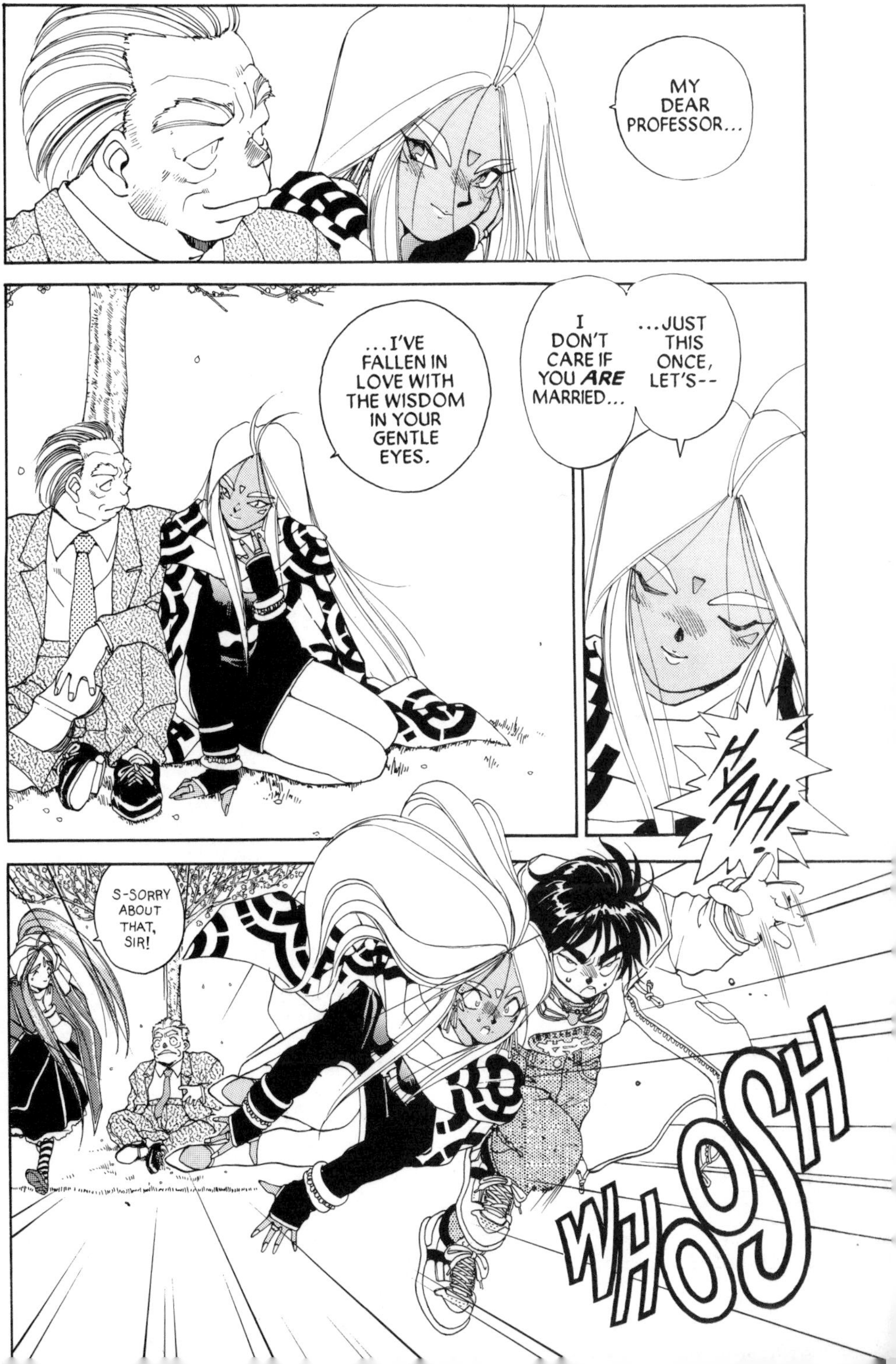
MY DEAR PROFESSOR...
...I'VE FALLEN IN LOVE WITH THE WISDOM IN YOUR GENTLE EYES.
I DON'T CARE IF YOU ***ARE*** MARRIED...
...JUST THIS ONCE, LET'S--
HYAH!
S-SORRY ABOUT THAT, SIR!
WHOOSH

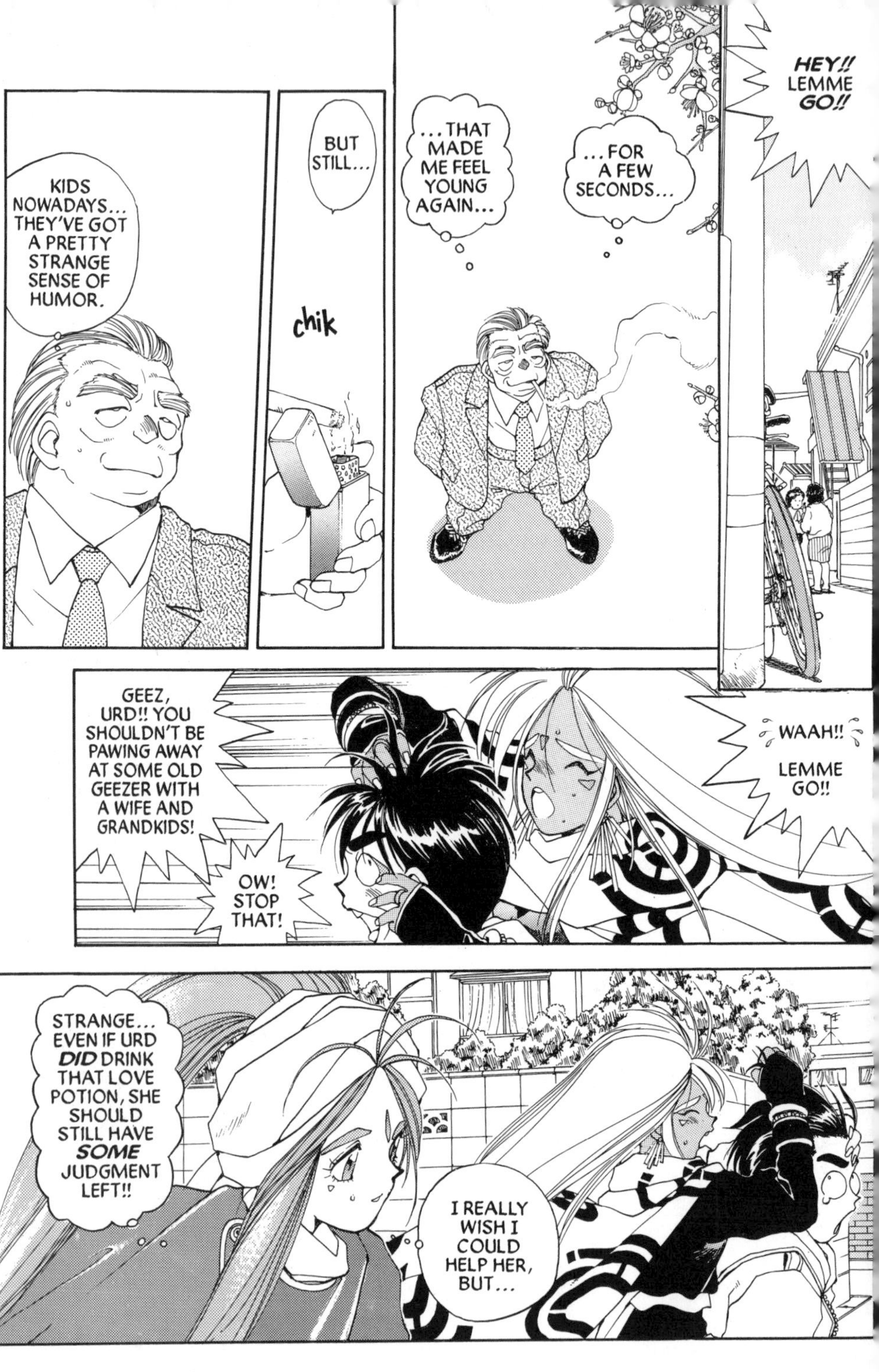
KIDS NOWADAYS... THEY'VE GOT A PRETTY STRANGE SENSE OF HUMOR.
BUT STILL...
chik
...THAT MADE ME FEEL YOUNG AGAIN...
...FOR A FEW SECONDS...
HEY!! LEMME GO!!
GEEZ, URD!! YOU SHOULDN'T BE PAWING AWAY AT SOME OLD GEEZER WITH A WIFE AND GRANDKIDS!
OW! STOP THAT!
WAAH!!
LEMME GO!!
STRANGE... EVEN IF URD *DID* DRINK THAT LOVE POTION, SHE SHOULD STILL HAVE *SOME* JUDGMENT LEFT!!
I REALLY WISH I COULD HELP HER, BUT...

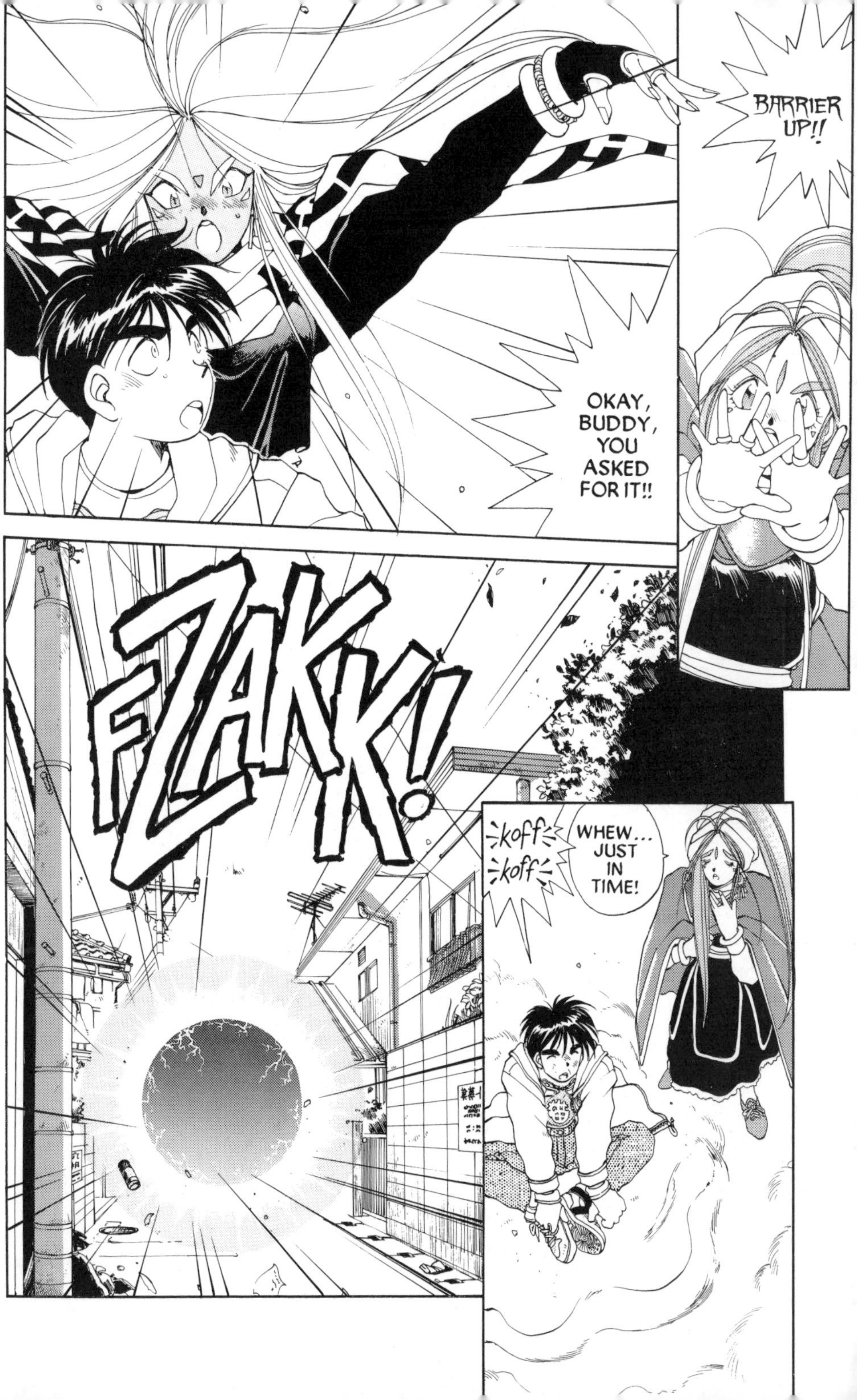
OKAY, BUDDY, YOU ASKED FOR IT!!
BARRIER UP!!
FZAKK!
koff
koff
WHEW... JUST IN TIME!

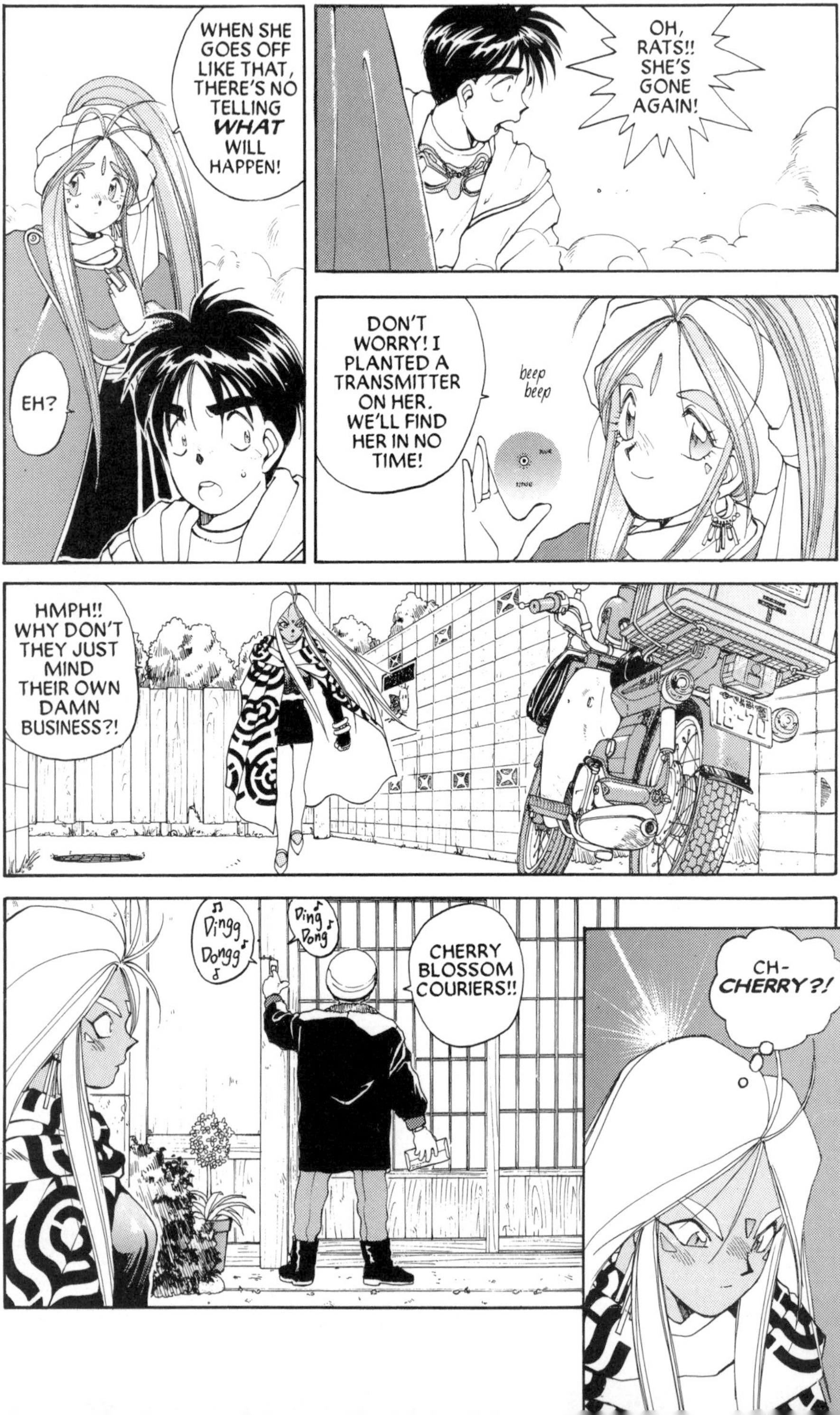
WHEN SHE GOES OFF LIKE THAT, THERE'S NO TELLING WHAT WILL HAPPEN!
EH?
OH, RATS!! SHE'S GONE AGAIN!
DON'T WORRY! I PLANTED A TRANSMITTER ON HER. WE'LL FIND HER IN NO TIME!
beep beep
HMPH!! WHY DON'T THEY JUST MIND THEIR OWN DAMN BUSINESS?!
Dingg Dongg
Ding Dong
CHERRY BLOSSOM COURIERS!!
CH-CHERRY?!

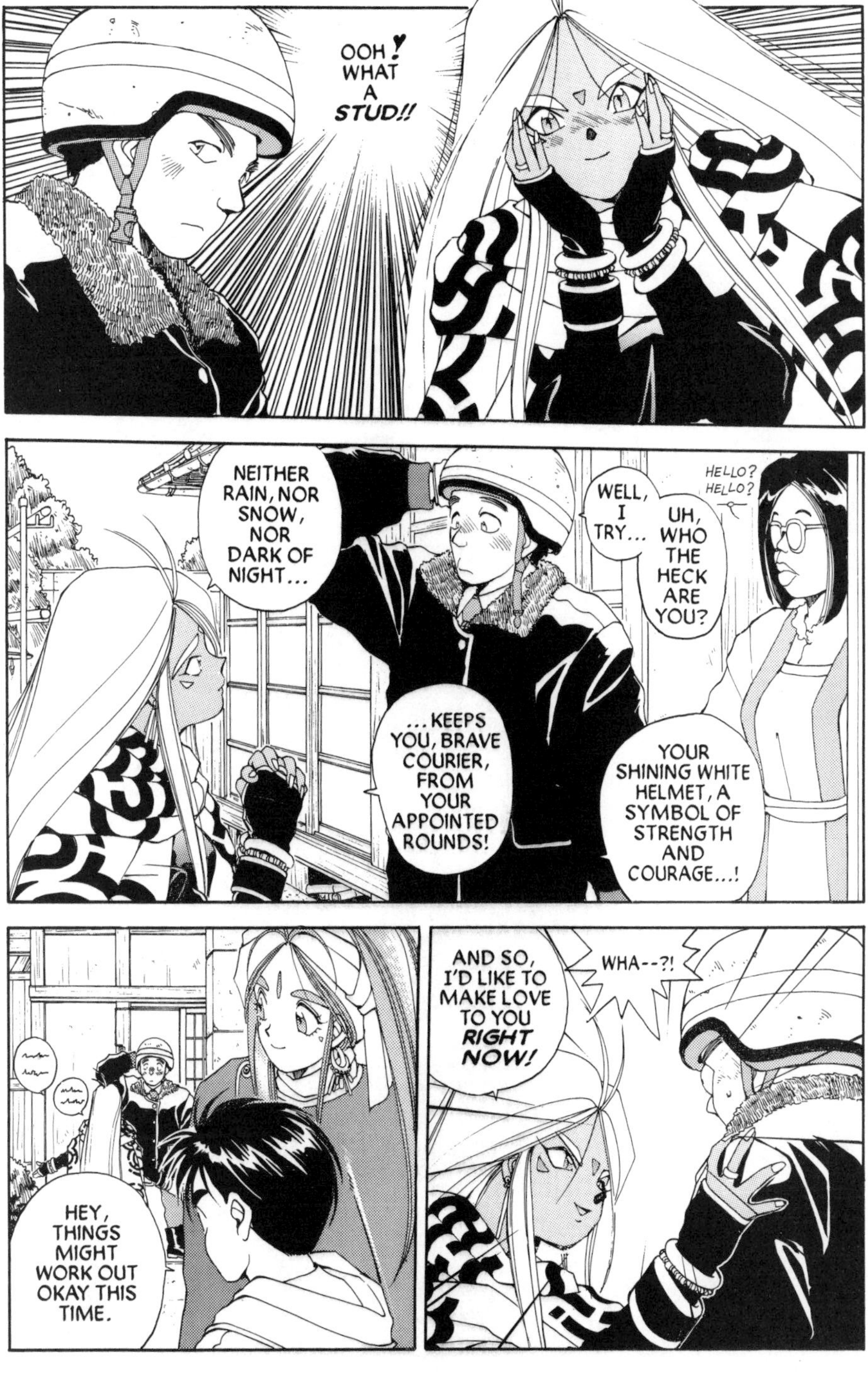
OOH! WHAT A STUD!!
NEITHER RAIN, NOR SNOW, NOR DARK OF NIGHT...
WELL, I TRY...
UH, WHO THE HECK ARE YOU?
HELLO? HELLO?
...KEEPS YOU, BRAVE COURIER, FROM YOUR APPOINTED ROUNDS!
YOUR SHINING WHITE HELMET, A SYMBOL OF STRENGTH AND COURAGE...!
HEY, THINGS MIGHT WORK OUT OKAY THIS TIME.
AND SO, I'D LIKE TO MAKE LOVE TO YOU RIGHT NOW!
WHA--?!

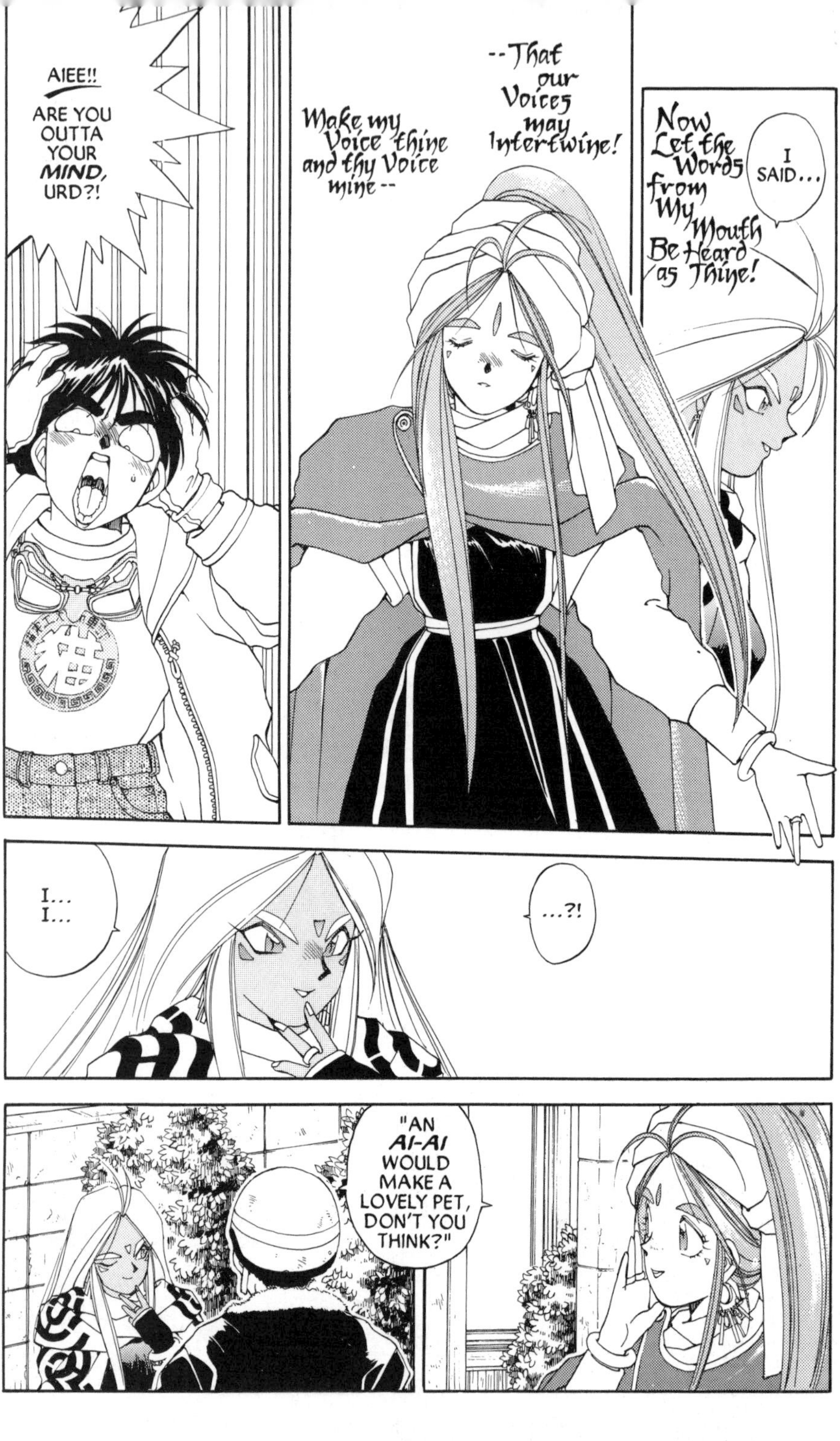
AIEE!!
ARE YOU OUTTA YOUR MIND, URD?!
Make my Voice thine and thy Voice mine --
--That our Voices may Intertwine!
Now Let the Words from My Mouth Be Heard as Thine!
I SAID...
I... I...
...?!
"AN AI-AI WOULD MAKE A LOVELY PET, DON'T YOU THINK?"

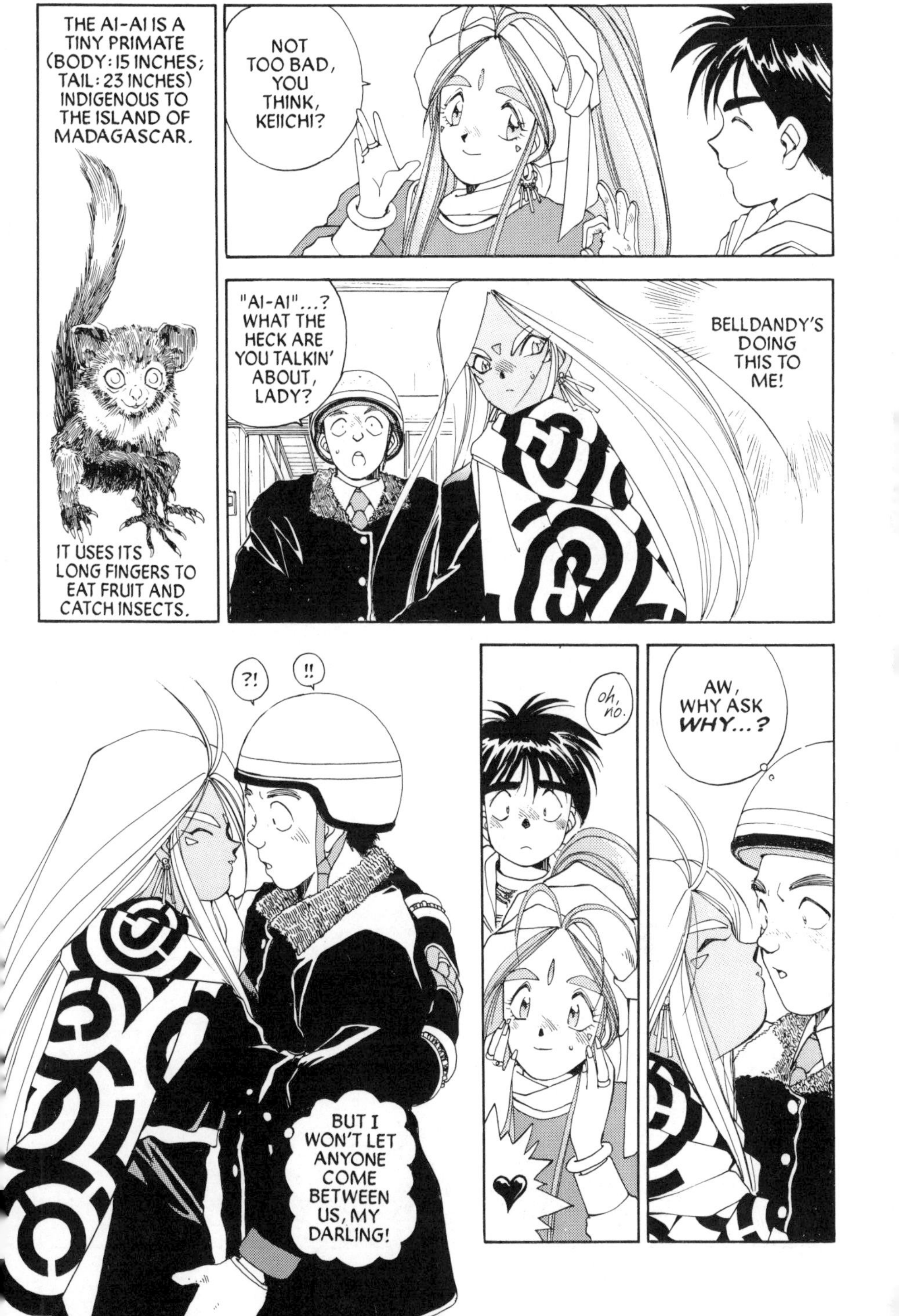
THE AI-AI IS A TINY PRIMATE (BODY: 15 INCHES; TAIL: 23 INCHES) INDIGENOUS TO THE ISLAND OF MADAGASCAR.
IT USES ITS LONG FINGERS TO EAT FRUIT AND CATCH INSECTS.
NOT TOO BAD, YOU THINK, KEIICHI?
"AI-AI"...? WHAT THE HECK ARE YOU TALKIN' ABOUT, LADY?
BELLDANDY'S DOING THIS TO ME!
?!
!!
BUT I WON'T LET ANYONE COME BETWEEN US, MY DARLING!
oh, no.
AW, WHY ASK WHY...?

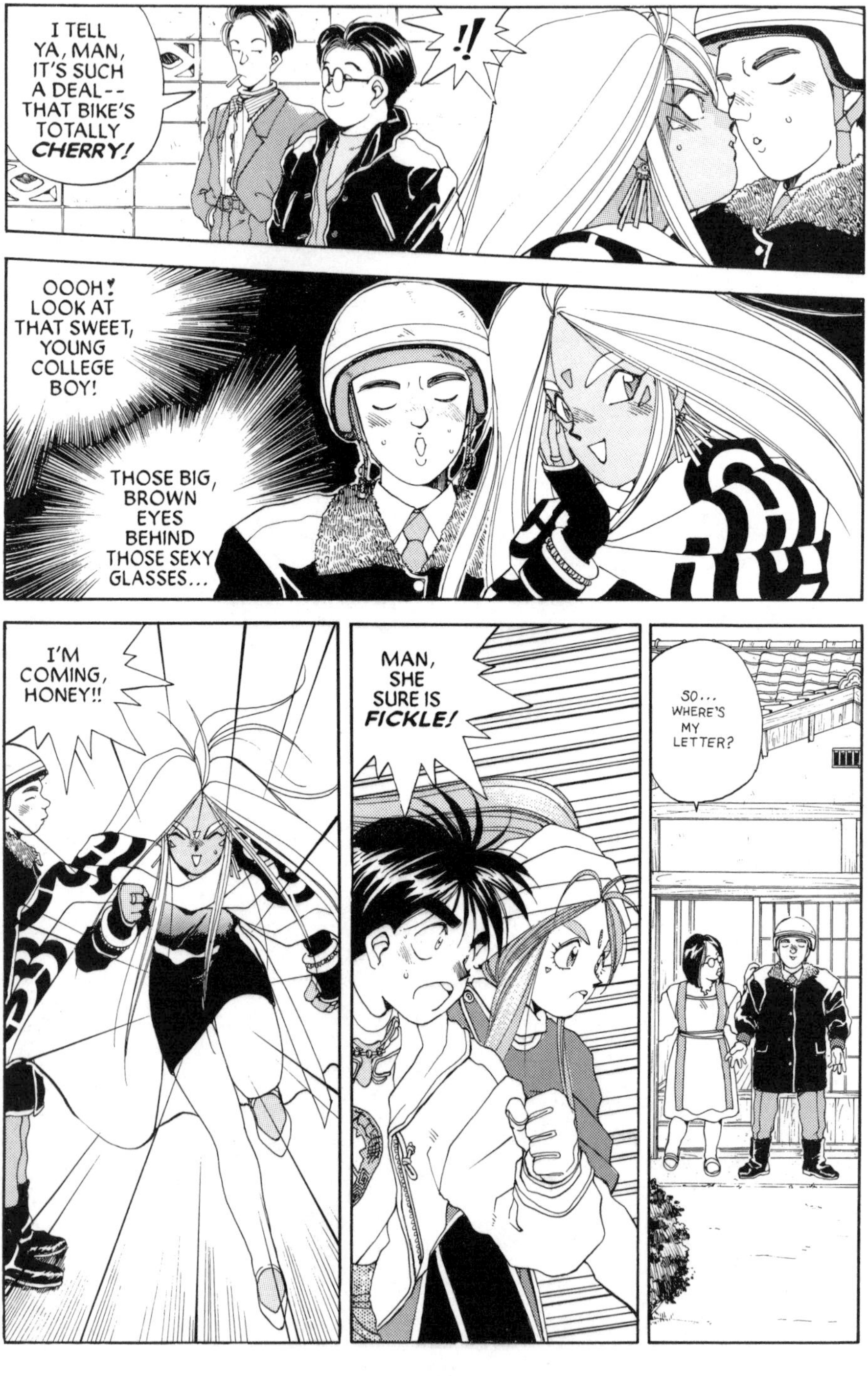
I TELL YA, MAN, IT'S SUCH A DEAL-- THAT BIKE'S TOTALLY CHERRY!
!!
OOOH♥ LOOK AT THAT SWEET, YOUNG COLLEGE BOY!
THOSE BIG, BROWN EYES BEHIND THOSE SEXY GLASSES...
I'M COMING, HONEY!!
MAN, SHE SURE IS FICKLE!
SO... WHERE'S MY LETTER?

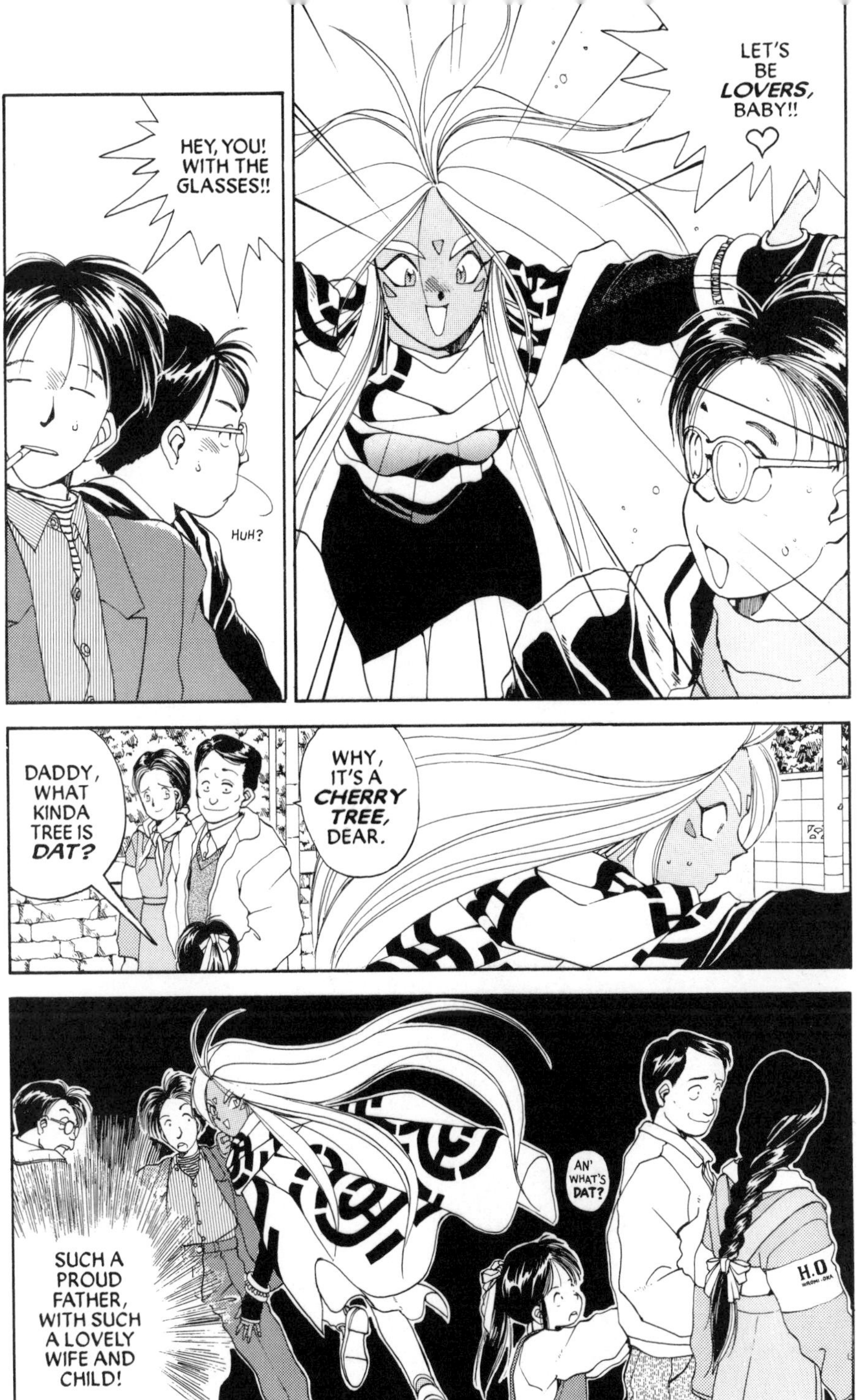

HEY, YOU! WITH THE GLASSES!!
HUH?
LET'S BE LOVERS, BABY!! ♡
DADDY, WHAT KINDA TREE IS DAT?
WHY, IT'S A CHERRY TREE, DEAR.
AN' WHAT'S DAT?
SUCH A PROUD FATHER, WITH SUCH A LOVELY WIFE AND CHILD!
H.O

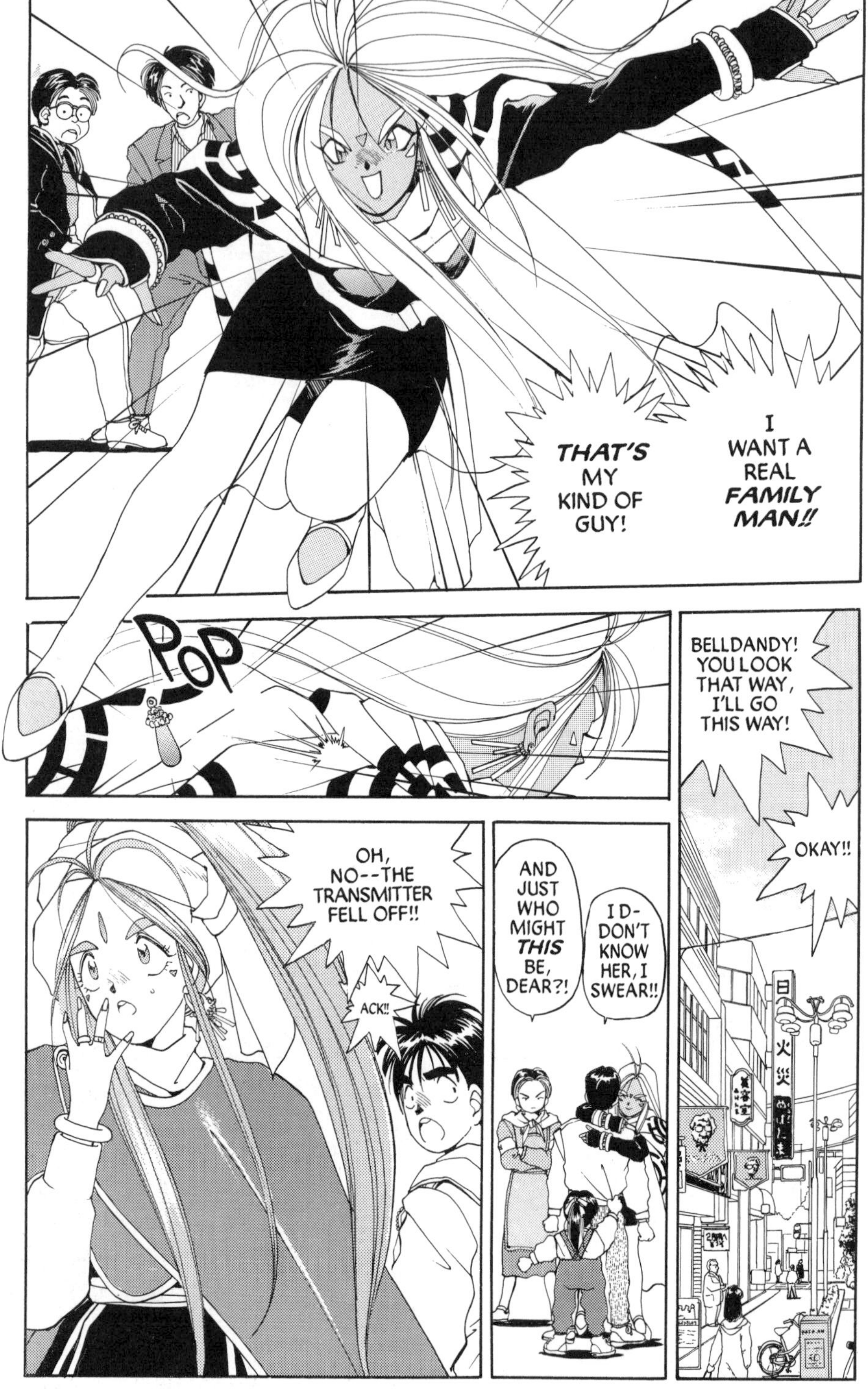
THAT'S MY KIND OF GUY!
I WANT A REAL FAMILY MAN!!
POP
OH, NO--THE TRANSMITTER FELL OFF!!
ACK!!
AND JUST WHO MIGHT THIS BE, DEAR?!
I D-DON'T KNOW HER, I SWEAR!!
BELLDANDY! YOU LOOK THAT WAY, I'LL GO THIS WAY!
OKAY!!

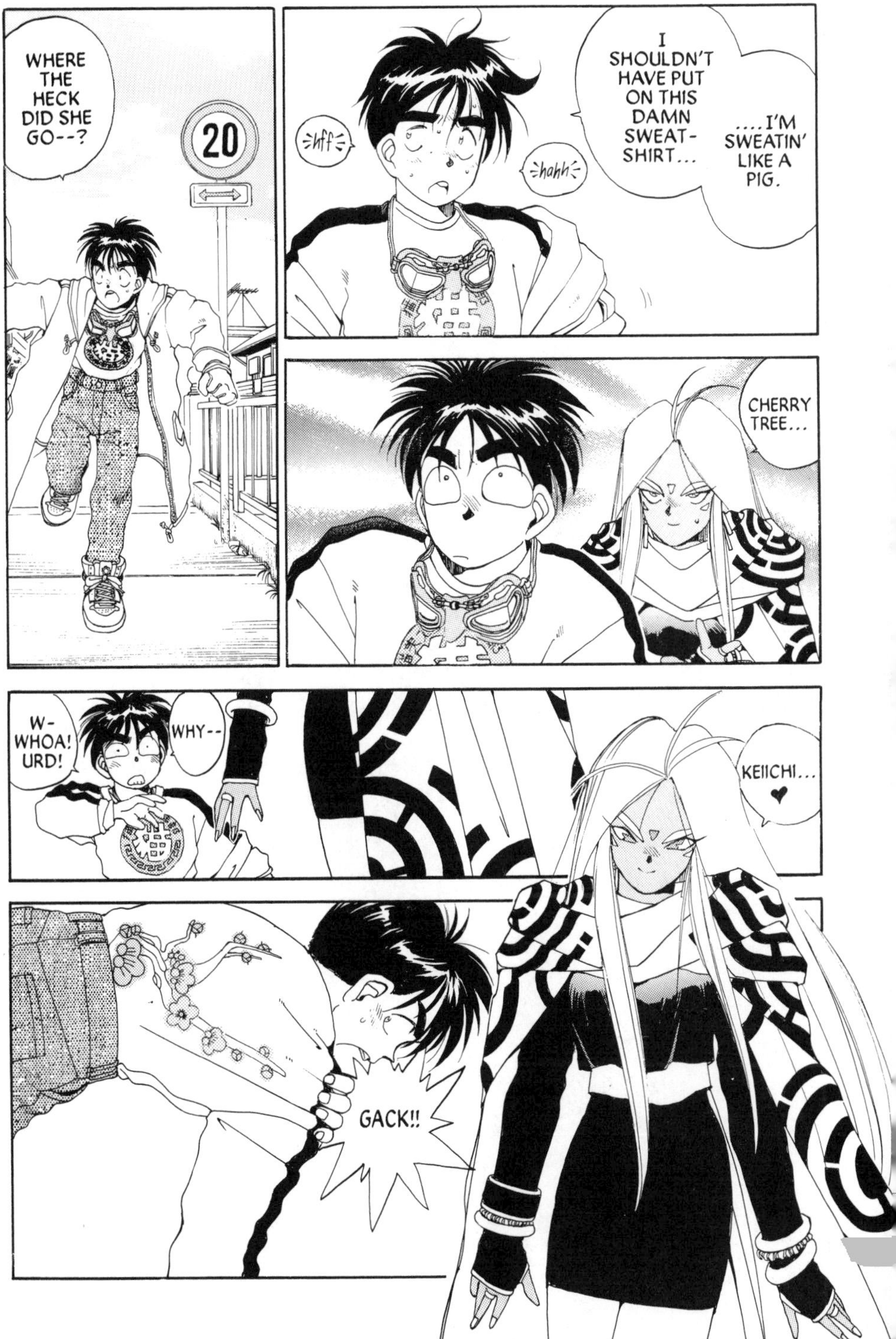
WHERE THE HECK DID SHE GO--?
20
hff
hahh
I SHOULDN'T HAVE PUT ON THIS DAMN SWEAT-SHIRT...
....I'M SWEATIN' LIKE A PIG.
CHERRY TREE...
W-WHOA! URD!
WHY--
KEIICHI... ♥
GACK!!

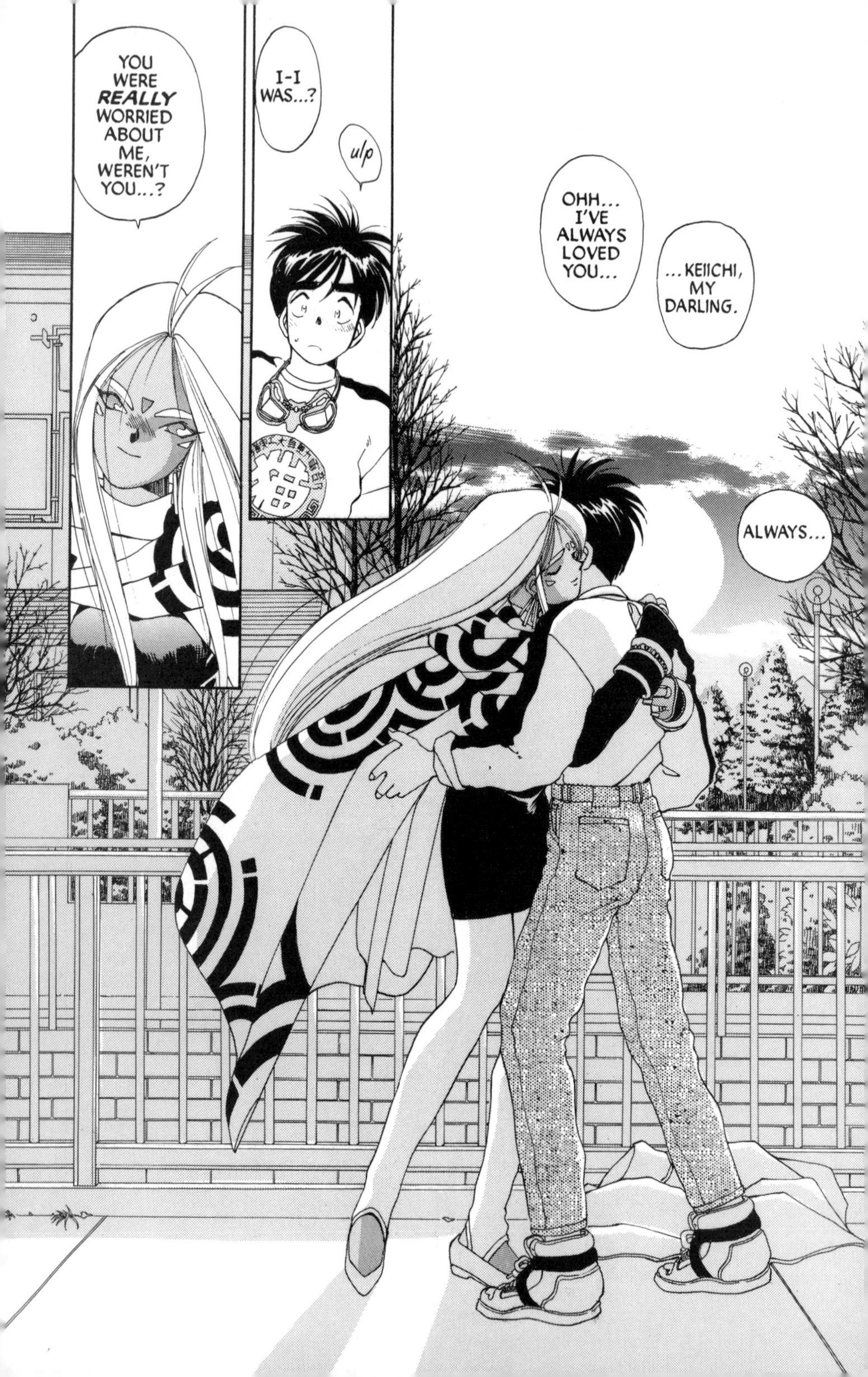
YOU WERE ***REALLY*** WORRIED ABOUT ME, WEREN'T YOU...?
I-I WAS...?
u/p
OHH... I'VE ALWAYS LOVED YOU...
...KEIICHI, MY DARLING.
ALWAYS...

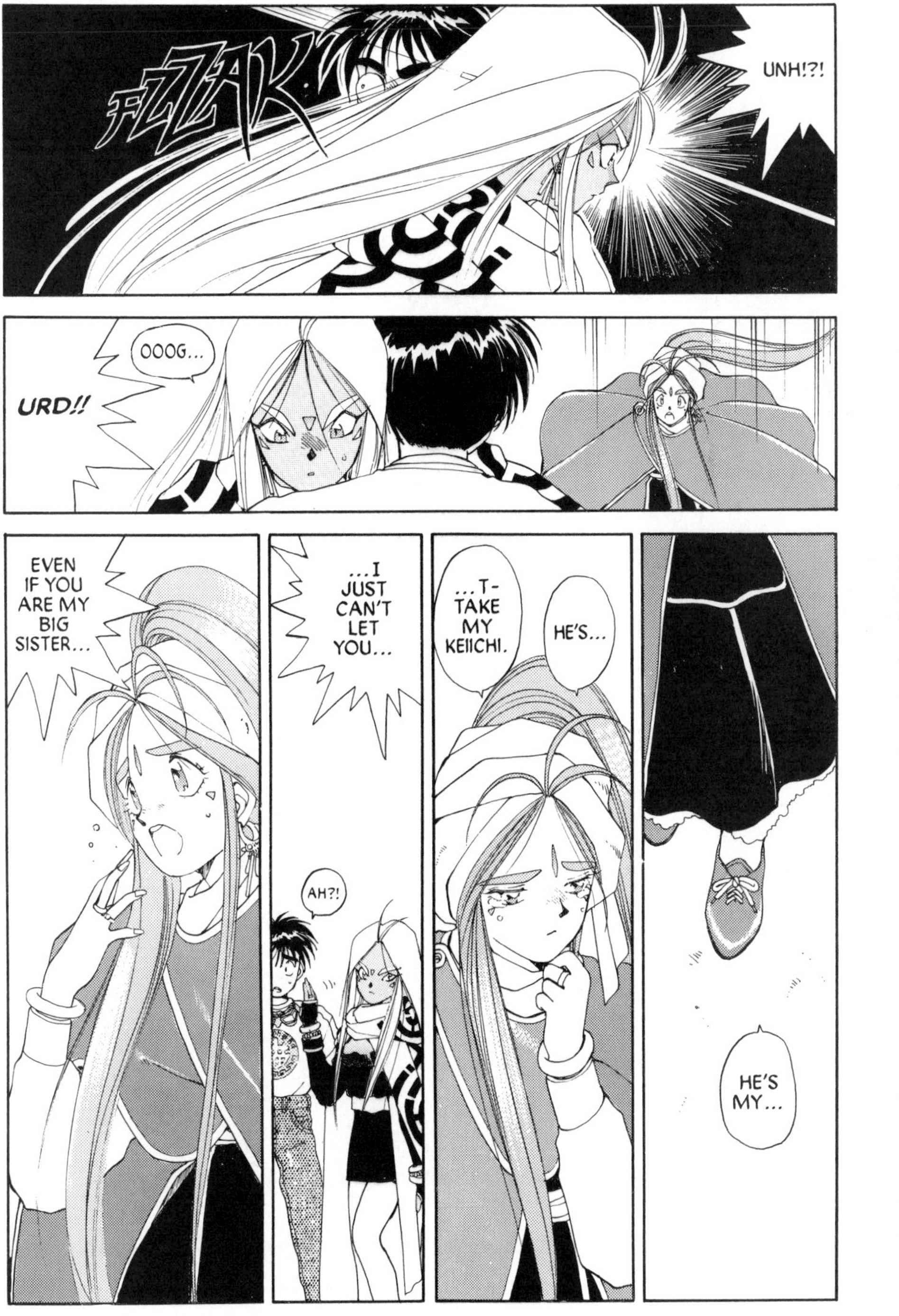
FZZAK
UNH!?!
URD!!
OOOG...
EVEN IF YOU ARE MY BIG SISTER...
...I JUST CAN'T LET YOU...
AH?!
...T-TAKE MY KEIICHI.
HE'S...
HE'S MY...

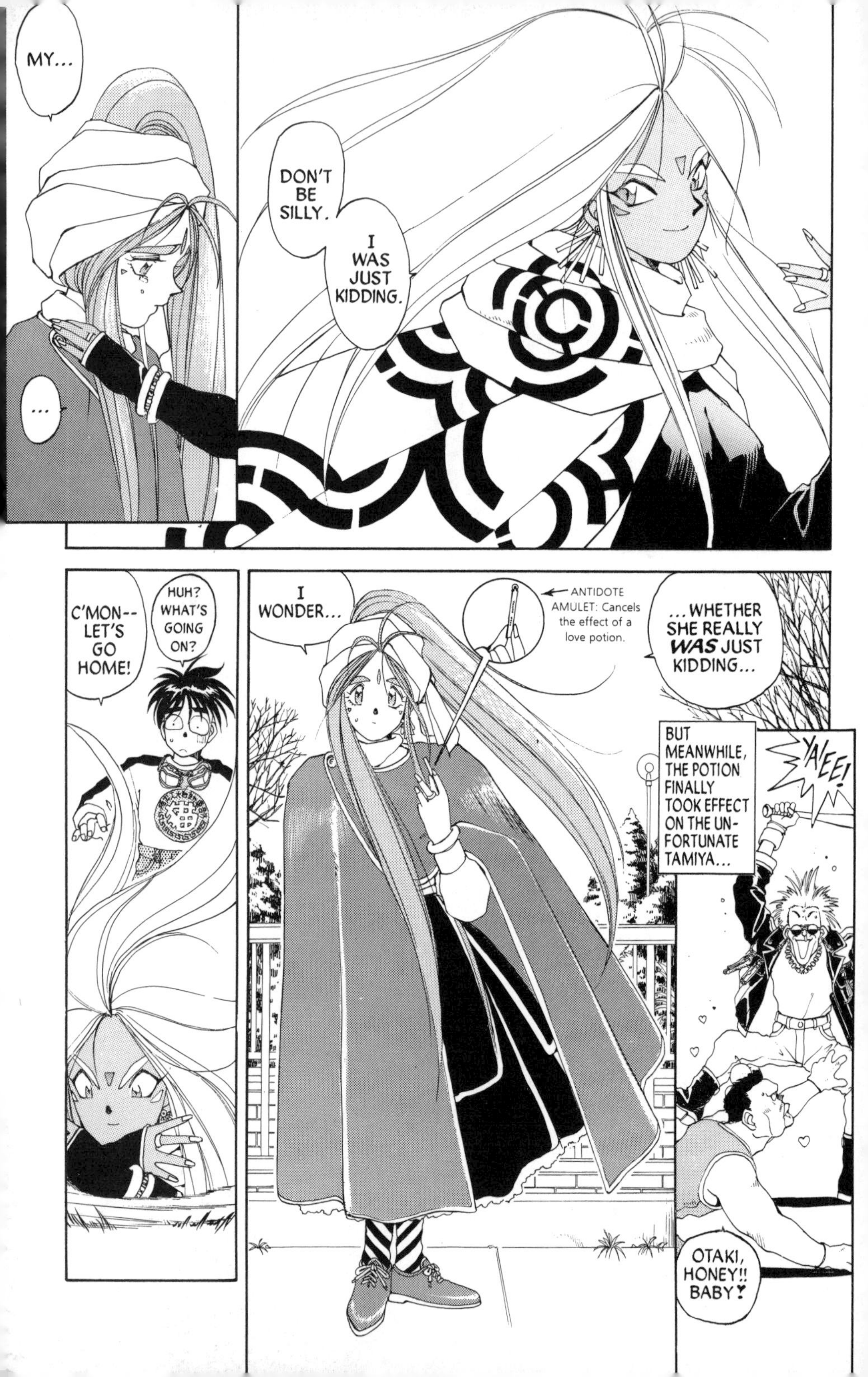
MY...
...
DON'T BE SILLY.
I WAS JUST KIDDING.
C'MON-- LET'S GO HOME!
HUH? WHAT'S GOING ON?
I WONDER...
ANTIDOTE AMULET: Cancels the effect of a love potion.
...WHETHER SHE REALLY WAS JUST KIDDING...
BUT MEANWHILE, THE POTION FINALLY TOOK EFFECT ON THE UNFORTUNATE TAMIYA...
YAIEE!
OTAKI, HONEY!! BABY!

THE CD FROM HELL

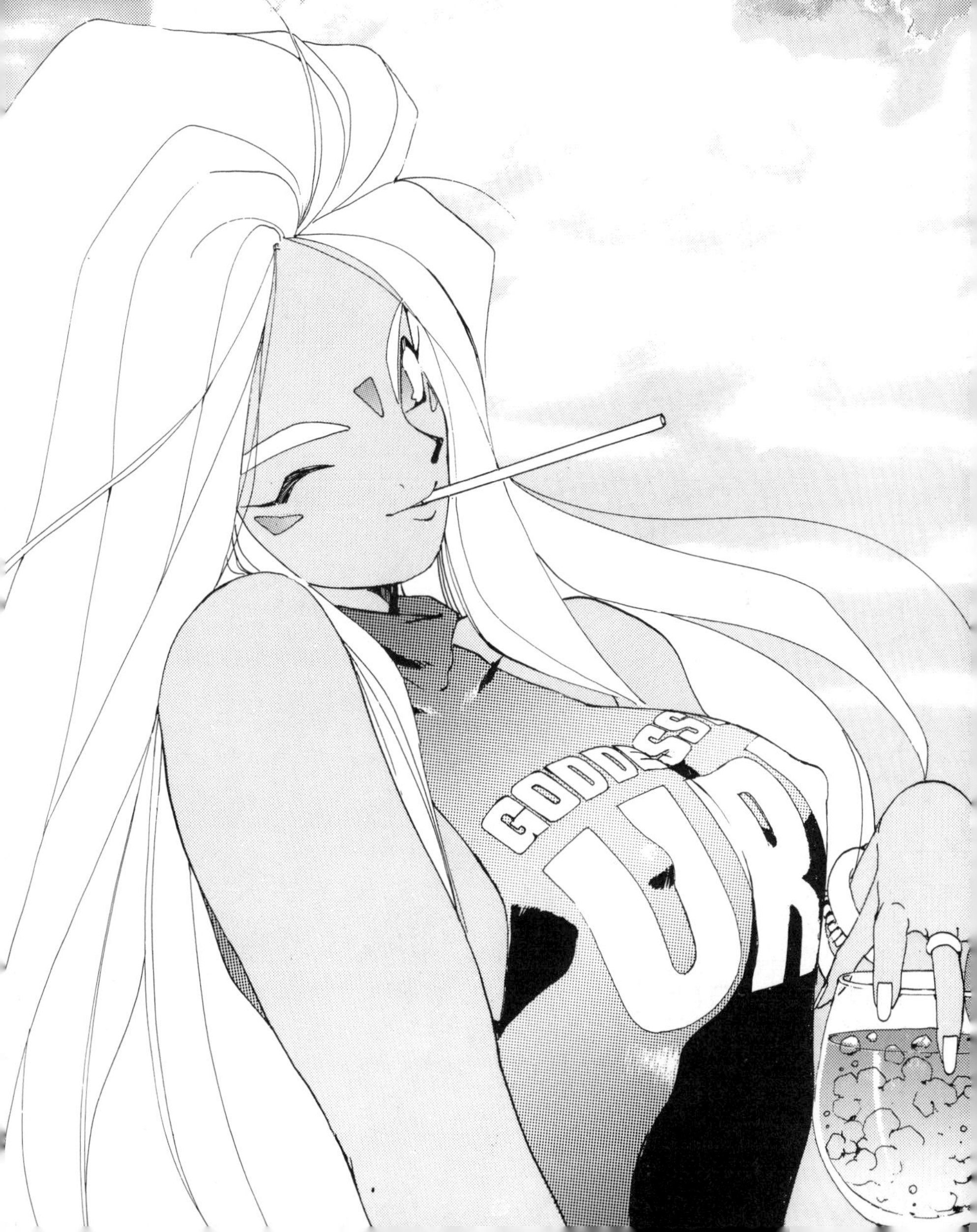
GODDESS
URD

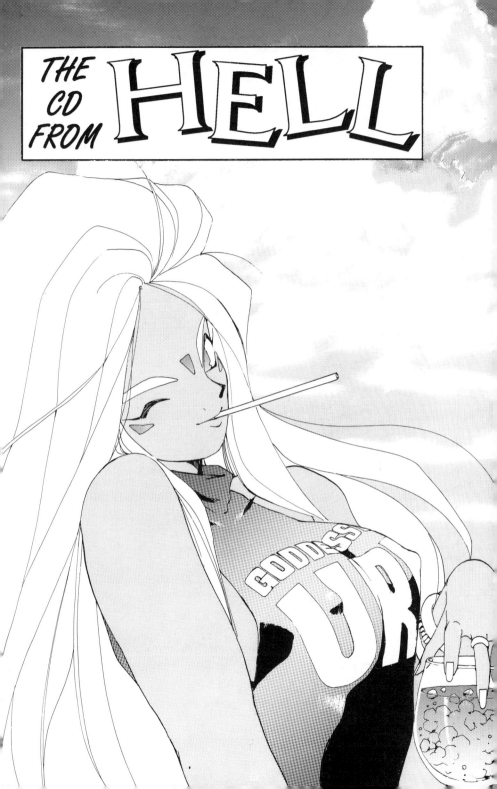

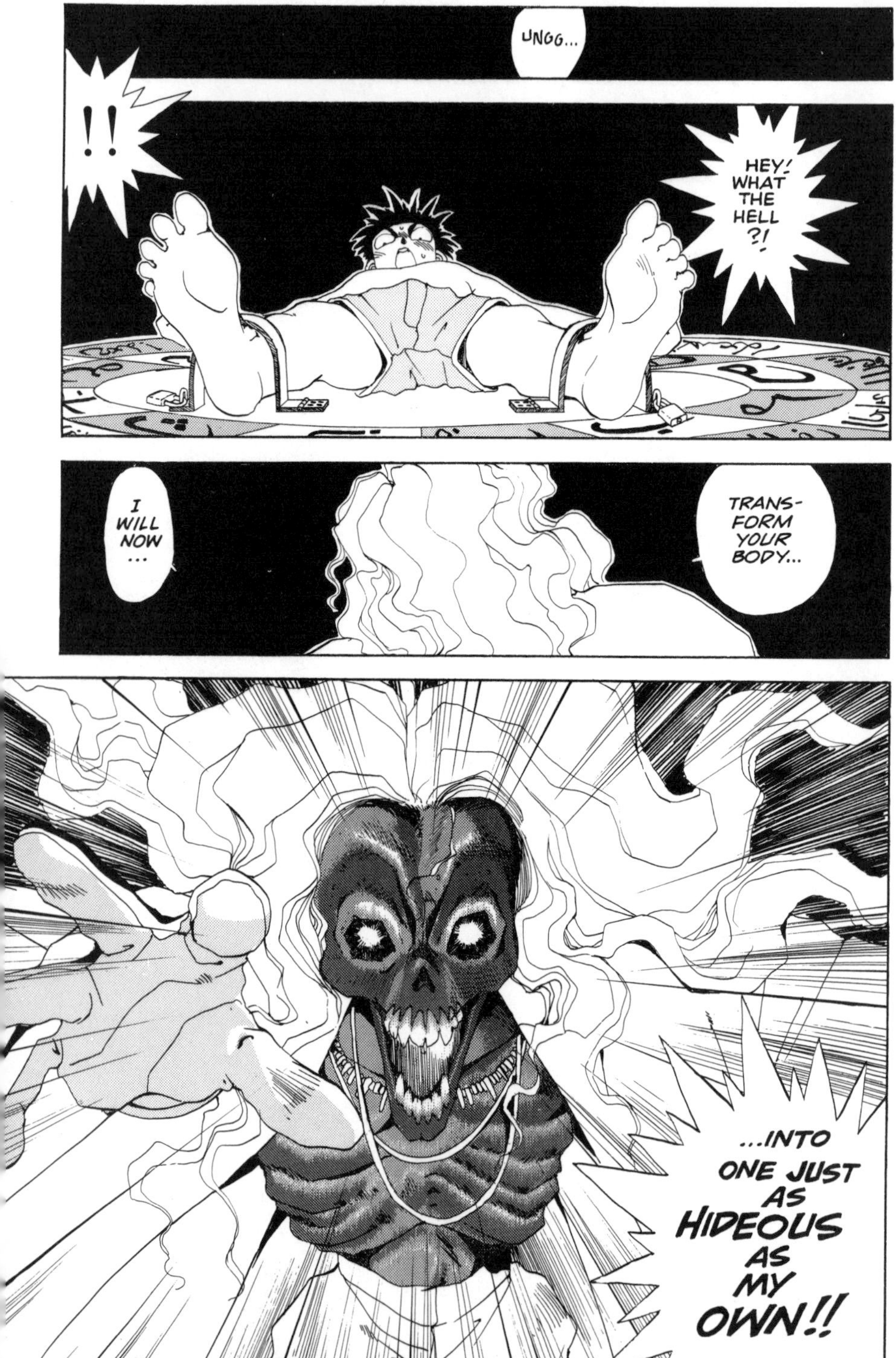
UNGG...
!!
HEY! WHAT THE HELL ?!
I WILL NOW ...
TRANS-FORM YOUR BODY...
...INTO ONE JUST AS HIDEOUS AS MY OWN!!

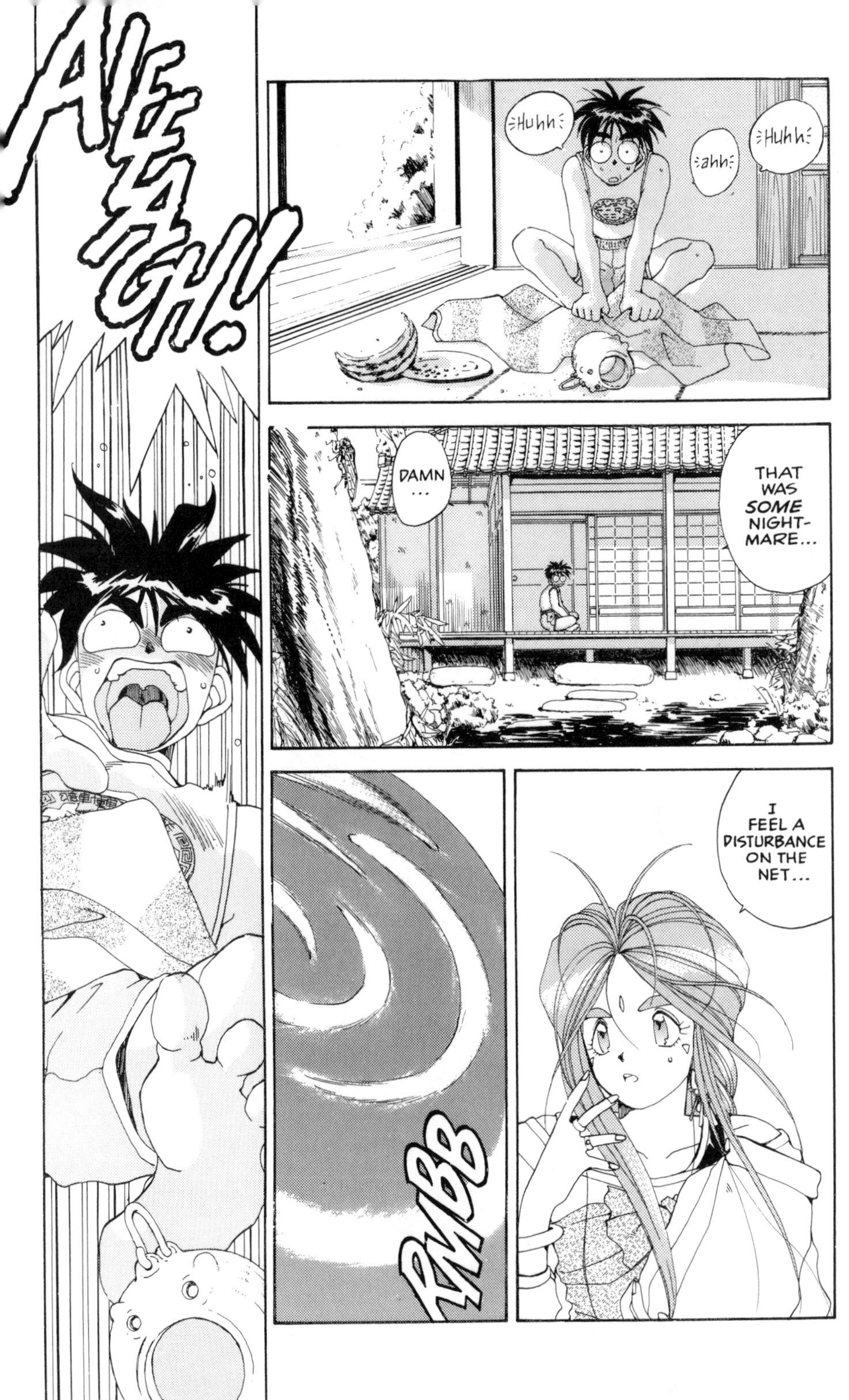
AIEEAGH!!
Huhh
ahh
Huhh
DAMN ...
THAT WAS SOME NIGHT-MARE...
RMBB
I FEEL A DISTURBANCE ON THE NET...

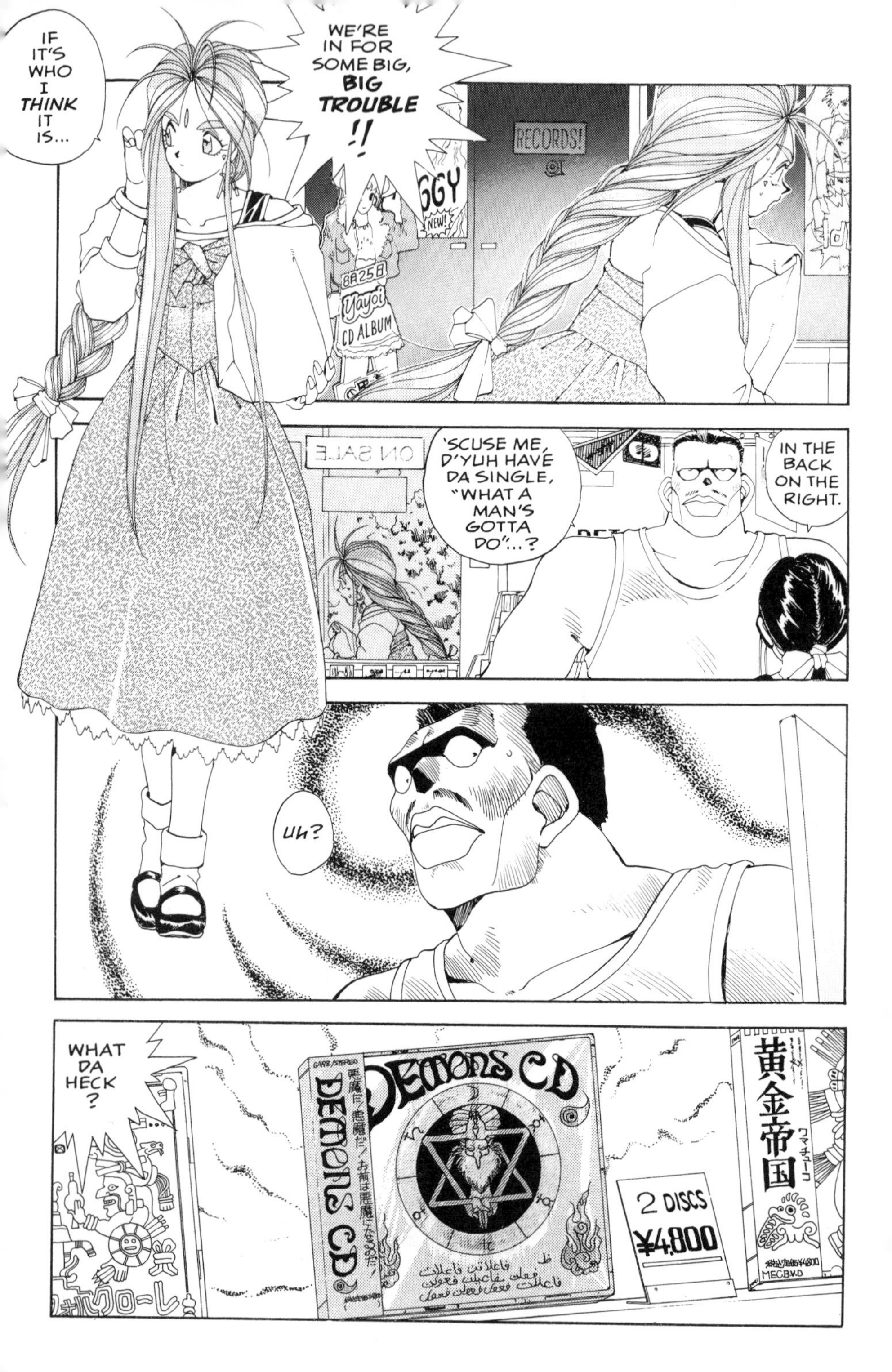
IF IT'S WHO I *THINK* IT IS...
WE'RE IN FOR SOME BIG, **BIG TROUBLE** !!
RECORDS!
GGY
NEW!
8月25日
Yayoi
CD ALBUM
'SCUSE ME, D'YUH HAVE DA SINGLE, "WHAT A MAN'S GOTTA DO"...?
IN THE BACK ON THE RIGHT.
UH?
WHAT DA HECK?
DEMONS CD
DEMONS CD
2 DISCS
¥4,800
黄金帝国
MEC.B.V.D

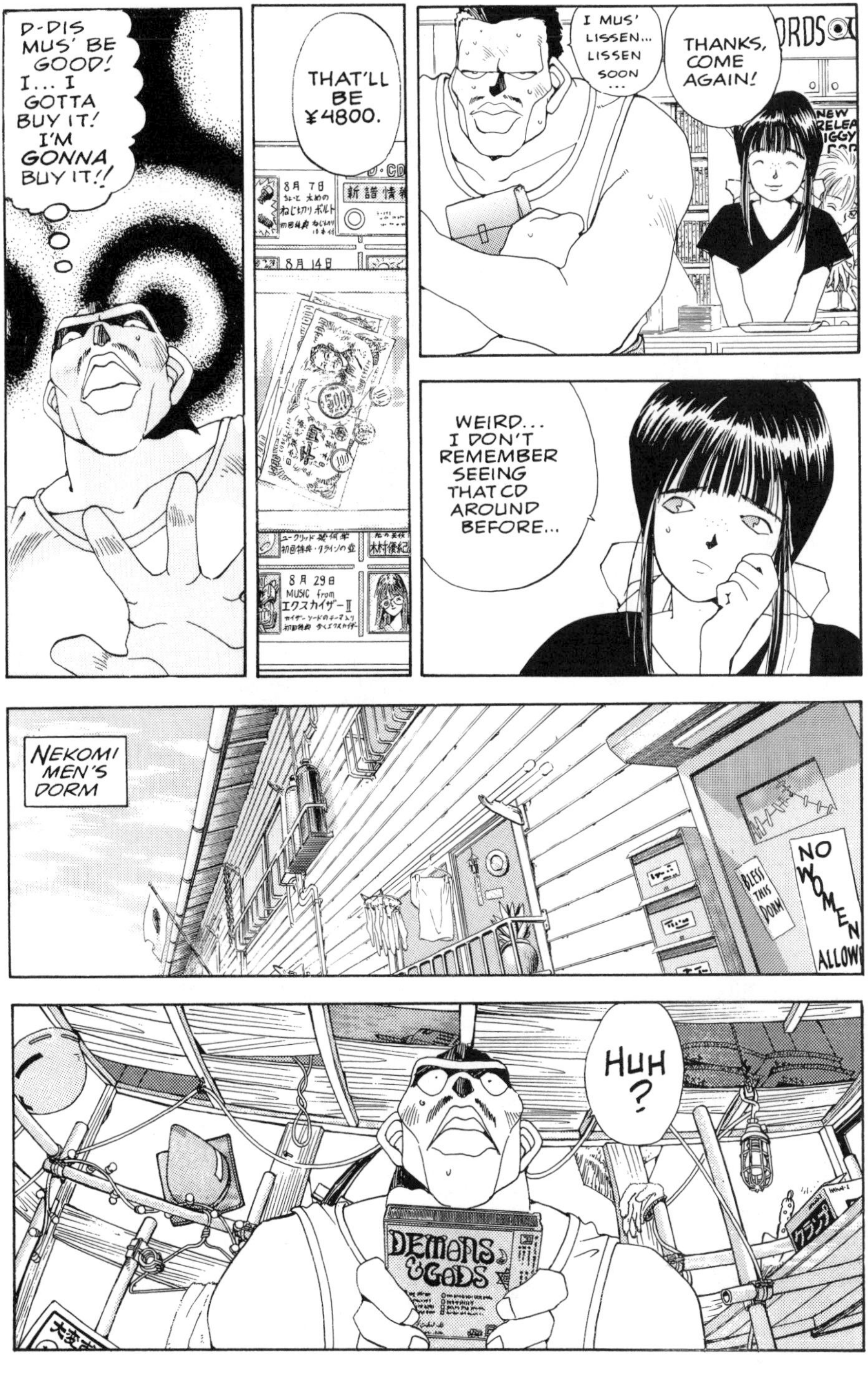
D-DIS MUS' BE GOOD! I... I GOTTA BUY IT! I'M GONNA BUY IT!!
THAT'LL BE ¥4800.
I MUS' LISSEN... LISSEN SOON...
THANKS, COME AGAIN!
WEIRD... I DON'T REMEMBER SEEING THAT CD AROUND BEFORE...
NEKOMI MEN'S DORM
BLESS THIS DORM
NO WOMEN ALLOW
HUH?
DEMONS & GODS

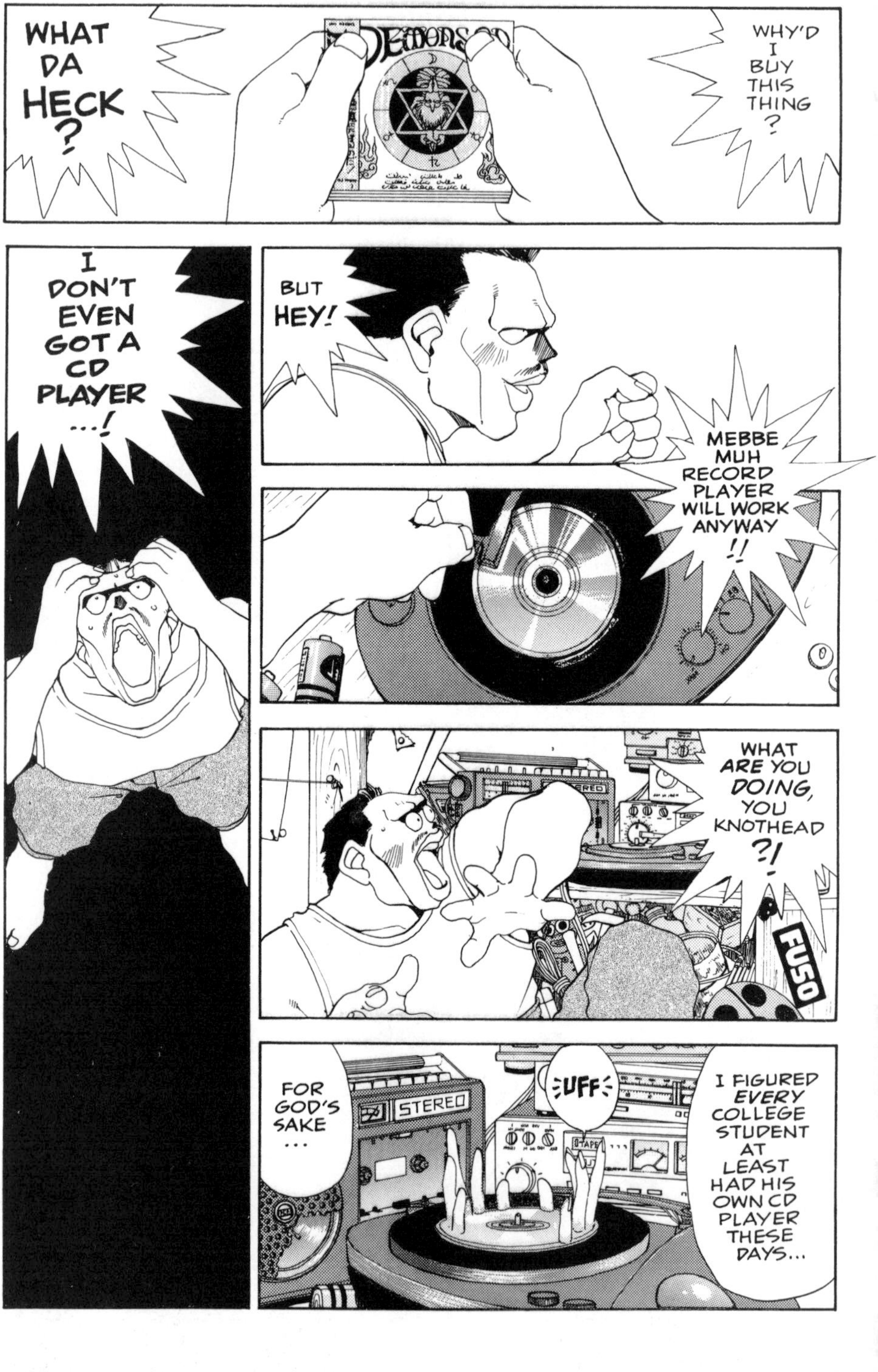
WHAT DA HECK?
DEMONS CD
WHY'D I BUY THIS THING?
I DON'T EVEN GOT A CD PLAYER...!
BUT HEY!
MEBBE MUH RECORD PLAYER WILL WORK ANYWAY!!
WHAT ARE YOU DOING, YOU KNOTHEAD?!
FUSO
STEREO
FOR GOD'S SAKE...
UFF
I FIGURED EVERY COLLEGE STUDENT AT LEAST HAD HIS OWN CD PLAYER THESE DAYS...

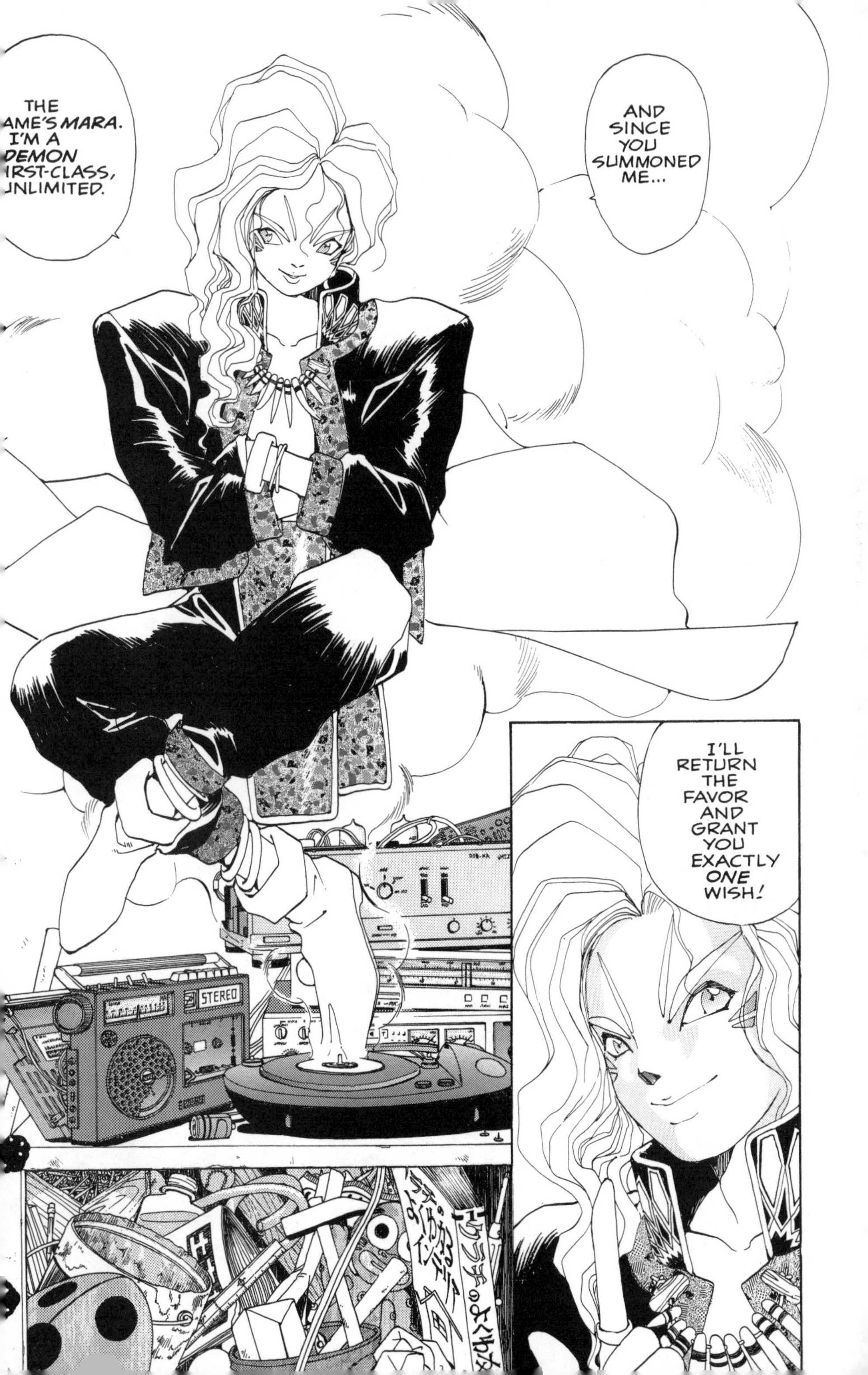
THE AME'S MARA. I'M A DEMON IRST-CLASS, JNLIMITED.
AND SINCE YOU SUMMONED ME...
I'LL RETURN THE FAVOR AND GRANT YOU EXACTLY ONE WISH!

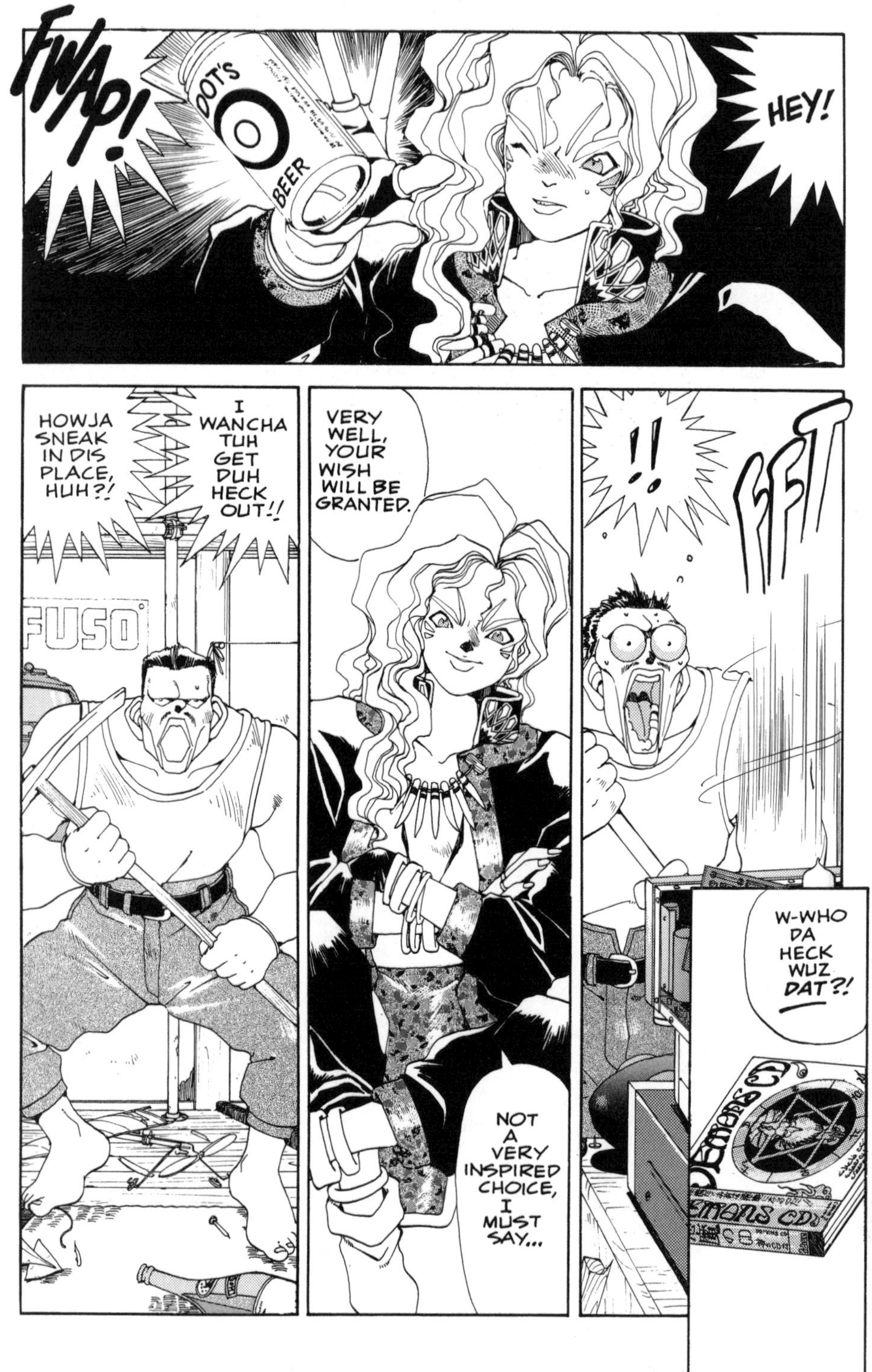
FWAP!
DOT'S
BEER
HEY!
HOWJA SNEAK IN DIS PLACE, HUH?!
I WANCHA TUH GET DUH HECK OUT!!
FUSO
VERY WELL, YOUR WISH WILL BE GRANTED.
NOT A VERY INSPIRED CHOICE, I MUST SAY...
!!
FFT
W-WHO DA HECK WUZ DAT?!
DEMONS CD

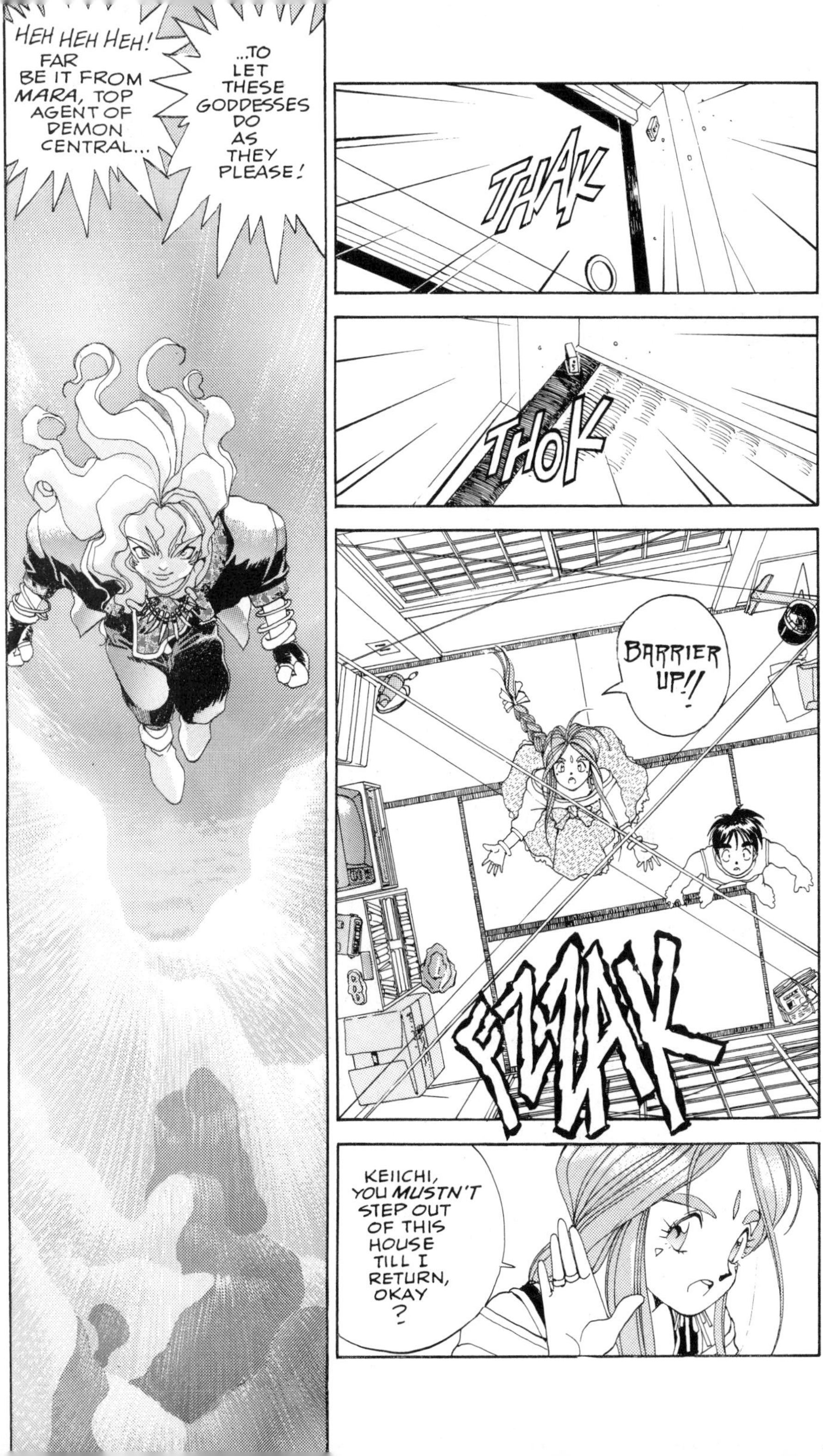
HEH HEH HEH! FAR BE IT FROM MARA, TOP AGENT OF DEMON CENTRAL...
...TO LET THESE GODDESSES DO AS THEY PLEASE!
THAK
THOK
BARRIER UP!!
FZZAK
KEIICHI, YOU MUSTN'T STEP OUT OF THIS HOUSE TILL I RETURN, OKAY?

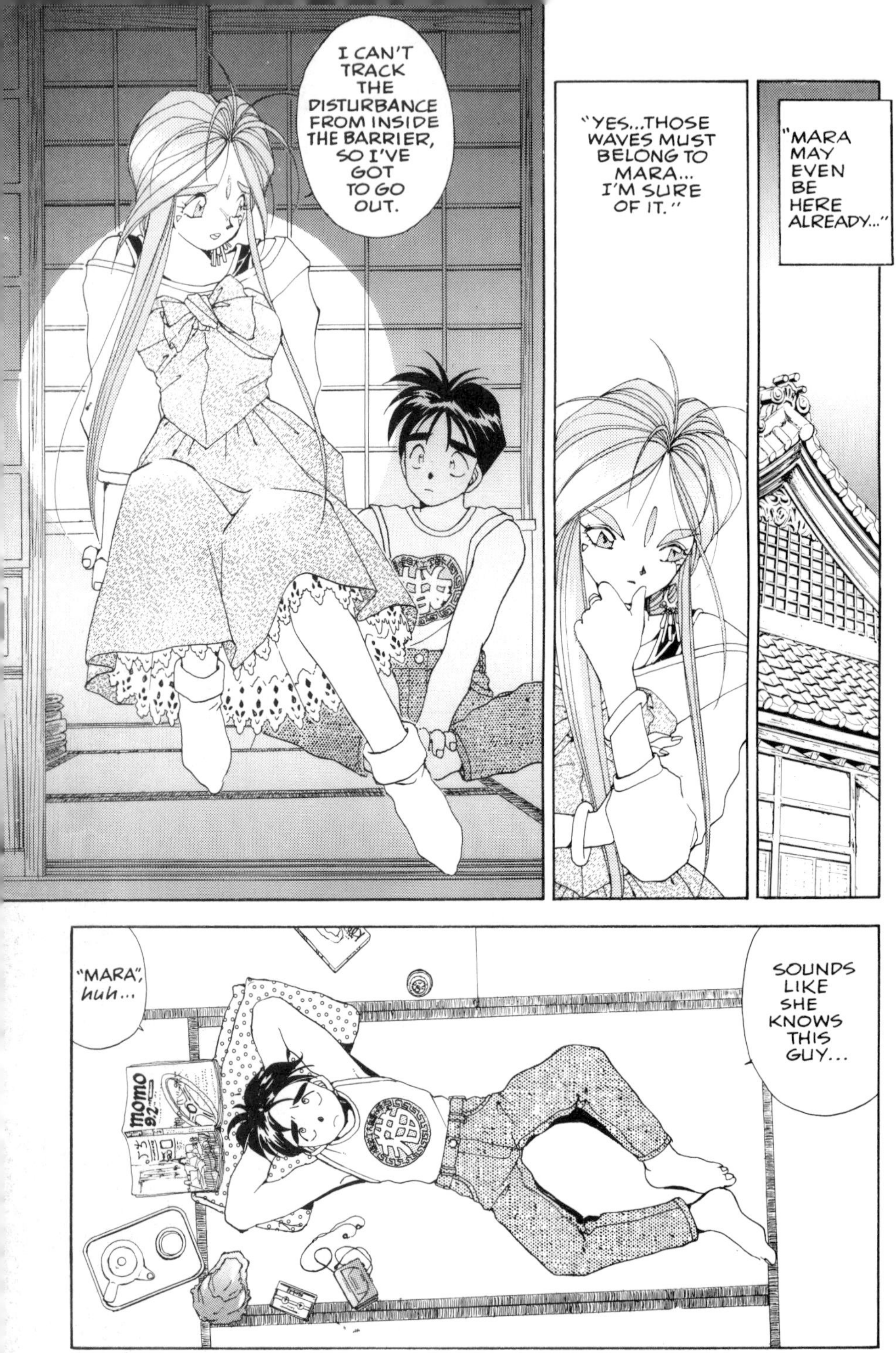
I CAN'T TRACK THE DISTURBANCE FROM INSIDE THE BARRIER, SO I'VE GOT TO GO OUT.
"YES...THOSE WAVES MUST BELONG TO MARA... I'M SURE OF IT."
"MARA MAY EVEN BE HERE ALREADY..."
"MARA", huh...
SOUNDS LIKE SHE KNOWS THIS GUY...

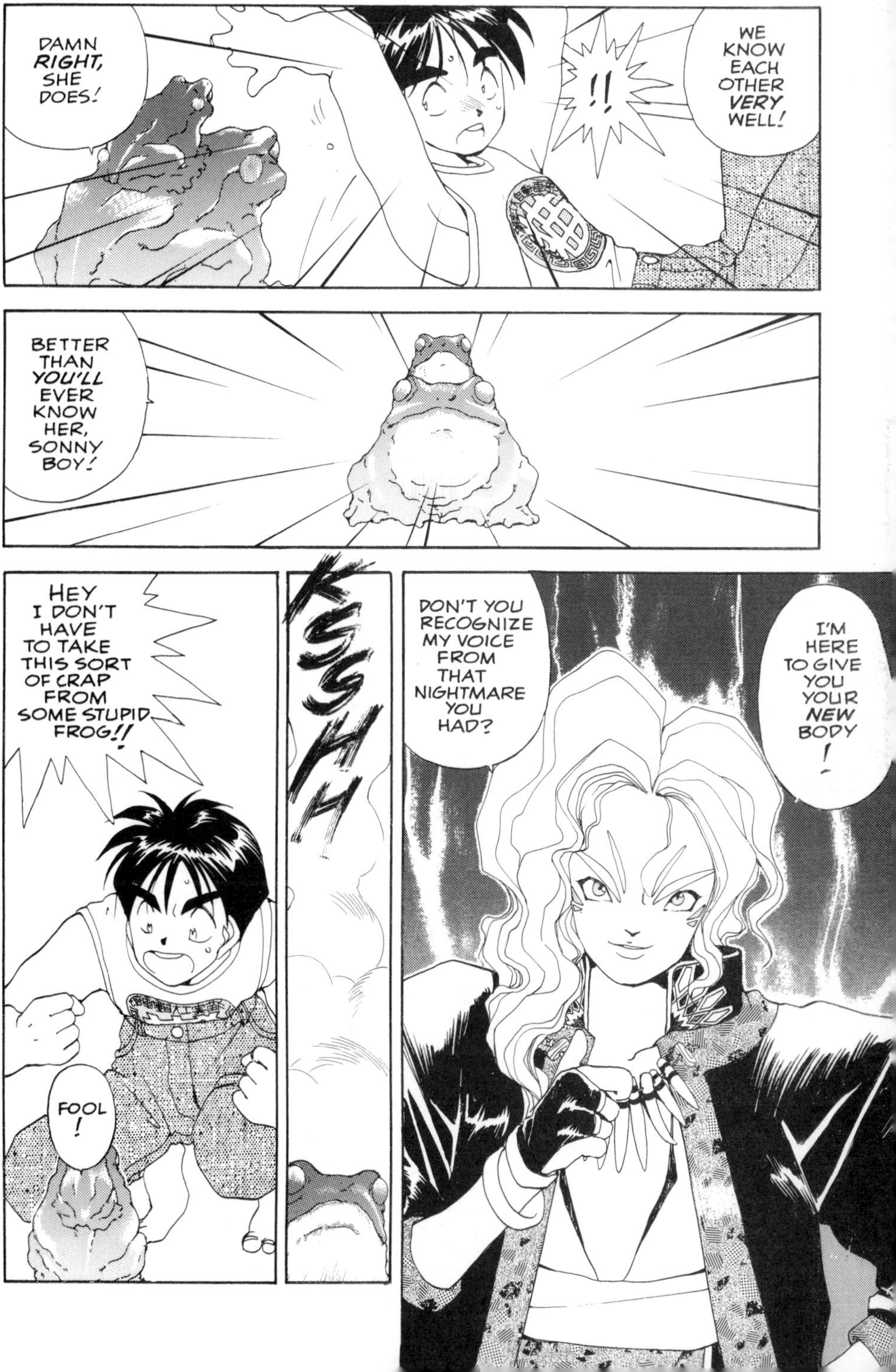

DAMN RIGHT, SHE DOES!
!!
WE KNOW EACH OTHER VERY WELL!
BETTER THAN YOU'LL EVER KNOW HER, SONNY BOY!
HEY I DON'T HAVE TO TAKE THIS SORT OF CRAP FROM SOME STUPID FROG!!
FOOL!
KSSHH
DON'T YOU RECOGNIZE MY VOICE FROM THAT NIGHTMARE YOU HAD?
I'M HERE TO GIVE YOU YOUR NEW BODY!

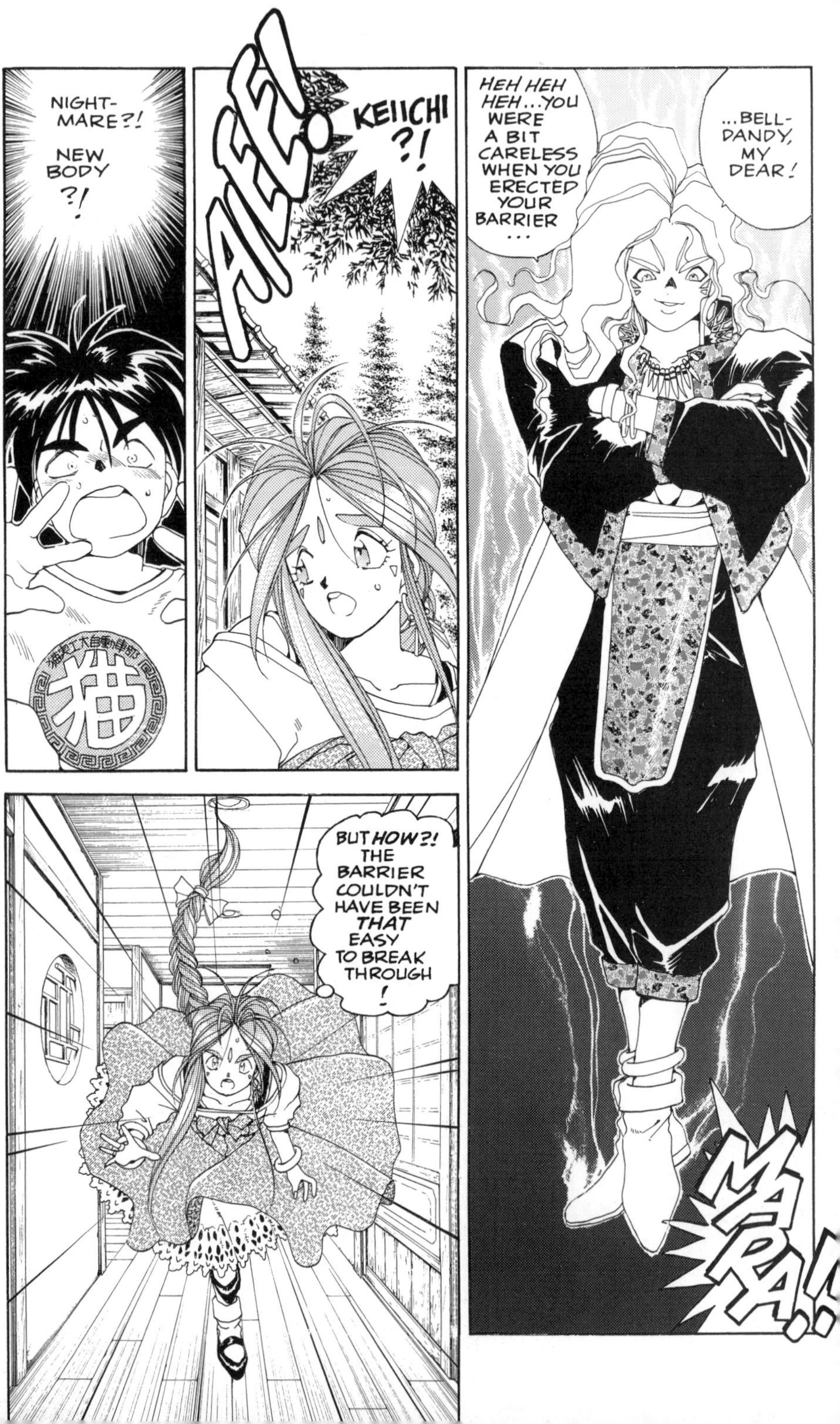
NIGHT-MARE?!
NEW BODY ?!
AIEE!
KEIICHI ?!
BUT *HOW*?! THE BARRIER COULDN'T HAVE BEEN *THAT* EASY TO BREAK THROUGH!
HEH HEH HEH...YOU WERE A BIT CARELESS WHEN YOU ERECTED YOUR BARRIER...
...BELL-DANDY, MY DEAR!
MARA!!

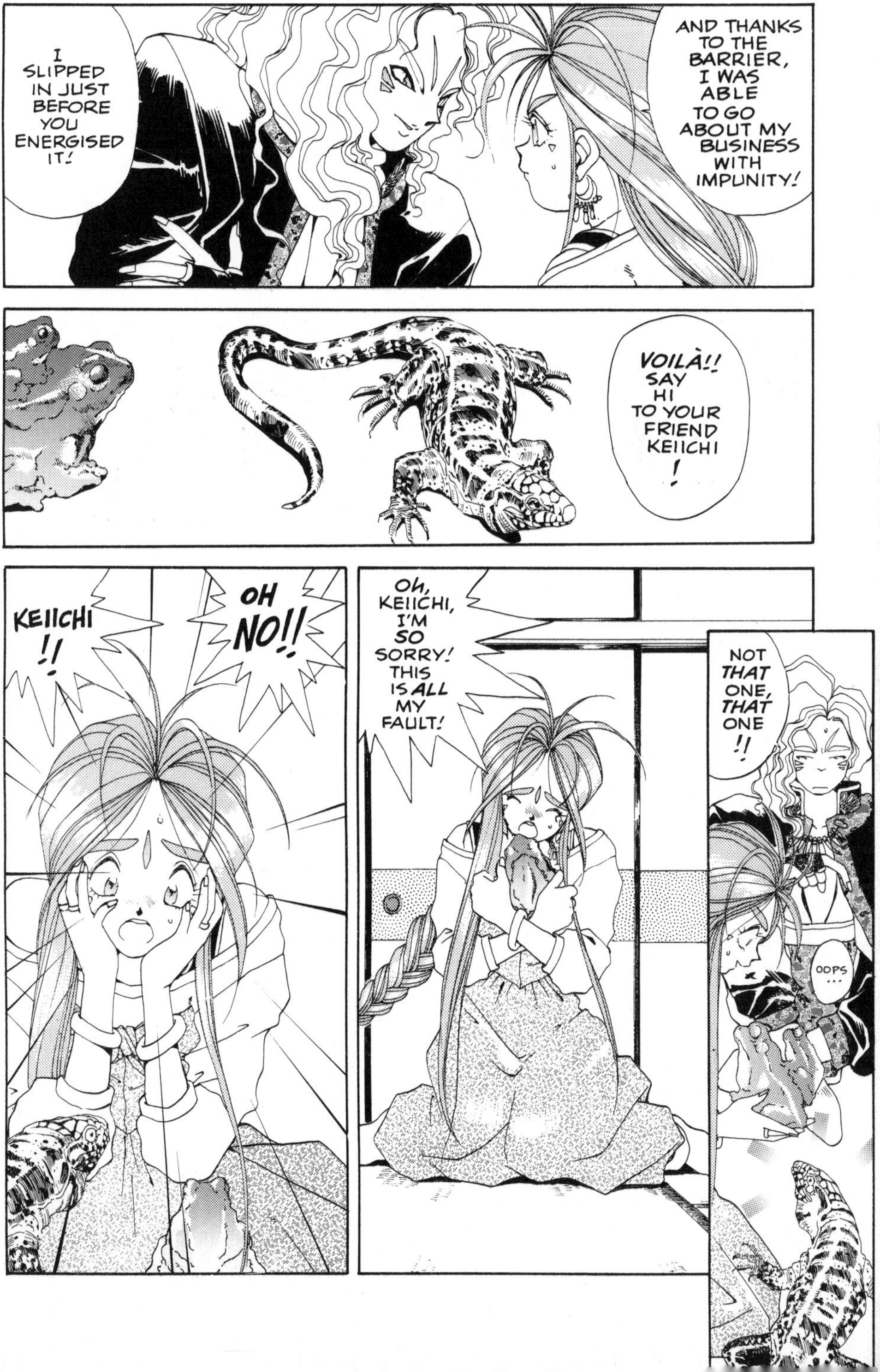
AND THANKS TO THE BARRIER, I WAS ABLE TO GO ABOUT MY BUSINESS WITH IMPUNITY!
I SLIPPED IN JUST BEFORE YOU ENERGISED IT!
VOILÀ!! SAY HI TO YOUR FRIEND KEIICHI !
OH NO!!
KEIICHI !!
Oh, KEIICHI, I'M SO SORRY! THIS IS ALL MY FAULT!
NOT THAT ONE, THAT ONE !!
OOPS ...

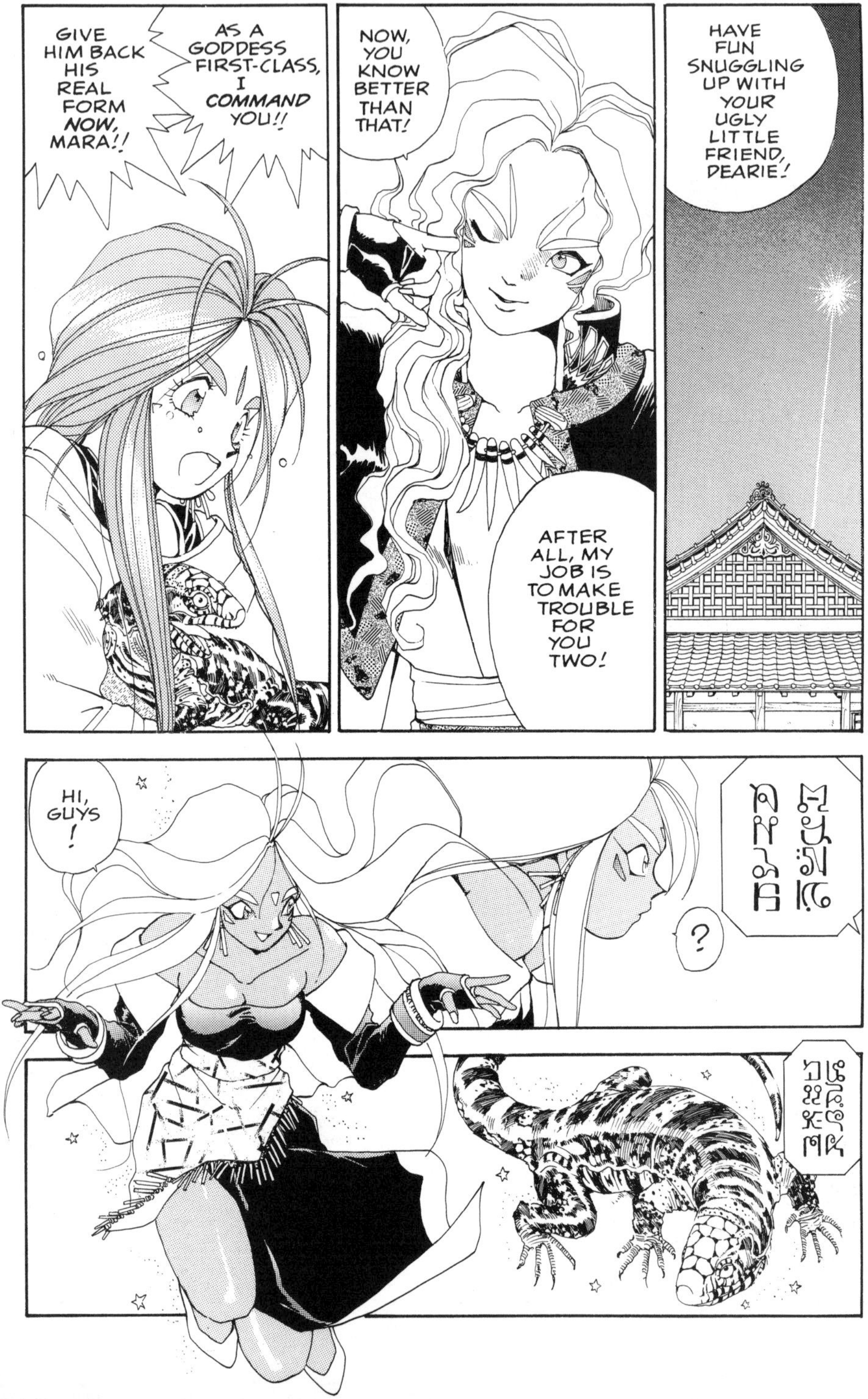
GIVE HIM BACK HIS REAL FORM *NOW*, MARA!!
AS A GODDESS FIRST-CLASS, I *COMMAND* YOU!!
NOW, YOU KNOW BETTER THAN THAT!
AFTER ALL, MY JOB IS TO MAKE TROUBLE FOR YOU TWO!
HAVE FUN SNUGGLING UP WITH *YOUR* UGLY LITTLE FRIEND, DEARIE!
HI, GUYS!
?

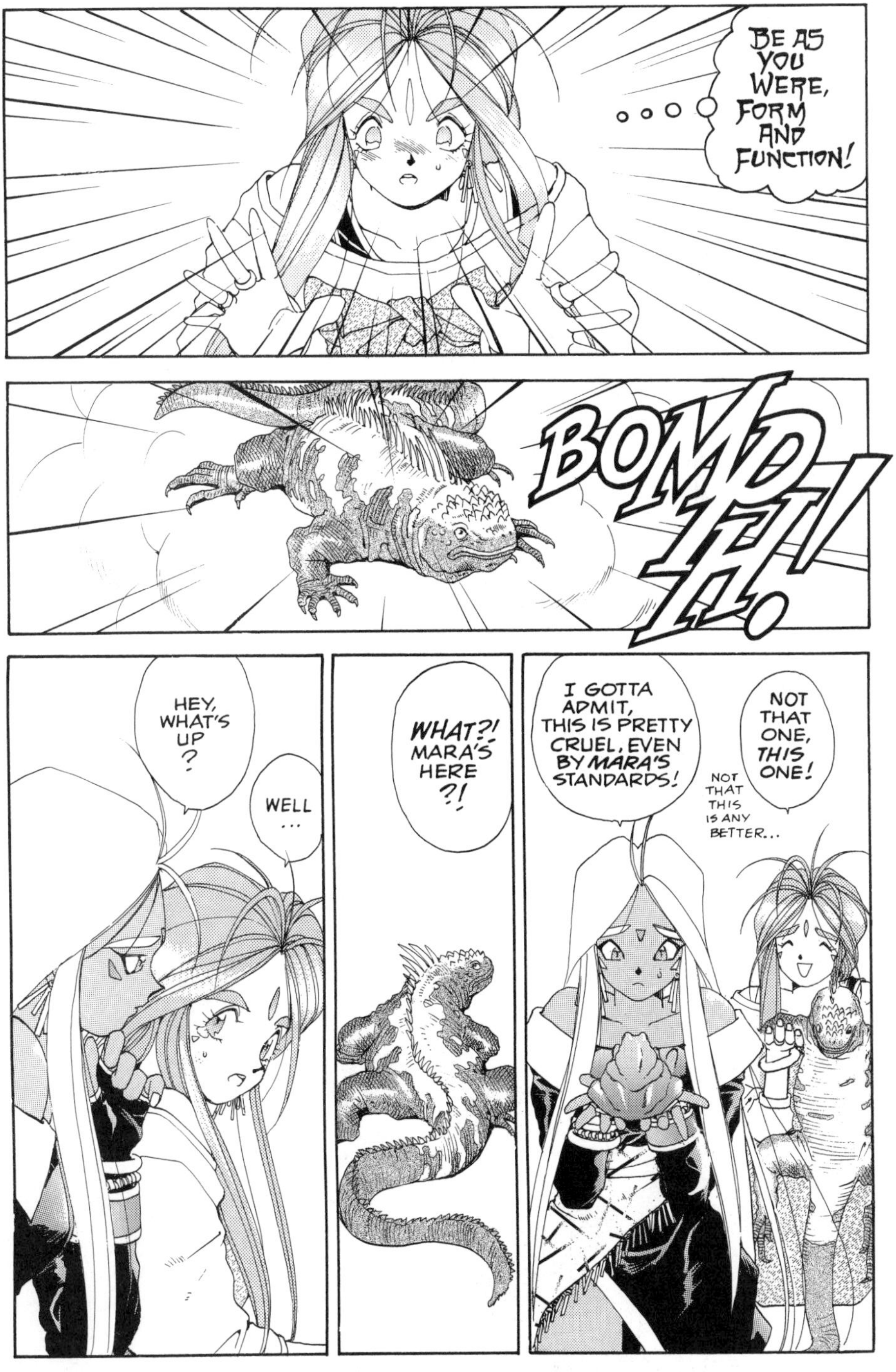
BE AS YOU WERE, FORM AND FUNCTION!
BOMPH!
HEY, WHAT'S UP?
WELL...
WHAT?! MARA'S HERE?!
I GOTTA ADMIT, THIS IS PRETTY CRUEL, EVEN BY MARA'S STANDARDS!
NOT THAT ONE, THIS ONE!
NOT THAT THIS IS ANY BETTER...

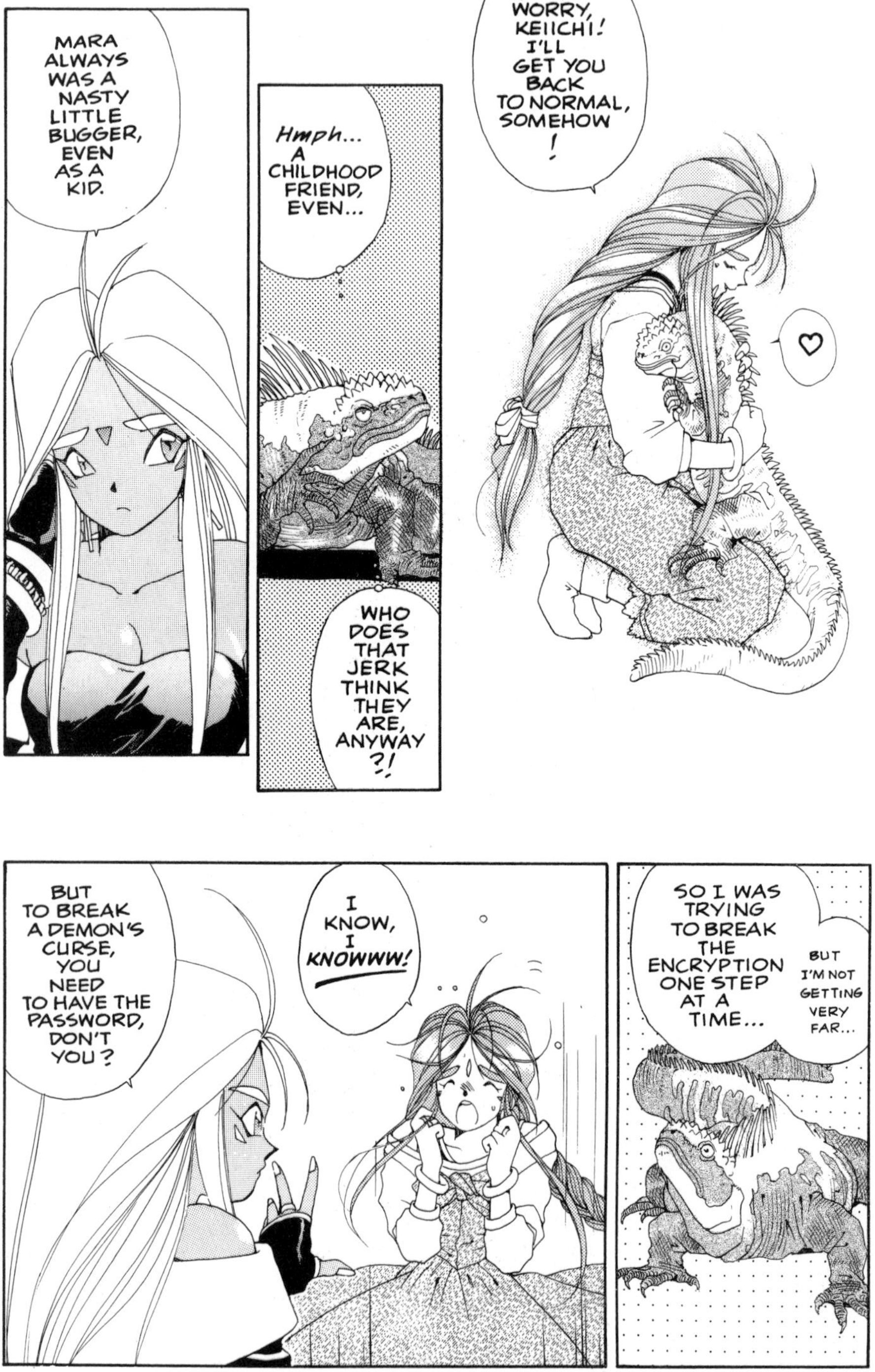
MARA ALWAYS WAS A NASTY LITTLE BUGGER, EVEN AS A KID.
Hmph... A CHILDHOOD FRIEND, EVEN...
WHO DOES THAT JERK THINK THEY ARE, ANYWAY ?!
DON'T WORRY, KEIICHI! I'LL GET YOU BACK TO NORMAL, SOMEHOW !
♡
BUT TO BREAK A DEMON'S CURSE, YOU NEED TO HAVE THE PASSWORD, DON'T YOU ?
I KNOW, I KNOWWW!
SO I WAS TRYING TO BREAK THE ENCRYPTION ONE STEP AT A TIME...
BUT I'M NOT GETTING VERY FAR...

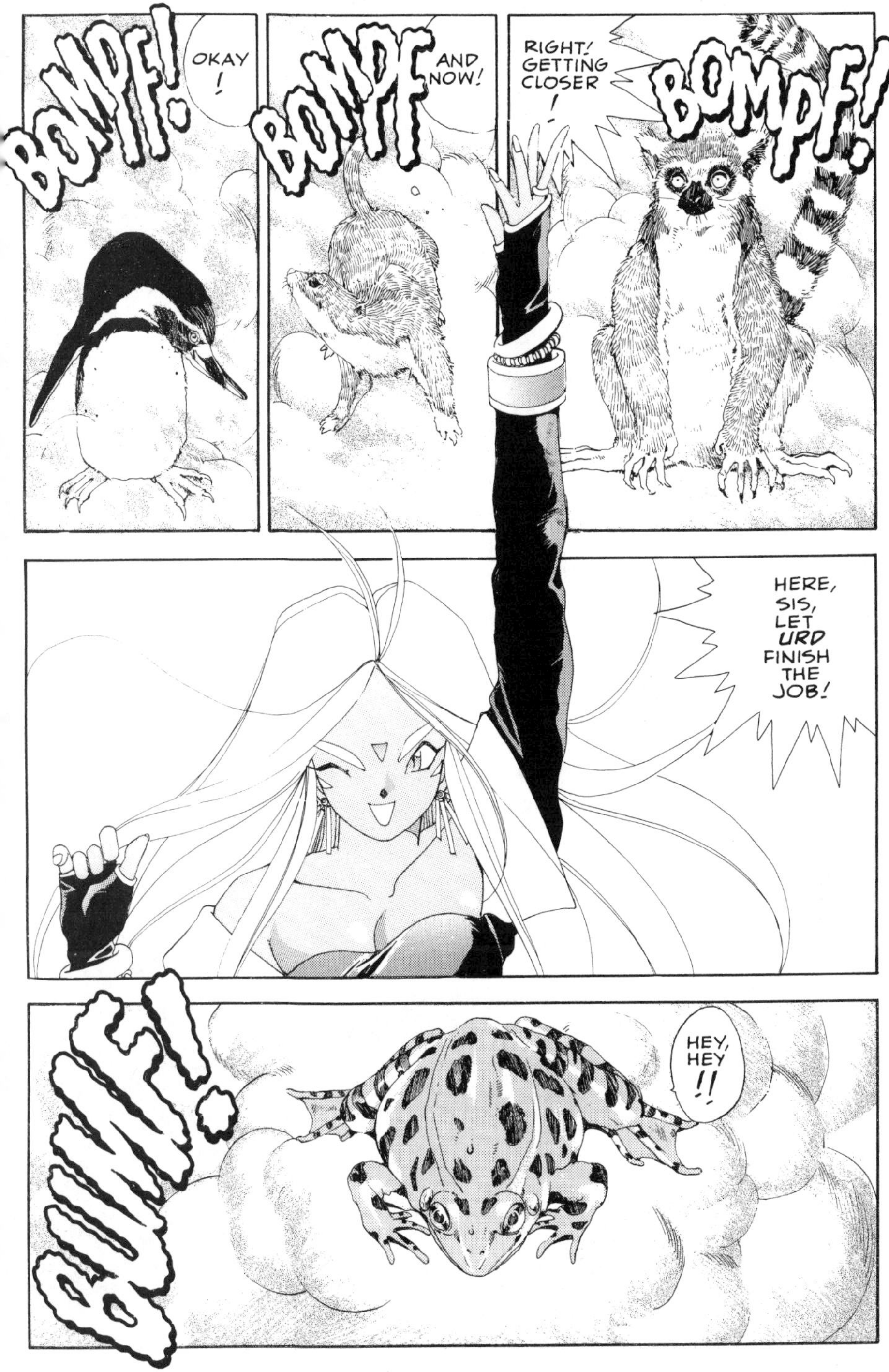
BOMPF!
OKAY!
BOMPF
AND NOW!
RIGHT! GETTING CLOSER!
BOMPF!
HERE, SIS, LET URD FINISH THE JOB!
BUMF!
HEY, HEY!!

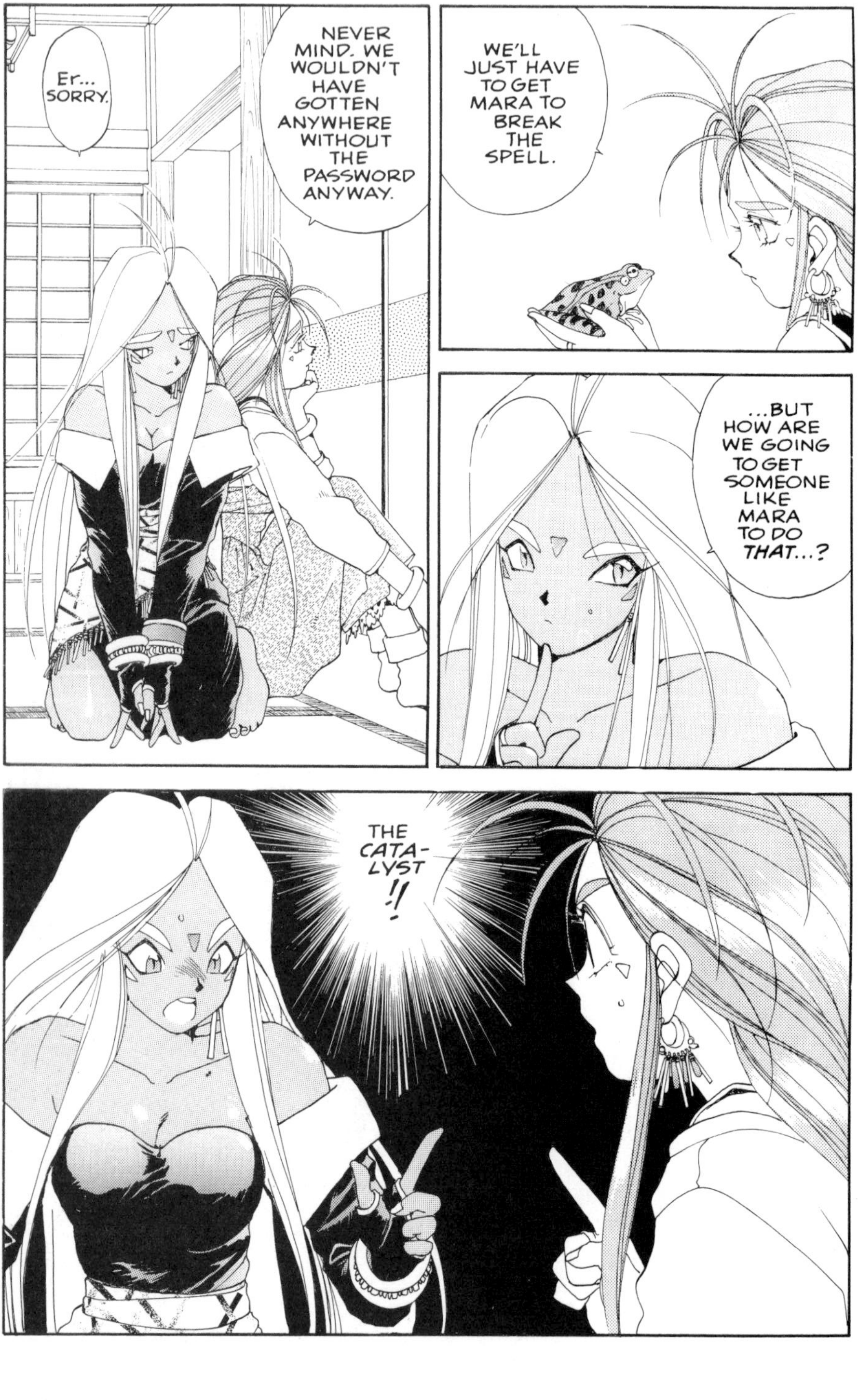
Er... SORRY.
NEVER MIND. WE WOULDN'T HAVE GOTTEN ANYWHERE WITHOUT THE PASSWORD ANYWAY.
WE'LL JUST HAVE TO GET MARA TO BREAK THE SPELL.
...BUT HOW ARE WE GOING TO GET SOMEONE LIKE MARA TO DO *THAT*...?
THE *CATA-LYST* !!

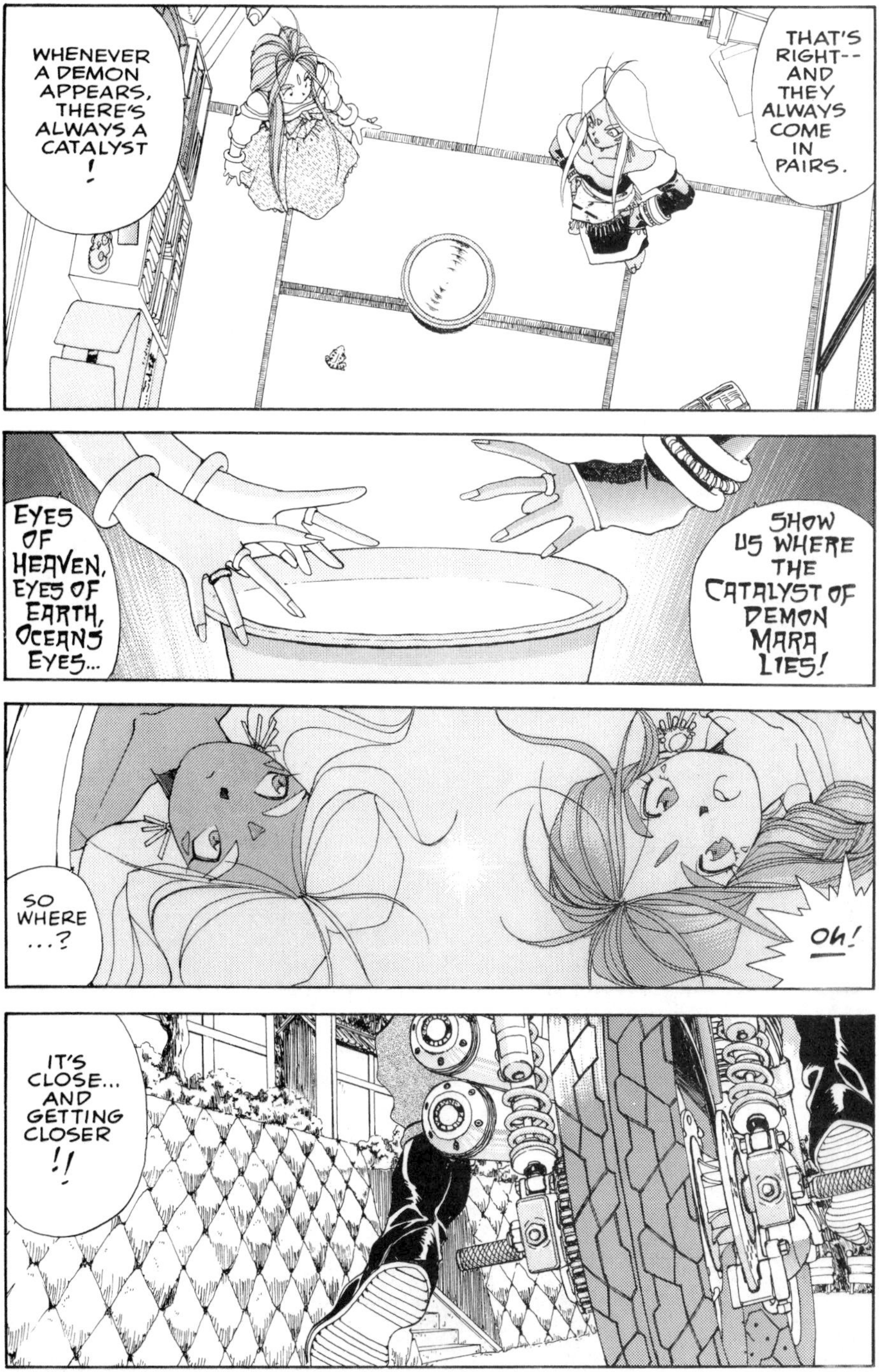
WHENEVER A DEMON APPEARS, THERE'S ALWAYS A CATALYST!
THAT'S RIGHT-- AND THEY ALWAYS COME IN PAIRS.
EYES OF HEAVEN, EYES OF EARTH, OCEANS EYES...
SHOW US WHERE THE CATALYST OF DEMON MARA LIES!
SO WHERE ...?
Oh!
IT'S CLOSE... AND GETTING CLOSER!!

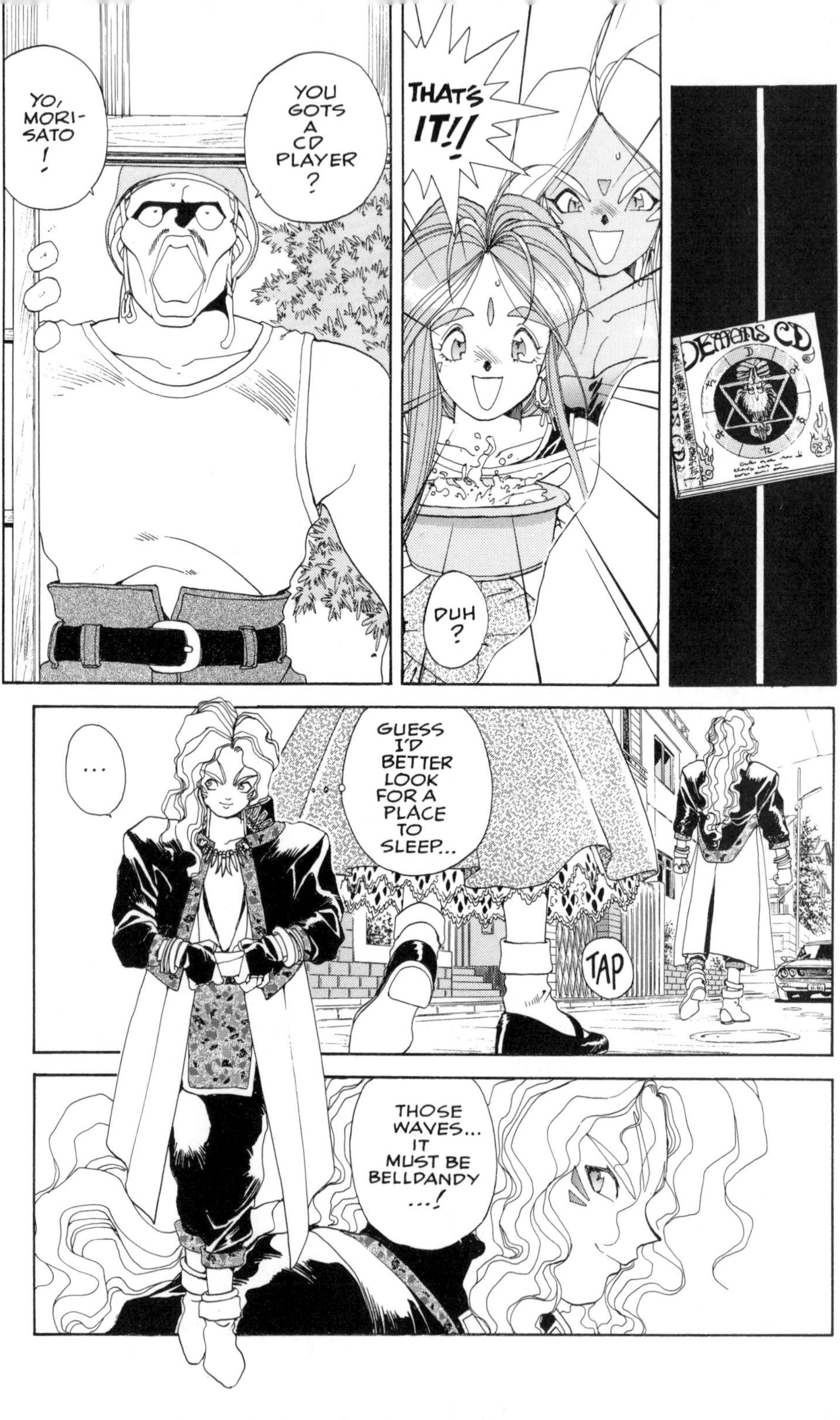
YO, MORI-SATO!
YOU GOTS A CD PLAYER?
THAT'S IT!!
DUH?
...
GUESS I'D BETTER LOOK FOR A PLACE TO SLEEP...
TAP
THOSE WAVES... IT MUST BE BELLDANDY...!

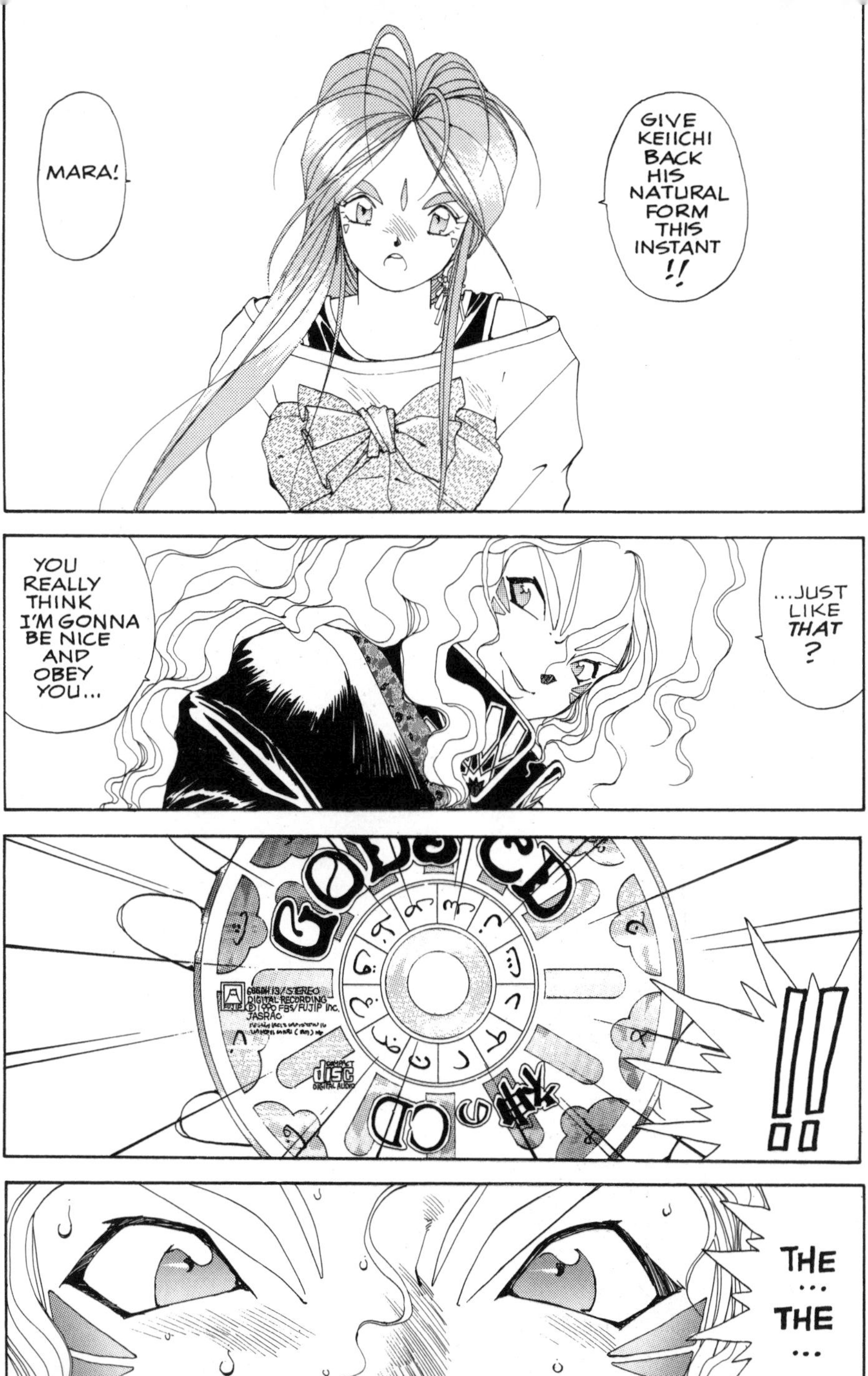
MARA!
GIVE KEIICHI BACK HIS NATURAL FORM THIS INSTANT !!
YOU REALLY THINK I'M GONNA BE NICE AND OBEY YOU...
...JUST LIKE *THAT*?
GODS CD
G86AH 13/STEREO
DIGITAL RECORDING
©1990 FBS/FUJIP Inc.
JASRAC
COMPACT disc DIGITAL AUDIO
!!
THE ... THE ...

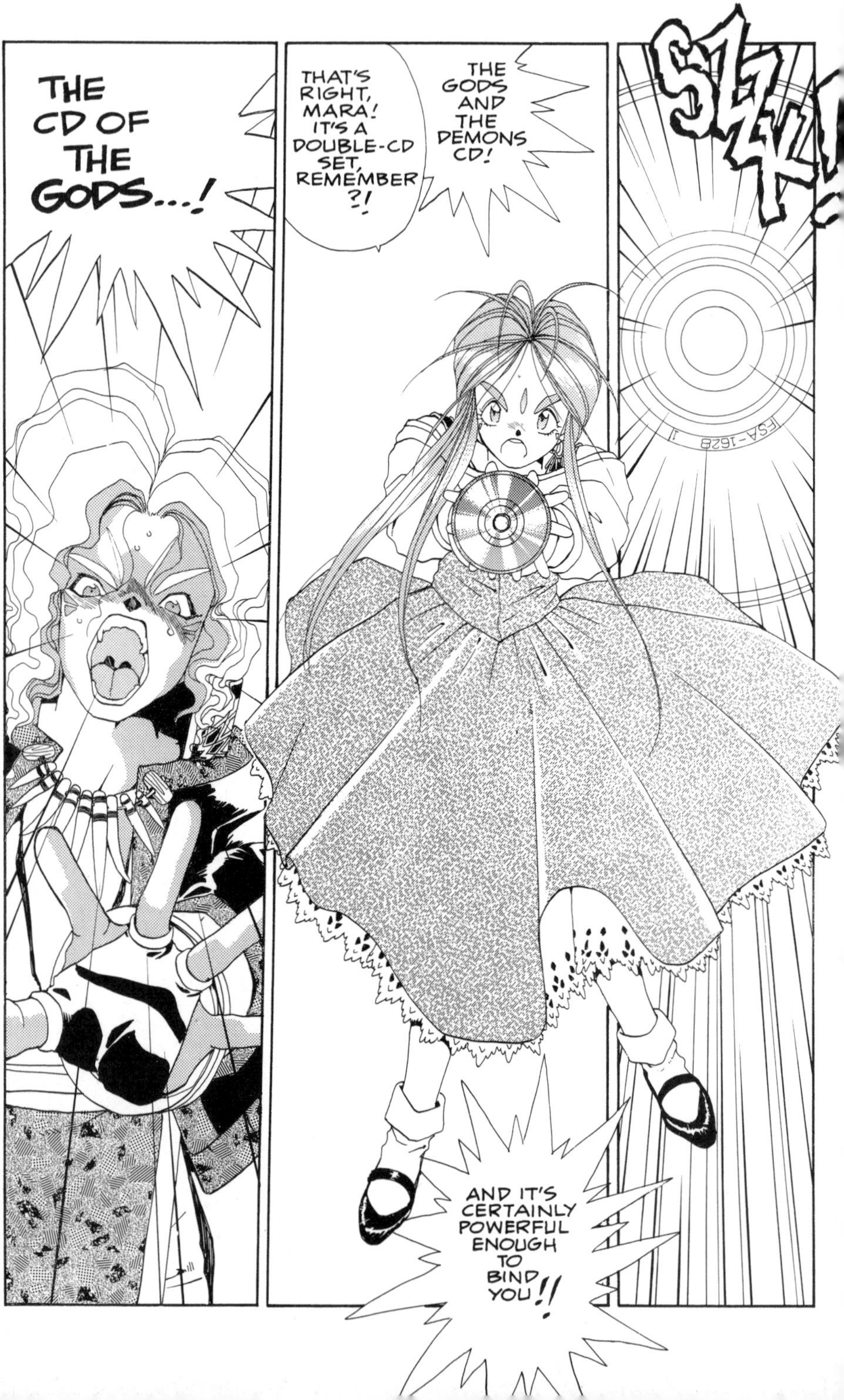
THE CD OF THE GODS...!
THAT'S RIGHT, MARA! IT'S A DOUBLE-CD SET, REMEMBER?!
THE GODS AND THE DEMONS CD!
AND IT'S CERTAINLY POWERFUL ENOUGH TO BIND YOU!!
SZZK!

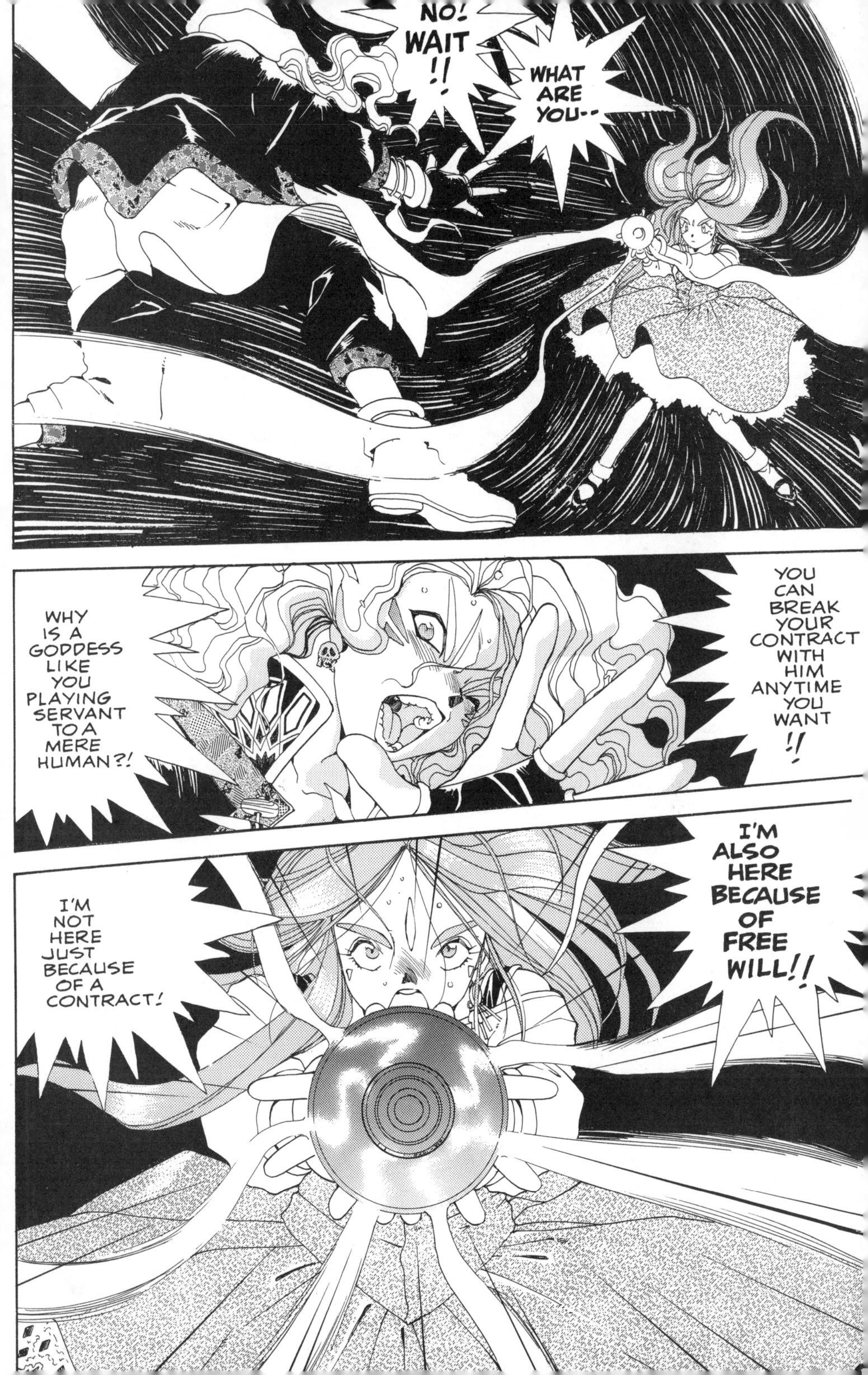
NO! WAIT!!
WHAT ARE YOU--
WHY IS A GODDESS LIKE YOU PLAYING SERVANT TO A MERE HUMAN?!
YOU CAN BREAK YOUR CONTRACT WITH HIM ANYTIME YOU WANT!!
I'M NOT HERE JUST BECAUSE OF A CONTRACT!
I'M ALSO HERE BECAUSE OF FREE WILL!!

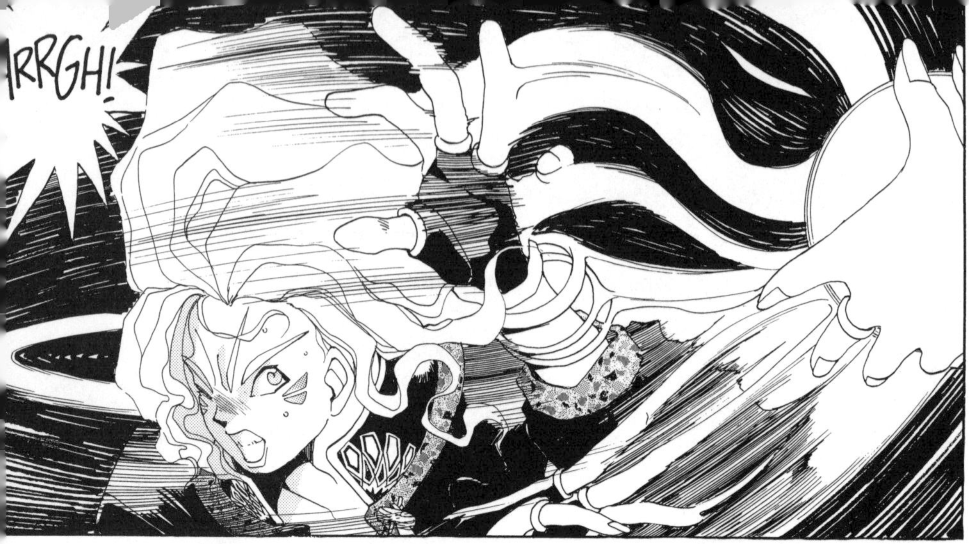
RRGH!

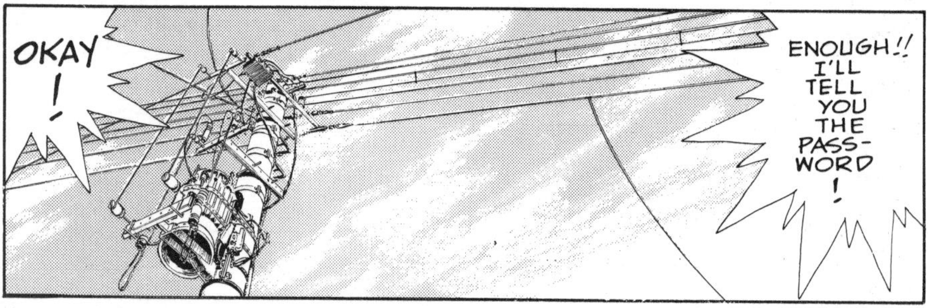
OKAY!
ENOUGH!! I'LL TELL YOU THE PASS-WORD!

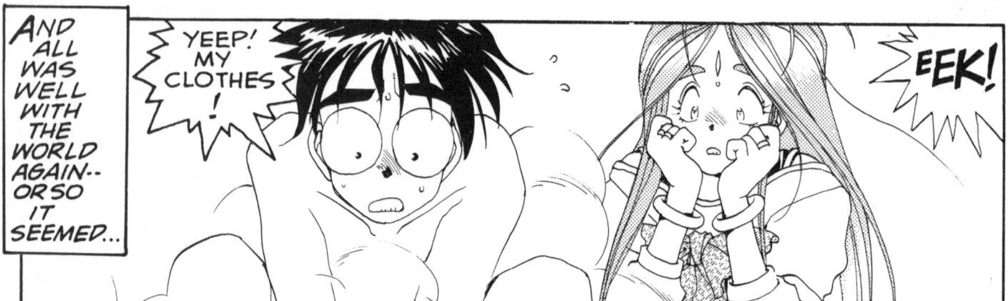
AND ALL WAS WELL WITH THE WORLD AGAIN-- OR SO IT SEEMED...
YEEP! MY CLOTHES!
EEK!

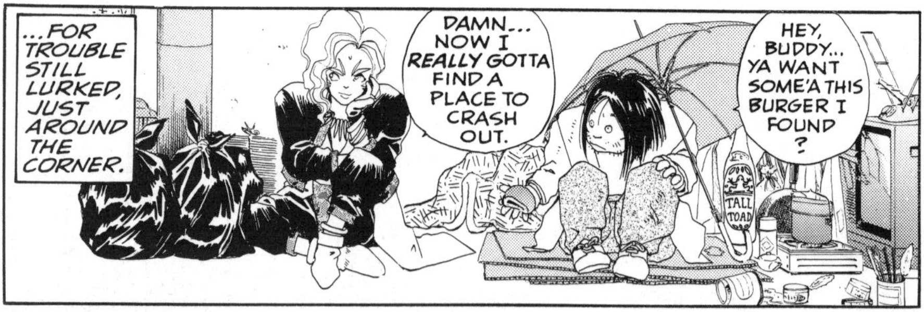
...FOR TROUBLE STILL LURKED, JUST AROUND THE CORNER.
DAMN... NOW I REALLY GOTTA FIND A PLACE TO CRASH OUT.
HEY, BUDDY... YA WANT SOME'A THIS BURGER I FOUND?
TALL TOAD

MARA STRIKES BACK!!

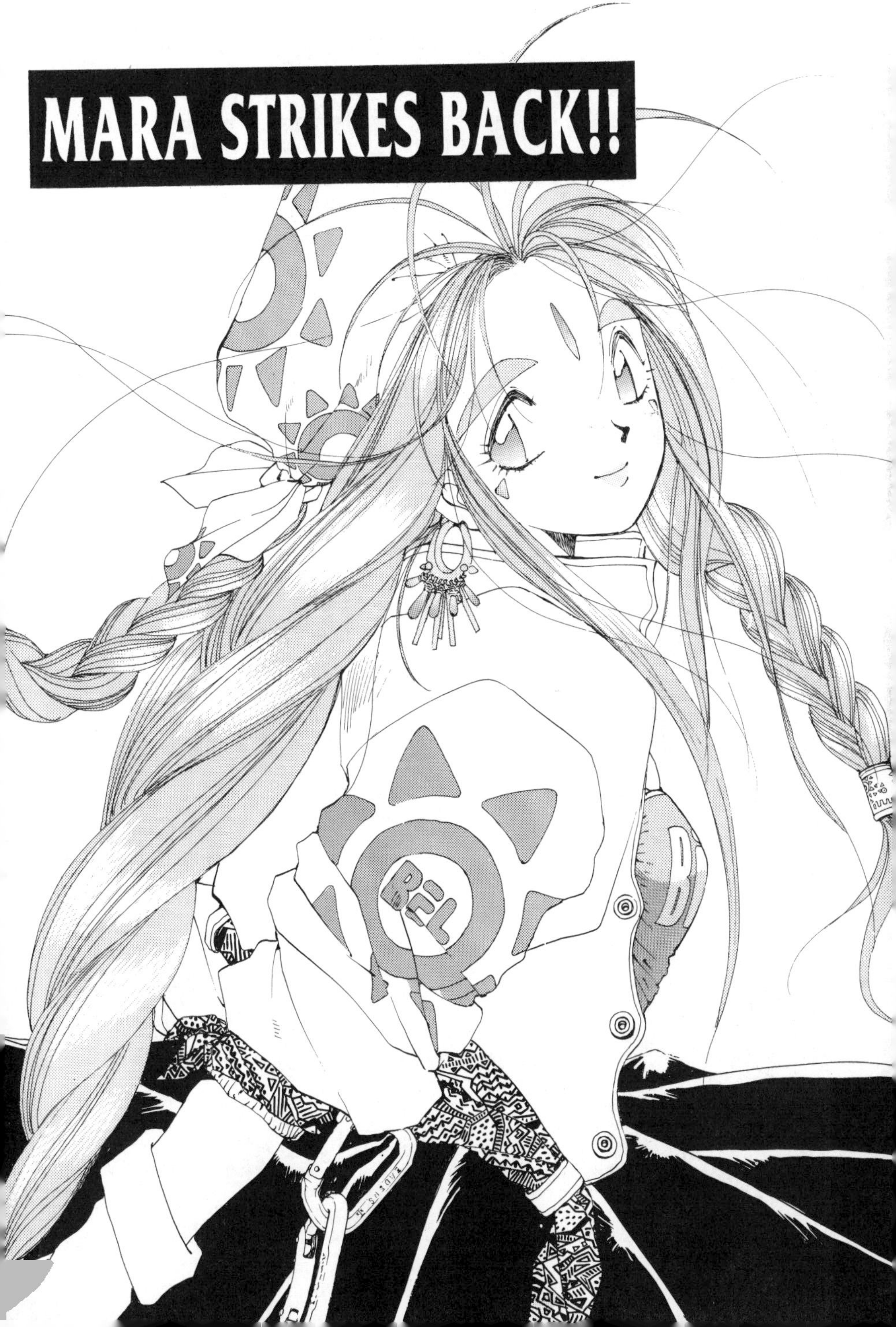

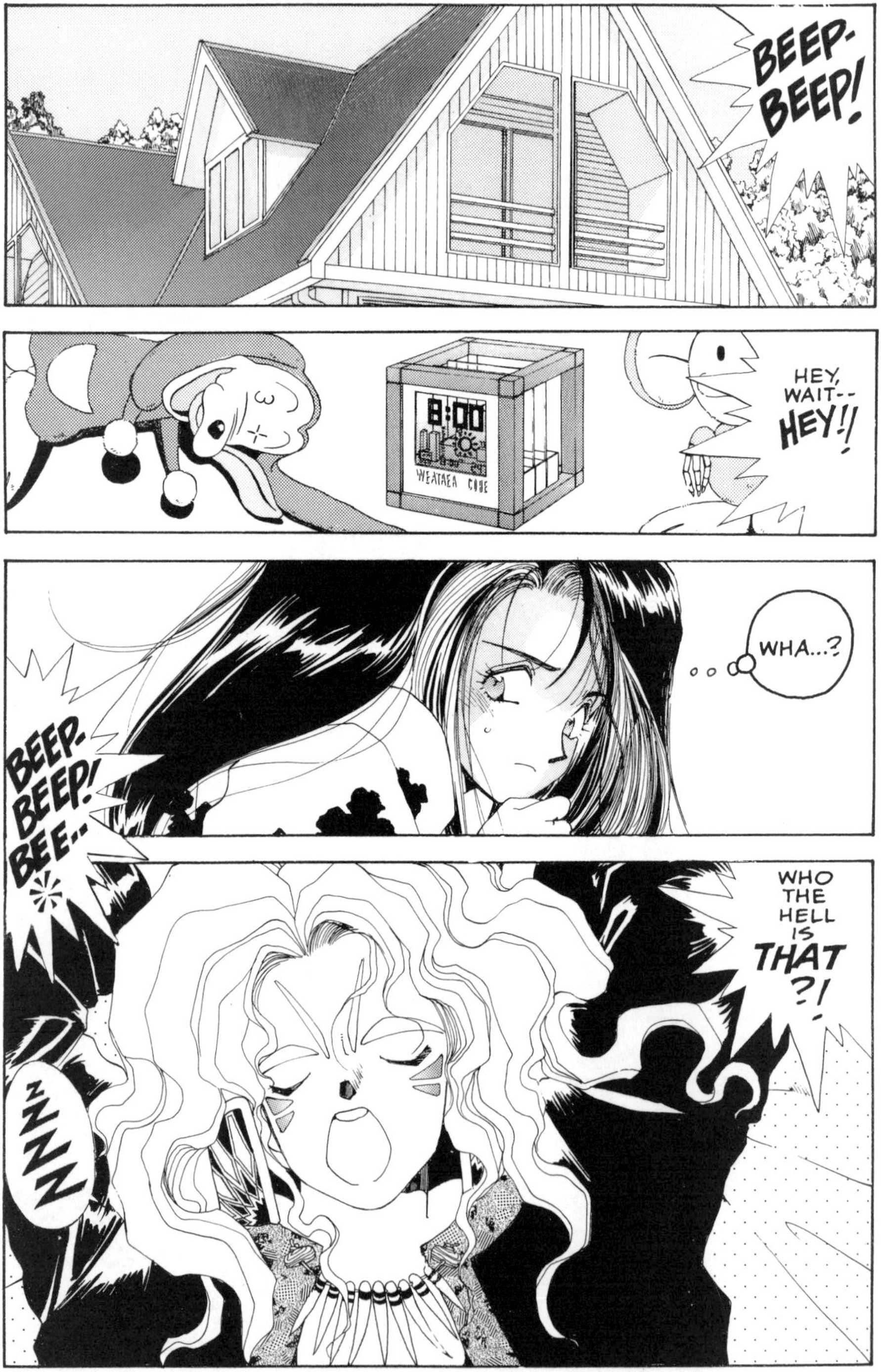
BEEP-BEEP!
8:00
HEY, WAIT-- HEY!!
WHA...?
BEEP-BEEP! BEE...
WHO THE HELL IS THAT?!
ZZZZ

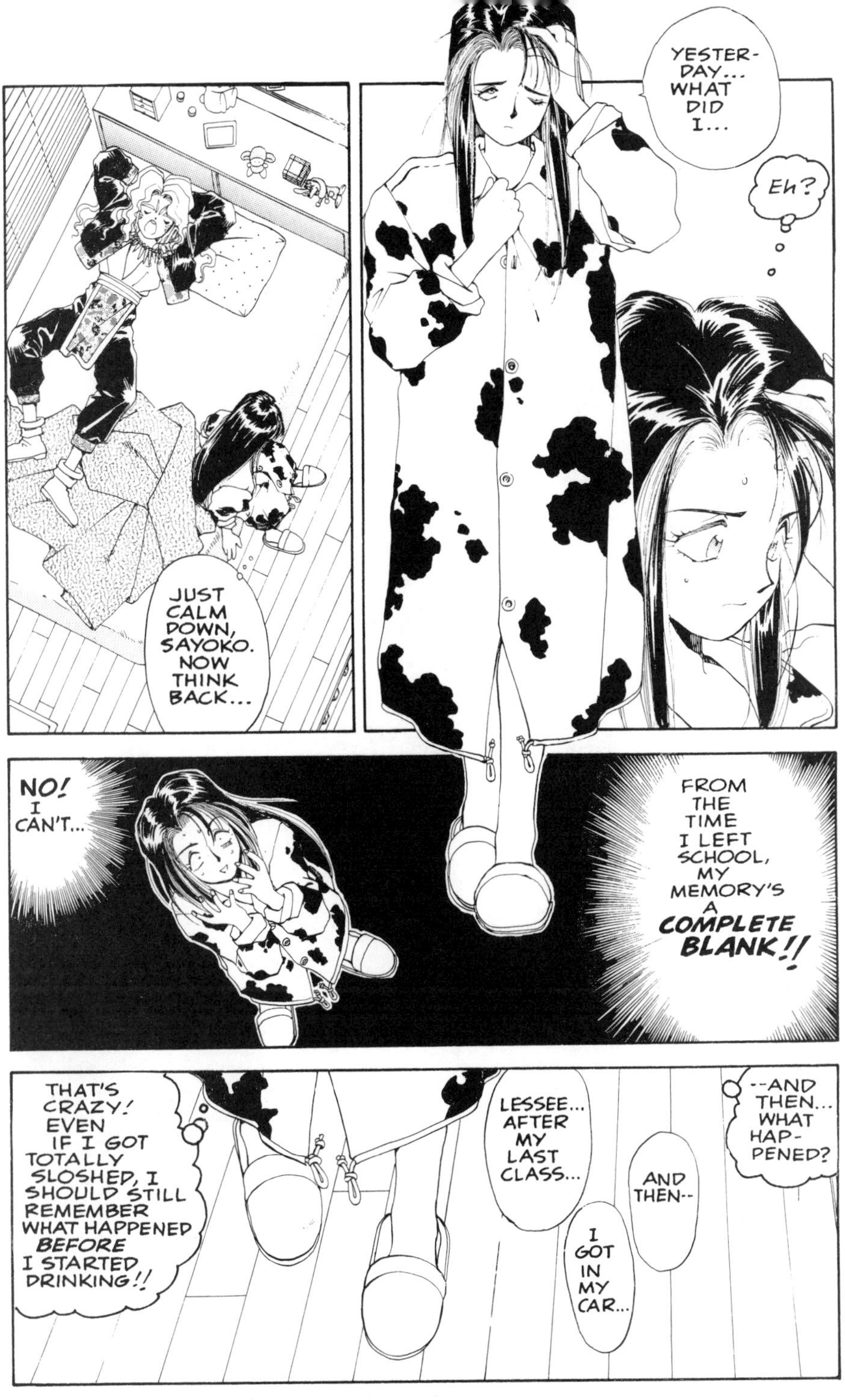
JUST CALM DOWN, SAYOKO. NOW THINK BACK...
YESTER-DAY... WHAT DID I...
Eh?
NO! I CAN'T...
FROM THE TIME I LEFT SCHOOL, MY MEMORY'S A **COMPLETE BLANK!!**
THAT'S CRAZY! EVEN IF I GOT TOTALLY SLOSHED, I SHOULD STILL REMEMBER WHAT HAPPENED *BEFORE* I STARTED DRINKING!!
LESSEE... AFTER MY LAST CLASS...
I GOT IN MY CAR...
AND THEN--
--AND THEN... WHAT HAP-PENED?

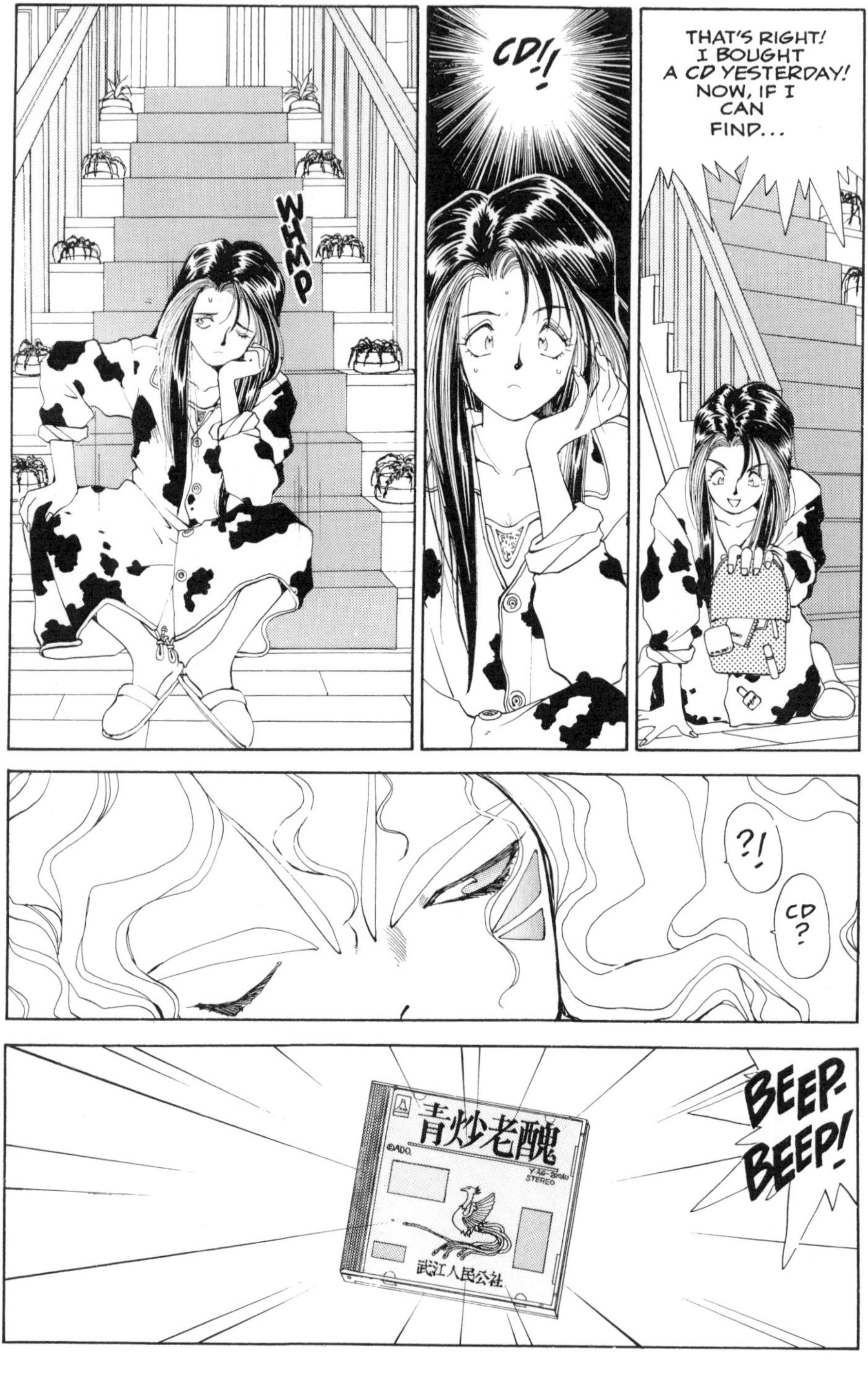
WHMP
CD?!
THAT'S RIGHT! I BOUGHT A CD YESTERDAY! NOW, IF I CAN FIND...
?!
CD?
青炒老醜
©ADO.
STEREO
武江人民公社
BEEP-BEEP!

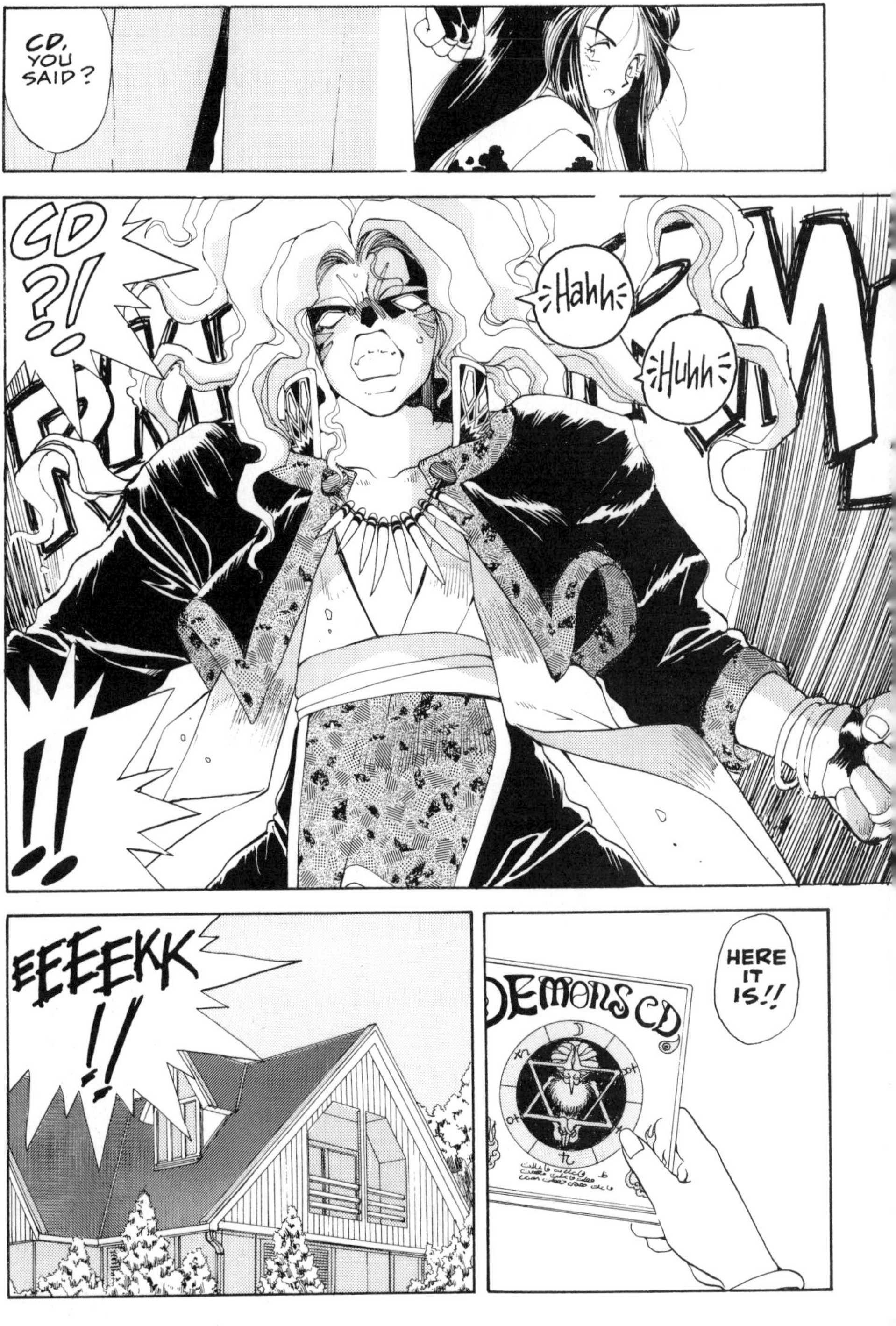
CD, YOU SAID?
CD?!
!!
Hahh
Huhh
EEEEKK!!
DEMONS CD
HERE IT IS!!

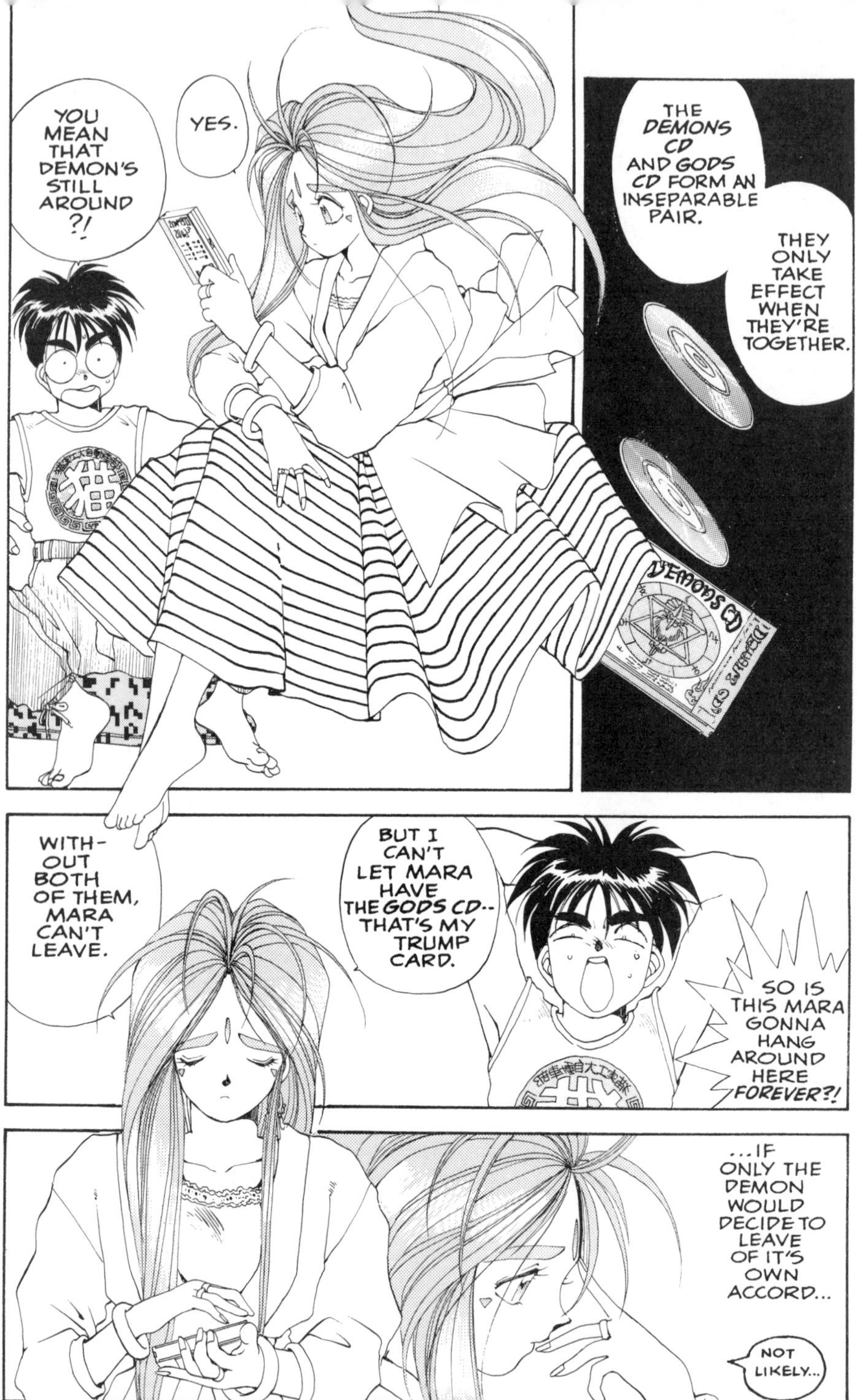
YOU MEAN THAT DEMON'S STILL AROUND ?!
YES.
THE DEMONS CD AND GODS CD FORM AN INSEPARABLE PAIR.
THEY ONLY TAKE EFFECT WHEN THEY'RE TOGETHER.
DEMONS CD
WITH-OUT BOTH OF THEM, MARA CAN'T LEAVE.
BUT I CAN'T LET MARA HAVE THE GODS CD-- THAT'S MY TRUMP CARD.
SO IS THIS MARA GONNA HANG AROUND HERE FOREVER?!
...IF ONLY THE DEMON WOULD DECIDE TO LEAVE OF IT'S OWN ACCORD...
NOT LIKELY...

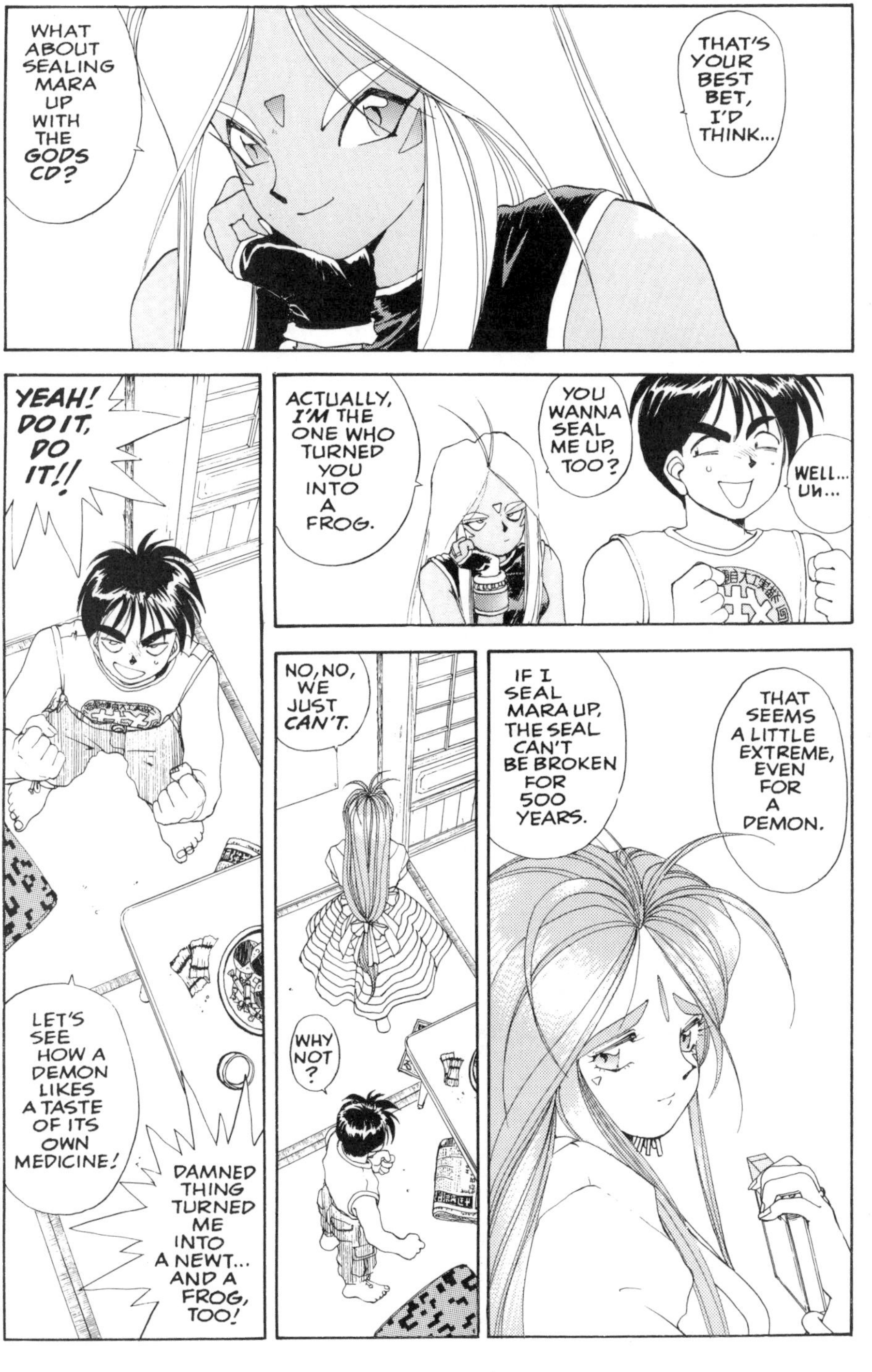
WHAT ABOUT SEALING MARA UP WITH THE GODS CD?
THAT'S YOUR BEST BET, I'D THINK...
YEAH! DO IT, DO IT!!
LET'S SEE HOW A DEMON LIKES A TASTE OF ITS OWN MEDICINE!
DAMNED THING TURNED ME INTO A NEWT... AND A FROG, TOO!
ACTUALLY, *I'M* THE ONE WHO TURNED YOU INTO A FROG.
YOU WANNA SEAL ME UP, TOO?
WELL... UH...
NO, NO, WE JUST *CAN'T*.
WHY NOT?
IF I SEAL MARA UP, THE SEAL CAN'T BE BROKEN FOR 500 YEARS.
THAT SEEMS A LITTLE EXTREME, EVEN FOR A DEMON.

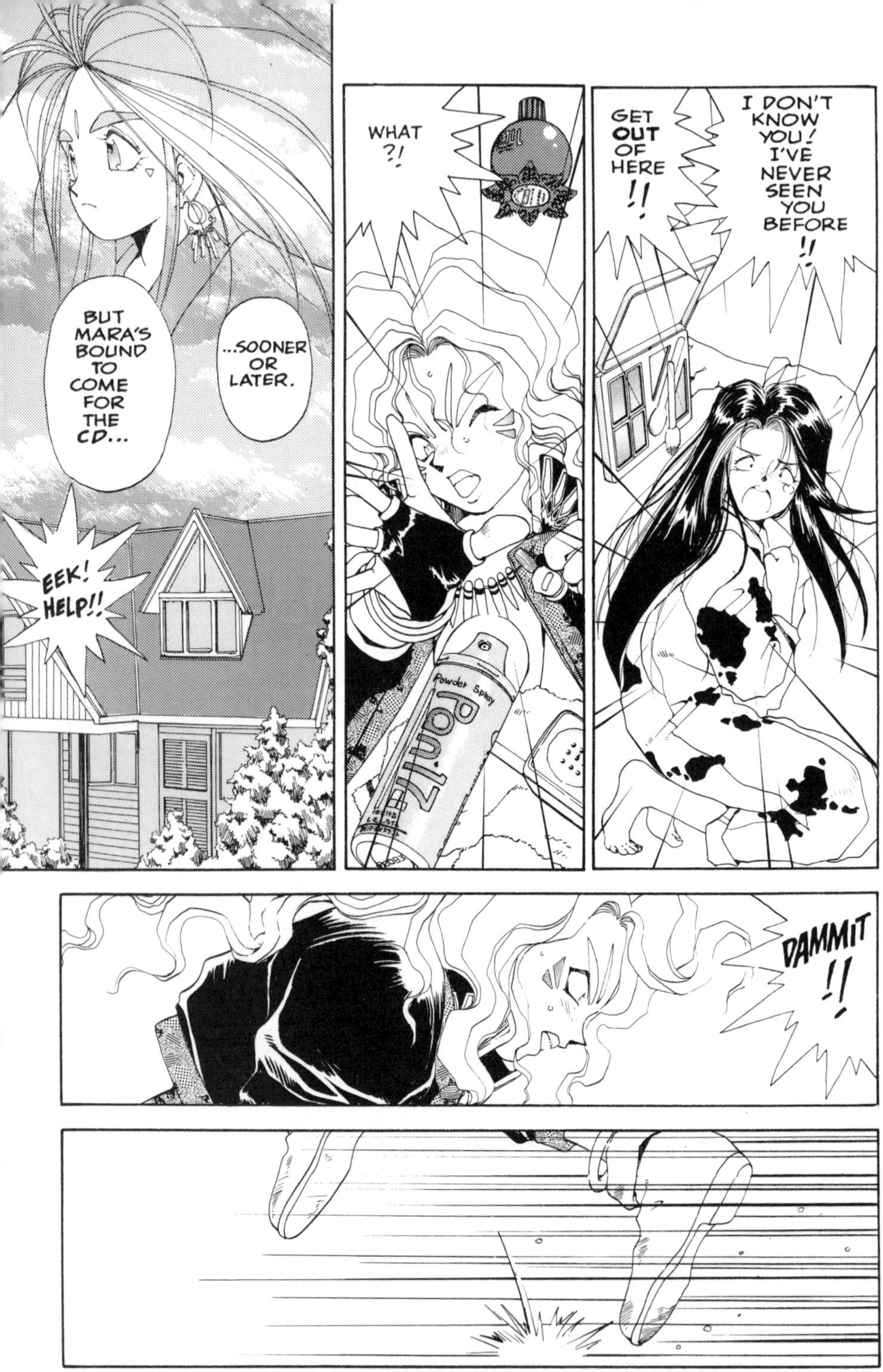
BUT MARA'S BOUND TO COME FOR THE CD...
...SOONER OR LATER.
EEK! HELP!!
WHAT?!
Powder Spray
GET OUT OF HERE!!
I DON'T KNOW YOU! I'VE NEVER SEEN YOU BEFORE!!
DAMMIT!!

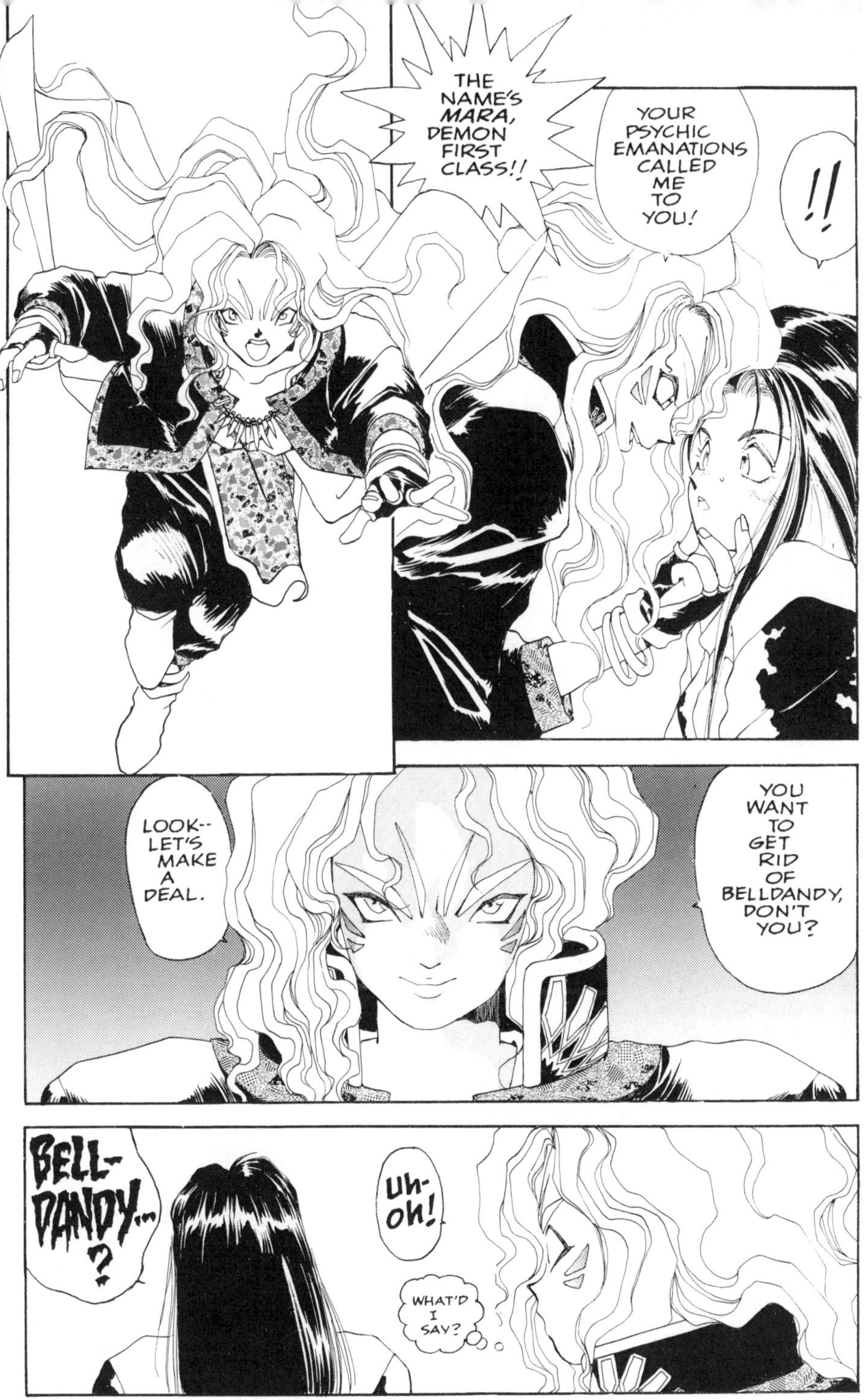

THE NAME'S MARA, DEMON FIRST CLASS!!
YOUR PSYCHIC EMANATIONS CALLED ME TO YOU!
!!
LOOK-- LET'S MAKE A DEAL.
YOU WANT TO GET RID OF BELLDANDY, DON'T YOU?
BELL- DANDY...?
Uh-oh!
WHAT'D I SAY?

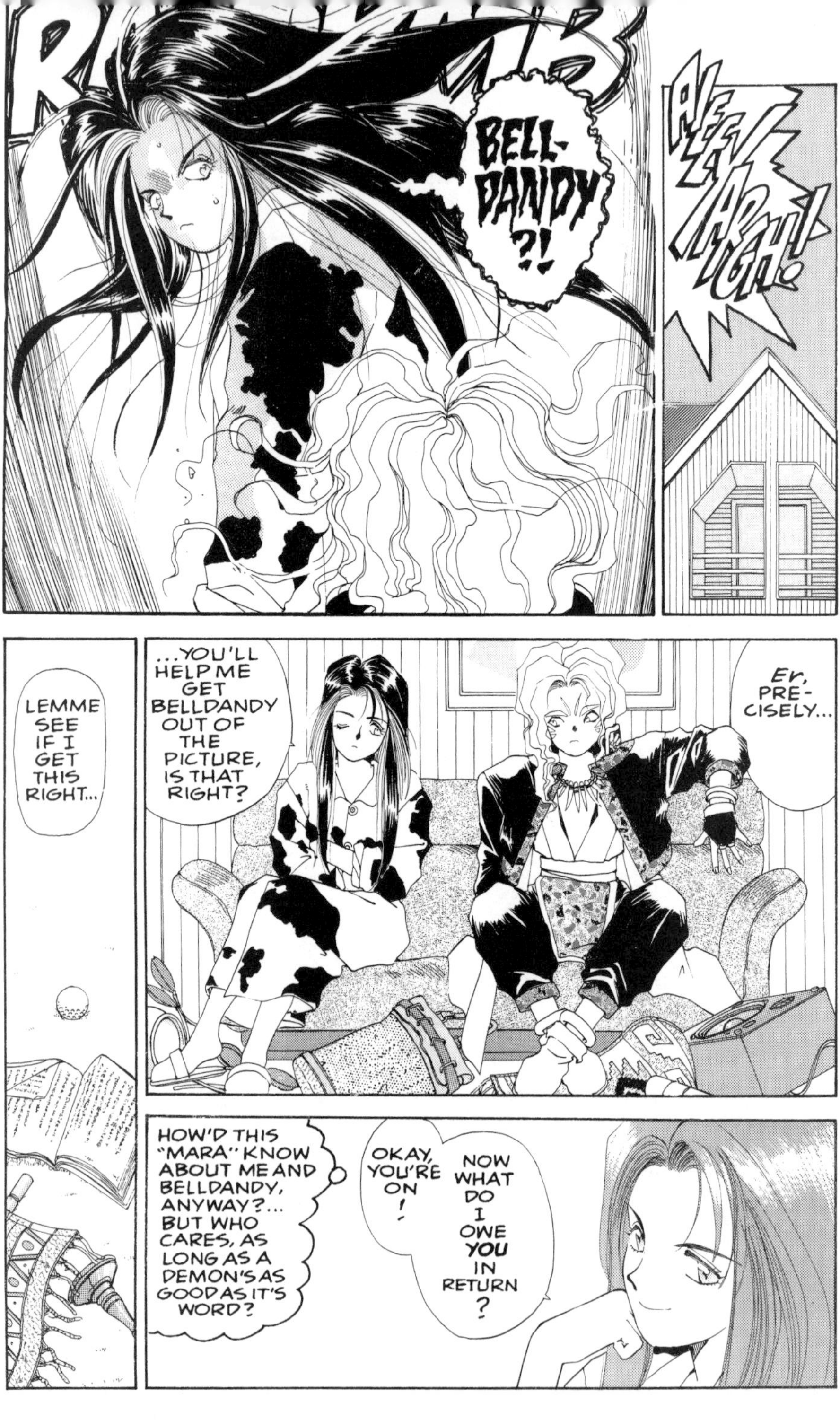
BELL-DANDY ?!
AIEEYAAARGH!
LEMME SEE IF I GET THIS RIGHT...
...YOU'LL HELP ME GET BELLDANDY OUT OF THE PICTURE, IS THAT RIGHT?
Er, PRE-CISELY...
HOW'D THIS "MARA" KNOW ABOUT ME AND BELLDANDY, ANYWAY?... BUT WHO CARES, AS LONG AS A DEMON'S AS GOOD AS IT'S WORD?
OKAY, YOU'RE ON!
NOW WHAT DO I OWE **YOU** IN RETURN?

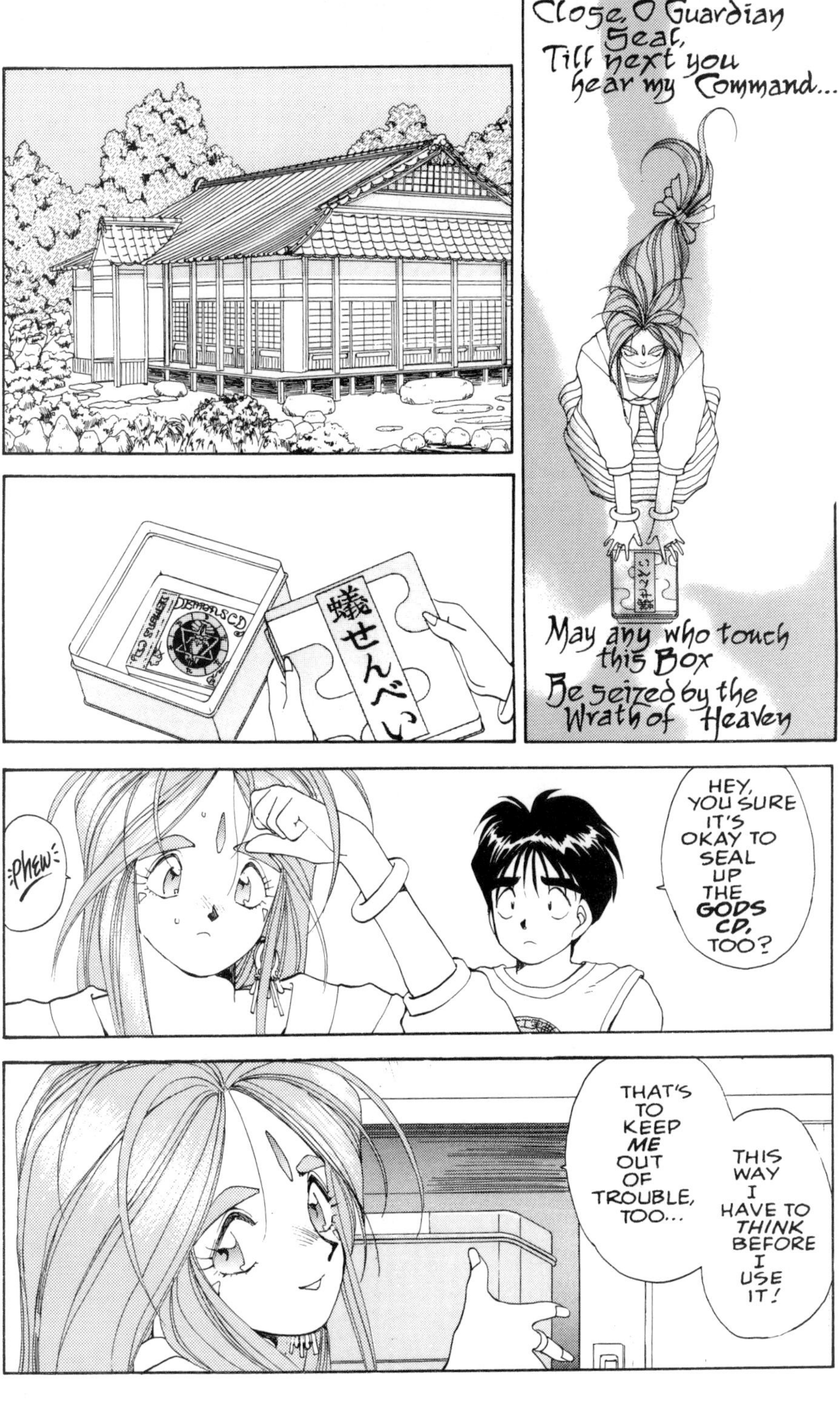
DEMONS CD
せんべい
Close O Guardian Seal, Till next you hear my Command...
May any who touch this Box Be seized by the Wrath of Heaven
phew
HEY, YOU SURE IT'S OKAY TO SEAL UP THE **GODS CD,** TOO?
THAT'S TO KEEP *ME* OUT OF TROUBLE, TOO...
THIS WAY I HAVE TO *THINK* BEFORE I USE IT!

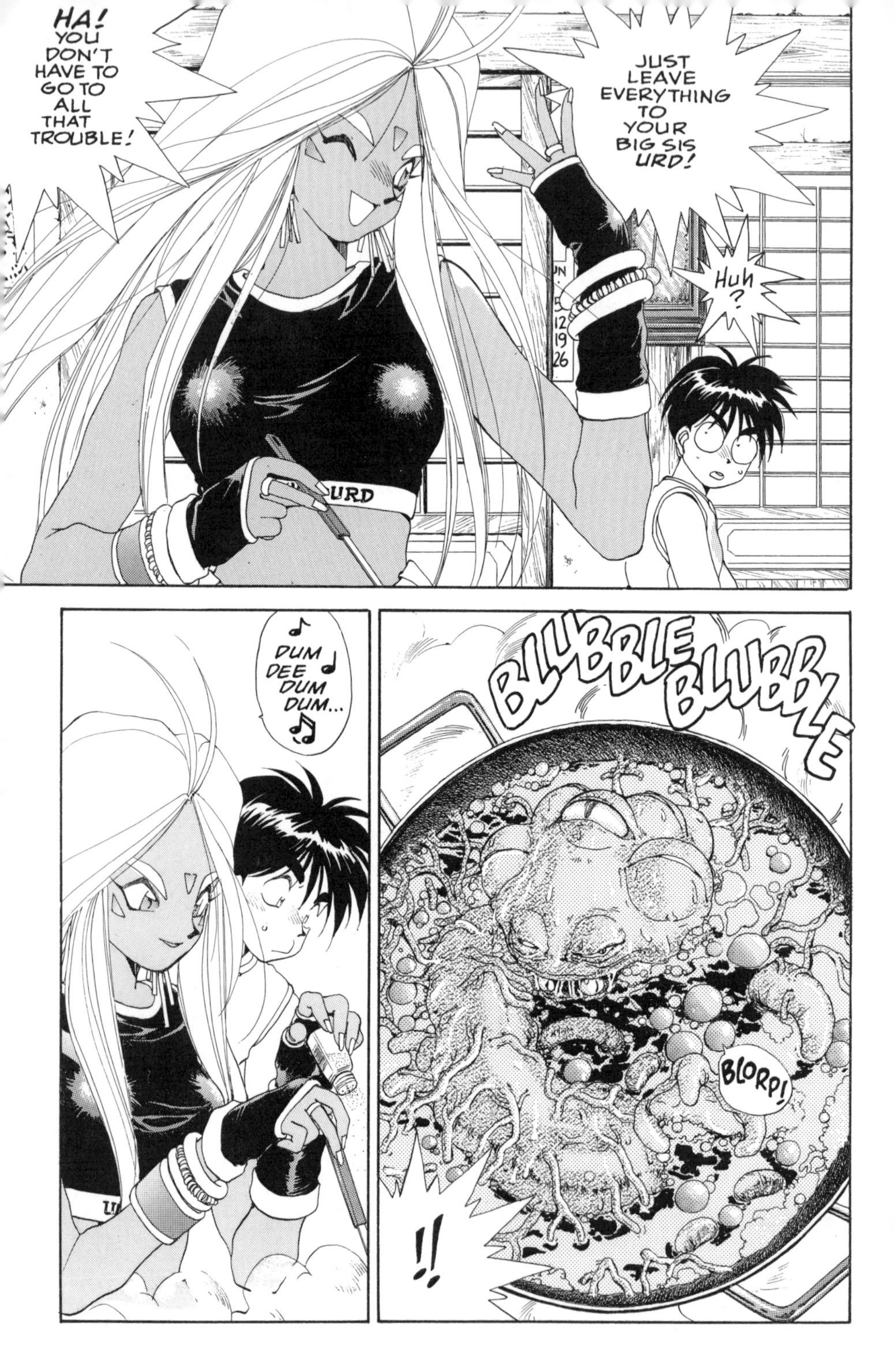

HA! YOU DON'T HAVE TO GO TO ALL THAT TROUBLE!
JUST LEAVE EVERYTHING TO YOUR BIG SIS URD!
Huh?
DUM DEE DUM DUM...
BLUBBLE BLUBBLE
BLORP!
!!

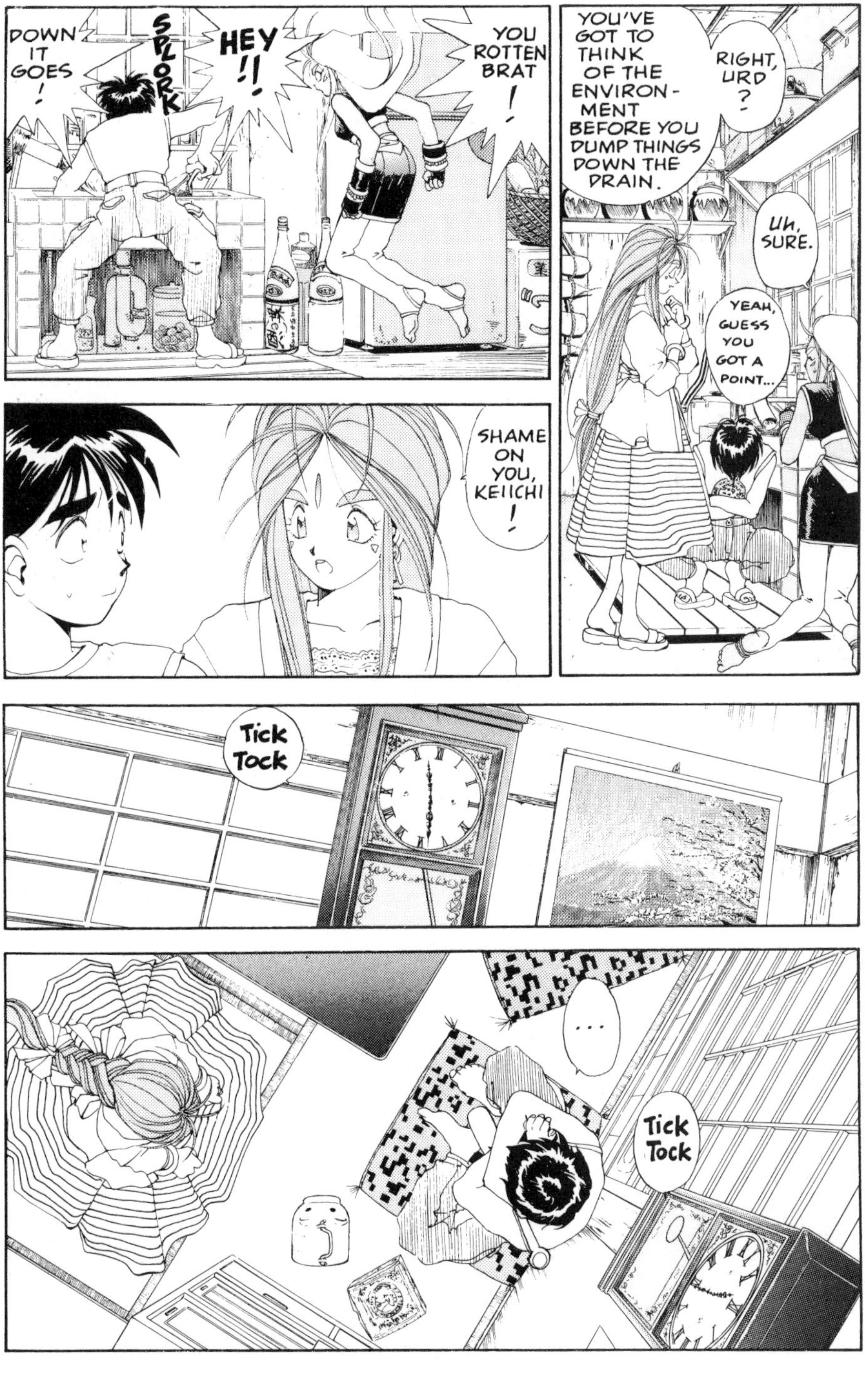
DOWN IT GOES!
SPLORK
HEY!!
YOU ROTTEN BRAT!
SHAME ON YOU, KEIICHI!
YOU'VE GOT TO THINK OF THE ENVIRONMENT BEFORE YOU DUMP THINGS DOWN THE DRAIN.
RIGHT, URD?
Uh, SURE.
YEAH, GUESS YOU GOT A POINT...
Tick Tock
...
Tick Tock

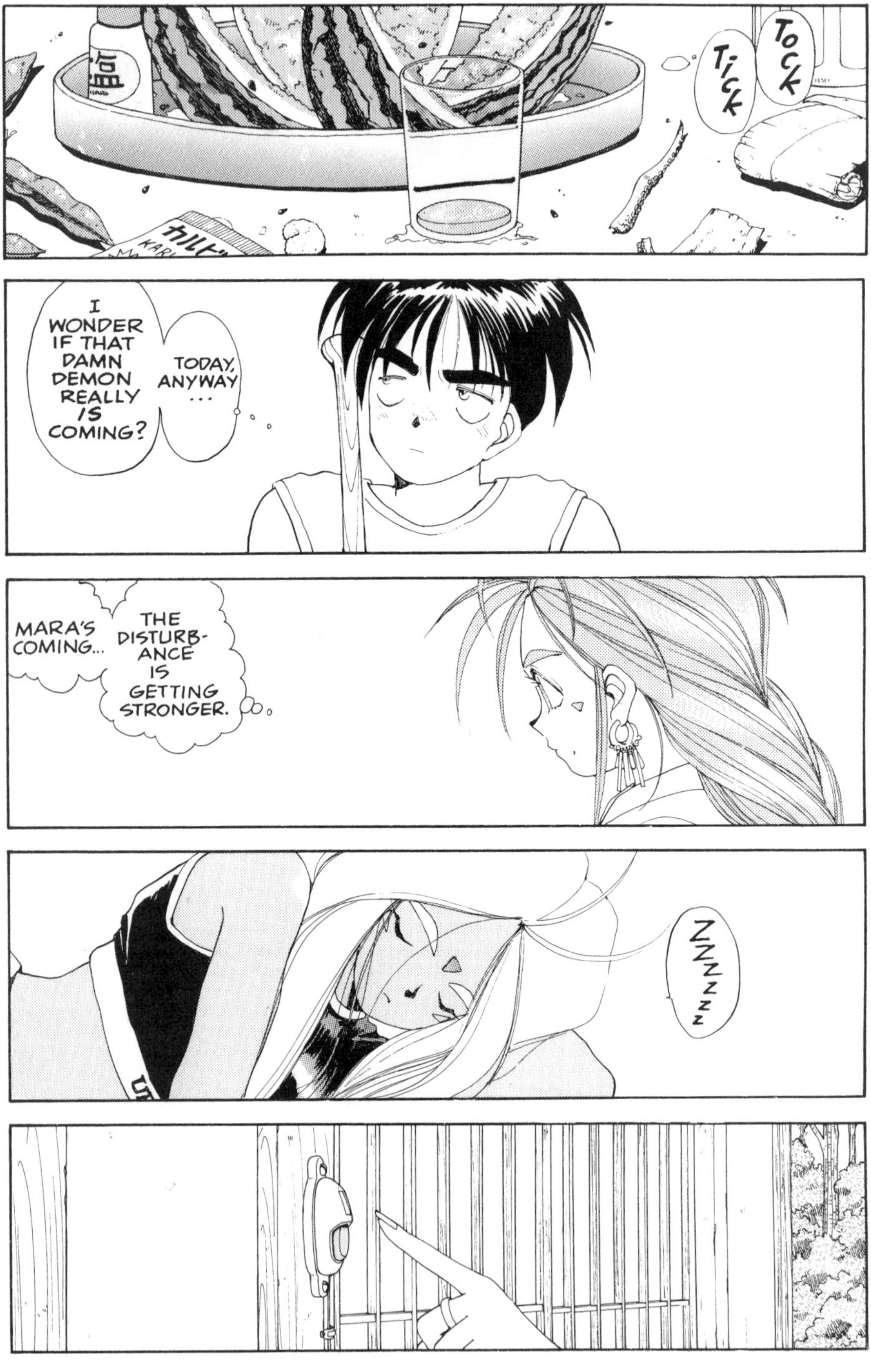
塩
TICK
TOCK
I WONDER IF THAT DAMN DEMON REALLY IS COMING?
TODAY, ANYWAY . . .
MARA'S COMING...
THE DISTURB-ANCE IS GETTING STRONGER.
ZZZZZZ

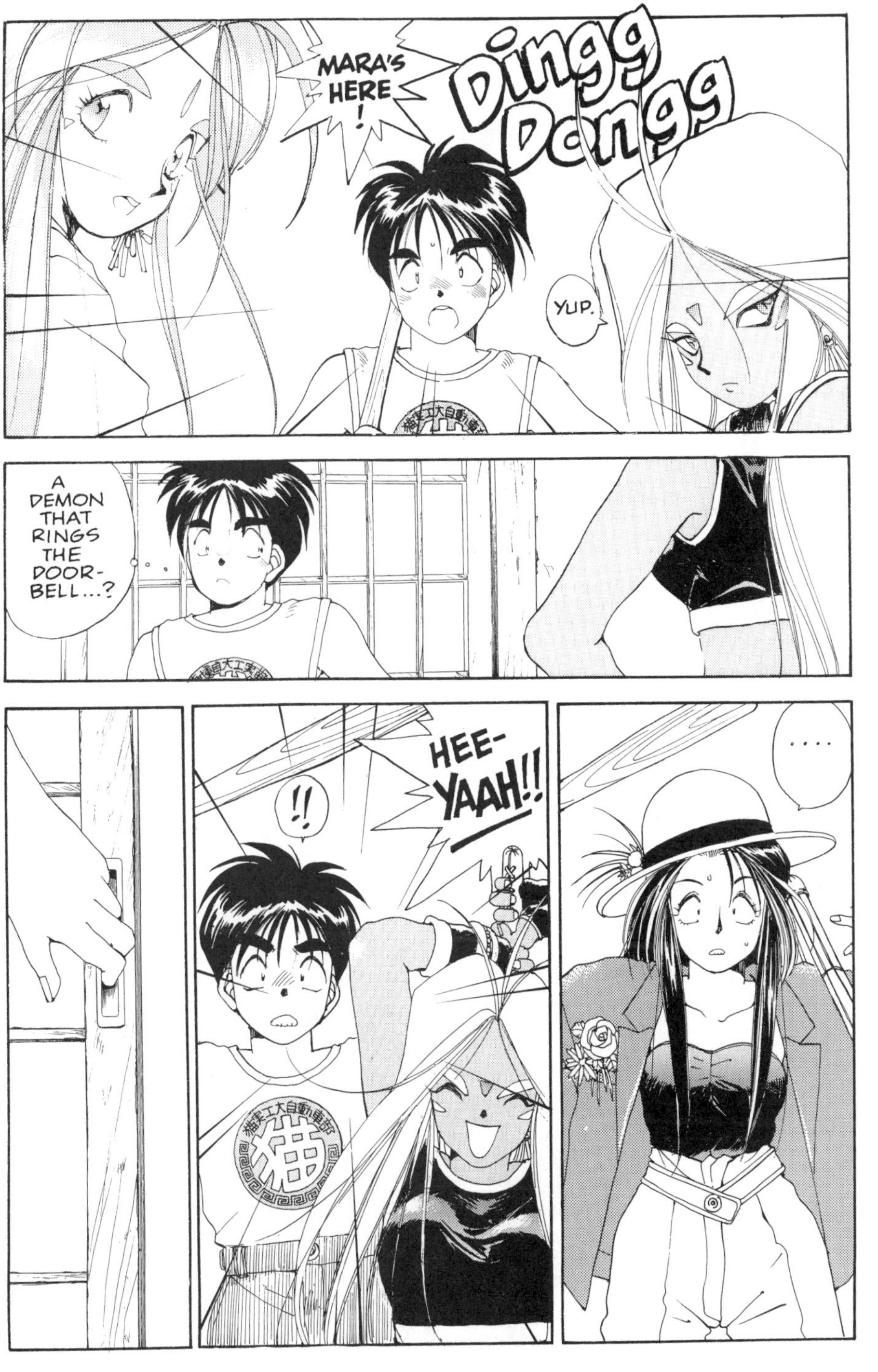
MARA'S HERE!
Dingg Dongg
YUP.
A DEMON THAT RINGS THE DOOR-BELL...?
!!
HEE-YAAH!!
....

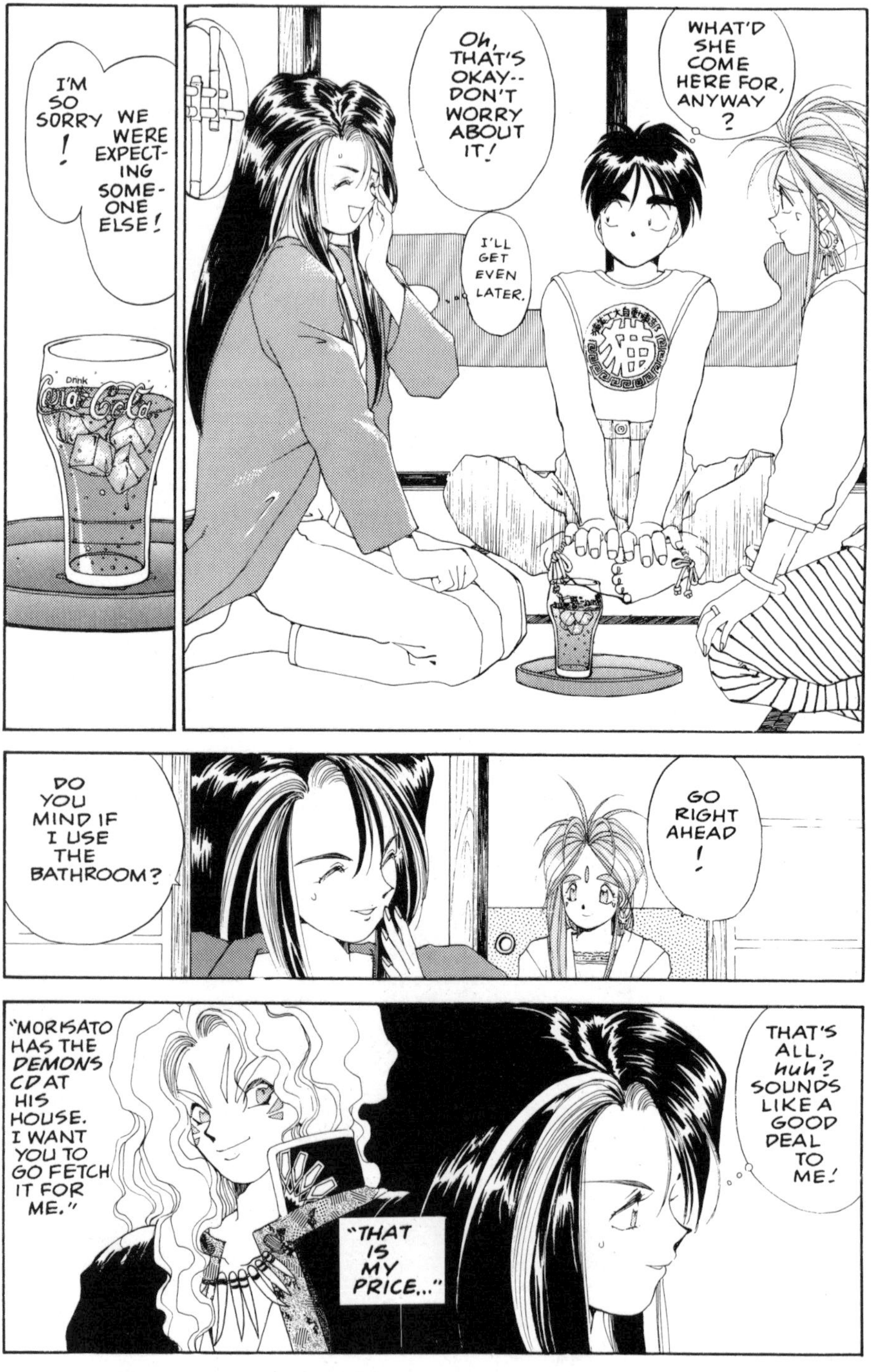
I'M SO SORRY! WE WERE EXPECTING SOME-ONE ELSE!
Drink Coca-Cola
Oh, THAT'S OKAY-- DON'T WORRY ABOUT IT!
WHAT'D SHE COME HERE FOR, ANYWAY?
I'LL GET EVEN LATER.
DO YOU MIND IF I USE THE BATHROOM?
GO RIGHT AHEAD!
"MORISATO HAS THE DEMONS CD AT HIS HOUSE. I WANT YOU TO GO FETCH IT FOR ME."
"THAT IS MY PRICE..."
THAT'S ALL, huh? SOUNDS LIKE A GOOD DEAL TO ME!

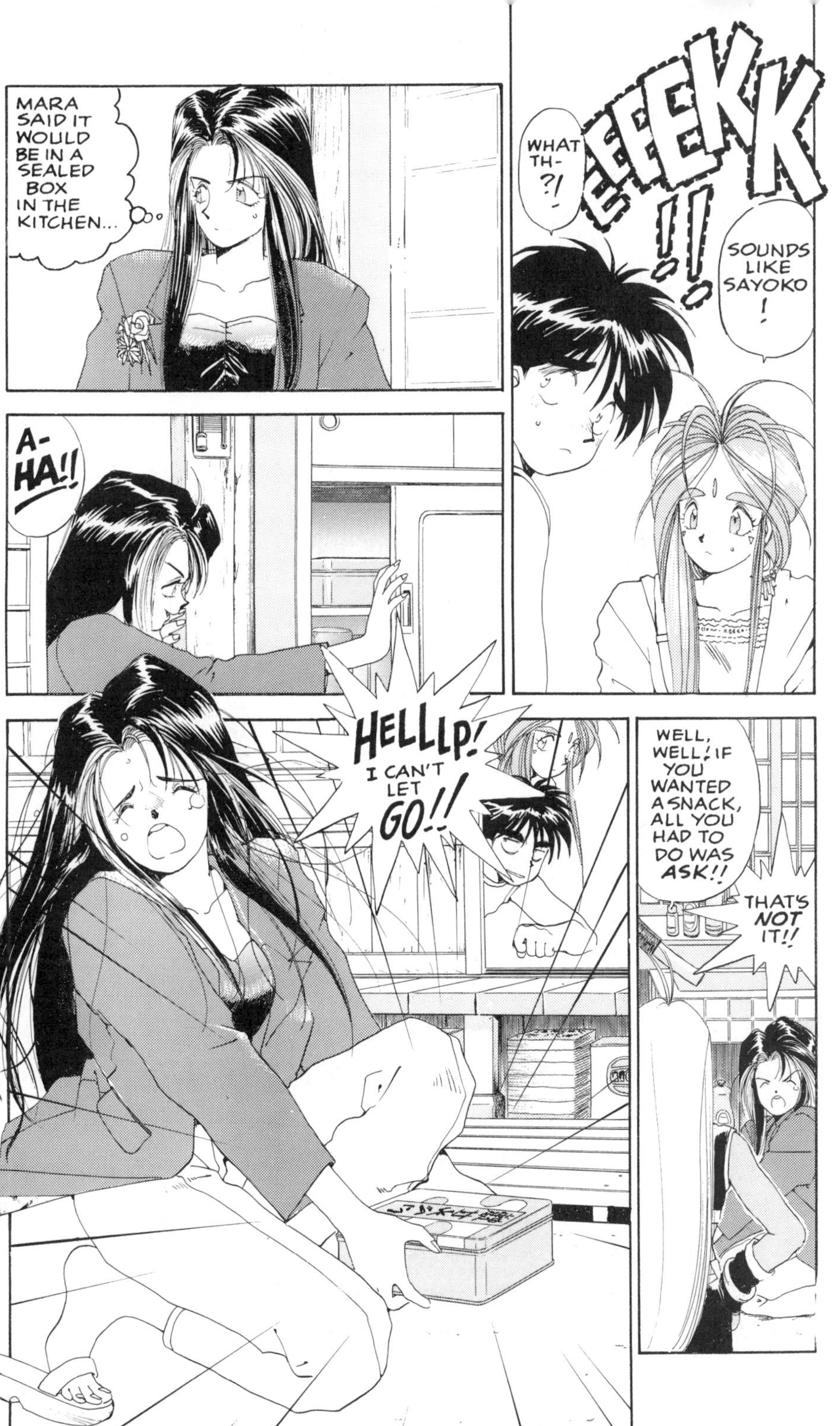
MARA SAID IT WOULD BE IN A SEALED BOX IN THE KITCHEN...
A-HA!!
WHAT TH-?!
EEEKK!!
SOUNDS LIKE SAYOKO!
HELLLP! I CAN'T LET GO!!
WELL, WELL! IF YOU WANTED A SNACK, ALL YOU HAD TO DO WAS ASK!!
THAT'S NOT IT!!

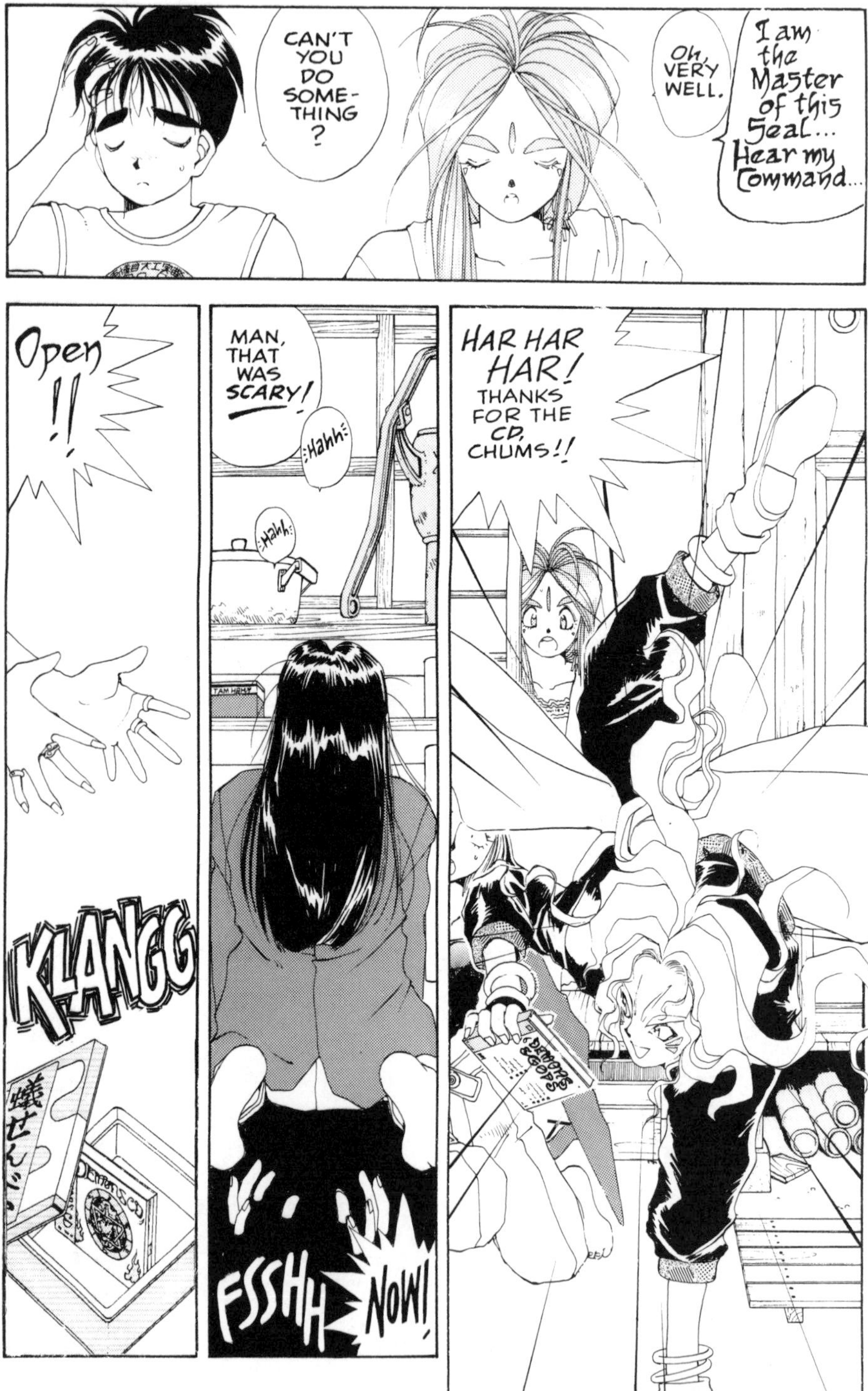
CAN'T YOU DO SOMETHING?
Oh, VERY WELL.
I am the Master of this Seal... Hear my Command...
Open!!
KLANGG
MAN, THAT WAS SCARY!
Hahh
Hahh
FSSHH
NOW!
HAR HAR HAR! THANKS FOR THE CD, CHUMS!!

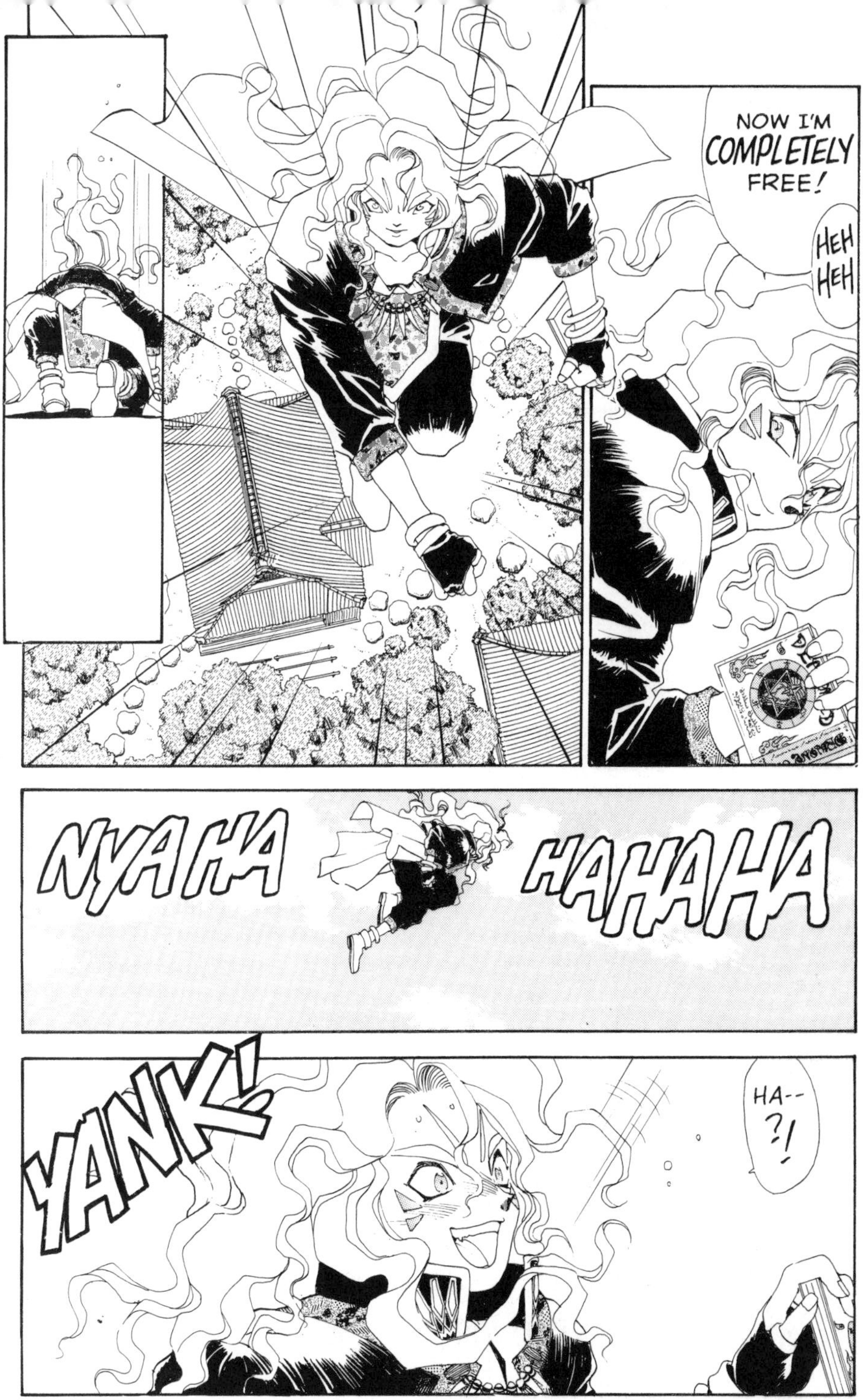
NOW I'M COMPLETELY FREE!
HEH HEH
NYAHA
HAHAHA
YANK!
HA-- ?!

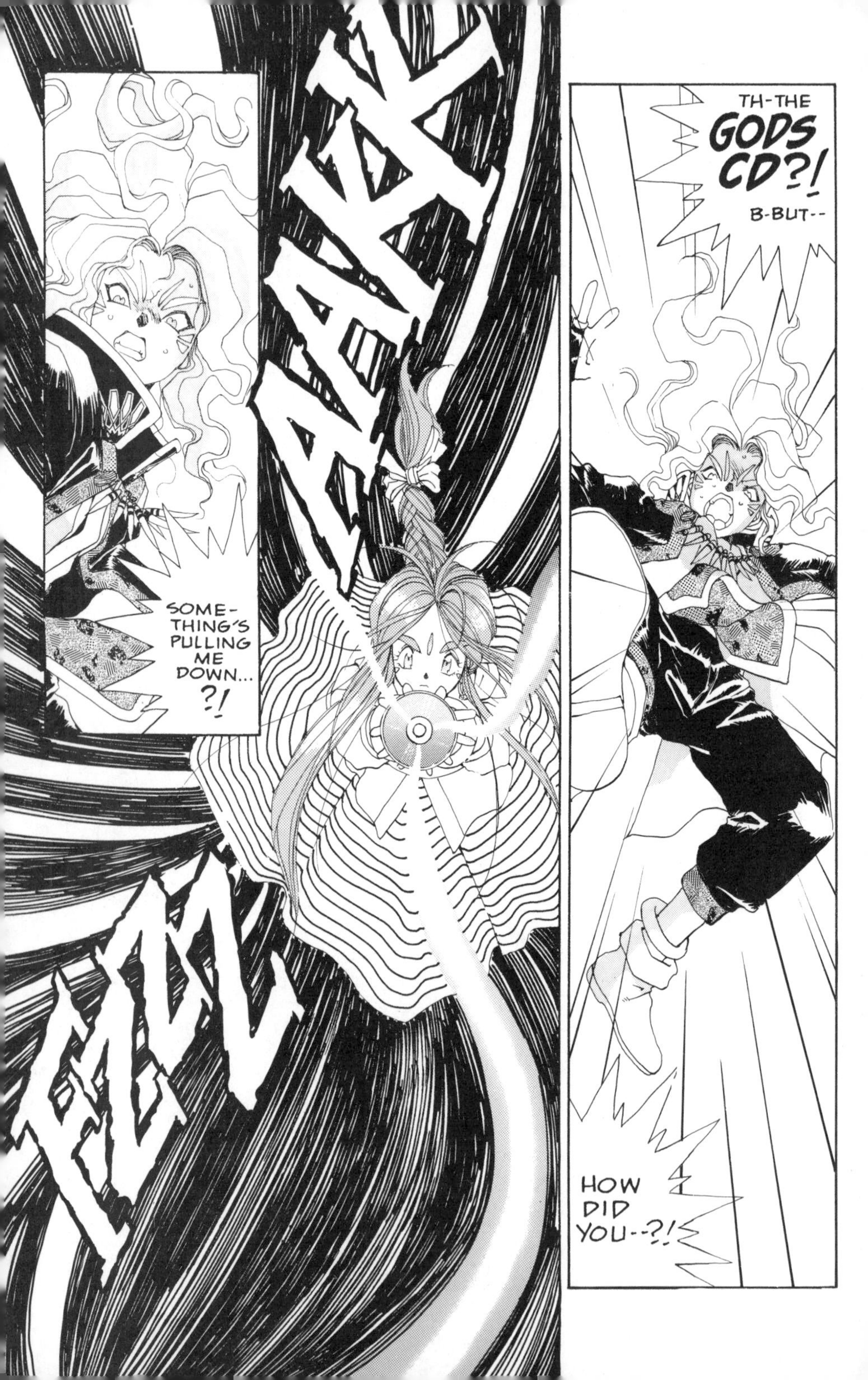
SOME-THING'S PULLING ME DOWN...?!
TH-THE GODS CD?!
B-BUT--
HOW DID YOU--?!

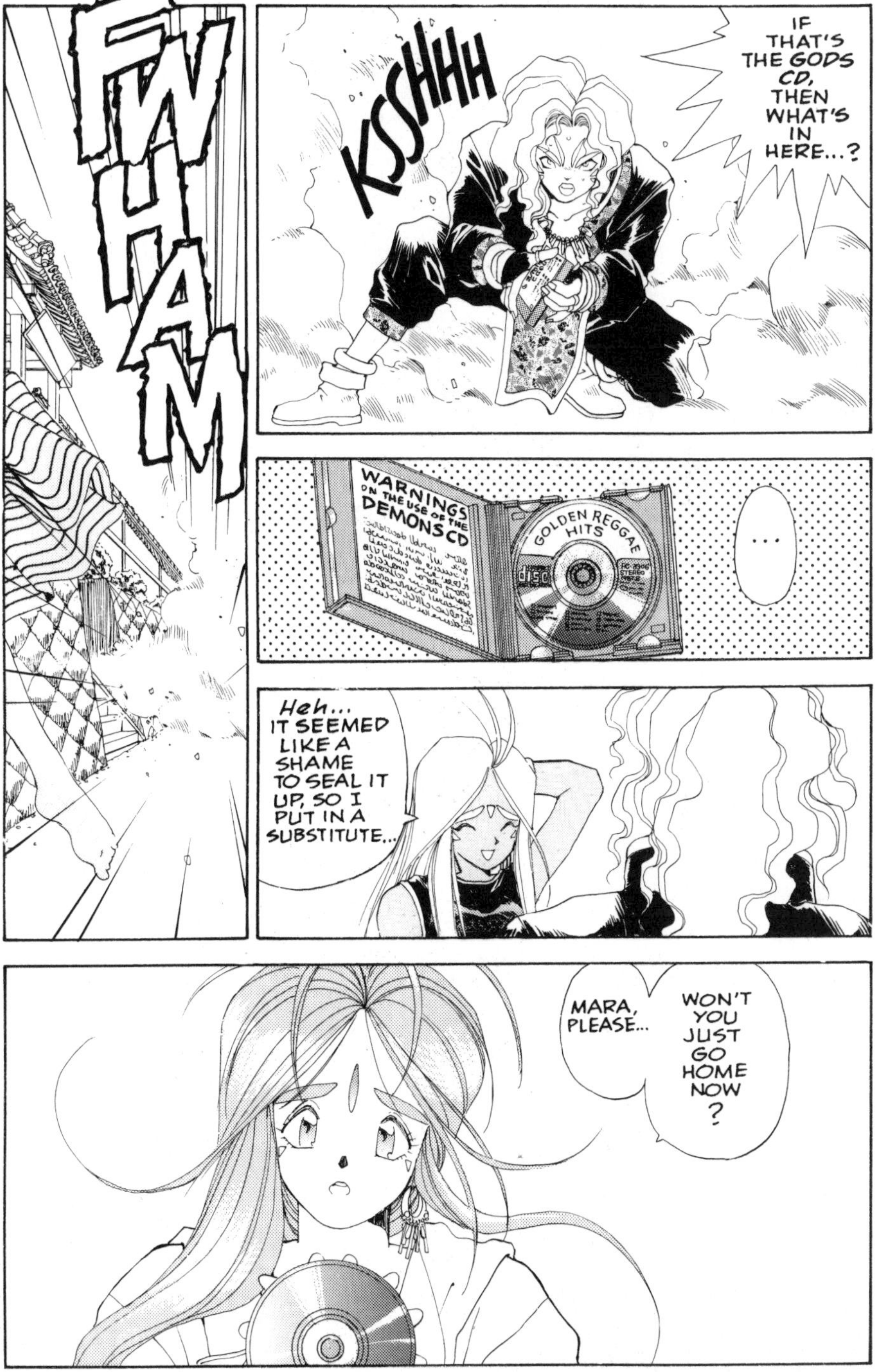
FWHAM
KSSHHH
IF THAT'S THE GODS CD, THEN WHAT'S IN HERE...?
WARNINGS ON THE USE OF THE DEMONS CD
GOLDEN REGGAE HITS
disc
...
Heh... IT SEEMED LIKE A SHAME TO SEAL IT UP, SO I PUT IN A SUBSTITUTE...
MARA, PLEASE...
WON'T YOU JUST GO HOME NOW ?

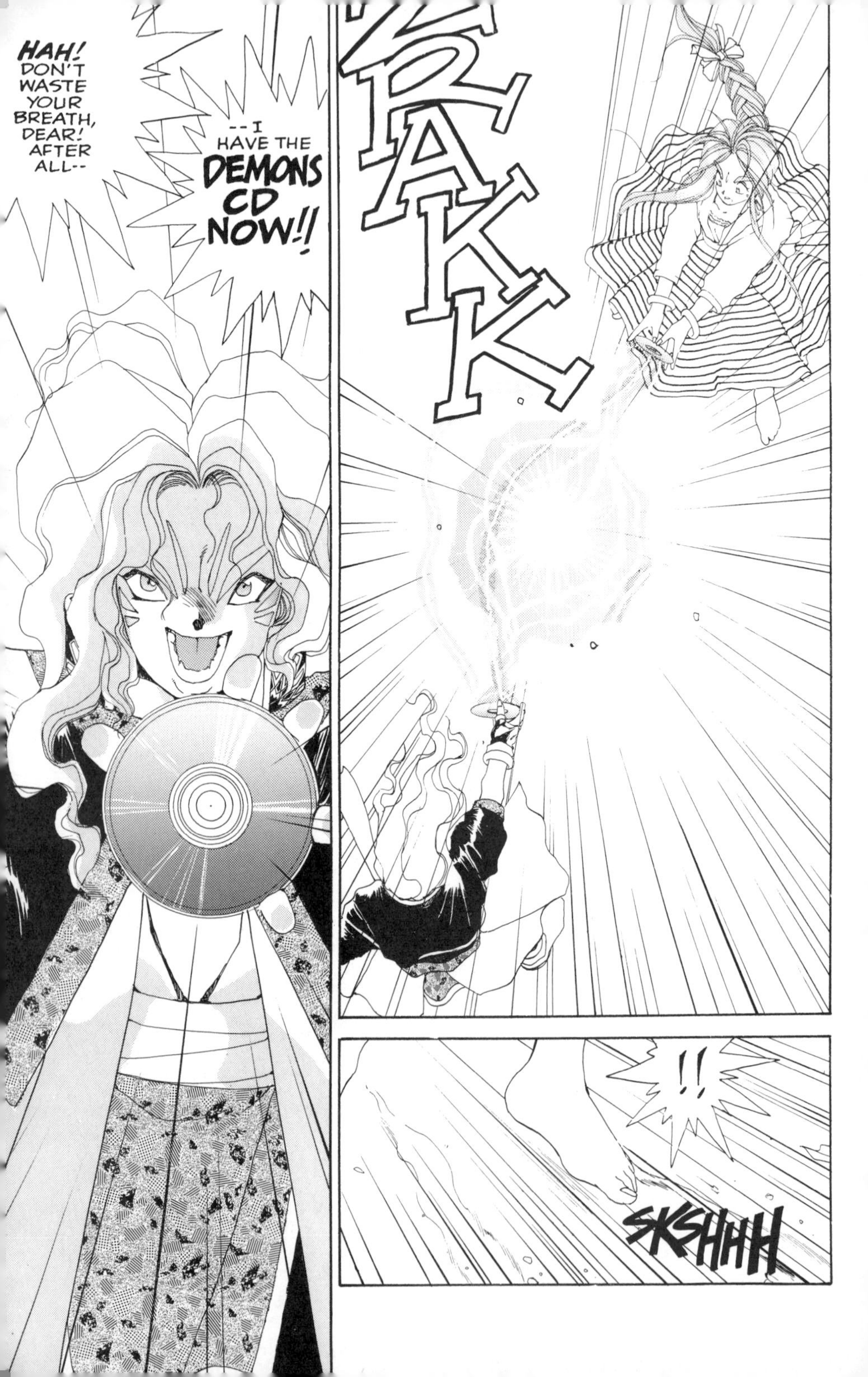
HAH! DON'T WASTE YOUR BREATH, DEAR! AFTER ALL--
--I HAVE THE DEMONS CD NOW!!
KRAKK
!!
SKSHHH

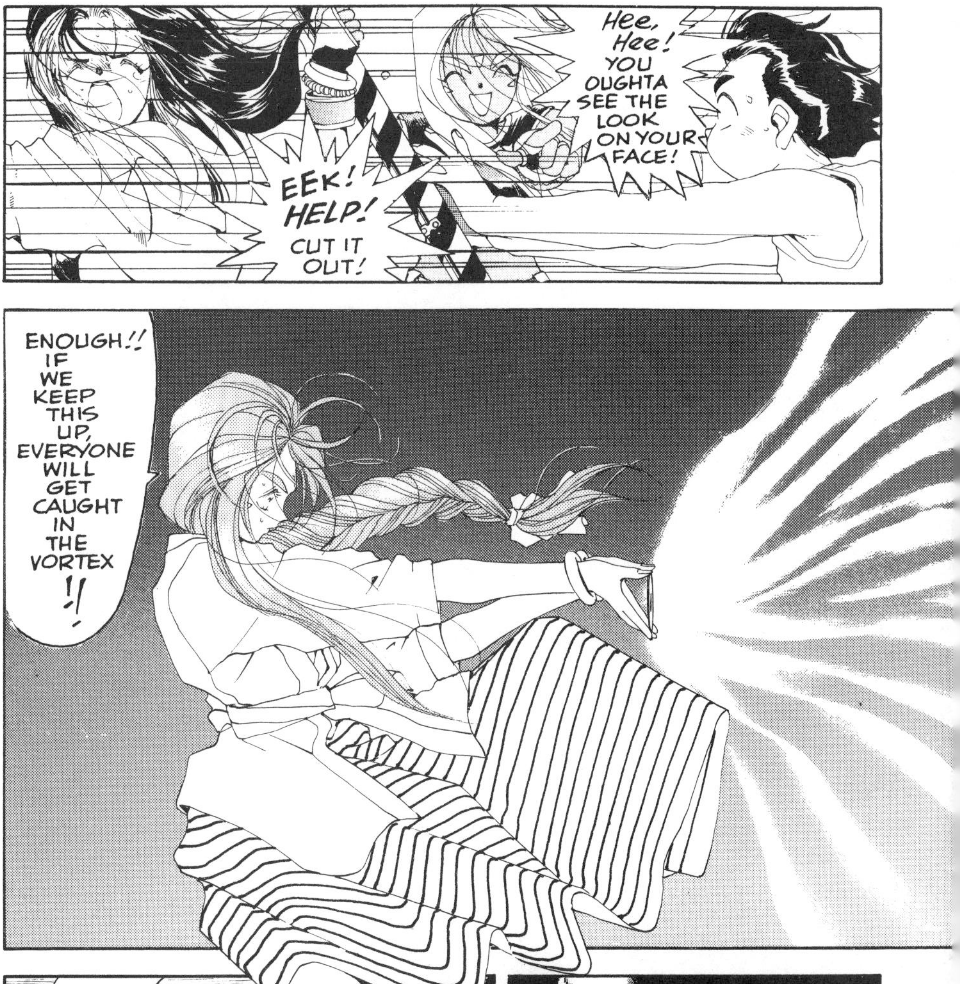
EEK! HELP! CUT IT OUT!
Hee, Hee! YOU OUGHTA SEE THE LOOK ON YOUR FACE!
ENOUGH!! IF WE KEEP THIS UP, EVERYONE WILL GET CAUGHT IN THE VORTEX!!
IS THAT WHAT YOU WANT?!
BLUBB BLUBB
....
GBLORP

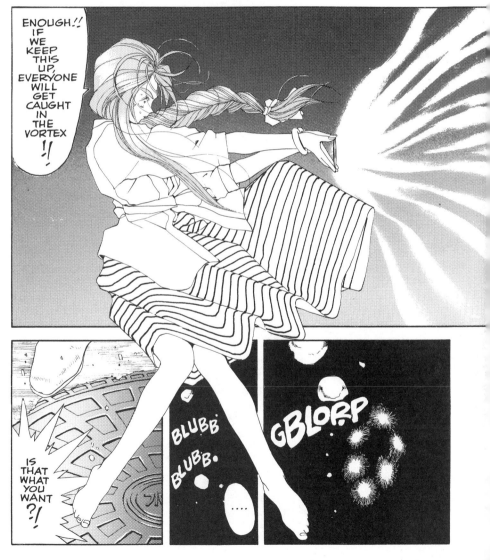

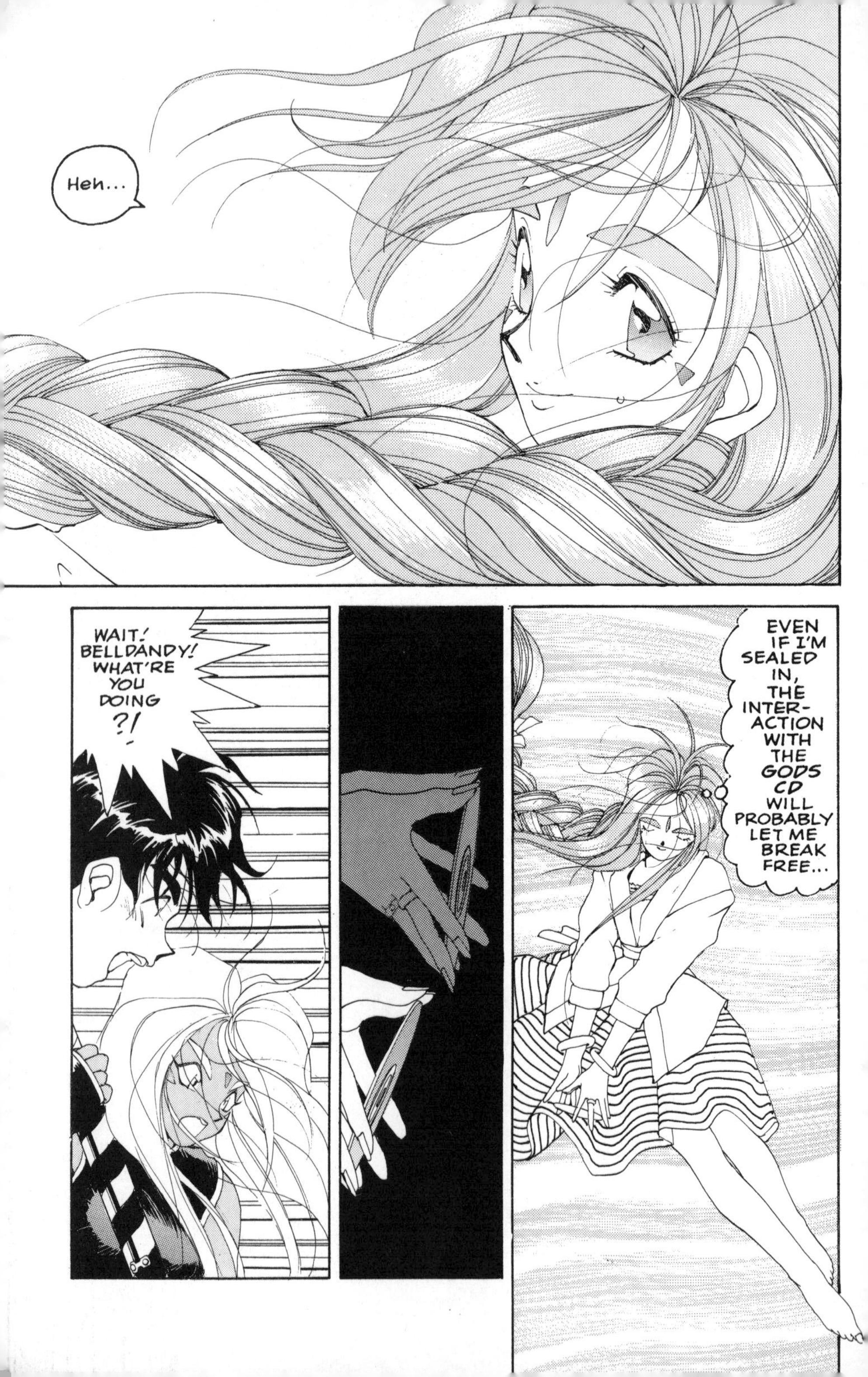

Heh...
WAIT! BELLDANDY! WHAT'RE YOU DOING ?!
EVEN IF I'M SEALED IN, THE INTER-ACTION WITH THE GODS CD WILL PROBABLY LET ME BREAK FREE...

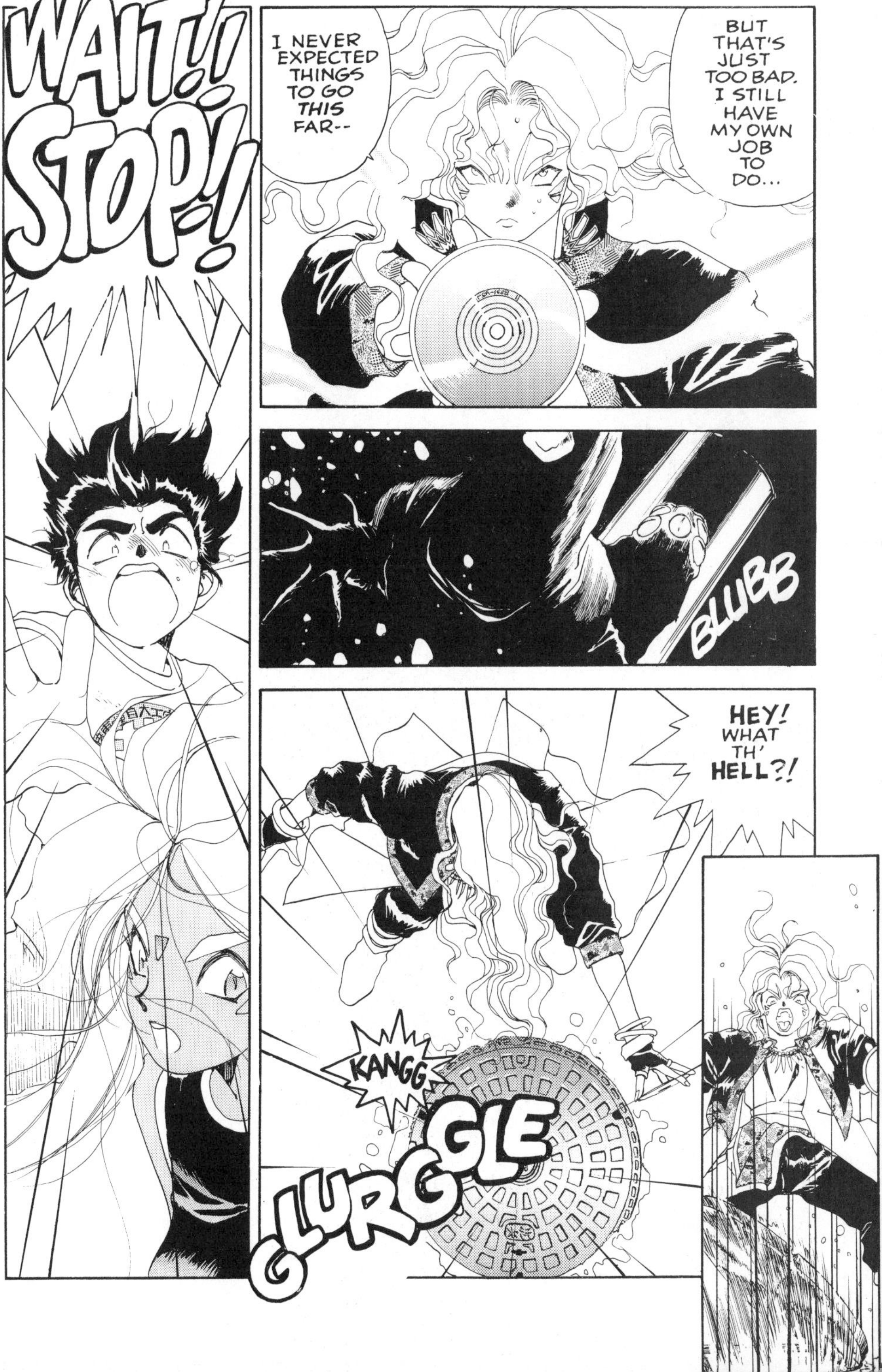
WAIT!! STOP!!
I NEVER EXPECTED THINGS TO GO THIS FAR--
BUT THAT'S JUST TOO BAD. I STILL HAVE MY OWN JOB TO DO...
BLUBB
KANGG
GLURGGLE
HEY! WHAT TH' HELL?!

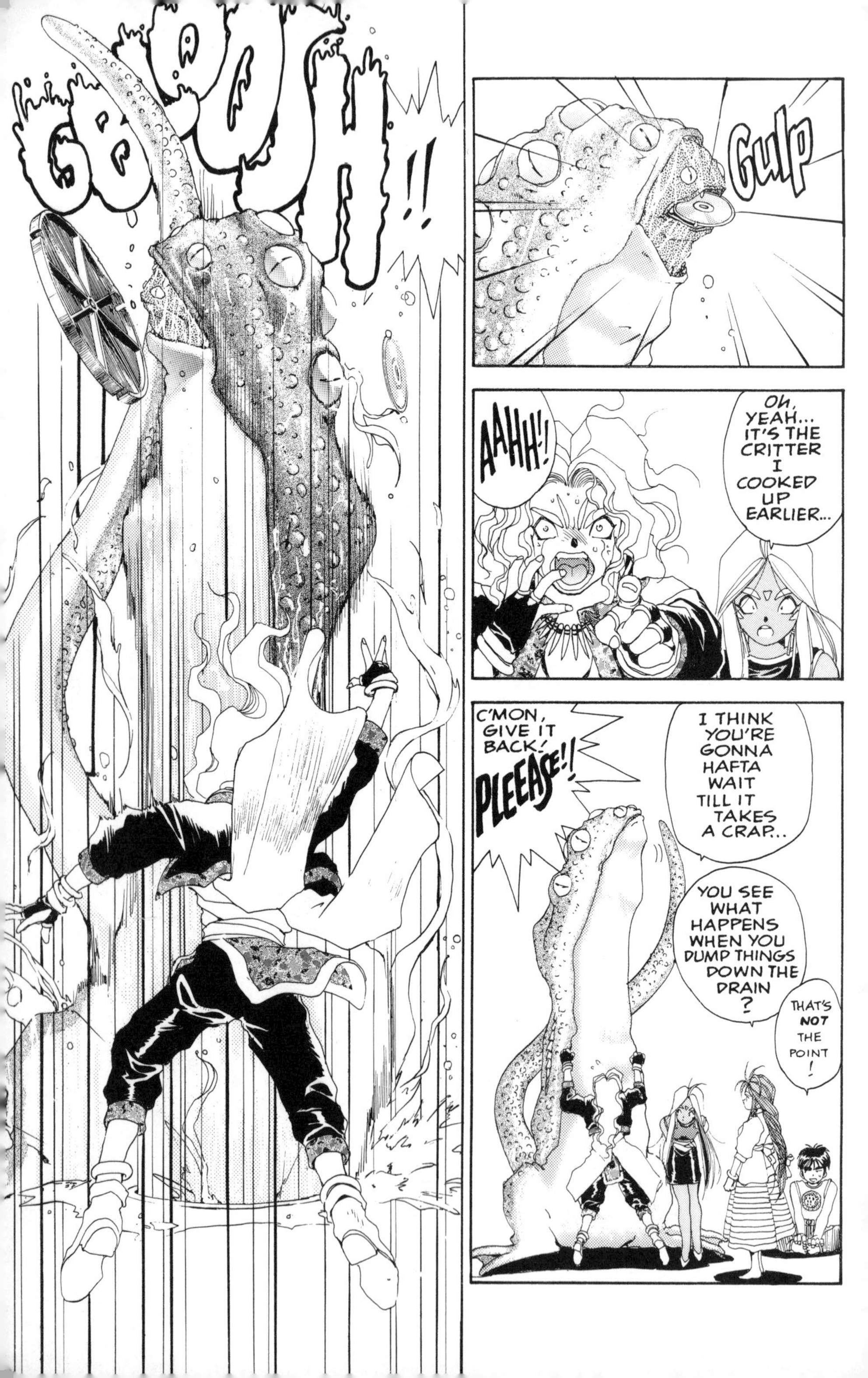
GBOUSH!!
Gulp
AAHH!!
Oh, YEAH... IT'S THE CRITTER I COOKED UP EARLIER...
C'MON, GIVE IT BACK! PLEEASE!!
I THINK YOU'RE GONNA HAFTA WAIT TILL IT TAKES A CRAP...
YOU SEE WHAT HAPPENS WHEN YOU DUMP THINGS DOWN THE DRAIN ?
THAT'S NOT THE POINT !

Oh My Goddess!

ああ女神さま

Love Potion No. 9

Cover Gallery

Following are some of Kosuke Fujishima's covers to the comics collected here. In fact, we liked the cover for *Oh My Goddess!* Part II issue 8 so much we put it on the cover — again!

Oh My Goddess! Part I issue 4

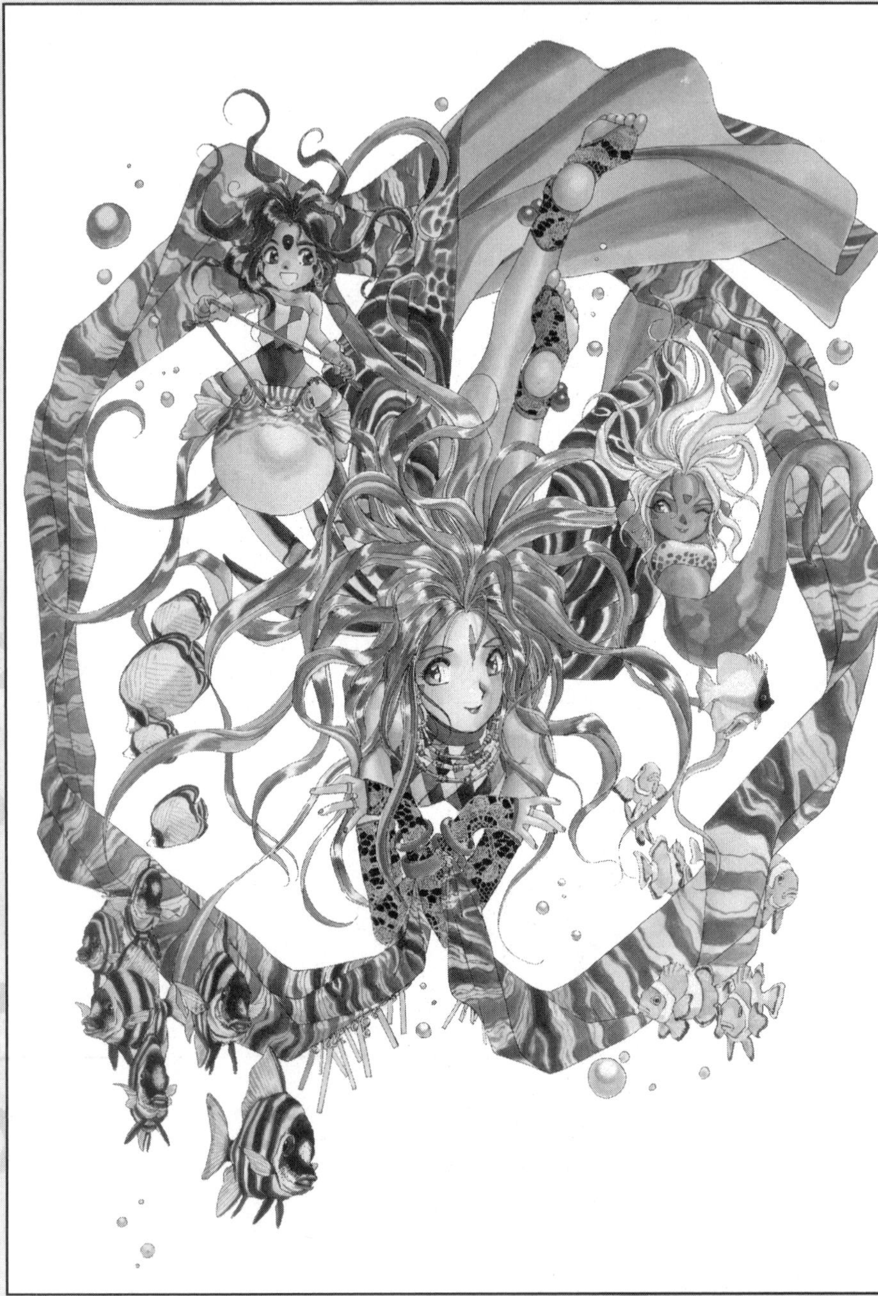

Oh My Goddess! Part I issue 5

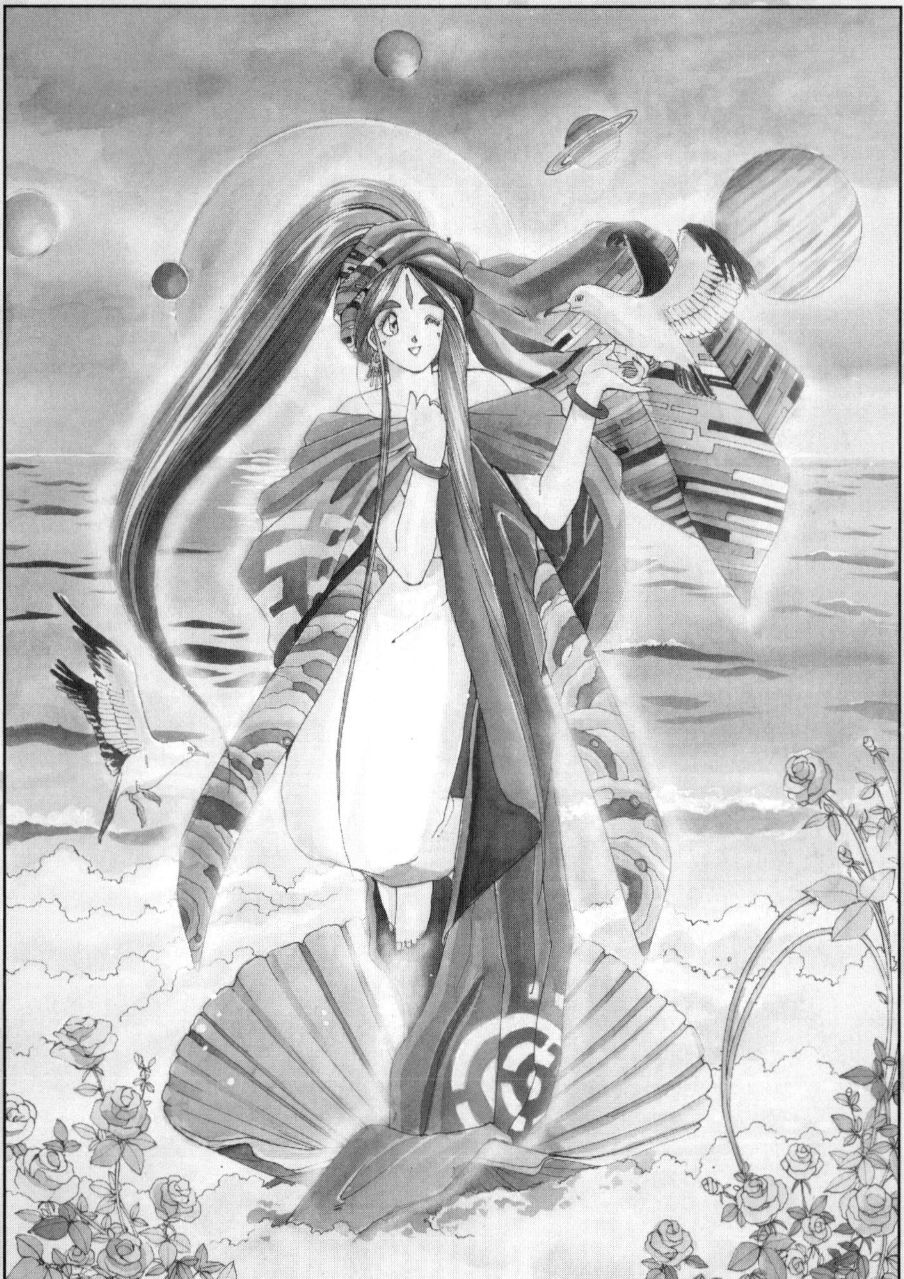

Oh My Goddess! Part II issue 7